THE AMORTIZATION BOOK

5% THRU 25%

The amount of monthly
payments required to amortize a loan

UNITED FINANCIAL PUBLISHERS
Post Office Box 701
San Angelo, Texas 76902
Printed in U.S.A.

ISBN 0-943605-01-6

Publication No. 98

DATA

RATE OF INTEREST
5% thru 25% by .25%

TERMS IN YEARS
1 to 5 years by 1/2 yr.
6 to 16 years by 1 yr.
Also 20, 30, 40, & 50 yrs.

DOLLAR AMOUNTS
$100 to $1,000 by $100
$2,000 to $10,000 by $1,000
$15,000 to $50,000 by $5,000
$60,000, $75,000, $100,000
$125,000 to $200,000 by $25,000
Also $250,000

FORWARD

A great variety of rates have been published in this one book; from 5% to 25%. These computations show directly the minimum monthly payment needed to amortize a loan.

To assure, in every case, the payment will be adequate for complete amortization, fractions of a cent have been increased to the next highest cent.

Amount	1.0 Year	1.5 Years	2.0 Years	2.5 Years	3.0 Years	3.5 Years	4.0 Years	4.5 Years	5.0 Years	6.0 Years	7.0 Years	8.0 Years	Amount
100	8.57	5.78	4.39	3.56	3.00	2.61	2.31	2.08	1.89	1.62	1.42	1.27	100
200	17.13	11.56	8.78	7.11	6.00	5.21	4.61	4.15	3.78	3.23	2.83	2.54	200
300	25.69	17.34	13.17	10.66	8.99	7.81	6.91	6.22	5.67	4.84	4.25	3.80	300
400	34.25	23.12	17.55	14.22	11.99	10.41	9.22	8.29	7.55	6.45	5.66	5.07	400
500	42.81	28.90	21.94	17.77	14.99	13.01	11.52	10.36	9.44	8.06	7.07	6.33	500
600	51.37	34.67	26.33	21.32	17.99	15.61	13.82	12.44	11.33	9.67	8.49	7.60	600
700	59.93	40.45	30.71	24.88	20.98	18.21	16.13	14.51	13.21	11.28	9.90	8.87	700
800	68.49	46.23	35.10	28.43	23.98	20.81	18.43	16.58	15.10	12.89	11.31	10.13	800
900	77.05	52.01	39.49	31.98	26.98	23.41	20.73	18.65	16.99	14.50	12.73	11.40	900
1000	85.61	57.79	43.88	35.53	29.98	26.01	23.03	20.72	18.88	16.11	14.14	12.66	1000
2000	171.22	115.57	87.75	71.06	59.95	52.01	46.06	41.44	37.75	32.21	28.27	25.32	2000
3000	256.83	173.35	131.62	106.59	89.92	78.01	69.09	62.16	56.62	48.32	42.41	37.98	3000
4000	342.43	231.13	175.49	142.12	119.89	104.02	92.12	82.88	75.49	64.42	56.54	50.64	4000
5000	428.04	288.91	219.36	177.65	149.86	130.02	115.15	103.60	94.36	80.53	70.67	63.30	5000
6000	513.65	346.69	263.23	213.18	179.83	156.02	138.18	124.31	113.23	96.63	84.81	75.96	6000
7000	599.26	404.47	307.10	248.71	209.80	182.03	161.21	145.03	132.10	112.74	98.94	88.62	7000
8000	684.86	462.25	350.98	284.24	239.77	208.03	184.24	165.75	150.97	128.84	113.08	101.28	8000
9000	770.47	520.03	394.85	319.77	269.74	234.03	207.27	186.47	169.85	144.95	127.21	113.94	9000
10000	856.08	577.81	438.72	355.30	299.71	260.04	230.30	207.19	188.72	161.05	141.34	126.60	10000
15000	1284.12	866.71	658.08	532.95	449.57	390.05	345.44	310.78	283.07	241.58	212.01	189.90	15000
20000	1712.15	1155.62	877.43	710.59	599.42	520.07	460.59	414.37	377.43	322.10	282.68	253.20	20000
25000	2140.19	1444.52	1096.79	888.24	749.28	650.08	575.74	517.96	471.79	402.63	353.35	316.50	25000
30000	2568.23	1733.42	1316.15	1065.89	899.13	780.10	690.88	621.55	566.14	483.15	424.02	379.80	30000
35000	2996.27	2022.32	1535.50	1243.53	1048.99	910.11	806.03	725.15	660.50	563.68	494.69	443.10	35000
40000	3424.30	2311.23	1754.86	1421.18	1198.84	1040.13	921.18	828.74	754.85	644.20	565.36	506.40	40000
45000	3852.34	2600.13	1974.22	1598.83	1348.70	1170.14	1036.32	932.33	849.21	724.73	636.03	569.70	45000
50000	4280.38	2889.03	2193.57	1776.47	1498.55	1300.16	1151.47	1035.92	943.57	805.25	706.70	633.00	50000
60000	5136.45	3466.84	2632.29	2131.77	1798.26	1560.19	1381.76	1243.10	1132.28	966.30	848.04	759.60	60000
75000	6420.57	4333.55	3290.36	2664.71	2247.82	1950.23	1727.20	1553.88	1415.35	1207.87	1060.05	949.50	75000
100000	8560.75	5778.06	4387.14	3552.94	2997.09	2600.31	2302.93	2071.84	1887.13	1610.50	1413.40	1266.00	100000
125000	10700.94	7222.57	5483.93	4441.18	3746.37	3250.38	2878.67	2589.79	2358.91	2013.12	1766.74	1582.50	125000
150000	12841.13	8667.09	6580.71	5329.41	4495.64	3900.46	3454.40	3107.75	2830.69	2415.74	2120.09	1898.99	150000
175000	14981.31	10111.60	7677.50	6217.64	5244.91	4550.54	4030.13	3625.71	3302.47	2818.37	2473.44	2215.49	175000
200000	17121.50	11556.11	8774.28	7105.88	5994.18	5200.61	4605.86	4143.67	3774.25	3220.99	2826.79	2531.99	200000
250000	21401.88	14445.14	10967.85	8882.35	7492.73	6500.76	5757.33	5179.58	4717.81	4026.24	3533.48	3164.99	250000

Amount	9.0 Years	10.0 Years	11.0 Years	12.0 Years	13.0 Years	14.0 Years	15.0 Years	16.0 Years	20.0 Years	30.0 Years	40.0 Years	50.0 Years	Amount
100	1.16	1.07	0.99	0.93	0.88	0.83	0.80	0.76	0.66	0.54	0.49	0.46	100
200	2.31	2.13	1.98	1.85	1.75	1.66	1.59	1.52	1.32	1.08	0.97	0.91	200
300	3.46	3.19	2.96	2.78	2.62	2.49	2.38	2.28	1.98	1.62	1.45	1.37	300
400	4.61	4.25	3.95	3.70	3.50	3.32	3.17	3.04	2.64	2.15	1.93	1.82	400
500	5.76	5.31	4.94	4.63	4.37	4.15	3.96	3.79	3.30	2.69	2.42	2.28	500
600	6.92	6.37	5.92	5.55	5.24	4.98	4.75	4.55	3.96	3.23	2.90	2.73	600
700	8.07	7.43	6.91	6.48	6.12	5.81	5.54	5.31	4.62	3.76	3.38	3.18	700
800	9.22	8.49	7.90	7.40	6.99	6.64	6.33	6.07	5.28	4.30	3.86	3.64	800
900	10.37	9.55	8.88	8.33	7.86	7.46	7.12	6.82	5.94	4.84	4.34	4.09	900
1000	11.52	10.61	9.87	9.25	8.74	8.29	7.91	7.58	6.60	5.37	4.83	4.55	1000
2000	23.04	21.22	19.73	18.50	17.47	16.58	15.82	15.16	13.20	10.74	9.65	9.09	2000
3000	34.56	31.82	29.60	27.75	26.20	24.87	23.73	22.74	19.80	16.11	14.47	13.63	3000
4000	46.07	42.43	39.46	37.00	34.93	33.16	31.64	30.31	26.40	21.48	19.29	18.17	4000
5000	57.59	53.04	49.33	46.25	43.66	41.45	39.54	37.89	33.00	26.85	24.11	22.71	5000
6000	69.11	63.64	59.19	55.50	52.39	49.74	47.45	45.47	39.60	32.21	28.94	27.25	6000
7000	80.63	74.25	69.06	64.75	61.12	58.03	55.36	53.04	46.20	37.58	33.76	31.79	7000
8000	92.14	84.86	78.92	74.00	69.85	66.31	63.27	60.62	52.80	42.95	38.58	36.34	8000
9000	103.66	95.46	88.79	83.25	78.58	74.60	71.18	68.20	59.40	48.32	43.40	40.88	9000
10000	115.18	106.07	98.65	92.49	87.31	82.89	79.08	75.77	66.00	53.69	48.22	45.42	10000
15000	172.76	159.10	147.97	138.74	130.96	124.34	118.62	113.66	99.00	80.53	72.33	68.13	15000
20000	230.35	212.14	197.29	184.98	174.62	165.78	158.16	151.54	132.00	107.37	96.44	90.83	20000
25000	287.94	265.17	246.62	231.23	218.27	207.22	197.70	189.43	164.99	134.21	120.55	113.54	25000
30000	345.52	318.20	295.94	277.47	261.92	248.67	237.24	227.31	197.99	161.05	144.66	136.25	30000
35000	403.11	371.23	345.26	323.72	305.58	290.11	276.78	265.19	230.99	187.89	168.77	158.95	35000
40000	460.70	424.27	394.58	369.96	349.23	331.55	316.32	303.08	263.99	214.73	192.88	181.66	40000
45000	518.28	477.30	443.91	416.21	392.88	373.00	355.86	340.96	296.99	241.57	216.99	204.37	45000
50000	575.87	530.33	493.23	462.45	436.53	414.44	395.40	378.85	329.98	268.42	241.10	227.07	50000
60000	691.04	636.40	591.87	554.94	523.84	497.33	474.48	454.61	395.98	322.10	289.32	272.49	60000
75000	863.80	795.50	739.84	693.67	654.80	621.66	593.10	568.27	494.97	402.62	361.65	340.61	75000
100000	1151.73	1060.66	986.45	924.90	873.06	828.88	790.80	757.69	659.96	536.83	482.20	454.14	100000
125000	1439.66	1325.82	1233.07	1156.12	1091.33	1036.09	988.50	947.11	824.95	671.03	602.75	567.68	125000
150000	1727.60	1590.99	1479.68	1387.34	1309.59	1243.31	1186.20	1136.53	989.94	805.24	723.30	681.21	150000
175000	2015.53	1856.15	1726.29	1618.56	1527.86	1450.53	1383.89	1325.95	1154.93	939.44	843.85	794.75	175000
200000	2303.46	2121.32	1972.90	1849.79	1746.12	1657.75	1581.59	1515.37	1319.92	1073.65	964.40	908.28	200000
250000	2879.32	2651.64	2466.13	2312.23	2182.65	2072.18	1976.99	1894.21	1649.89	1342.06	1205.50	1135.35	250000

Amount	1.0 Year	1.5 Years	2.0 Years	2.5 Years	3.0 Years	3.5 Years	4.0 Years	4.5 Years	5.0 Years	6.0 Years	7.0 Years	8.0 Years	Amount
100	8.58	5.79	4.40	3.57	3.01	2.62	2.32	2.09	1.90	1.63	1.43	1.28	100
200	17.15	11.58	8.80	7.13	6.02	5.23	4.63	4.17	3.80	3.25	2.86	2.56	200
300	25.72	17.37	13.20	10.70	9.03	7.84	6.95	6.25	5.70	4.87	4.28	3.84	300
400	34.29	23.16	17.60	14.26	12.04	10.45	9.26	8.34	7.60	6.49	5.71	5.12	400
500	42.87	28.95	22.00	17.83	15.05	13.06	11.58	10.42	9.50	8.12	7.13	6.39	500
600	51.44	34.74	26.40	21.39	18.05	15.67	13.89	12.50	11.40	9.74	8.56	7.67	600
700	60.01	40.53	30.79	24.95	21.06	18.29	16.20	14.59	13.30	11.36	9.98	8.95	700
800	68.58	46.32	35.19	28.52	24.07	20.90	18.52	16.67	15.19	12.98	11.41	10.23	800
900	77.15	52.11	39.59	32.08	27.08	23.51	20.83	18.75	17.09	14.60	12.83	11.51	900
1000	85.73	57.90	43.99	35.65	30.09	26.12	23.15	20.84	18.99	16.23	14.26	12.78	1000
2000	171.45	115.79	87.97	71.29	60.17	52.24	46.29	41.67	37.98	32.45	28.51	25.56	2000
3000	257.17	173.68	131.96	106.93	90.25	78.35	69.43	62.50	56.96	48.67	42.76	38.34	3000
4000	342.89	231.58	175.94	142.57	120.34	104.47	92.58	83.33	75.95	64.89	57.01	51.12	4000
5000	428.62	289.47	219.92	178.21	150.42	130.58	115.72	104.17	94.93	81.11	71.26	63.90	5000
6000	514.34	347.36	263.91	213.85	180.50	156.70	138.86	125.00	113.92	97.33	85.52	76.68	6000
7000	600.06	405.26	307.89	249.50	210.59	182.82	162.00	145.83	132.91	113.55	99.77	89.46	7000
8000	685.78	463.15	351.87	285.14	240.67	208.93	185.15	166.66	151.89	129.77	114.02	102.24	8000
9000	771.50	521.04	395.86	320.78	270.75	235.05	208.29	187.50	170.88	146.00	128.27	115.02	9000
10000	857.23	578.94	439.84	356.42	300.84	261.16	231.43	208.33	189.86	162.22	142.52	127.80	10000
15000	1285.84	868.40	659.76	534.63	451.25	391.74	347.15	312.49	284.79	243.32	213.78	191.69	15000
20000	1714.45	1157.87	879.67	712.83	601.67	522.32	462.86	416.65	379.72	324.43	285.04	255.59	20000
25000	2143.06	1447.33	1099.59	891.04	752.09	652.90	578.57	520.81	474.65	405.53	356.30	319.49	25000
30000	2571.67	1736.80	1319.51	1069.25	902.50	783.48	694.29	624.98	569.58	486.64	427.56	383.38	30000
35000	3000.28	2026.26	1539.43	1247.46	1052.92	914.06	810.00	729.14	664.51	567.75	498.81	447.28	35000
40000	3428.89	2315.73	1759.34	1425.66	1203.34	1044.64	925.71	833.30	759.44	648.85	570.07	511.18	40000
45000	3857.50	2605.20	1979.26	1603.87	1353.75	1175.22	1041.43	937.46	854.37	729.96	641.33	575.07	45000
50000	4286.11	2894.66	2199.18	1782.08	1504.17	1305.80	1157.14	1041.62	949.30	811.06	712.59	638.97	50000
60000	5143.33	3473.59	2639.01	2138.49	1805.00	1566.96	1388.57	1249.95	1139.16	973.27	855.11	766.76	60000
75000	6429.16	4341.99	3298.76	2673.11	2256.25	1958.70	1735.71	1562.43	1423.95	1216.59	1068.88	958.45	75000
100000	8572.21	5789.32	4398.35	3564.15	3008.33	2611.59	2314.28	2083.24	1898.60	1622.12	1425.17	1277.93	100000
125000	10715.27	7236.65	5497.93	4455.18	3760.41	3264.49	2892.84	2604.05	2373.25	2027.65	1781.46	1597.42	125000
150000	12858.32	8683.98	6597.52	5346.22	4512.50	3917.39	3471.41	3124.86	2847.90	2433.18	2137.75	1916.90	150000
175000	15001.37	10131.30	7697.11	6237.26	5264.58	4570.28	4049.98	3645.67	3322.55	2838.71	2494.05	2236.38	175000
200000	17144.42	11578.63	8796.69	7128.29	6016.66	5223.18	4628.55	4166.48	3797.20	3244.24	2850.34	2555.86	200000
250000	21430.53	14473.29	10995.86	8910.36	7520.82	6528.97	5785.68	5208.10	4746.50	4055.29	3562.92	3194.83	250000

Amount	9.0 Years	10.0 Years	11.0 Years	12.0 Years	13.0 Years	14.0 Years	15.0 Years	16.0 Years	20.0 Years	30.0 Years	40.0 Years	50.0 Years	Amount
100	1.17	1.08	1.00	0.94	0.89	0.85	0.81	0.78	0.68	0.56	0.50	0.48	100
200	2.33	2.15	2.00	1.88	1.78	1.69	1.61	1.55	1.35	1.11	1.00	0.95	200
300	3.50	3.22	3.00	2.82	2.66	2.53	2.42	2.32	2.03	1.66	1.50	1.42	300
400	4.66	4.30	4.00	3.75	3.55	3.37	3.22	3.09	2.70	2.21	2.00	1.89	400
500	5.82	5.37	5.00	4.69	4.43	4.21	4.02	3.86	3.37	2.77	2.50	2.36	500
600	6.99	6.44	6.00	5.63	5.32	5.06	4.83	4.63	4.05	3.32	3.00	2.84	600
700	8.15	7.52	7.00	6.57	6.21	5.90	5.63	5.40	4.72	3.87	3.50	3.31	700
800	9.32	8.59	8.00	7.50	7.09	6.74	6.44	6.17	5.40	4.42	4.00	3.78	800
900	10.48	9.66	8.99	8.44	7.98	7.58	7.24	6.94	6.07	4.97	4.49	4.25	900
1000	11.64	10.73	9.99	9.38	8.86	8.42	8.04	7.71	6.74	5.53	4.99	4.72	1000
2000	23.28	21.46	19.98	18.75	17.72	16.84	16.08	15.42	13.48	11.05	9.98	9.44	2000
3000	34.92	32.19	29.97	28.13	26.58	25.26	24.12	23.13	20.22	16.57	14.97	14.16	3000
4000	46.56	42.92	39.96	37.50	35.44	33.68	32.16	30.84	26.96	22.09	19.96	18.88	4000
5000	58.20	53.65	49.95	46.88	44.30	42.09	40.20	38.55	33.70	27.62	24.95	23.60	5000
6000	69.83	64.38	59.94	56.25	53.15	50.51	48.24	46.26	40.44	33.14	29.94	28.32	6000
7000	81.47	75.11	69.93	65.63	62.01	58.93	56.28	53.97	47.17	38.66	34.93	33.04	7000
8000	93.11	85.84	79.92	75.00	70.87	67.35	64.32	61.68	53.91	44.18	39.91	37.76	8000
9000	104.75	96.57	89.90	84.38	79.73	75.77	72.35	69.39	60.65	49.70	44.90	42.47	9000
10000	116.39	107.30	99.89	93.75	88.58	84.18	80.39	77.10	67.39	55.23	49.89	47.19	10000
15000	174.58	160.94	149.84	140.63	132.88	126.27	120.59	115.64	101.08	82.84	74.84	70.79	15000
20000	232.77	214.59	199.78	187.50	177.17	168.36	160.78	154.19	134.77	110.45	99.78	94.38	20000
25000	290.96	268.23	249.72	234.38	221.46	210.45	200.97	192.74	168.47	138.06	124.72	117.97	25000
30000	349.15	321.88	299.67	281.25	265.75	252.54	241.17	231.28	202.16	165.67	149.67	141.57	30000
35000	407.34	375.53	349.61	328.12	310.04	294.63	281.36	269.83	235.85	193.28	174.61	165.16	35000
40000	465.54	429.17	399.56	375.00	354.33	336.72	321.56	308.38	269.54	220.89	199.55	188.76	40000
45000	523.73	482.82	449.50	421.87	398.62	378.81	361.75	346.92	303.23	248.50	224.50	212.35	45000
50000	581.92	536.46	499.44	468.75	442.91	420.90	401.94	385.47	336.93	276.11	249.44	235.94	50000
60000	698.30	643.76	599.33	562.49	531.49	505.08	482.33	462.56	404.31	331.33	299.33	283.13	60000
75000	872.87	804.69	749.16	703.12	664.37	631.35	602.91	578.20	505.39	414.16	374.16	353.91	75000
100000	1163.83	1072.92	998.88	937.49	885.82	841.80	803.88	770.93	673.85	552.21	498.88	471.88	100000
125000	1454.79	1341.15	1248.60	1171.86	1107.27	1052.24	1004.85	963.67	842.31	690.26	623.59	589.85	125000
150000	1745.74	1609.38	1498.32	1406.23	1328.73	1262.69	1205.82	1156.40	1010.77	828.31	748.31	707.82	150000
175000	2036.70	1877.61	1748.04	1640.60	1550.18	1473.14	1406.79	1349.13	1179.23	966.36	873.03	825.79	175000
200000	2327.66	2145.84	1997.76	1874.97	1771.64	1683.59	1607.76	1541.86	1347.69	1104.41	997.75	943.76	200000
250000	2909.57	2682.30	2497.19	2343.71	2214.54	2104.48	2009.70	1927.33	1684.62	1380.51	1247.18	1179.70	250000

Amount	1.0 Year	1.5 Years	2.0 Years	2.5 Years	3.0 Years	3.5 Years	4.0 Years	4.5 Years	5.0 Years	6.0 Years	7.0 Years	8.0 Years	Amount
100	8.59	5.81	4.41	3.58	3.02	2.63	2.33	2.10	1.92	1.64	1.44	1.29	100
200	17.17	11.61	8.82	7.16	6.04	5.25	4.66	4.19	3.83	3.27	2.88	2.58	200
300	25.76	17.41	13.23	10.73	9.06	7.87	6.98	6.29	5.74	4.91	4.32	3.87	300
400	34.34	23.21	17.64	14.31	12.08	10.50	9.31	8.38	7.65	6.54	5.75	5.16	400
500	42.92	29.01	22.05	17.88	15.10	13.12	11.63	10.48	9.56	8.17	7.19	6.45	500
600	51.51	34.81	26.46	21.46	18.12	15.74	13.96	12.57	11.47	9.81	8.63	7.74	600
700	60.09	40.61	30.87	25.03	21.14	18.37	16.28	14.67	13.38	11.44	10.06	9.03	700
800	68.67	46.41	35.28	28.61	24.16	20.99	18.61	16.76	15.29	13.08	11.50	10.32	800
900	77.26	52.21	39.69	32.18	27.18	23.61	20.94	18.86	17.20	14.71	12.94	11.61	900
1000	85.84	58.01	44.10	35.76	30.20	26.23	23.26	20.95	19.11	16.34	14.38	12.90	1000
2000	171.68	116.02	88.20	71.51	60.40	52.46	46.52	41.90	38.21	32.68	28.75	25.80	2000
3000	257.52	174.02	132.29	107.27	90.59	78.69	69.77	62.85	57.31	49.02	43.12	38.70	3000
4000	343.35	232.03	176.39	143.02	120.79	104.92	93.03	83.79	76.41	65.36	57.49	51.60	4000
5000	429.19	290.03	220.48	178.77	150.98	131.15	116.29	104.74	95.51	81.69	71.86	64.50	5000
6000	515.03	348.04	264.58	214.53	181.18	157.38	139.54	125.69	114.61	98.03	86.23	77.40	6000
7000	600.86	406.05	308.67	250.28	211.38	183.61	162.80	146.63	133.71	114.37	100.60	90.30	7000
8000	686.70	464.05	352.77	286.03	241.57	209.84	186.06	167.58	152.81	130.71	114.97	103.20	8000
9000	772.54	522.06	396.87	321.79	271.77	236.07	209.31	188.53	171.92	147.05	129.34	116.10	9000
10000	858.37	580.06	440.96	357.54	301.96	262.30	232.57	209.47	191.02	163.38	143.71	129.00	10000
15000	1287.56	870.09	661.44	536.31	452.94	393.44	348.85	314.21	286.52	245.07	215.56	193.49	15000
20000	1716.74	1160.12	881.92	715.08	603.92	524.59	465.13	418.94	382.03	326.76	287.41	257.99	20000
25000	2145.92	1450.15	1102.40	893.85	754.90	655.73	581.42	523.68	477.53	408.45	359.26	322.49	25000
30000	2575.11	1740.18	1322.87	1072.62	905.88	786.88	697.70	628.41	573.04	490.14	431.11	386.98	30000
35000	3004.29	2030.21	1543.35	1251.38	1056.86	918.02	813.98	733.14	668.55	571.83	502.96	451.48	35000
40000	3433.48	2320.24	1763.83	1430.15	1207.84	1049.17	930.26	837.88	764.05	653.52	574.81	515.98	40000
45000	3862.66	2610.27	1984.31	1608.92	1358.82	1180.31	1046.55	942.61	859.56	735.21	646.66	580.47	45000
50000	4291.84	2900.30	2204.79	1787.69	1509.80	1311.46	1162.83	1047.35	955.06	816.90	718.51	644.97	50000
60000	5150.21	3480.36	2645.74	2145.23	1811.76	1573.75	1395.39	1256.81	1146.07	980.28	862.21	773.96	60000
75000	6437.76	4350.45	3307.18	2681.53	2264.70	1967.18	1744.24	1571.02	1432.59	1225.35	1077.76	967.45	75000
100000	8583.68	5800.59	4409.57	3575.38	3019.60	2622.91	2325.65	2094.69	1910.12	1633.79	1437.01	1289.94	100000
125000	10729.60	7250.74	5511.96	4469.22	3774.49	3278.63	2907.06	2618.36	2387.65	2042.24	1796.26	1612.42	125000
150000	12875.52	8700.89	6614.35	5363.06	4529.39	3934.36	3488.48	3142.03	2865.18	2450.69	2155.51	1934.90	150000
175000	15021.44	10151.03	7716.74	6256.90	5284.29	4590.08	4069.89	3665.70	3342.71	2859.14	2514.76	2257.39	175000
200000	17167.36	11601.18	8819.14	7150.75	6039.19	5245.81	4651.30	4189.37	3820.24	3267.58	2874.01	2579.87	200000
250000	21459.20	14501.47	11023.92	8938.43	7548.98	6557.26	5814.12	5236.71	4775.30	4084.48	3592.52	3224.84	250000

Amount	9.0 Years	10.0 Years	11.0 Years	12.0 Years	13.0 Years	14.0 Years	15.0 Years	16.0 Years	20.0 Years	30.0 Years	40.0 Years	50.0 Years	Amount
100	1.18	1.09	1.02	0.96	0.90	0.86	0.82	0.79	0.69	0.57	0.52	0.49	100
200	2.36	2.18	2.03	1.91	1.80	1.71	1.64	1.57	1.38	1.14	1.04	0.98	200
300	3.53	3.26	3.04	2.86	2.70	2.57	2.46	2.36	2.07	1.71	1.55	1.47	300
400	4.71	4.35	4.05	3.81	3.60	3.42	3.27	3.14	2.76	2.28	2.07	1.96	400
500	5.88	5.43	5.06	4.76	4.50	4.28	4.09	3.93	3.44	2.84	2.58	2.45	500
600	7.06	6.52	6.07	5.71	5.40	5.13	4.91	4.71	4.13	3.41	3.10	2.94	600
700	8.24	7.60	7.08	6.66	6.30	5.99	5.72	5.50	4.82	3.98	3.62	3.43	700
800	9.41	8.69	8.10	7.61	7.19	6.84	6.54	6.28	5.51	4.55	4.13	3.92	800
900	10.59	9.77	9.11	8.56	8.09	7.70	7.36	7.06	6.20	5.12	4.65	4.41	900
1000	11.76	10.86	10.12	9.51	8.99	8.55	8.18	7.85	6.88	5.68	5.16	4.90	1000
2000	23.52	21.71	20.23	19.01	17.98	17.10	16.35	15.69	13.76	11.36	10.32	9.80	2000
3000	35.28	32.56	30.35	28.51	26.97	25.65	24.52	23.53	20.64	17.04	15.48	14.70	3000
4000	47.04	43.42	40.46	38.01	35.95	34.20	32.69	31.38	27.52	22.72	20.64	19.60	4000
5000	58.80	54.27	50.57	47.51	44.94	42.75	40.86	39.22	34.40	28.39	25.79	24.50	5000
6000	70.56	65.12	60.69	57.02	53.93	51.29	49.03	47.06	41.28	34.07	30.95	29.40	6000
7000	82.32	75.97	70.80	66.52	62.91	59.84	57.20	54.91	48.16	39.75	36.11	34.29	7000
8000	94.08	86.83	80.92	76.02	71.90	68.39	65.37	62.75	55.04	45.43	41.27	39.19	8000
9000	105.84	97.68	91.03	85.52	80.89	76.94	73.54	70.59	61.91	51.11	46.42	44.09	9000
10000	117.60	108.53	101.14	95.02	89.87	85.49	81.71	78.44	68.79	56.78	51.58	48.99	10000
15000	176.40	162.79	151.71	142.53	134.81	128.23	122.57	117.65	103.19	85.17	77.37	73.48	15000
20000	235.20	217.06	202.28	190.04	179.74	170.97	163.42	156.87	137.58	113.56	103.16	97.97	20000
25000	294.00	271.32	252.85	237.55	224.67	213.71	204.28	196.08	171.98	141.95	128.95	122.47	25000
30000	352.80	325.58	303.42	285.06	269.61	256.45	245.13	235.30	206.37	170.34	154.74	146.96	30000
35000	411.60	379.85	353.99	332.57	314.54	299.19	285.98	274.51	240.77	198.73	180.52	171.45	35000
40000	470.40	434.11	404.56	380.07	359.48	341.94	326.84	313.73	275.16	227.12	206.31	195.94	40000
45000	529.20	488.37	455.13	427.58	404.41	384.68	367.69	352.94	309.55	255.51	232.10	220.44	45000
50000	588.00	542.64	505.70	475.09	449.34	427.42	408.55	392.16	343.95	283.90	257.89	244.93	50000
60000	705.60	651.16	606.84	570.11	539.21	512.90	490.26	470.59	412.74	340.68	309.47	293.91	60000
75000	882.00	813.95	758.55	712.63	674.01	641.12	612.82	588.23	515.92	425.85	386.83	367.39	75000
100000	1176.00	1085.27	1011.40	950.18	898.68	854.83	817.09	784.31	687.89	567.79	515.78	489.85	100000
125000	1470.00	1356.58	1264.25	1187.72	1123.35	1068.54	1021.36	980.38	859.86	709.74	644.72	612.31	125000
150000	1764.00	1627.90	1517.09	1425.26	1348.02	1282.24	1225.63	1176.46	1031.84	851.69	773.66	734.77	150000
175000	2058.00	1899.21	1769.94	1662.81	1572.69	1495.95	1429.90	1372.54	1203.81	993.64	902.60	857.23	175000
200000	2352.00	2170.53	2022.79	1900.35	1797.36	1709.66	1634.17	1568.61	1375.78	1135.58	1031.55	979.70	200000
250000	2940.00	2713.16	2528.49	2375.44	2246.70	2137.07	2042.71	1960.76	1719.72	1419.48	1289.43	1224.62	250000

5.50%   Page 6   **Monthly Payment Required To Amortize A Loan**   Page 6   **5.50%**

Amount	1.0 Year	1.5 Years	2.0 Years	2.5 Years	3.0 Years	3.5 Years	4.0 Years	4.5 Years	5.0 Years	6.0 Years	7.0 Years	8.0 Years	Amount
100	8.60	5.82	4.43	3.59	3.04	2.64	2.34	2.11	1.93	1.65	1.45	1.31	100
200	17.20	11.63	8.85	7.18	6.07	5.27	4.68	4.22	3.85	3.30	2.90	2.61	200
300	25.79	17.44	13.27	10.76	9.10	7.91	7.02	6.32	5.77	4.94	4.35	3.91	300
400	34.39	23.25	17.69	14.35	12.13	10.54	9.35	8.43	7.69	6.59	5.80	5.21	400
500	42.98	29.06	22.11	17.94	15.16	13.18	11.69	10.54	9.61	8.23	7.25	6.52	500
600	51.58	34.88	26.53	21.52	18.19	15.81	14.03	12.64	11.54	9.88	8.70	7.82	600
700	60.17	40.69	30.95	25.11	21.22	18.44	16.36	14.75	13.46	11.52	10.15	9.12	700
800	68.77	46.50	35.37	28.70	24.25	21.08	18.70	16.85	15.38	13.17	11.60	10.42	800
900	77.36	52.31	39.79	32.28	27.28	23.71	21.04	18.96	17.30	14.81	13.05	11.72	900
1000	85.96	58.12	44.21	35.87	30.31	26.35	23.38	21.07	19.22	16.46	14.49	13.03	1000
2000	171.91	116.24	88.42	71.74	60.62	52.69	46.75	42.13	38.44	32.92	28.98	26.05	2000
3000	257.86	174.36	132.63	107.60	90.93	79.03	70.12	63.19	57.66	49.37	43.47	39.07	3000
4000	343.81	232.48	176.84	143.47	121.24	105.37	93.49	84.25	76.87	65.83	57.96	52.09	4000
5000	429.76	290.60	221.05	179.34	151.55	131.72	116.86	105.31	96.09	82.28	72.45	65.11	5000
6000	515.71	348.72	265.25	215.20	181.86	158.06	140.23	126.37	115.31	98.74	86.94	78.13	6000
7000	601.67	406.84	309.46	251.07	212.17	184.40	163.60	147.44	134.52	115.19	101.43	91.15	7000
8000	687.62	464.95	353.67	286.93	242.48	210.74	186.97	168.50	153.74	131.65	115.92	104.17	8000
9000	773.57	523.07	397.88	322.80	272.78	237.09	210.34	189.56	172.96	148.10	130.41	117.19	9000
10000	859.52	581.19	442.09	358.67	303.09	263.43	233.71	210.62	192.17	164.56	144.90	130.21	10000
15000	1289.28	871.79	663.13	538.00	454.64	395.14	350.56	315.93	288.26	246.83	217.34	195.31	15000
20000	1719.04	1162.38	884.17	717.33	606.18	526.85	467.42	421.24	384.34	329.11	289.79	260.41	20000
25000	2148.79	1452.97	1105.21	896.66	757.72	658.57	584.27	526.55	480.42	411.38	362.23	325.51	25000
30000	2578.55	1743.57	1326.25	1075.99	909.27	790.28	701.12	631.85	576.51	493.66	434.68	390.61	30000
35000	3008.31	2034.16	1547.29	1255.32	1060.81	921.99	817.98	737.16	672.59	575.93	507.12	455.71	35000
40000	3438.07	2324.75	1768.33	1434.65	1212.36	1053.70	934.83	842.47	768.68	658.21	579.57	520.81	40000
45000	3867.83	2615.35	1989.37	1613.98	1363.90	1185.42	1051.68	947.78	864.76	740.49	652.01	585.91	45000
50000	4297.58	2905.94	2210.41	1793.32	1515.44	1317.13	1168.53	1053.09	960.84	822.76	724.46	651.01	50000
60000	5157.10	3487.13	2652.49	2151.98	1818.53	1580.55	1402.24	1263.70	1153.01	987.31	869.35	781.21	60000
75000	6446.37	4358.91	3315.61	2689.97	2273.16	1975.69	1752.80	1579.63	1441.26	1234.14	1086.68	976.51	75000
100000	8595.16	5811.88	4420.81	3586.63	3030.88	2634.25	2337.06	2106.17	1921.68	1645.52	1448.91	1302.01	100000
125000	10743.95	7264.85	5526.01	4483.28	3788.60	3292.81	2921.33	2632.71	2402.10	2056.90	1811.13	1627.51	125000
150000	12892.74	8717.82	6631.21	5379.94	4546.32	3951.38	3505.59	3159.25	2882.52	2468.27	2173.36	1953.01	150000
175000	15041.53	10170.78	7736.41	6276.59	5304.04	4609.94	4089.86	3685.79	3362.94	2879.65	2535.58	2278.51	175000
200000	17190.32	11623.75	8841.61	7173.25	6061.76	5268.50	4674.12	4212.33	3843.36	3291.03	2897.81	2604.01	200000
250000	21487.90	14529.69	11052.02	8966.56	7577.20	6585.62	5842.65	5265.42	4804.20	4113.79	3622.26	3255.01	250000

Amount	9.0 Years	10.0 Years	11.0 Years	12.0 Years	13.0 Years	14.0 Years	15.0 Years	16.0 Years	20.0 Years	30.0 Years	40.0 Years	50.0 Years	Amount
100	1.19	1.10	1.03	0.97	0.92	0.87	0.84	0.80	0.71	0.59	0.54	0.51	100
200	2.38	2.20	2.05	1.93	1.83	1.74	1.67	1.60	1.41	1.17	1.07	1.02	200
300	3.57	3.30	3.08	2.89	2.74	2.61	2.50	2.40	2.11	1.76	1.60	1.53	300
400	4.76	4.40	4.10	3.86	3.65	3.48	3.33	3.20	2.81	2.34	2.14	2.04	400
500	5.95	5.49	5.13	4.82	4.56	4.34	4.16	3.99	3.52	2.92	2.67	2.55	500
600	7.13	6.59	6.15	5.78	5.47	5.21	4.99	4.79	4.22	3.51	3.20	3.05	600
700	8.32	7.69	7.17	6.75	6.39	6.08	5.82	5.59	4.92	4.09	3.74	3.56	700
800	9.51	8.79	8.20	7.71	7.30	6.95	6.65	6.39	5.62	4.67	4.27	4.07	800
900	10.70	9.88	9.22	8.67	8.21	7.82	7.48	7.19	6.32	5.26	4.80	4.58	900
1000	11.89	10.98	10.25	9.63	9.12	8.68	8.31	7.98	7.03	5.84	5.33	5.09	1000
2000	23.77	21.96	20.49	19.26	18.24	17.36	16.61	15.96	14.05	11.68	10.66	10.17	2000
3000	35.65	32.94	30.73	28.89	27.35	26.04	24.92	23.94	21.07	17.51	15.99	15.25	3000
4000	47.53	43.91	40.97	38.52	36.47	34.72	33.22	31.92	28.09	23.35	21.32	20.33	4000
5000	59.42	54.89	51.21	48.15	45.59	43.40	41.53	39.90	35.11	29.18	26.65	25.41	5000
6000	71.30	65.87	61.45	57.78	54.70	52.08	49.83	47.87	42.13	35.02	31.98	30.49	6000
7000	83.18	76.84	71.69	67.41	63.82	60.76	58.13	55.85	49.15	40.86	37.31	35.57	7000
8000	95.06	87.82	81.93	77.04	72.94	69.44	66.44	63.83	56.17	46.69	42.64	40.65	8000
9000	106.95	98.80	92.17	86.67	82.05	78.12	74.74	71.81	63.19	52.53	47.96	45.73	9000
10000	118.83	109.77	102.41	96.30	91.17	86.80	83.05	79.79	70.21	58.36	53.29	50.81	10000
15000	178.24	164.66	153.61	144.45	136.75	130.20	124.57	119.68	105.32	87.54	79.94	76.21	15000
20000	237.65	219.54	204.81	192.60	182.33	173.60	166.09	159.57	140.42	116.72	106.58	101.61	20000
25000	297.07	274.43	256.01	240.75	227.92	217.00	207.61	199.46	175.53	145.90	133.23	127.01	25000
30000	356.48	329.31	307.21	288.89	273.50	260.40	249.13	239.35	210.63	175.08	159.87	152.41	30000
35000	415.89	384.20	358.41	337.04	319.08	303.80	290.65	279.24	245.73	204.26	186.52	177.81	35000
40000	475.30	439.08	409.61	385.19	364.66	347.19	332.17	319.13	280.84	233.43	213.16	203.21	40000
45000	534.72	493.97	460.81	433.34	410.25	390.59	373.69	359.02	315.94	262.61	239.80	228.62	45000
50000	594.13	548.85	512.01	481.49	455.83	433.99	415.21	398.91	351.05	291.79	266.45	254.02	50000
60000	712.95	658.62	614.41	577.78	546.99	520.79	498.25	478.69	421.26	350.15	319.74	304.82	60000
75000	891.19	823.27	768.01	722.23	683.74	650.99	622.81	598.36	526.57	437.68	399.67	381.02	75000
100000	1188.25	1097.70	1024.01	962.97	911.65	867.98	830.42	797.81	702.09	583.58	532.89	508.03	100000
125000	1485.32	1372.12	1280.01	1203.71	1139.56	1084.97	1038.02	997.26	877.61	729.47	666.11	635.04	125000
150000	1782.38	1646.54	1536.01	1444.45	1367.48	1301.97	1245.62	1196.72	1053.13	875.36	799.34	762.04	150000
175000	2079.44	1920.97	1792.01	1685.19	1595.39	1518.96	1453.22	1396.17	1228.65	1021.26	932.56	889.05	175000
200000	2376.50	2195.39	2048.01	1925.93	1823.30	1735.95	1660.83	1595.62	1404.17	1167.15	1065.78	1016.05	200000
250000	2970.63	2744.24	2560.01	2407.41	2279.12	2169.94	2076.03	1994.52	1755.21	1458.94	1332.22	1270.07	250000

Amount	1.0 Year	1.5 Years	2.0 Years	2.5 Years	3.0 Years	3.5 Years	4.0 Years	4.5 Years	5.0 Years	6.0 Years	7.0 Years	8.0 Years	Amount
100	8.61	5.83	4.44	3.60	3.05	2.65	2.35	2.12	1.94	1.66	1.47	1.32	100
200	17.22	11.65	8.87	7.20	6.09	5.30	4.70	4.24	3.87	3.32	2.93	2.63	200
300	25.82	17.47	13.30	10.80	9.13	7.94	7.05	6.36	5.80	4.98	4.39	3.95	300
400	34.43	23.30	17.73	14.40	12.17	10.59	9.40	8.48	7.74	6.63	5.85	5.26	400
500	43.04	29.12	22.17	17.99	15.22	13.23	11.75	10.59	9.67	8.29	7.31	6.58	500
600	51.64	34.94	26.60	21.59	18.26	15.88	14.10	12.71	11.60	9.95	8.77	7.89	600
700	60.25	40.77	31.03	25.19	21.30	18.52	16.44	14.83	13.54	11.61	10.23	9.20	700
800	68.86	46.59	35.46	28.79	24.34	21.17	18.79	16.95	15.47	13.26	11.69	10.52	800
900	77.46	52.41	39.89	32.39	27.38	23.82	21.14	19.06	17.40	14.92	13.15	11.83	900
1000	86.07	58.24	44.33	35.98	30.43	26.46	23.49	21.18	19.34	16.58	14.61	13.15	1000
2000	172.14	116.47	88.65	71.96	60.85	52.92	46.98	42.36	38.67	33.15	29.22	26.29	2000
3000	258.20	174.70	132.97	107.94	91.27	79.37	70.46	63.54	58.00	49.72	43.83	39.43	3000
4000	344.27	232.93	177.29	143.92	121.69	105.83	93.95	84.71	77.34	66.30	58.44	52.57	4000
5000	430.34	291.16	221.61	179.90	152.11	132.29	117.43	105.89	96.67	82.87	73.05	65.71	5000
6000	516.40	349.40	265.93	215.88	182.54	158.74	140.92	127.07	116.00	99.44	87.66	78.85	6000
7000	602.47	407.63	310.25	251.86	212.96	185.20	164.40	148.24	135.33	116.02	102.26	92.00	7000
8000	688.54	465.86	354.57	287.84	243.38	211.65	187.89	169.42	154.67	132.59	116.87	105.14	8000
9000	774.60	524.09	398.89	323.82	273.80	238.11	211.37	190.60	174.00	149.16	131.48	118.28	9000
10000	860.67	582.32	443.21	359.79	304.22	264.57	234.86	211.77	193.33	165.73	146.09	131.42	10000
15000	1291.00	873.48	664.81	539.69	456.33	396.85	352.28	317.66	290.00	248.60	219.13	197.13	15000
20000	1721.33	1164.64	886.42	719.58	608.44	529.13	469.71	423.54	386.66	331.46	292.18	262.83	20000
25000	2151.67	1455.80	1108.02	899.48	760.55	661.41	587.13	529.43	483.33	414.33	365.22	328.54	25000
30000	2582.00	1746.96	1329.62	1079.37	912.66	793.69	704.56	635.31	579.99	497.19	438.26	394.25	30000
35000	3012.33	2038.12	1551.23	1259.27	1064.77	925.97	821.98	741.20	676.65	580.06	511.30	459.96	35000
40000	3442.66	2329.27	1772.83	1439.16	1216.88	1058.25	939.41	847.08	773.32	662.92	584.35	525.66	40000
45000	3872.99	2620.43	1994.43	1619.06	1368.99	1190.53	1056.83	952.96	869.98	745.78	657.39	591.37	45000
50000	4303.33	2911.59	2216.04	1798.95	1521.10	1322.82	1174.26	1058.85	966.65	828.65	730.43	657.08	50000
60000	5163.99	3493.91	2659.24	2158.74	1825.32	1587.38	1409.11	1270.62	1159.97	994.38	876.52	788.49	60000
75000	6454.99	4367.38	3324.05	2698.42	2281.65	1984.22	1761.38	1588.27	1449.97	1242.97	1095.65	985.61	75000
100000	8606.65	5823.18	4432.07	3597.90	3042.20	2645.63	2348.51	2117.69	1933.29	1657.29	1460.86	1314.15	100000
125000	10758.31	7278.97	5540.08	4497.37	3802.75	3307.03	2935.63	2647.11	2416.61	2071.62	1826.07	1642.68	125000
150000	12909.97	8734.76	6648.10	5396.84	4563.30	3968.44	3522.76	3176.53	2899.93	2485.94	2191.29	1971.22	150000
175000	15061.63	10190.56	7756.11	6296.32	5323.84	4629.84	4109.89	3705.96	3383.25	2900.26	2556.50	2299.76	175000
200000	17213.29	11646.35	8864.13	7195.79	6084.39	5291.25	4697.01	4235.38	3866.57	3314.58	2921.72	2628.29	200000
250000	21516.61	14557.94	11080.16	8994.73	7605.49	6614.06	5871.26	5294.22	4833.21	4143.23	3652.14	3285.36	250000

Amount	9.0 Years	10.0 Years	11.0 Years	12.0 Years	13.0 Years	14.0 Years	15.0 Years	16.0 Years	20.0 Years	30.0 Years	40.0 Years	50.0 Years	Amount
100	1.21	1.12	1.04	0.98	0.93	0.89	0.85	0.82	0.72	0.60	0.56	0.53	100
200	2.41	2.23	2.08	1.96	1.85	1.77	1.69	1.63	1.44	1.20	1.11	1.06	200
300	3.61	3.34	3.12	2.93	2.78	2.65	2.54	2.44	2.15	1.80	1.66	1.58	300
400	4.81	4.45	4.15	3.91	3.70	3.53	3.38	3.25	2.87	2.40	2.21	2.11	400
500	6.01	5.56	5.19	4.88	4.63	4.41	4.22	4.06	3.59	3.00	2.76	2.64	500
600	7.21	6.67	6.23	5.86	5.55	5.29	5.07	4.87	4.30	3.60	3.31	3.16	600
700	8.41	7.78	7.26	6.84	6.48	6.17	5.91	5.69	5.02	4.20	3.86	3.69	700
800	9.61	8.89	8.30	7.81	7.40	7.05	6.76	6.50	5.74	4.80	4.41	4.22	800
900	10.81	10.00	9.34	8.79	8.33	7.94	7.60	7.31	6.45	5.40	4.96	4.74	900
1000	12.01	11.11	10.37	9.76	9.25	8.82	8.44	8.12	7.17	6.00	5.51	5.27	1000
2000	24.02	22.21	20.74	19.52	18.50	17.63	16.88	16.23	14.33	12.00	11.01	10.53	2000
3000	36.02	33.31	31.11	29.28	27.75	26.44	25.32	24.35	21.50	17.99	16.51	15.80	3000
4000	48.03	44.41	41.47	39.04	36.99	35.25	33.76	32.46	28.66	23.99	22.01	21.06	4000
5000	60.03	55.52	51.84	48.80	46.24	44.07	42.20	40.58	35.83	29.98	27.52	26.33	5000
6000	72.04	66.62	62.21	58.56	55.49	52.88	50.64	48.69	42.99	35.98	33.02	31.59	6000
7000	84.05	77.72	72.57	68.31	64.74	61.69	59.07	56.81	50.16	41.97	38.52	36.85	7000
8000	96.05	88.82	82.94	78.07	73.98	70.50	67.51	64.92	57.32	47.97	44.02	42.12	8000
9000	108.06	99.92	93.31	87.83	83.23	79.32	75.95	73.03	64.48	53.96	49.52	47.38	9000
10000	120.06	111.03	103.68	97.59	92.48	88.13	84.39	81.15	71.65	59.96	55.03	52.65	10000
15000	180.09	166.54	155.51	146.38	138.71	132.19	126.58	121.72	107.47	89.94	82.54	78.97	15000
20000	240.12	222.05	207.35	195.18	184.95	176.25	168.78	162.29	143.29	119.92	110.05	105.29	20000
25000	300.15	277.56	259.18	243.97	231.19	220.31	210.97	202.86	179.11	149.89	137.56	131.61	25000
30000	360.18	333.07	311.02	292.76	277.42	264.38	253.16	243.44	214.93	179.87	165.07	157.93	30000
35000	420.21	388.58	362.85	341.55	323.66	308.44	295.35	284.01	250.76	209.85	192.58	184.25	35000
40000	480.23	444.09	414.69	390.35	369.89	352.50	337.55	324.58	286.58	239.83	220.09	210.57	40000
45000	540.26	499.60	466.52	439.14	416.13	396.56	379.74	365.15	322.40	269.80	247.60	236.89	45000
50000	600.29	555.11	518.36	487.93	462.37	440.62	421.93	405.72	358.22	299.78	275.11	263.21	50000
60000	720.35	666.13	622.03	585.52	554.84	528.75	506.32	486.87	429.86	359.74	330.13	315.85	60000
75000	900.44	832.66	777.53	731.89	693.55	660.93	632.90	608.58	537.33	449.67	412.67	394.81	75000
100000	1200.58	1110.21	1036.71	975.86	924.73	881.24	843.86	811.44	716.44	599.56	550.22	526.41	100000
125000	1500.72	1387.76	1295.88	1219.82	1155.91	1101.55	1054.83	1014.30	895.54	749.44	687.77	658.01	125000
150000	1800.87	1665.31	1555.06	1463.78	1387.09	1321.86	1265.79	1217.16	1074.65	899.33	825.33	789.61	150000
175000	2101.01	1942.86	1814.24	1707.74	1618.27	1542.17	1476.75	1420.02	1253.76	1049.22	962.88	921.21	175000
200000	2401.15	2220.42	2073.41	1951.71	1849.45	1762.48	1687.72	1622.88	1432.87	1199.11	1100.43	1052.81	200000
250000	3001.44	2775.52	2591.76	2439.63	2311.81	2203.09	2109.65	2028.60	1791.08	1498.88	1375.54	1316.02	250000

Amount	1.0 Year	1.5 Years	2.0 Years	2.5 Years	3.0 Years	3.5 Years	4.0 Years	4.5 Years	5.0 Years	6.0 Years	7.0 Years	8.0 Years	Amount
100	8.62	5.84	4.45	3.61	3.06	2.66	2.36	2.13	1.95	1.67	1.48	1.33	100
200	17.24	11.67	8.89	7.22	6.11	5.32	4.72	4.26	3.89	3.34	2.95	2.66	200
300	25.86	17.51	13.34	10.83	9.17	7.98	7.08	6.39	5.84	5.01	4.42	3.98	300
400	34.48	23.34	17.78	14.44	12.22	10.63	9.44	8.52	7.78	6.68	5.90	5.31	400
500	43.10	29.18	22.22	18.05	15.27	13.29	11.80	10.65	9.73	8.35	7.37	6.64	500
600	51.71	35.01	26.67	21.66	18.33	15.95	14.16	12.78	11.67	10.02	8.84	7.96	600
700	60.33	40.85	31.11	25.27	21.38	18.60	16.52	14.91	13.62	11.69	10.32	9.29	700
800	68.95	46.68	35.55	28.88	24.43	21.26	18.88	17.04	15.56	13.36	11.79	10.62	800
900	77.57	52.52	40.00	32.49	27.49	23.92	21.24	19.17	17.51	15.03	13.26	11.94	900
1000	86.19	58.35	44.44	36.10	30.54	26.58	23.60	21.30	19.45	16.70	14.73	13.27	1000
2000	172.37	116.69	88.87	72.19	61.08	53.15	47.20	42.59	38.90	33.39	29.46	26.53	2000
3000	258.55	175.04	133.31	108.28	91.61	79.72	70.80	63.88	58.35	50.08	44.19	39.80	3000
4000	344.73	233.38	177.74	144.37	122.15	106.29	94.40	85.17	77.80	66.77	58.92	53.06	4000
5000	430.91	291.73	222.17	180.46	152.68	132.86	118.00	106.47	97.25	83.46	73.65	66.32	5000
6000	517.09	350.07	266.61	216.56	183.22	159.43	141.60	127.76	116.70	100.15	88.38	79.59	6000
7000	603.27	408.42	311.04	252.65	213.75	186.00	165.20	149.05	136.15	116.84	103.11	92.85	7000
8000	689.46	466.76	355.47	288.74	244.29	212.57	188.80	170.34	155.60	133.53	117.83	106.11	8000
9000	775.64	525.11	399.91	324.83	274.82	239.14	212.40	191.64	175.05	150.23	132.56	119.38	9000
10000	861.82	583.45	444.34	360.92	305.36	265.71	236.00	212.93	194.50	166.92	147.29	132.64	10000
15000	1292.73	875.18	666.51	541.38	458.04	398.56	354.00	319.39	291.74	250.37	220.94	198.96	15000
20000	1723.63	1166.90	888.67	721.84	610.71	531.41	472.00	425.85	388.99	333.83	294.58	265.27	20000
25000	2154.54	1458.63	1110.84	902.30	763.39	664.26	590.00	532.32	486.24	417.28	368.22	331.59	25000
30000	2585.45	1750.35	1333.01	1082.76	916.07	797.11	708.00	638.78	583.48	500.74	441.87	397.91	30000
35000	3016.35	2042.07	1555.17	1263.22	1068.74	929.96	826.00	745.24	680.73	584.20	515.51	464.23	35000
40000	3447.26	2333.80	1777.34	1443.68	1221.42	1062.82	944.00	851.70	777.98	667.65	589.15	530.54	40000
45000	3878.17	2625.52	1999.51	1624.14	1374.10	1195.67	1062.00	958.17	875.22	751.11	662.80	596.86	45000
50000	4309.07	2917.25	2221.67	1804.60	1526.77	1328.52	1180.00	1064.63	972.47	834.56	736.44	663.18	50000
60000	5170.89	3500.70	2666.01	2165.52	1832.13	1594.22	1415.99	1277.55	1166.96	1001.47	883.73	795.81	60000
75000	6463.61	4375.87	3332.51	2706.89	2290.16	1992.77	1769.99	1596.94	1458.70	1251.84	1104.66	994.77	75000
100000	8618.14	5834.49	4443.34	3609.19	3053.54	2657.03	2359.99	2129.25	1944.93	1669.12	1472.87	1326.35	100000
125000	10772.68	7293.11	5554.17	4511.49	3816.92	3321.29	2949.98	2661.56	2431.16	2086.40	1841.09	1657.94	125000
150000	12927.21	8751.73	6665.01	5413.78	4580.31	3985.54	3539.98	3193.87	2917.39	2503.68	2209.31	1989.53	150000
175000	15081.75	10210.35	7775.84	6316.08	5343.69	4649.80	4129.97	3726.19	3403.63	2920.96	2577.53	2321.12	175000
200000	17236.28	11668.98	8886.67	7218.37	6107.07	5314.06	4719.97	4258.50	3889.86	3338.24	2945.74	2652.70	200000
250000	21545.35	14586.22	11108.34	9022.97	7633.84	6642.57	5899.96	5323.12	4862.32	4172.79	3682.18	3315.88	250000

Amount	9.0 Years	10.0 Years	11.0 Years	12.0 Years	13.0 Years	14.0 Years	15.0 Years	16.0 Years	20.0 Years	30.0 Years	40.0 Years	50.0 Years	Amount
100	1.22	1.13	1.05	0.99	0.94	0.90	0.86	0.83	0.74	0.62	0.57	0.55	100
200	2.43	2.25	2.10	1.98	1.88	1.79	1.72	1.66	1.47	1.24	1.14	1.09	200
300	3.64	3.37	3.15	2.97	2.82	2.69	2.58	2.48	2.20	1.85	1.71	1.64	300
400	4.86	4.50	4.20	3.96	3.76	3.58	3.43	3.31	2.93	2.47	2.28	2.18	400
500	6.07	5.62	5.25	4.95	4.69	4.48	4.29	4.13	3.66	3.08	2.84	2.73	500
600	7.28	6.74	6.30	5.94	5.63	5.37	5.15	4.96	4.39	3.70	3.41	3.27	600
700	8.50	7.86	7.35	6.93	6.57	6.27	6.01	5.78	5.12	4.32	3.98	3.82	700
800	9.71	8.99	8.40	7.92	7.51	7.16	6.86	6.61	5.85	4.93	4.55	4.36	800
900	10.92	10.11	9.45	8.90	8.45	8.06	7.72	7.43	6.58	5.55	5.11	4.91	900
1000	12.13	11.23	10.50	9.89	9.38	8.95	8.58	8.26	7.31	6.16	5.68	5.45	1000
2000	24.26	22.46	20.99	19.78	18.76	17.90	17.15	16.51	14.62	12.32	11.36	10.90	2000
3000	36.39	33.69	31.49	29.67	28.14	26.84	25.73	24.76	21.93	18.48	17.04	16.35	3000
4000	48.52	44.92	41.98	39.56	37.52	35.79	34.30	33.01	29.24	24.63	22.71	21.80	4000
5000	60.65	56.15	52.48	49.45	46.90	44.74	42.88	41.26	36.55	30.79	28.39	27.25	5000
6000	72.78	67.37	62.97	59.34	56.28	53.68	51.45	49.52	43.86	36.95	34.07	32.70	6000
7000	84.91	78.60	73.47	69.22	65.66	62.63	60.02	57.77	51.17	43.11	39.75	38.15	7000
8000	97.04	89.83	83.96	79.11	75.04	71.57	68.60	66.02	58.48	49.26	45.42	43.60	8000
9000	109.17	101.06	94.46	89.00	84.42	80.52	77.17	74.27	65.79	55.42	51.10	49.05	9000
10000	121.30	112.29	104.95	98.89	93.80	89.47	85.75	82.53	73.10	61.58	56.78	54.50	10000
15000	181.95	168.43	157.43	148.33	140.69	134.20	128.62	123.78	109.64	92.36	85.17	81.75	15000
20000	242.60	224.57	209.90	197.77	187.59	178.93	171.49	165.04	146.19	123.15	113.55	109.00	20000
25000	303.25	280.71	262.38	247.21	234.48	223.66	214.36	206.30	182.74	153.93	141.94	136.25	25000
30000	363.90	336.85	314.85	296.66	281.38	268.39	257.23	247.56	219.28	184.72	170.33	163.50	30000
35000	424.55	392.99	367.33	346.10	328.27	313.12	300.10	288.82	255.83	215.51	198.71	190.75	35000
40000	485.20	449.13	419.80	395.54	375.17	357.85	342.97	330.08	292.38	246.29	227.10	217.99	40000
45000	545.84	505.27	472.28	444.98	422.06	402.58	385.85	371.34	328.92	277.08	255.49	245.24	45000
50000	606.49	561.41	524.75	494.42	468.96	447.31	428.72	412.60	365.47	307.86	283.87	272.49	50000
60000	727.79	673.69	629.70	593.31	562.75	536.77	514.46	495.12	438.56	369.44	340.65	326.99	60000
75000	909.74	842.11	787.13	741.63	703.43	670.96	643.07	618.90	548.20	461.79	425.81	408.73	75000
100000	1212.98	1122.81	1049.50	988.84	937.91	894.62	857.43	825.20	730.93	615.72	567.74	544.98	100000
125000	1516.22	1403.51	1311.87	1236.05	1172.39	1118.27	1071.78	1031.50	913.67	769.65	709.68	681.22	125000
150000	1819.47	1684.21	1574.25	1483.26	1406.86	1341.92	1286.14	1237.80	1096.40	923.58	851.61	817.46	150000
175000	2122.71	1964.91	1836.62	1730.47	1641.34	1565.57	1500.50	1444.09	1279.13	1077.51	993.55	953.71	175000
200000	2425.96	2245.61	2098.99	1977.68	1875.81	1789.23	1714.85	1650.39	1461.86	1231.44	1135.48	1089.95	200000
250000	3032.44	2807.01	2623.74	2472.10	2344.77	2236.53	2143.56	2062.99	1827.33	1539.30	1419.35	1362.44	250000

Amount	1.0 Year	1.5 Years	2.0 Years	2.5 Years	3.0 Years	3.5 Years	4.0 Years	4.5 Years	5.0 Years	6.0 Years	7.0 Years	8.0 Years	Amount
100	8.63	5.85	4.46	3.63	3.07	2.67	2.38	2.15	1.96	1.69	1.49	1.34	100
200	17.26	11.70	8.91	7.25	6.13	5.34	4.75	4.29	3.92	3.37	2.97	2.68	200
300	25.89	17.54	13.37	10.87	9.20	8.01	7.12	6.43	5.87	5.05	4.46	4.02	300
400	34.52	23.39	17.82	14.49	12.26	10.68	9.49	8.57	7.83	6.73	5.94	5.36	400
500	43.15	29.23	22.28	18.11	15.33	13.35	11.86	10.71	9.79	8.41	7.43	6.70	500
600	51.78	35.08	26.73	21.73	18.39	16.02	14.23	12.85	11.74	10.09	8.91	8.04	600
700	60.41	40.93	31.19	25.35	21.46	18.68	16.61	14.99	13.70	11.77	10.40	9.38	700
800	69.04	46.77	35.64	28.97	24.52	21.35	18.98	17.13	15.66	13.45	11.88	10.71	800
900	77.67	52.62	40.10	32.59	27.59	24.02	21.35	19.27	17.61	15.13	13.37	12.05	900
1000	86.30	58.46	44.55	36.21	30.65	26.69	23.72	21.41	19.57	16.81	14.85	13.39	1000
2000	172.60	116.92	89.10	72.41	61.30	53.37	47.43	42.82	39.14	33.62	29.70	26.78	2000
3000	258.89	175.38	133.64	108.62	91.95	80.06	71.15	64.23	58.70	50.43	44.55	40.16	3000
4000	345.19	233.84	178.19	144.82	122.60	106.74	94.86	85.64	78.27	67.24	59.40	53.55	4000
5000	431.49	292.30	222.74	181.03	153.25	133.43	118.58	107.05	97.84	84.05	74.25	66.94	5000
6000	517.78	350.75	267.28	217.23	183.90	160.11	142.29	128.46	117.40	100.86	89.10	80.32	6000
7000	604.08	409.21	311.83	253.44	214.55	186.80	166.00	149.86	136.97	117.67	103.95	93.71	7000
8000	690.38	467.67	356.38	289.64	245.20	213.48	189.72	171.27	156.53	134.48	118.80	107.09	8000
9000	776.67	526.13	400.92	325.85	275.85	240.17	213.44	192.68	176.10	151.29	133.65	120.48	9000
10000	862.97	584.59	445.47	362.05	306.50	266.85	237.15	214.09	195.67	168.10	148.50	133.87	10000
15000	1294.45	876.88	668.20	543.08	459.74	400.27	355.73	321.13	293.50	252.15	222.75	200.80	15000
20000	1725.93	1169.17	890.93	724.10	612.99	533.70	474.30	428.17	391.33	336.20	296.99	267.73	20000
25000	2157.42	1461.46	1113.66	905.13	766.23	667.12	592.88	535.22	489.16	420.25	371.24	334.66	25000
30000	2588.90	1753.75	1336.39	1086.15	919.48	800.54	711.45	642.26	586.99	504.30	445.49	401.59	30000
35000	3020.38	2046.04	1559.12	1267.18	1072.72	933.97	830.03	749.30	684.82	588.35	519.74	468.52	35000
40000	3451.86	2338.33	1781.86	1448.20	1225.97	1067.39	948.60	856.34	782.65	672.40	593.98	535.45	40000
45000	3883.34	2630.62	2004.59	1629.23	1379.21	1200.81	1067.18	963.39	880.48	756.45	668.23	602.39	45000
50000	4314.83	2922.91	2227.32	1810.25	1532.46	1334.24	1185.75	1070.43	978.31	840.50	742.48	669.32	50000
60000	5177.79	3507.49	2672.78	2172.30	1838.95	1601.08	1422.90	1284.51	1173.97	1008.60	890.97	803.18	60000
75000	6472.24	4384.36	3340.97	2715.38	2298.68	2001.35	1778.63	1605.64	1467.47	1260.75	1113.71	1003.97	75000
100000	8629.65	5845.82	4454.63	3620.50	3064.91	2668.47	2371.50	2140.85	1956.62	1681.00	1484.95	1338.63	100000
125000	10787.06	7307.27	5568.29	4525.63	3831.13	3335.58	2964.37	2676.06	2445.77	2101.25	1856.18	1673.28	125000
150000	12944.47	8768.72	6681.94	5430.75	4597.36	4002.70	3557.25	3211.27	2934.93	2521.49	2227.42	2007.94	150000
175000	15101.88	10230.17	7795.60	6335.88	5363.58	4669.81	4150.12	3746.48	3424.08	2941.74	2598.66	2342.60	175000
200000	17259.29	11691.63	8909.26	7241.00	6129.81	5336.93	4743.00	4281.69	3913.23	3361.99	2969.89	2677.25	200000
250000	21574.11	14614.53	11136.57	9051.25	7662.26	6671.16	5928.74	5352.12	4891.54	4202.49	3712.36	3346.56	250000

Amount	9.0 Years	10.0 Years	11.0 Years	12.0 Years	13.0 Years	14.0 Years	15.0 Years	16.0 Years	20.0 Years	30.0 Years	40.0 Years	50.0 Years	Amount
100	1.23	1.14	1.07	1.01	0.96	0.91	0.88	0.84	0.75	0.64	0.59	0.57	100
200	2.46	2.28	2.13	2.01	1.91	1.82	1.75	1.68	1.50	1.27	1.18	1.13	200
300	3.68	3.41	3.19	3.01	2.86	2.73	2.62	2.52	2.24	1.90	1.76	1.70	300
400	4.91	4.55	4.25	4.01	3.81	3.64	3.49	3.36	2.99	2.53	2.35	2.26	400
500	6.13	5.68	5.32	5.01	4.76	4.55	4.36	4.20	3.73	3.17	2.93	2.82	500
600	7.36	6.82	6.38	6.02	5.71	5.45	5.23	5.04	4.48	3.80	3.52	3.39	600
700	8.58	7.95	7.44	7.02	6.66	6.36	6.10	5.88	5.22	4.43	4.10	3.95	700
800	9.81	9.09	8.50	8.02	7.61	7.27	6.97	6.72	5.97	5.06	4.69	4.51	800
900	11.03	10.22	9.57	9.02	8.57	8.18	7.84	7.56	6.72	5.69	5.27	5.08	900
1000	12.26	11.36	10.63	10.02	9.52	9.09	8.72	8.40	7.46	6.33	5.86	5.64	1000
2000	24.51	22.71	21.25	20.04	19.03	18.17	17.43	16.79	14.92	12.65	11.71	11.28	2000
3000	36.77	34.07	31.88	30.06	28.54	27.25	26.14	25.18	22.37	18.97	17.57	16.92	3000
4000	49.02	45.42	42.50	40.08	38.05	36.33	34.85	33.57	29.83	25.29	23.42	22.55	4000
5000	61.28	56.78	53.12	50.10	47.56	45.41	43.56	41.96	37.28	31.61	29.28	28.19	5000
6000	73.53	68.13	63.75	60.12	57.08	54.49	52.27	50.35	44.74	37.93	35.13	33.83	6000
7000	85.79	79.49	74.37	70.14	66.59	63.57	60.98	58.74	52.20	44.25	40.99	39.47	7000
8000	98.04	90.84	85.00	80.16	76.10	72.65	69.69	67.13	59.65	50.57	46.84	45.10	8000
9000	110.30	102.20	95.62	90.18	85.61	81.73	78.40	75.52	67.11	56.89	52.70	50.74	9000
10000	122.55	113.55	106.24	100.20	95.12	90.81	87.12	83.91	74.56	63.21	58.55	56.38	10000
15000	183.82	170.33	159.36	150.29	142.68	136.22	130.67	125.87	111.84	94.82	87.82	84.56	15000
20000	245.10	227.10	212.48	200.39	190.24	181.62	174.23	167.82	149.12	126.42	117.10	112.75	20000
25000	306.37	283.87	265.60	250.49	237.80	227.03	217.78	209.77	186.40	158.02	146.37	140.93	25000
30000	367.64	340.65	318.72	300.58	285.36	272.43	261.34	251.73	223.68	189.63	175.64	169.12	30000
35000	428.91	397.42	371.84	350.68	332.92	317.84	304.89	293.68	260.96	221.23	204.91	197.31	35000
40000	490.19	454.20	424.96	400.77	380.48	363.24	348.45	335.64	298.23	252.83	234.19	225.49	40000
45000	551.46	510.97	478.07	450.87	428.04	408.65	392.00	377.59	335.51	284.44	263.46	253.68	45000
50000	612.73	567.74	531.19	500.97	475.60	454.05	435.56	419.54	372.79	316.04	292.73	281.86	50000
60000	735.28	681.29	637.43	601.16	570.72	544.86	522.67	503.45	447.35	379.25	351.28	338.24	60000
75000	919.09	851.61	796.79	751.45	713.40	681.08	653.34	629.31	559.18	474.06	439.10	422.79	75000
100000	1225.46	1135.48	1062.38	1001.93	951.20	908.10	871.11	839.08	745.58	632.07	585.46	563.72	100000
125000	1531.82	1419.35	1327.98	1252.41	1188.99	1135.13	1088.89	1048.85	931.97	790.09	731.83	704.65	125000
150000	1838.18	1703.22	1593.57	1502.89	1426.79	1362.15	1306.67	1258.62	1118.36	948.11	878.19	845.58	150000
175000	2144.55	1987.09	1859.16	1753.37	1664.59	1589.17	1524.44	1468.39	1304.76	1106.12	1024.55	986.51	175000
200000	2450.91	2270.96	2124.76	2003.85	1902.39	1816.20	1742.22	1678.16	1491.15	1264.14	1170.92	1127.44	200000
250000	3063.63	2838.70	2655.95	2504.81	2377.98	2270.25	2177.77	2097.69	1863.94	1580.18	1463.65	1409.30	250000

Amount	1.0 Year	1.5 Years	2.0 Years	2.5 Years	3.0 Years	3.5 Years	4.0 Years	4.5 Years	5.0 Years	6.0 Years	7.0 Years	8.0 Years	Amount
100	8.65	5.86	4.47	3.64	3.08	2.68	2.39	2.16	1.97	1.70	1.50	1.36	100
200	17.29	11.72	8.94	7.27	6.16	5.36	4.77	4.31	3.94	3.39	3.00	2.71	200
300	25.93	17.58	13.40	10.90	9.23	8.04	7.15	6.46	5.91	5.08	4.50	4.06	300
400	34.57	23.43	17.87	14.53	12.31	10.72	9.54	8.61	7.88	6.78	5.99	5.41	400
500	43.21	29.29	22.33	18.16	15.39	13.40	11.92	10.77	9.85	8.47	7.49	6.76	500
600	51.85	35.15	26.80	21.80	18.46	16.08	14.30	12.92	11.82	10.16	8.99	8.11	600
700	60.49	41.01	31.27	25.43	21.54	18.76	16.69	15.07	13.78	11.86	10.48	9.46	700
800	69.13	46.86	35.73	29.06	24.62	21.44	19.07	17.22	15.75	13.55	11.98	10.81	800
900	77.78	52.72	40.20	32.69	27.69	24.12	21.45	19.38	17.72	15.24	13.48	12.16	900
1000	86.42	58.58	44.66	36.32	30.77	26.80	23.84	21.53	19.69	16.93	14.98	13.51	1000
2000	172.83	117.15	89.32	72.64	61.53	53.60	47.67	43.05	39.37	33.86	29.95	27.02	2000
3000	259.24	175.72	133.98	108.96	92.29	80.40	71.50	64.58	59.06	50.79	44.92	40.53	3000
4000	345.65	234.29	178.64	145.28	123.06	107.20	95.33	86.10	78.74	67.72	59.89	54.04	4000
5000	432.06	292.86	223.30	181.60	153.82	134.00	119.16	107.63	98.42	84.65	74.86	67.55	5000
6000	518.47	351.43	267.96	217.92	184.58	160.80	142.99	129.15	118.11	101.58	89.83	81.06	6000
7000	604.89	410.01	312.62	254.23	215.35	187.60	166.82	150.68	137.79	118.51	104.80	94.57	7000
8000	691.30	468.58	357.28	290.55	246.11	214.40	190.65	172.20	157.47	135.44	119.77	108.08	8000
9000	777.71	527.15	401.94	326.87	276.87	241.20	214.48	193.73	177.16	152.37	134.74	121.59	9000
10000	864.12	585.72	446.60	363.19	307.63	268.00	238.31	215.25	196.84	169.30	149.71	135.10	10000
15000	1296.18	878.58	669.89	544.78	461.45	401.99	357.46	322.88	295.26	253.94	224.57	202.65	15000
20000	1728.24	1171.43	893.19	726.37	615.26	535.99	476.61	430.50	393.67	338.59	299.42	270.20	20000
25000	2160.29	1464.29	1116.49	907.96	769.08	669.99	595.77	538.13	492.09	423.24	374.27	337.75	25000
30000	2592.35	1757.15	1339.78	1089.56	922.89	803.98	714.92	645.75	590.51	507.88	449.13	405.29	30000
35000	3024.41	2050.01	1563.08	1271.15	1076.71	937.98	834.07	753.37	688.93	592.53	523.98	472.84	35000
40000	3456.47	2342.86	1786.38	1452.74	1230.52	1071.98	953.22	861.00	787.34	677.17	598.84	540.39	40000
45000	3888.52	2635.72	2009.67	1634.33	1384.34	1205.97	1072.37	968.62	885.76	761.82	673.69	607.94	45000
50000	4320.58	2928.58	2232.97	1815.92	1538.15	1339.97	1191.53	1076.25	984.18	846.47	748.54	675.49	50000
60000	5184.70	3514.29	2679.56	2179.11	1845.78	1607.96	1429.83	1291.49	1181.01	1015.76	898.25	810.58	60000
75000	6480.87	4392.87	3349.45	2723.88	2307.22	2009.95	1787.29	1614.37	1476.26	1269.70	1122.81	1013.23	75000
100000	8641.16	5857.15	4465.94	3631.84	3076.30	2679.93	2383.05	2152.49	1968.35	1692.93	1497.08	1350.97	100000
125000	10801.45	7321.44	5582.42	4539.80	3845.37	3349.91	2978.81	2690.61	2460.44	2116.16	1871.35	1688.71	125000
150000	12961.74	8785.73	6698.90	5447.76	4614.44	4019.89	3574.57	3228.73	2952.52	2539.39	2245.62	2026.45	150000
175000	15122.02	10250.01	7815.39	6355.71	5383.52	4689.87	4170.33	3766.85	3444.61	2962.62	2619.89	2364.19	175000
200000	17282.31	11714.30	8931.87	7263.67	6152.59	5359.86	4766.09	4304.97	3936.70	3385.85	2994.16	2701.93	200000
250000	21602.89	14642.87	11164.84	9079.59	7690.74	6699.82	5957.61	5381.21	4920.87	4232.31	3742.70	3377.42	250000

Amount	9.0 Years	10.0 Years	11.0 Years	12.0 Years	13.0 Years	14.0 Years	15.0 Years	16.0 Years	20.0 Years	30.0 Years	40.0 Years	50.0 Years	Amount
100	1.24	1.15	1.08	1.02	0.97	0.93	0.89	0.86	0.77	0.65	0.61	0.59	100
200	2.48	2.30	2.16	2.04	1.93	1.85	1.77	1.71	1.53	1.30	1.21	1.17	200
300	3.72	3.45	3.23	3.05	2.90	2.77	2.66	2.56	2.29	1.95	1.82	1.75	300
400	4.96	4.60	4.31	4.07	3.86	3.69	3.54	3.42	3.05	2.60	2.42	2.34	400
500	6.20	5.75	5.38	5.08	4.83	4.61	4.43	4.27	3.81	3.25	3.02	2.92	500
600	7.43	6.89	6.46	6.10	5.79	5.54	5.31	5.12	4.57	3.90	3.63	3.50	600
700	8.67	8.04	7.53	7.11	6.76	6.46	6.20	5.98	5.33	4.55	4.23	4.08	700
800	9.91	9.19	8.61	8.13	7.72	7.38	7.08	6.83	6.09	5.19	4.83	4.67	800
900	11.15	10.34	9.68	9.14	8.69	8.30	7.97	7.68	6.85	5.84	5.44	5.25	900
1000	12.39	11.49	10.76	10.16	9.65	9.22	8.85	8.54	7.61	6.49	6.04	5.83	1000
2000	24.77	22.97	21.51	20.31	19.30	18.44	17.70	17.07	15.21	12.98	12.07	11.66	2000
3000	37.15	34.45	32.27	30.46	28.94	27.66	26.55	25.60	22.82	19.46	18.11	17.48	3000
4000	49.53	45.93	43.02	40.61	38.59	36.87	35.40	34.13	30.42	25.95	24.14	23.31	4000
5000	61.91	57.42	53.77	50.76	48.23	46.09	44.25	42.66	38.02	32.43	30.17	29.14	5000
6000	74.29	68.90	64.53	60.91	57.88	55.31	53.10	51.19	45.63	38.92	36.21	34.96	6000
7000	86.67	80.38	75.28	71.06	67.53	64.52	61.95	59.72	53.23	45.41	42.24	40.79	7000
8000	99.05	91.86	86.03	81.21	77.17	73.74	70.80	68.25	60.83	51.89	48.27	46.62	8000
9000	111.43	103.35	96.79	91.36	86.82	82.95	79.65	76.78	68.44	58.38	54.31	52.44	9000
10000	123.81	114.83	107.54	101.52	96.46	92.17	88.50	85.31	76.04	64.86	60.34	58.27	10000
15000	185.71	172.24	161.31	152.27	144.69	138.26	132.74	127.97	114.06	97.29	90.51	87.40	15000
20000	247.61	229.65	215.07	203.03	192.92	184.34	176.99	170.62	152.08	129.72	120.68	116.53	20000
25000	309.51	287.07	268.84	253.78	241.15	230.43	221.23	213.28	190.10	162.15	150.84	145.66	25000
30000	371.41	344.48	322.61	304.54	289.38	276.51	265.48	255.93	228.11	194.58	181.01	174.79	30000
35000	433.31	401.89	376.38	355.29	337.61	322.60	309.72	298.58	266.13	227.01	211.18	203.92	35000
40000	495.21	459.30	430.14	406.05	385.84	368.68	353.97	341.24	304.15	259.44	241.35	233.06	40000
45000	557.11	516.71	483.91	456.80	434.07	414.77	398.21	383.89	342.17	291.87	271.52	262.19	45000
50000	619.01	574.13	537.68	507.56	482.30	460.85	442.46	426.55	380.19	324.30	301.68	291.32	50000
60000	742.81	688.95	645.21	609.07	578.75	553.02	530.95	511.85	456.22	389.16	362.02	349.58	60000
75000	928.51	861.19	806.52	761.33	723.44	691.27	663.69	639.82	570.28	486.45	452.52	436.97	75000
100000	1238.01	1148.25	1075.35	1015.11	964.59	921.70	884.91	853.09	760.37	648.60	603.36	582.63	100000
125000	1547.51	1435.31	1344.19	1268.88	1205.73	1152.12	1106.14	1066.36	950.46	810.75	754.20	728.29	125000
150000	1857.01	1722.37	1613.03	1522.66	1446.88	1382.54	1327.37	1279.63	1140.55	972.90	905.04	873.94	150000
175000	2166.51	2009.43	1881.87	1776.43	1688.02	1612.97	1548.60	1492.90	1330.64	1135.05	1055.88	1019.60	175000
200000	2476.01	2296.49	2150.70	2030.21	1929.17	1843.39	1769.82	1706.17	1520.73	1297.20	1206.72	1165.26	200000
250000	3095.01	2870.61	2688.38	2537.76	2411.46	2304.24	2212.28	2132.71	1900.92	1621.50	1508.40	1456.57	250000

Amount	1.0 Year	1.5 Years	2.0 Years	2.5 Years	3.0 Years	3.5 Years	4.0 Years	4.5 Years	5.0 Years	6.0 Years	7.0 Years	8.0 Years	Amount
100	8.66	5.87	4.48	3.65	3.09	2.70	2.40	2.17	1.99	1.71	1.51	1.37	100
200	17.31	11.74	8.96	7.29	6.18	5.39	4.79	4.33	3.97	3.41	3.02	2.73	200
300	25.96	17.61	13.44	10.93	9.27	8.08	7.19	6.50	5.95	5.12	4.53	4.10	300
400	34.62	23.48	17.91	14.58	12.36	10.77	9.58	8.66	7.93	6.82	6.04	5.46	400
500	43.27	29.35	22.39	18.22	15.44	13.46	11.98	10.83	9.91	8.53	7.55	6.82	500
600	51.92	35.22	26.87	21.86	18.53	16.15	14.37	12.99	11.89	10.23	9.06	8.19	600
700	60.57	41.08	31.35	25.51	21.62	18.84	16.77	15.15	13.87	11.94	10.57	9.55	700
800	69.23	46.95	35.82	29.15	24.71	21.54	19.16	17.32	15.85	13.64	12.08	10.91	800
900	77.88	52.82	40.30	32.79	27.79	24.23	21.56	19.48	17.83	15.35	13.59	12.28	900
1000	86.53	58.69	44.78	36.44	30.88	26.92	23.95	21.65	19.81	17.05	15.10	13.64	1000
2000	173.06	117.37	89.55	72.87	61.76	53.83	47.90	43.29	39.61	34.10	30.19	27.27	2000
3000	259.59	176.06	134.32	109.30	92.64	80.75	71.84	64.93	59.41	51.15	45.28	40.91	3000
4000	346.11	234.74	179.10	145.73	123.51	107.66	95.79	86.57	79.21	68.20	60.38	54.54	4000
5000	432.64	293.43	223.87	182.16	154.39	134.58	119.74	108.21	99.01	85.25	75.47	68.17	5000
6000	519.17	352.11	268.64	218.60	185.27	161.49	143.68	129.85	118.81	102.30	90.56	81.81	6000
7000	605.69	410.80	313.41	255.03	216.14	188.40	167.63	151.50	138.61	119.35	105.65	95.44	7000
8000	692.22	469.48	358.19	291.46	247.02	215.32	191.57	173.14	158.41	136.40	120.75	109.07	8000
9000	778.75	528.17	402.96	327.89	277.90	242.23	215.52	194.78	178.22	153.45	135.84	122.71	9000
10000	865.27	586.85	447.73	364.32	308.78	269.15	239.47	216.42	198.02	170.50	150.93	136.34	10000
15000	1297.91	880.28	671.59	546.48	463.16	403.72	359.20	324.63	297.02	255.74	226.40	204.51	15000
20000	1730.54	1173.70	895.46	728.64	617.55	538.29	478.93	432.84	396.03	340.99	301.86	272.68	20000
25000	2163.17	1467.13	1119.32	910.80	771.93	672.86	598.66	541.04	495.03	426.23	377.32	340.85	25000
30000	2595.81	1760.55	1343.18	1092.96	926.32	807.43	718.39	649.25	594.04	511.48	452.79	409.02	30000
35000	3028.44	2053.98	1567.05	1275.12	1080.70	942.00	838.12	757.46	693.05	596.72	528.25	477.19	35000
40000	3461.07	2347.40	1790.91	1457.28	1235.09	1076.57	957.85	865.67	792.05	681.97	603.71	545.35	40000
45000	3893.71	2640.83	2014.77	1639.44	1389.47	1211.14	1077.59	973.88	891.06	767.21	679.18	613.52	45000
50000	4326.34	2934.25	2238.63	1821.60	1543.86	1345.72	1197.32	1082.08	990.06	852.46	754.64	681.69	50000
60000	5191.61	3521.10	2686.36	2185.92	1852.63	1614.86	1436.78	1298.50	1188.08	1022.95	905.57	818.03	60000
75000	6489.51	4401.38	3357.95	2732.40	2315.79	2018.57	1795.97	1623.12	1485.09	1278.68	1131.96	1022.53	75000
100000	8652.68	5868.50	4477.26	3643.20	3087.71	2691.43	2394.63	2164.16	1980.12	1704.91	1509.27	1363.38	100000
125000	10815.85	7335.63	5596.58	4553.99	3859.64	3364.28	2993.29	2705.20	2475.15	2131.13	1886.59	1704.22	125000
150000	12979.02	8802.75	6715.89	5464.79	4631.57	4037.14	3591.94	3246.24	2970.18	2557.36	2263.91	2045.06	150000
175000	15142.19	10269.88	7835.21	6375.59	5403.50	4709.99	4190.60	3787.28	3465.21	2983.58	2641.22	2385.91	175000
200000	17305.35	11737.00	8954.52	7286.39	6175.42	5382.85	4789.25	4328.32	3960.24	3409.81	3018.54	2726.75	200000
250000	21631.69	14671.25	11193.15	9107.98	7719.28	6728.56	5986.57	5410.40	4950.30	4262.26	3773.17	3408.43	250000

Amount	9.0 Years	10.0 Years	11.0 Years	12.0 Years	13.0 Years	14.0 Years	15.0 Years	16.0 Years	20.0 Years	30.0 Years	40.0 Years	50.0 Years	Amount
100	1.26	1.17	1.09	1.03	0.98	0.94	0.90	0.87	0.78	0.67	0.63	0.61	100
200	2.51	2.33	2.18	2.06	1.96	1.88	1.80	1.74	1.56	1.34	1.25	1.21	200
300	3.76	3.49	3.27	3.09	2.94	2.81	2.70	2.61	2.33	2.00	1.87	1.81	300
400	5.01	4.65	4.36	4.12	3.92	3.75	3.60	3.47	3.11	2.67	2.49	2.41	400
500	6.26	5.81	5.45	5.15	4.90	4.68	4.50	4.34	3.88	3.33	3.11	3.01	500
600	7.51	6.97	6.54	6.18	5.87	5.62	5.40	5.21	4.66	4.00	3.73	3.62	600
700	8.76	8.13	7.62	7.20	6.85	6.55	6.30	6.08	5.43	4.66	4.36	4.22	700
800	10.01	9.29	8.71	8.23	7.83	7.49	7.20	6.94	6.21	5.33	4.98	4.82	800
900	11.26	10.45	9.80	9.26	8.81	8.42	8.09	7.81	6.98	5.99	5.60	5.42	900
1000	12.51	11.62	10.89	10.29	9.79	9.36	8.99	8.68	7.76	6.66	6.22	6.02	1000
2000	25.02	23.23	21.77	20.57	19.57	18.71	17.98	17.35	15.51	13.31	12.43	12.04	2000
3000	37.52	34.84	32.66	30.86	29.35	28.07	26.97	26.02	23.26	19.96	18.65	18.06	3000
4000	50.03	46.45	43.54	41.14	39.13	37.42	35.96	34.69	31.02	26.62	24.86	24.07	4000
5000	62.54	58.06	54.43	51.42	48.91	46.78	44.95	43.37	38.77	33.27	31.08	30.09	5000
6000	75.04	69.67	65.31	61.71	58.69	56.13	53.93	52.04	46.52	39.92	37.29	36.11	6000
7000	87.55	81.28	76.19	71.99	68.47	65.48	62.92	60.71	54.28	46.58	43.51	42.12	7000
8000	100.06	92.89	87.08	82.28	78.25	74.84	71.91	69.38	62.03	53.23	49.72	48.14	8000
9000	112.56	104.50	97.96	92.56	88.03	84.19	80.90	78.05	69.78	59.88	55.93	54.16	9000
10000	125.07	116.11	108.85	102.84	97.81	93.55	89.89	86.73	77.53	66.54	62.15	60.17	10000
15000	187.60	174.17	163.27	154.26	146.72	140.32	134.83	130.09	116.30	99.80	93.22	90.26	15000
20000	250.13	232.22	217.69	205.68	195.62	187.09	179.77	173.45	155.06	133.07	124.29	120.34	20000
25000	312.66	290.28	272.11	257.10	244.52	233.86	224.71	216.81	193.83	166.33	155.36	150.43	25000
30000	375.19	348.33	326.53	308.52	293.43	280.63	269.65	260.17	232.59	199.60	186.43	180.51	30000
35000	437.72	406.38	380.95	359.94	342.33	327.40	314.59	303.53	271.36	232.86	217.51	210.60	35000
40000	500.26	464.44	435.37	411.36	391.23	374.17	359.54	346.89	310.12	266.13	248.58	240.68	40000
45000	562.79	522.49	489.79	462.78	440.14	420.94	404.48	390.25	348.89	299.39	279.65	270.76	45000
50000	625.32	580.55	544.21	514.20	489.04	467.71	449.42	433.61	387.65	332.66	310.72	300.85	50000
60000	750.38	696.66	653.05	617.03	586.85	561.25	539.30	520.33	465.18	399.19	372.86	361.02	60000
75000	937.98	870.82	816.31	771.29	733.56	701.56	674.13	650.41	581.48	498.98	466.08	451.27	75000
100000	1250.63	1161.09	1088.42	1028.39	978.08	935.41	898.83	867.21	775.30	665.31	621.44	601.69	100000
125000	1563.29	1451.36	1360.52	1285.48	1222.60	1169.26	1123.54	1084.02	969.13	831.63	776.79	752.12	125000
150000	1875.95	1741.63	1632.62	1542.58	1467.12	1403.11	1348.25	1300.82	1162.95	997.96	932.15	902.54	150000
175000	2188.60	2031.90	1904.72	1799.67	1711.63	1636.96	1572.95	1517.62	1356.78	1164.28	1087.51	1052.96	175000
200000	2501.26	2322.17	2176.83	2056.77	1956.15	1870.81	1797.66	1734.42	1550.60	1330.61	1242.87	1203.38	200000
250000	3126.57	2902.72	2721.03	2570.96	2445.19	2338.51	2247.08	2168.03	1938.25	1663.26	1553.58	1504.23	250000

Amount	1.0 Year	1.5 Years	2.0 Years	2.5 Years	3.0 Years	3.5 Years	4.0 Years	4.5 Years	5.0 Years	6.0 Years	7.0 Years	8.0 Years	Amount
100	8.67	5.88	4.49	3.66	3.10	2.71	2.41	2.18	2.00	1.72	1.53	1.38	100
200	17.33	11.76	8.98	7.31	6.20	5.41	4.82	4.36	3.99	3.44	3.05	2.76	200
300	26.00	17.64	13.47	10.97	9.30	8.11	7.22	6.53	5.98	5.16	4.57	4.13	300
400	34.66	23.52	17.96	14.62	12.40	10.82	9.63	8.71	7.97	6.87	6.09	5.51	400
500	43.33	29.40	22.45	18.28	15.50	13.52	12.04	10.88	9.96	8.59	7.61	6.88	500
600	51.99	35.28	26.94	21.93	18.60	16.22	14.44	13.06	11.96	10.31	9.13	8.26	600
700	60.65	41.16	31.43	25.59	21.70	18.93	16.85	15.24	13.95	12.02	10.66	9.64	700
800	69.32	47.04	35.91	29.24	24.80	21.63	19.25	17.41	15.94	13.74	12.18	11.01	800
900	77.98	52.92	40.40	32.90	27.90	24.33	21.66	19.59	17.93	15.46	13.70	12.39	900
1000	86.65	58.80	44.89	36.55	31.00	27.03	24.07	21.76	19.92	17.17	15.22	13.76	1000
2000	173.29	117.60	89.78	73.10	61.99	54.06	48.13	43.52	39.84	34.34	30.44	27.52	2000
3000	259.93	176.40	134.66	109.64	92.98	81.09	72.19	65.28	59.76	51.51	45.65	41.28	3000
4000	346.57	235.20	179.55	146.19	123.97	108.12	96.25	87.04	79.68	68.68	60.87	55.04	4000
5000	433.22	294.00	224.44	182.73	154.96	135.15	120.32	108.80	99.60	85.85	76.08	68.80	5000
6000	519.86	352.80	269.32	219.28	185.95	162.18	144.38	130.56	119.52	103.02	91.30	82.56	6000
7000	606.50	411.60	314.21	255.82	216.95	189.21	168.44	152.32	139.44	120.19	106.51	96.31	7000
8000	693.14	470.39	359.09	292.37	247.94	216.24	192.50	174.07	159.36	137.36	121.73	110.07	8000
9000	779.78	529.19	403.98	328.92	278.93	243.27	216.57	195.83	179.28	154.53	136.94	123.83	9000
10000	866.43	587.99	448.87	365.46	309.92	270.30	240.63	217.59	199.20	171.70	152.16	137.59	10000
15000	1299.64	881.98	673.30	548.19	464.88	405.45	360.94	326.39	298.80	257.54	228.23	206.38	15000
20000	1732.85	1175.98	897.73	730.92	619.84	540.59	481.25	435.18	398.39	343.39	304.31	275.17	20000
25000	2166.06	1469.97	1122.16	913.65	774.79	675.74	601.57	543.97	497.99	429.24	380.38	343.97	25000
30000	2599.27	1763.96	1346.59	1096.38	929.75	810.89	721.88	652.77	597.59	515.08	456.46	412.76	30000
35000	3032.48	2057.96	1571.02	1279.10	1084.71	946.04	842.19	761.56	697.18	600.93	532.54	481.55	35000
40000	3465.69	2351.95	1795.45	1461.83	1239.67	1081.18	962.50	870.35	796.78	686.78	608.61	550.34	40000
45000	3898.90	2645.94	2019.88	1644.56	1394.62	1216.33	1082.81	979.15	896.38	772.62	684.69	619.14	45000
50000	4332.11	2939.94	2244.31	1827.29	1549.58	1351.48	1203.13	1087.94	995.97	858.47	760.76	687.93	50000
60000	5198.53	3527.92	2693.17	2192.75	1859.50	1621.77	1443.75	1305.53	1195.17	1030.16	912.92	825.51	60000
75000	6498.16	4409.90	3366.46	2740.93	2324.37	2027.21	1804.69	1631.91	1493.96	1287.70	1141.14	1031.89	75000
100000	8664.21	5879.87	4488.61	3654.57	3099.16	2702.95	2406.25	2175.88	1991.94	1716.94	1521.52	1375.85	100000
125000	10830.26	7349.83	5610.76	4568.22	3873.95	3378.69	3007.81	2719.84	2489.93	2146.17	1901.90	1719.81	125000
150000	12996.31	8819.80	6732.91	5481.86	4648.73	4054.42	3609.37	3263.81	2987.91	2575.40	2282.28	2063.77	150000
175000	15162.36	10289.76	7855.06	6395.50	5423.52	4730.16	4210.93	3807.78	3485.89	3004.63	2662.66	2407.74	175000
200000	17328.41	11759.73	8977.21	7309.14	6198.31	5405.89	4812.49	4351.75	3983.88	3433.87	3043.04	2751.70	200000
250000	21660.51	14699.66	11221.51	9136.43	7747.89	6757.37	6015.61	5439.68	4979.85	4292.33	3803.80	3439.62	250000

Amount	9.0 Years	10.0 Years	11.0 Years	12.0 Years	13.0 Years	14.0 Years	15.0 Years	16.0 Years	20.0 Years	30.0 Years	40.0 Years	50.0 Years	Amount
100	1.27	1.18	1.11	1.05	1.00	0.95	0.92	0.89	0.80	0.69	0.64	0.63	100
200	2.53	2.35	2.21	2.09	1.99	1.90	1.83	1.77	1.59	1.37	1.28	1.25	200
300	3.79	3.53	3.31	3.13	2.98	2.85	2.74	2.65	2.38	2.05	1.92	1.87	300
400	5.06	4.70	4.41	4.17	3.97	3.80	3.66	3.53	3.17	2.73	2.56	2.49	400
500	6.32	5.88	5.51	5.21	4.96	4.75	4.57	4.41	3.96	3.42	3.20	3.11	500
600	7.58	7.05	6.61	6.26	5.96	5.70	5.48	5.29	4.75	4.10	3.84	3.73	600
700	8.85	8.22	7.72	7.30	6.95	6.65	6.40	6.18	5.54	4.78	4.48	4.35	700
800	10.11	9.40	8.82	8.34	7.94	7.60	7.31	7.06	6.33	5.46	5.12	4.97	800
900	11.37	10.57	9.92	9.38	8.93	8.55	8.22	7.94	7.12	6.14	5.76	5.59	900
1000	12.64	11.75	11.02	10.42	9.92	9.50	9.13	8.82	7.91	6.83	6.40	6.21	1000
2000	25.27	23.49	22.04	20.84	19.84	18.99	18.26	17.63	15.81	13.65	12.80	12.42	2000
3000	37.90	35.23	33.05	31.26	29.76	28.48	27.39	26.45	23.72	20.47	19.20	18.63	3000
4000	50.54	46.97	44.07	41.68	39.67	37.97	36.52	35.26	31.62	27.29	25.59	24.84	4000
5000	63.17	58.71	55.08	52.09	49.59	47.47	45.65	44.08	39.52	34.11	31.99	31.05	5000
6000	75.80	70.45	66.10	62.51	59.51	56.96	54.78	52.89	47.43	40.94	38.39	37.26	6000
7000	88.44	82.19	77.11	72.93	69.42	66.45	63.91	61.71	55.33	47.76	44.78	43.47	7000
8000	101.07	93.93	88.13	83.35	79.34	75.94	73.03	70.52	63.24	54.58	51.18	49.68	8000
9000	113.70	105.67	99.15	93.76	89.26	85.43	82.16	79.34	71.14	61.40	57.58	55.89	9000
10000	126.34	117.41	110.16	104.18	99.17	94.93	91.29	88.15	79.04	68.22	63.97	62.09	10000
15000	189.50	176.11	165.24	156.27	148.76	142.39	136.93	132.22	118.56	102.33	95.96	93.14	15000
20000	252.67	234.81	220.32	208.36	198.34	189.85	182.58	176.30	158.08	136.44	127.94	124.18	20000
25000	315.84	293.51	275.40	260.44	247.92	237.31	228.22	220.37	197.60	170.55	159.92	155.23	25000
30000	379.00	352.21	330.47	312.53	297.51	284.77	273.86	264.44	237.12	204.66	191.91	186.27	30000
35000	442.17	410.91	385.55	364.62	347.09	332.23	319.51	308.52	276.64	238.77	223.89	217.32	35000
40000	505.34	469.61	440.63	416.71	396.67	379.69	365.15	352.59	316.16	272.88	255.87	248.36	40000
45000	568.50	528.31	495.71	468.80	446.26	427.15	410.79	396.66	355.67	306.98	287.86	279.41	45000
50000	631.67	587.01	550.79	520.88	495.84	474.61	456.44	440.73	395.19	341.09	319.84	310.45	50000
60000	758.00	704.41	660.94	625.06	595.01	569.54	547.72	528.88	474.23	409.31	383.81	372.54	60000
75000	947.50	880.51	826.18	781.32	743.76	711.92	684.65	661.10	592.79	511.64	479.76	465.68	75000
100000	1263.33	1174.02	1101.57	1041.76	991.68	949.22	912.87	881.46	790.38	682.18	639.68	620.90	100000
125000	1579.16	1467.52	1376.96	1302.20	1239.59	1186.53	1141.08	1101.83	987.97	852.73	799.59	776.12	125000
150000	1895.00	1761.02	1652.35	1562.64	1487.51	1423.83	1369.30	1322.19	1185.57	1023.27	959.51	931.35	150000
175000	2210.83	2054.52	1927.74	1823.08	1735.43	1661.14	1597.52	1542.56	1383.16	1193.81	1119.43	1086.57	175000
200000	2526.66	2348.03	2203.13	2083.52	1983.35	1898.44	1825.73	1762.92	1580.76	1364.36	1279.35	1241.79	200000
250000	3158.32	2935.03	2753.91	2604.39	2479.18	2373.05	2282.16	2203.65	1975.94	1705.45	1599.18	1552.24	250000

Amount	1.0 Year	1.5 Years	2.0 Years	2.5 Years	3.0 Years	3.5 Years	4.0 Years	4.5 Years	5.0 Years	6.0 Years	7.0 Years	8.0 Years	Amount
100	8.68	5.90	4.50	3.67	3.12	2.72	2.42	2.19	2.01	1.73	1.54	1.39	100
200	17.36	11.79	9.00	7.34	6.23	5.43	4.84	4.38	4.01	3.46	3.07	2.78	200
300	26.03	17.68	13.50	11.00	9.34	8.15	7.26	6.57	6.02	5.19	4.61	4.17	300
400	34.71	23.57	18.00	14.67	12.45	10.86	9.68	8.76	8.02	6.92	6.14	5.56	400
500	43.38	29.46	22.50	18.33	15.56	13.58	12.09	10.94	10.02	8.65	7.67	6.95	500
600	52.06	35.35	27.00	22.00	18.67	16.29	14.51	13.13	12.03	10.38	9.21	8.34	600
700	60.74	41.24	31.50	25.67	21.78	19.01	16.93	15.32	14.03	12.11	10.74	9.72	700
800	69.41	47.13	36.00	29.33	24.89	21.72	19.35	17.51	16.04	13.84	12.28	11.11	800
900	78.09	53.03	40.50	33.00	28.00	24.44	21.77	19.69	18.04	15.57	13.81	12.50	900
1000	86.76	58.92	45.00	36.66	31.11	27.15	24.18	21.88	20.04	17.30	15.34	13.89	1000
2000	173.52	117.83	90.00	73.32	62.22	54.29	48.36	43.76	40.08	34.59	30.68	27.77	2000
3000	260.28	176.74	135.00	109.98	93.32	81.44	72.54	65.63	60.12	51.88	46.02	41.66	3000
4000	347.03	235.65	180.00	146.64	124.43	108.58	96.72	87.51	80.16	69.17	61.36	55.54	4000
5000	433.79	294.57	225.00	183.30	155.54	135.73	120.90	109.39	100.19	86.46	76.70	69.42	5000
6000	520.55	353.48	270.00	219.96	186.64	162.87	145.08	131.26	120.23	103.75	92.03	83.31	6000
7000	607.31	412.39	315.00	256.62	217.75	190.02	169.26	153.14	140.27	121.04	107.37	97.19	7000
8000	694.06	471.30	360.00	293.28	248.85	217.16	193.44	175.01	160.31	138.33	122.71	111.08	8000
9000	780.82	530.22	405.00	329.94	279.96	244.31	217.62	196.89	180.35	155.62	138.05	124.96	9000
10000	867.58	589.13	450.00	366.60	311.07	271.45	241.79	218.77	200.38	172.91	153.39	138.84	10000
15000	1301.37	883.69	675.00	549.90	466.60	407.18	362.69	328.15	300.57	259.36	230.08	208.26	15000
20000	1735.15	1178.25	900.00	733.20	622.13	542.90	483.58	437.53	400.76	345.81	306.77	277.68	20000
25000	2168.94	1472.81	1124.99	916.50	777.66	678.63	604.48	546.91	500.95	432.26	383.46	347.10	25000
30000	2602.73	1767.38	1349.99	1099.80	933.19	814.35	725.37	656.29	601.14	518.71	460.15	416.52	30000
35000	3036.51	2061.94	1574.99	1283.09	1088.72	950.08	846.27	765.67	701.33	605.16	536.84	485.94	35000
40000	3470.30	2356.50	1799.99	1466.39	1244.25	1085.80	967.16	875.05	801.52	691.61	613.54	555.36	40000
45000	3904.09	2651.06	2024.99	1649.69	1399.78	1221.53	1088.06	984.44	901.71	778.06	690.23	624.78	45000
50000	4337.88	2945.62	2249.98	1832.99	1555.32	1357.25	1208.95	1093.82	1001.90	864.51	766.92	694.20	50000
60000	5205.45	3534.75	2699.98	2199.59	1866.38	1628.70	1450.74	1312.58	1202.28	1037.41	920.30	833.04	60000
75000	6506.81	4418.43	3374.97	2749.48	2332.97	2035.88	1813.42	1640.72	1502.85	1296.76	1150.38	1041.30	75000
100000	8675.75	5891.24	4499.96	3665.97	3110.63	2714.50	2417.90	2187.63	2003.80	1729.02	1533.83	1388.39	100000
125000	10844.68	7364.05	5624.95	4582.47	3888.28	3393.13	3022.37	2734.53	2504.75	2161.27	1917.29	1735.49	125000
150000	13013.62	8836.86	6749.94	5498.96	4665.94	4071.75	3626.84	3281.44	3005.70	2593.52	2300.75	2082.59	150000
175000	15182.55	10309.67	7874.93	6415.45	5443.59	4750.38	4231.31	3828.35	3506.65	3025.77	2684.20	2429.68	175000
200000	17351.49	11782.48	8999.92	7331.94	6221.25	5429.00	4835.79	4375.25	4007.59	3458.03	3067.66	2776.78	200000
250000	21689.36	14728.10	11249.90	9164.93	7776.56	6786.25	6044.73	5469.06	5009.49	4322.53	3834.57	3470.97	250000

Amount	9.0 Years	10.0 Years	11.0 Years	12.0 Years	13.0 Years	14.0 Years	15.0 Years	16.0 Years	20.0 Years	30.0 Years	40.0 Years	50.0 Years	Amount
100	1.28	1.19	1.12	1.06	1.01	0.97	0.93	0.90	0.81	0.70	0.66	0.65	100
200	2.56	2.38	2.23	2.12	2.02	1.93	1.86	1.80	1.62	1.40	1.32	1.29	200
300	3.83	3.57	3.35	3.17	3.02	2.89	2.79	2.69	2.42	2.10	1.98	1.93	300
400	5.11	4.75	4.46	4.23	4.03	3.86	3.71	3.59	3.23	2.80	2.64	2.57	400
500	6.39	5.94	5.58	5.28	5.03	4.82	4.64	4.48	4.03	3.50	3.30	3.21	500
600	7.66	7.13	6.69	6.34	6.04	5.78	5.57	5.38	4.84	4.20	3.95	3.85	600
700	8.94	8.31	7.81	7.39	7.04	6.75	6.49	6.28	5.64	4.90	4.61	4.49	700
800	10.21	9.50	8.92	8.45	8.05	7.71	7.42	7.17	6.45	5.60	5.27	5.13	800
900	11.49	10.69	10.04	9.50	9.05	8.67	8.35	8.07	7.26	6.30	5.93	5.77	900
1000	12.77	11.88	11.15	10.56	10.06	9.64	9.28	8.96	8.06	7.00	6.59	6.41	1000
2000	25.53	23.75	22.30	21.11	20.11	19.27	18.55	17.92	16.12	13.99	13.17	12.81	2000
3000	38.29	35.62	33.45	31.66	30.17	28.90	27.82	26.88	24.17	20.98	19.75	19.21	3000
4000	51.05	47.49	44.60	42.21	40.22	38.53	37.09	35.84	32.23	27.97	26.33	25.61	4000
5000	63.81	59.36	55.75	52.77	50.27	48.16	46.36	44.80	40.28	34.97	32.91	32.02	5000
6000	76.57	71.23	66.89	63.32	60.33	57.79	55.63	53.75	48.34	41.96	39.49	38.42	6000
7000	89.33	83.10	78.04	73.87	70.38	67.43	64.90	62.71	56.40	48.95	46.07	44.82	7000
8000	102.09	94.97	89.19	84.42	80.43	77.06	74.17	71.67	64.45	55.94	52.65	51.22	8000
9000	114.85	106.84	100.34	94.98	90.49	86.69	83.44	80.63	72.51	62.93	59.23	57.63	9000
10000	127.62	118.71	111.49	105.53	100.54	96.32	92.71	89.59	80.56	69.93	65.81	64.03	10000
15000	191.42	178.06	167.23	158.29	150.81	144.48	139.06	134.38	120.84	104.89	98.72	96.04	15000
20000	255.23	237.41	222.97	211.05	201.08	192.63	185.41	179.17	161.12	139.85	131.62	128.05	20000
25000	319.03	296.76	278.71	263.81	251.35	240.79	231.76	223.96	201.40	174.81	164.52	160.06	25000
30000	382.84	356.11	334.45	316.57	301.62	288.95	278.11	268.75	241.68	209.77	197.43	192.08	30000
35000	446.64	415.46	390.19	369.33	351.88	337.11	324.46	313.54	281.96	244.73	230.33	224.09	35000
40000	510.45	474.81	445.93	422.10	402.15	385.26	370.81	358.34	322.24	279.69	263.23	256.10	40000
45000	574.25	534.16	501.67	474.86	452.42	433.42	417.16	403.13	362.52	314.65	296.14	288.11	45000
50000	638.06	593.51	557.41	527.62	502.69	481.58	463.51	447.92	402.80	349.61	329.04	320.12	50000
60000	765.67	712.22	668.89	633.14	603.23	577.89	556.21	537.50	483.36	419.53	394.85	384.15	60000
75000	957.08	890.27	836.11	791.42	754.03	722.36	695.26	671.88	604.20	524.42	493.56	480.18	75000
100000	1276.11	1187.02	1114.81	1055.23	1005.38	963.15	927.02	895.83	805.60	699.22	658.08	640.24	100000
125000	1595.13	1483.78	1393.51	1319.04	1256.72	1203.93	1158.77	1119.79	1007.00	874.02	822.59	800.30	125000
150000	1914.16	1780.53	1672.21	1582.84	1508.06	1444.72	1390.52	1343.75	1208.39	1048.83	987.11	960.36	150000
175000	2233.18	2077.29	1950.91	1846.65	1759.40	1685.51	1622.28	1567.70	1409.79	1223.63	1151.63	1120.41	175000
200000	2552.21	2374.04	2229.61	2110.46	2010.75	1926.29	1854.03	1791.66	1611.19	1398.43	1316.15	1280.47	200000
250000	3190.26	2967.55	2787.01	2638.07	2513.43	2407.86	2317.54	2239.57	2013.99	1748.04	1645.18	1600.59	250000

Amount	1.0 Year	1.5 Years	2.0 Years	2.5 Years	3.0 Years	3.5 Years	4.0 Years	4.5 Years	5.0 Years	6.0 Years	7.0 Years	8.0 Years	Amount
100	8.69	5.91	4.52	3.68	3.13	2.73	2.43	2.20	2.02	1.75	1.55	1.41	100
200	17.38	11.81	9.03	7.36	6.25	5.46	4.86	4.40	4.04	3.49	3.10	2.81	200
300	26.07	17.71	13.54	11.04	9.37	8.18	7.29	6.60	6.05	5.23	4.64	4.21	300
400	34.75	23.62	18.05	14.71	12.49	10.91	9.72	8.80	8.07	6.97	6.19	5.61	400
500	43.44	29.52	22.56	18.39	15.62	13.64	12.15	11.00	10.08	8.71	7.74	7.01	500
600	52.13	35.42	27.07	22.07	18.74	16.36	14.58	13.20	12.10	10.45	9.28	8.41	600
700	60.82	41.32	31.58	25.75	21.86	19.09	17.01	15.40	14.11	12.19	10.83	9.81	700
800	69.50	47.23	36.10	29.42	24.98	21.81	19.44	17.60	16.13	13.93	12.37	11.21	800
900	78.19	53.13	40.61	33.10	28.10	24.54	21.87	19.80	18.15	15.68	13.92	12.61	900
1000	86.88	59.03	45.12	36.78	31.23	27.27	24.30	22.00	20.16	17.42	15.47	14.01	1000
2000	173.75	118.06	90.23	73.55	62.45	54.53	48.60	43.99	40.32	34.83	30.93	28.02	2000
3000	260.62	177.08	135.35	110.33	93.67	81.79	72.89	65.99	60.48	52.24	46.39	42.03	3000
4000	347.50	236.11	180.46	147.10	124.89	109.05	97.19	87.98	80.63	69.65	61.85	56.04	4000
5000	434.37	295.14	225.57	183.87	156.11	136.31	121.48	109.98	100.79	87.06	77.31	70.05	5000
6000	521.24	354.16	270.69	220.65	187.33	163.57	145.78	131.97	120.95	104.47	92.78	84.06	6000
7000	608.12	413.19	315.80	257.42	218.55	190.83	170.08	153.96	141.10	121.88	108.24	98.07	7000
8000	694.99	472.22	360.91	294.20	249.77	218.09	194.37	175.96	161.26	139.30	123.70	112.08	8000
9000	781.86	531.24	406.03	330.97	281.00	245.35	218.67	197.95	181.42	156.71	139.16	126.09	9000
10000	868.73	590.27	451.14	367.74	312.22	272.61	242.96	219.95	201.57	174.12	154.62	140.10	10000
15000	1303.10	885.40	676.71	551.61	468.32	408.92	364.44	329.92	302.36	261.18	231.93	210.15	15000
20000	1737.46	1180.53	902.27	735.48	624.43	545.22	485.92	439.89	403.14	348.23	309.24	280.20	20000
25000	2171.83	1475.66	1127.84	919.35	780.53	681.53	607.40	549.86	503.93	435.29	386.55	350.25	25000
30000	2606.19	1770.79	1353.41	1103.22	936.64	817.83	728.88	659.83	604.71	522.35	463.86	420.30	30000
35000	3040.56	2065.92	1578.97	1287.09	1092.75	954.13	850.36	769.80	705.50	609.40	541.17	490.35	35000
40000	3474.92	2361.06	1804.54	1470.96	1248.85	1090.44	971.83	879.77	806.28	696.46	618.48	560.40	40000
45000	3909.28	2656.19	2030.11	1654.83	1404.96	1226.74	1093.31	989.74	907.07	783.52	695.79	630.45	45000
50000	4343.65	2951.32	2255.67	1838.70	1561.06	1363.05	1214.79	1099.71	1007.85	870.58	773.10	700.50	50000
60000	5212.38	3541.58	2706.81	2206.44	1873.27	1635.65	1457.75	1319.65	1209.42	1044.69	927.72	840.60	60000
75000	6515.47	4426.98	3383.51	2758.05	2341.59	2044.57	1822.19	1649.57	1511.78	1305.86	1159.65	1050.75	75000
100000	8687.29	5902.63	4511.34	3677.39	3122.12	2726.09	2429.58	2199.42	2015.70	1741.15	1546.20	1401.00	100000
125000	10859.12	7378.29	5639.17	4596.74	3902.65	3407.61	3036.97	2749.27	2519.62	2176.43	1932.75	1751.25	125000
150000	13030.94	8853.95	6767.01	5516.09	4683.18	4089.13	3644.37	3299.13	3023.55	2611.72	2319.30	2101.50	150000
175000	15202.76	10329.60	7894.84	6435.44	5463.71	4770.65	4251.76	3848.98	3527.47	3047.00	2705.85	2451.75	175000
200000	17374.58	11805.26	9022.68	7354.78	6244.24	5452.17	4859.15	4398.83	4031.40	3482.29	3092.40	2801.99	200000
250000	21718.23	14756.57	11278.34	9193.48	7805.30	6815.21	6073.94	5498.54	5039.24	4352.86	3865.49	3502.49	250000

Amount	9.0 Years	10.0 Years	11.0 Years	12.0 Years	13.0 Years	14.0 Years	15.0 Years	16.0 Years	20.0 Years	30.0 Years	40.0 Years	50.0 Years	Amount
100	1.29	1.21	1.13	1.07	1.02	0.98	0.95	0.92	0.83	0.72	0.68	0.66	100
200	2.58	2.41	2.26	2.14	2.04	1.96	1.89	1.83	1.65	1.44	1.36	1.32	200
300	3.87	3.61	3.39	3.21	3.06	2.94	2.83	2.74	2.47	2.15	2.03	1.98	300
400	5.16	4.81	4.52	4.28	4.08	3.91	3.77	3.65	3.29	2.87	2.71	2.64	400
500	6.45	6.01	5.65	5.35	5.10	4.89	4.71	4.56	4.11	3.59	3.39	3.30	500
600	7.74	7.21	6.77	6.42	6.12	5.87	5.65	5.47	4.93	4.30	4.06	3.96	600
700	9.03	8.41	7.90	7.49	7.14	6.85	6.59	6.38	5.75	5.02	4.74	4.62	700
800	10.32	9.61	9.03	8.56	8.16	7.82	7.54	7.29	6.57	5.74	5.42	5.28	800
900	11.61	10.81	10.16	9.62	9.18	8.80	8.48	8.20	7.39	6.45	6.09	5.94	900
1000	12.89	12.01	11.29	10.69	10.20	9.78	9.42	9.11	8.21	7.17	6.77	6.60	1000
2000	25.78	24.01	22.57	21.38	20.39	19.55	18.83	18.21	16.42	14.33	13.54	13.20	2000
3000	38.67	36.01	33.85	32.07	30.58	29.32	28.24	27.31	24.63	21.50	20.30	19.80	3000
4000	51.56	48.01	45.13	42.76	40.77	39.09	37.66	36.42	32.84	28.66	27.07	26.39	4000
5000	64.45	60.01	56.41	53.44	50.96	48.86	47.07	45.52	41.05	35.83	33.84	32.99	5000
6000	77.34	72.01	67.69	64.13	61.16	58.64	56.48	54.62	49.26	42.99	40.60	39.59	6000
7000	90.23	84.01	78.97	74.82	71.35	68.41	65.89	63.73	57.47	50.15	47.37	46.18	7000
8000	103.12	96.01	90.26	85.51	81.54	78.18	75.31	72.83	65.68	57.32	54.13	52.78	8000
9000	116.01	108.01	101.54	96.20	91.73	87.95	84.72	81.93	73.89	64.48	60.90	59.38	9000
10000	128.90	120.02	112.82	106.88	101.92	97.72	94.13	91.04	82.10	71.65	67.67	65.97	10000
15000	193.35	180.02	169.22	160.32	152.88	146.58	141.20	136.55	123.15	107.47	101.50	98.96	15000
20000	257.79	240.03	225.63	213.76	203.84	195.44	188.26	182.07	164.19	143.29	135.33	131.94	20000
25000	322.24	300.03	282.04	267.20	254.80	244.30	235.32	227.58	205.24	179.11	169.16	164.93	25000
30000	386.69	360.04	338.44	320.64	305.76	293.16	282.39	273.10	246.29	214.93	202.99	197.91	30000
35000	451.14	420.04	394.85	374.08	356.72	342.02	329.45	318.62	287.34	250.75	236.82	230.90	35000
40000	515.58	480.05	451.26	427.52	407.67	390.88	376.52	364.13	328.38	286.57	270.65	263.88	40000
45000	580.03	540.05	507.66	480.96	458.63	439.73	423.58	409.65	369.43	322.39	304.48	296.87	45000
50000	644.48	600.06	564.07	534.40	509.59	488.59	470.64	455.16	410.48	358.21	338.31	329.85	50000
60000	773.37	720.07	676.88	641.28	611.51	586.31	564.77	546.20	492.57	429.85	405.98	395.82	60000
75000	966.72	900.08	846.10	801.60	764.38	732.89	705.96	682.74	615.72	537.31	507.47	494.78	75000
100000	1288.95	1200.11	1128.13	1068.80	1019.18	977.18	941.28	910.32	820.95	716.42	676.62	659.70	100000
125000	1611.19	1500.14	1410.17	1336.00	1273.97	1221.48	1176.60	1137.90	1026.19	895.52	845.78	824.63	125000
150000	1933.43	1800.16	1692.20	1603.19	1528.76	1465.77	1411.92	1365.48	1231.43	1074.62	1014.93	989.55	150000
175000	2255.67	2100.19	1974.23	1870.39	1783.56	1710.07	1647.24	1593.06	1436.66	1253.73	1184.09	1154.47	175000
200000	2577.90	2400.22	2256.26	2137.59	2038.35	1954.36	1882.56	1820.64	1641.90	1432.83	1353.24	1319.40	200000
250000	3222.38	3000.27	2820.33	2671.99	2547.93	2442.95	2353.19	2275.80	2052.38	1791.04	1691.55	1649.25	250000

Amount	1.0 Year	1.5 Years	2.0 Years	2.5 Years	3.0 Years	3.5 Years	4.0 Years	4.5 Years	5.0 Years	6.0 Years	7.0 Years	8.0 Years	Amount
100	8.70	5.92	4.53	3.69	3.14	2.74	2.45	2.22	2.03	1.76	1.56	1.42	100
200	17.40	11.83	9.05	7.38	6.27	5.48	4.89	4.43	4.06	3.51	3.12	2.83	200
300	26.10	17.75	13.57	11.07	9.41	8.22	7.33	6.64	6.09	5.26	4.68	4.25	300
400	34.80	23.66	18.10	14.76	12.54	10.96	9.77	8.85	8.12	7.02	6.24	5.66	400
500	43.50	29.58	22.62	18.45	15.67	13.69	12.21	11.06	10.14	8.77	7.80	7.07	500
600	52.20	35.49	27.14	22.14	18.81	16.43	14.65	13.27	12.17	10.52	9.36	8.49	600
700	60.90	41.40	31.66	25.83	21.94	19.17	17.09	15.48	14.20	12.28	10.92	9.90	700
800	69.60	47.32	36.19	29.52	25.07	21.91	19.54	17.69	16.23	14.03	12.47	11.31	800
900	78.29	53.23	40.71	33.20	28.21	24.64	21.98	19.91	18.25	15.78	14.03	12.73	900
1000	86.99	59.15	45.23	36.89	31.34	27.38	24.42	22.12	20.28	17.54	15.59	14.14	1000
2000	173.98	118.29	90.46	73.78	62.68	54.76	48.83	44.23	40.56	35.07	31.18	28.28	2000
3000	260.97	177.43	135.69	110.67	94.01	82.14	73.24	66.34	60.83	52.60	46.76	42.42	3000
4000	347.96	236.57	180.91	147.56	125.35	109.51	97.66	88.45	81.11	70.14	62.35	56.55	4000
5000	434.95	295.71	226.14	184.45	156.69	136.89	122.07	110.57	101.39	87.67	77.94	70.69	5000
6000	521.94	354.85	271.37	221.33	188.02	164.27	146.48	132.68	121.66	105.20	93.52	84.83	6000
7000	608.92	413.99	316.60	258.22	219.36	191.64	170.90	154.79	141.94	122.74	109.11	98.96	7000
8000	695.91	473.13	361.82	295.11	250.70	219.02	195.31	176.90	162.22	140.27	124.69	113.10	8000
9000	782.90	532.27	407.05	332.00	282.03	246.40	219.72	199.02	182.49	157.80	140.28	127.24	9000
10000	869.89	591.41	452.28	368.89	313.37	273.77	244.13	221.13	202.77	175.34	155.87	141.37	10000
15000	1304.83	887.11	678.41	553.33	470.05	410.66	366.20	331.69	304.15	263.00	233.80	212.06	15000
20000	1739.77	1182.81	904.55	737.77	626.73	547.54	488.26	442.25	405.53	350.67	311.73	282.74	20000
25000	2174.72	1478.51	1130.69	922.21	783.41	684.43	610.33	552.82	506.91	438.34	389.66	353.42	25000
30000	2609.66	1774.21	1356.82	1106.65	940.10	821.31	732.39	663.38	608.30	526.00	467.59	424.11	30000
35000	3044.60	2069.92	1582.96	1291.10	1096.78	958.20	854.46	773.94	709.68	613.67	545.52	494.79	35000
40000	3479.54	2365.62	1809.10	1475.54	1253.46	1095.08	976.52	884.50	811.06	701.33	623.45	565.47	40000
45000	3914.48	2661.32	2035.23	1659.98	1410.14	1231.97	1098.59	995.06	912.44	789.00	701.38	636.16	45000
50000	4349.43	2957.02	2261.37	1844.42	1566.83	1368.85	1220.65	1105.63	1013.82	876.67	779.32	706.84	50000
60000	5219.31	3548.42	2713.64	2213.30	1880.19	1642.62	1464.78	1326.75	1216.59	1052.00	935.18	848.21	60000
75000	6524.14	4435.53	3392.05	2766.63	2350.23	2053.28	1830.97	1658.44	1520.73	1315.00	1168.97	1060.26	75000
100000	8698.85	5914.03	4522.73	3688.84	3133.64	2737.70	2441.30	2211.25	2027.64	1753.33	1558.63	1413.67	100000
125000	10873.56	7392.54	5653.42	4611.05	3917.05	3422.13	3051.62	2764.06	2534.55	2191.66	1948.28	1767.09	125000
150000	13048.27	8871.05	6784.10	5533.25	4700.46	4106.55	3661.94	3316.87	3041.46	2629.99	2337.94	2120.51	150000
175000	15222.98	10349.56	7914.78	6455.46	5483.87	4790.98	4272.27	3869.68	3548.37	3068.32	2727.59	2473.92	175000
200000	17397.69	11828.06	9045.46	7377.67	6267.28	5475.40	4882.59	4422.49	4055.28	3506.65	3117.25	2827.34	200000
250000	21747.11	14785.08	11306.83	9222.09	7834.10	6844.25	6103.24	5528.11	5069.10	4383.32	3896.56	3534.17	250000

Amount	9.0 Years	10.0 Years	11.0 Years	12.0 Years	13.0 Years	14.0 Years	15.0 Years	16.0 Years	20.0 Years	30.0 Years	40.0 Years	50.0 Years	Amount
100	1.31	1.22	1.15	1.09	1.04	1.00	0.96	0.93	0.84	0.74	0.70	0.68	100
200	2.61	2.43	2.29	2.17	2.07	1.99	1.92	1.85	1.68	1.47	1.40	1.36	200
300	3.91	3.64	3.43	3.25	3.10	2.98	2.87	2.78	2.51	2.21	2.09	2.04	300
400	5.21	4.86	4.57	4.33	4.14	3.97	3.83	3.70	3.35	2.94	2.79	2.72	400
500	6.51	6.07	5.71	5.42	5.17	4.96	4.78	4.63	4.19	3.67	3.48	3.40	500
600	7.82	7.28	6.85	6.50	6.20	5.95	5.74	5.55	5.02	4.41	4.18	4.08	600
700	9.12	8.50	8.00	7.58	7.24	6.94	6.69	6.48	5.86	5.14	4.87	4.76	700
800	10.42	9.71	9.14	8.66	8.27	7.94	7.65	7.40	6.70	5.88	5.57	5.44	800
900	11.72	10.92	10.28	9.75	9.30	8.93	8.61	8.33	7.53	6.61	6.26	6.12	900
1000	13.02	12.14	11.42	10.83	10.34	9.92	9.56	9.25	8.37	7.34	6.96	6.80	1000
2000	26.04	24.27	22.84	21.65	20.67	19.83	19.12	18.50	16.73	14.68	13.91	13.59	2000
3000	39.06	36.40	34.25	32.48	31.00	29.74	28.67	27.75	25.10	22.02	20.86	20.38	3000
4000	52.08	48.54	45.67	43.30	41.33	39.66	38.23	37.00	33.46	29.36	27.82	27.18	4000
5000	65.10	60.67	57.08	54.13	51.66	49.57	47.79	46.25	41.83	36.69	34.77	33.97	5000
6000	78.12	72.80	68.50	64.95	61.99	59.48	57.34	55.50	50.19	44.03	41.72	40.76	6000
7000	91.14	84.93	79.91	75.78	72.32	69.40	66.90	64.75	58.56	51.37	48.68	47.55	7000
8000	104.15	97.07	91.33	86.60	82.65	79.31	76.46	74.00	66.92	58.71	55.63	54.35	8000
9000	117.17	109.20	102.74	97.43	92.98	89.22	86.01	83.25	75.28	66.04	62.58	61.14	9000
10000	130.19	121.33	114.16	108.25	103.31	99.14	95.57	92.50	83.65	73.38	69.54	67.93	10000
15000	195.29	182.00	171.24	162.37	154.97	148.70	143.35	138.74	125.47	110.07	104.30	101.90	15000
20000	260.38	242.66	228.31	216.50	206.62	198.27	191.14	184.99	167.29	146.76	139.07	135.86	20000
25000	325.47	303.32	285.39	270.62	258.27	247.83	238.92	231.24	209.12	183.45	173.83	169.82	25000
30000	390.57	363.99	342.47	324.74	309.93	297.40	286.70	277.48	250.94	220.13	208.60	203.79	30000
35000	455.66	424.65	399.55	378.86	361.58	346.97	334.48	323.73	292.76	256.82	243.36	237.75	35000
40000	520.75	485.32	456.62	432.99	413.23	396.53	382.27	369.98	334.58	293.51	278.13	271.71	40000
45000	585.85	545.98	513.70	487.11	464.89	446.10	430.05	416.22	376.40	330.20	312.90	305.68	45000
50000	650.94	606.64	570.78	541.23	516.54	495.66	477.83	462.47	418.23	366.89	347.66	339.64	50000
60000	781.13	727.97	684.93	649.48	619.85	594.80	573.40	554.96	501.87	440.26	417.19	407.57	60000
75000	976.41	909.96	856.16	811.84	774.81	743.49	716.74	693.70	627.34	550.33	521.49	509.46	75000
100000	1301.88	1213.28	1141.55	1082.46	1033.08	991.32	955.66	924.93	836.45	733.77	695.32	679.28	100000
125000	1627.34	1516.60	1426.94	1353.07	1291.35	1239.15	1194.57	1156.16	1045.56	917.21	869.14	849.10	125000
150000	1952.81	1819.92	1712.32	1623.68	1549.62	1486.98	1433.48	1387.39	1254.67	1100.65	1042.97	1018.92	150000
175000	2278.28	2123.24	1997.71	1894.30	1807.88	1734.81	1672.40	1618.62	1463.78	1284.09	1216.80	1188.73	175000
200000	2603.75	2426.56	2283.09	2164.92	2066.15	1982.64	1911.31	1849.86	1672.89	1467.53	1390.63	1358.55	200000
250000	3254.68	3033.19	2853.87	2706.14	2582.69	2478.30	2389.14	2312.32	2091.11	1834.42	1738.28	1698.19	250000

Amount	1.0 Year	1.5 Years	2.0 Years	2.5 Years	3.0 Years	3.5 Years	4.0 Years	4.5 Years	5.0 Years	6.0 Years	7.0 Years	8.0 Years	Amount
100	8.72	5.93	4.54	3.71	3.15	2.75	2.46	2.23	2.04	1.77	1.58	1.43	100
200	17.43	11.86	9.07	7.41	6.30	5.50	4.91	4.45	4.08	3.54	3.15	2.86	200
300	26.14	17.78	13.61	11.11	9.44	8.25	7.36	6.67	6.12	5.30	4.72	4.28	300
400	34.85	23.71	18.14	14.81	12.59	11.00	9.82	8.90	8.16	7.07	6.29	5.71	400
500	43.56	29.63	22.68	18.51	15.73	13.75	12.27	11.12	10.20	8.83	7.86	7.14	500
600	52.27	35.56	27.21	22.21	18.88	16.50	14.72	13.34	12.24	10.60	9.43	8.56	600
700	60.98	41.48	31.74	25.91	22.02	19.25	17.18	15.57	14.28	12.36	11.00	9.99	700
800	69.69	47.41	36.28	29.61	25.17	22.00	19.63	17.79	16.32	14.13	12.57	11.42	800
900	78.40	53.33	40.81	33.31	28.31	24.75	22.08	20.01	18.36	15.90	14.14	12.84	900
1000	87.11	59.26	45.35	37.01	31.46	27.50	24.54	22.24	20.40	17.66	15.72	14.27	1000
2000	174.21	118.51	90.69	74.01	62.91	54.99	49.07	44.47	40.80	35.32	31.43	28.53	2000
3000	261.32	177.77	136.03	111.01	94.36	82.49	73.60	66.70	61.19	52.97	47.14	42.80	3000
4000	348.42	237.02	181.37	148.02	125.81	109.98	98.13	88.93	81.59	70.63	62.85	57.06	4000
5000	435.53	296.28	226.71	185.02	157.26	137.47	122.66	111.16	101.99	88.28	78.56	71.33	5000
6000	522.63	355.53	272.05	222.02	188.72	164.97	147.19	133.39	122.38	105.94	94.27	85.59	6000
7000	609.73	414.79	317.39	259.03	220.17	192.46	171.72	155.62	142.78	123.59	109.98	99.85	7000
8000	696.84	474.04	362.74	296.03	251.62	219.95	196.25	177.85	163.18	141.25	125.69	114.12	8000
9000	783.94	533.30	408.08	333.03	283.07	247.45	220.78	200.08	183.57	158.91	141.40	128.38	9000
10000	871.05	592.55	453.42	370.03	314.52	274.94	245.31	222.32	203.97	176.56	157.12	142.65	10000
15000	1306.57	888.82	680.13	555.05	471.78	412.41	367.96	333.47	305.95	264.84	235.67	213.97	15000
20000	1742.09	1185.09	906.83	740.06	629.04	549.87	490.61	444.63	407.93	353.12	314.23	285.29	20000
25000	2177.61	1481.37	1133.54	925.08	786.30	687.34	613.27	555.78	509.91	441.39	392.78	356.61	25000
30000	2613.13	1777.64	1360.25	1110.09	943.56	824.81	735.92	666.94	611.89	529.67	471.34	427.93	30000
35000	3048.65	2073.91	1586.95	1295.11	1100.82	962.27	858.57	778.09	713.87	617.95	549.89	499.25	35000
40000	3484.17	2370.18	1813.66	1480.12	1258.08	1099.74	981.22	889.25	815.86	706.23	628.45	570.57	40000
45000	3919.69	2666.46	2040.37	1665.14	1415.34	1237.21	1103.87	1000.40	917.84	794.51	707.00	641.89	45000
50000	4355.21	2962.73	2267.07	1850.15	1572.60	1374.68	1226.53	1111.56	1019.82	882.78	785.56	713.21	50000
60000	5226.25	3555.27	2720.49	2220.18	1887.11	1649.61	1471.83	1333.87	1223.78	1059.34	942.67	855.85	60000
75000	6532.81	4444.09	3400.61	2775.23	2358.89	2062.01	1839.79	1667.34	1529.72	1324.17	1178.33	1069.81	75000
100000	8710.41	5925.45	4534.14	3700.30	3145.19	2749.35	2453.05	2223.11	2039.63	1765.56	1571.11	1426.41	100000
125000	10888.01	7406.81	5667.68	4625.38	3931.48	3436.68	3066.31	2778.89	2549.54	2206.95	1963.89	1783.01	125000
150000	13065.61	8888.17	6801.21	5550.45	4717.78	4124.02	3679.57	3334.67	3059.44	2648.34	2356.66	2139.62	150000
175000	15243.22	10369.53	7934.75	6475.52	5504.07	4811.35	4292.83	3890.45	3569.35	3089.73	2749.44	2496.22	175000
200000	17420.82	11850.89	9068.28	7400.60	6290.37	5498.69	4906.09	4446.22	4079.26	3531.12	3142.22	2852.82	200000
250000	21776.02	14813.62	11335.35	9250.75	7862.96	6873.36	6132.62	5557.78	5099.07	4413.90	3927.77	3566.02	250000

Amount	9.0 Years	10.0 Years	11.0 Years	12.0 Years	13.0 Years	14.0 Years	15.0 Years	16.0 Years	20.0 Years	30.0 Years	40.0 Years	50.0 Years	Amount
100	1.32	1.23	1.16	1.10	1.05	1.01	0.98	0.94	0.86	0.76	0.72	0.70	100
200	2.63	2.46	2.32	2.20	2.10	2.02	1.95	1.88	1.71	1.51	1.43	1.40	200
300	3.95	3.68	3.47	3.29	3.15	3.02	2.92	2.82	2.56	2.26	2.15	2.10	300
400	5.26	4.91	4.63	4.39	4.19	4.03	3.89	3.76	3.41	3.01	2.86	2.80	400
500	6.58	6.14	5.78	5.49	5.24	5.03	4.86	4.70	4.27	3.76	3.58	3.50	500
600	7.89	7.36	6.94	6.58	6.29	6.04	5.83	5.64	5.12	4.51	4.29	4.20	600
700	9.21	8.59	8.09	7.68	7.33	7.04	6.80	6.58	5.97	5.26	5.00	4.90	700
800	10.52	9.82	9.25	8.77	8.38	8.05	7.77	7.52	6.82	6.02	5.72	5.60	800
900	11.84	11.04	10.40	9.87	9.43	9.06	8.74	8.46	7.67	6.77	6.43	6.30	900
1000	13.15	12.27	11.56	10.97	10.48	10.06	9.71	9.40	8.53	7.52	7.15	6.99	1000
2000	26.30	24.54	23.11	21.93	20.95	20.12	19.41	18.80	17.05	15.03	14.29	13.98	2000
3000	39.45	36.80	34.66	32.89	31.42	30.17	29.11	28.19	25.57	22.54	21.43	20.97	3000
4000	52.60	49.07	46.21	43.85	41.89	40.23	38.81	37.59	34.09	30.06	28.57	27.96	4000
5000	65.75	61.33	57.76	54.82	52.36	50.28	48.51	46.99	42.61	37.57	35.71	34.95	5000
6000	78.90	73.60	69.31	65.78	62.83	60.34	58.21	56.38	51.13	45.08	42.85	41.94	6000
7000	92.05	85.86	80.86	76.74	73.30	70.39	67.91	65.78	59.65	52.59	49.99	48.93	7000
8000	105.19	98.13	92.41	87.70	83.77	80.45	77.62	75.18	68.17	60.11	57.14	55.92	8000
9000	118.34	110.39	103.96	98.66	94.24	90.51	87.32	84.57	76.69	67.62	64.28	62.91	9000
10000	131.49	122.66	115.51	109.63	104.71	100.56	97.02	93.97	85.21	75.13	71.42	69.90	10000
15000	197.24	183.98	173.26	164.44	157.07	150.84	145.53	140.95	127.81	112.69	107.13	104.85	15000
20000	262.98	245.31	231.01	219.25	209.42	201.12	194.03	187.94	170.42	150.26	142.83	139.80	20000
25000	328.72	306.64	288.77	274.06	261.77	251.40	242.54	234.92	213.02	187.82	178.54	174.74	25000
30000	394.47	367.96	346.52	328.87	314.13	301.67	291.05	281.90	255.62	225.38	214.25	209.69	30000
35000	460.21	429.29	404.27	383.68	366.48	351.95	339.55	328.88	298.23	262.95	249.95	244.64	35000
40000	525.95	490.62	462.02	438.49	418.84	402.23	388.06	375.87	340.83	300.51	285.66	279.59	40000
45000	591.70	551.94	519.78	493.30	471.19	452.51	436.57	422.85	383.43	338.07	321.37	314.54	45000
50000	657.44	613.27	577.53	548.11	523.54	502.79	485.08	469.83	426.04	375.64	357.07	349.48	50000
60000	788.93	735.92	693.03	657.73	628.25	603.34	582.09	563.80	511.24	450.76	428.49	419.38	60000
75000	986.16	919.90	866.29	822.16	785.31	754.18	727.61	704.74	639.05	563.45	535.61	524.22	75000
100000	1314.87	1226.53	1155.05	1096.21	1047.08	1005.57	970.15	939.66	852.07	751.27	714.14	698.96	100000
125000	1643.59	1533.16	1443.82	1370.26	1308.85	1256.96	1212.68	1174.57	1065.09	939.09	892.68	873.70	125000
150000	1972.31	1839.79	1732.58	1644.32	1570.62	1508.35	1455.22	1409.48	1278.10	1126.90	1071.21	1048.44	150000
175000	2301.02	2146.43	2021.34	1918.37	1832.39	1759.74	1697.75	1644.39	1491.12	1314.72	1249.75	1223.18	175000
200000	2629.74	2453.06	2310.10	2192.42	2094.16	2011.14	1940.29	1879.31	1704.14	1502.54	1428.28	1397.92	200000
250000	3287.17	3066.32	2887.63	2740.52	2617.70	2513.92	2425.36	2349.13	2130.17	1878.17	1785.35	1747.40	250000

8.25%   Page 28   Monthly Payment Required To Amortize A Loan   Page 28   **8.25%**

Amount	1.0 Year	1.5 Years	2.0 Years	2.5 Years	3.0 Years	3.5 Years	4.0 Years	4.5 Years	5.0 Years	6.0 Years	7.0 Years	8.0 Years	Amount
100	8.73	5.94	4.55	3.72	3.16	2.77	2.47	2.24	2.06	1.78	1.59	1.44	100
200	17.45	11.88	9.10	7.43	6.32	5.53	4.93	4.48	4.11	3.56	3.17	2.88	200
300	26.17	17.82	13.64	11.14	9.48	8.29	7.40	6.71	6.16	5.34	4.76	4.32	300
400	34.89	23.75	18.19	14.85	12.63	11.05	9.86	8.95	8.21	7.12	6.34	5.76	400
500	43.61	29.69	22.73	18.56	15.79	13.81	12.33	11.18	10.26	8.89	7.92	7.20	500
600	52.34	35.63	27.28	22.28	18.95	16.57	14.79	13.42	12.31	10.67	9.51	8.64	600
700	61.06	41.56	31.82	25.99	22.10	19.33	17.26	15.65	14.37	12.45	11.09	10.08	700
800	69.78	47.50	36.37	29.70	25.26	22.09	19.72	17.89	16.42	14.23	12.67	11.52	800
900	78.50	53.44	40.92	33.41	28.42	24.85	22.19	20.12	18.47	16.01	14.26	12.96	900
1000	87.22	59.37	45.46	37.12	31.57	27.62	24.65	22.36	20.52	17.78	15.84	14.40	1000
2000	174.44	118.74	90.92	74.24	63.14	55.23	49.30	44.71	41.04	35.56	31.68	28.79	2000
3000	261.66	178.11	136.37	111.36	94.71	82.84	73.95	67.06	61.55	53.34	47.51	43.18	3000
4000	348.88	237.48	181.83	148.48	126.28	110.45	98.60	89.41	82.07	71.12	63.35	57.57	4000
5000	436.10	296.85	227.28	185.59	157.84	138.06	123.25	111.76	102.59	88.90	79.19	71.97	5000
6000	523.32	356.22	272.74	222.71	189.41	165.67	147.89	134.11	123.10	106.68	95.02	86.36	6000
7000	610.54	415.59	318.19	259.83	220.98	193.28	172.54	156.46	143.62	124.45	110.86	100.75	7000
8000	697.76	474.95	363.65	296.95	252.55	220.89	197.19	178.81	164.14	142.23	126.70	115.14	8000
9000	784.98	534.32	409.11	334.07	284.11	248.50	221.84	201.16	184.65	160.01	142.53	129.53	9000
10000	872.20	593.69	454.56	371.18	315.68	276.11	246.49	223.51	205.17	177.79	158.37	143.93	10000
15000	1308.30	890.54	681.84	556.77	473.52	414.16	369.73	335.26	307.75	266.68	237.55	215.89	15000
20000	1744.40	1187.38	909.12	742.36	631.36	552.21	492.97	447.01	410.34	355.57	316.73	287.85	20000
25000	2180.50	1484.22	1136.40	927.95	789.19	690.26	616.21	558.76	512.92	444.46	395.92	359.81	25000
30000	2616.60	1781.07	1363.68	1113.54	947.03	828.31	739.45	670.51	615.50	533.36	475.10	431.77	30000
35000	3052.70	2077.91	1590.95	1299.13	1104.87	966.36	862.70	782.26	718.08	622.25	554.28	503.73	35000
40000	3488.80	2374.75	1818.23	1484.72	1262.71	1104.41	985.94	894.01	820.67	711.14	633.46	575.69	40000
45000	3924.90	2671.60	2045.51	1670.31	1420.54	1242.46	1109.18	1005.76	923.25	800.03	712.65	647.65	45000
50000	4360.99	2968.44	2272.79	1855.90	1578.38	1380.51	1232.42	1117.51	1025.83	888.92	791.83	719.61	50000
60000	5233.19	3562.13	2727.35	2227.07	1894.06	1656.61	1478.90	1341.01	1231.00	1066.71	950.19	863.53	60000
75000	6541.49	4452.66	3409.18	2783.84	2367.57	2070.77	1848.63	1676.27	1538.74	1333.38	1187.74	1079.41	75000
100000	8721.98	5936.88	4545.57	3711.79	3156.76	2761.02	2464.84	2235.02	2051.66	1777.84	1583.65	1439.22	100000
125000	10902.48	7421.10	5681.96	4639.73	3945.96	3451.27	3081.04	2793.77	2564.57	2222.30	1979.57	1799.02	125000
150000	13082.97	8905.31	6818.36	5567.68	4735.14	4141.53	3697.25	3352.53	3077.48	2666.76	2375.48	2158.82	150000
175000	15263.47	10389.53	7954.75	6495.62	5524.54	4831.78	4313.46	3911.28	3590.40	3111.22	2771.39	2518.63	175000
200000	17443.96	11873.75	9091.14	7423.57	6313.51	5522.03	4929.67	4470.03	4103.31	3555.68	3167.30	2878.43	200000
250000	21804.95	14842.19	11363.92	9279.46	7891.89	6902.54	6162.08	5587.54	5129.14	4444.60	3959.13	3598.04	250000

Amount	9.0 Years	10.0 Years	11.0 Years	12.0 Years	13.0 Years	14.0 Years	15.0 Years	16.0 Years	20.0 Years	30.0 Years	40.0 Years	50.0 Years	Amount
100	1.33	1.24	1.17	1.12	1.07	1.02	0.99	0.96	0.87	0.77	0.74	0.72	100
200	2.66	2.48	2.34	2.23	2.13	2.04	1.97	1.91	1.74	1.54	1.47	1.44	200
300	3.99	3.72	3.51	3.34	3.19	3.06	2.96	2.87	2.61	2.31	2.20	2.16	300
400	5.32	4.96	4.68	4.45	4.25	4.08	3.94	3.82	3.48	3.08	2.94	2.88	400
500	6.64	6.20	5.85	5.56	5.31	5.10	4.93	4.78	4.34	3.85	3.67	3.60	500
600	7.97	7.44	7.02	6.67	6.37	6.12	5.91	5.73	5.21	4.62	4.40	4.32	600
700	9.30	8.68	8.19	7.78	7.43	7.14	6.90	6.69	6.08	5.39	5.14	5.04	700
800	10.63	9.92	9.35	8.89	8.49	8.16	7.88	7.64	6.95	6.16	5.87	5.75	800
900	11.96	11.16	10.52	10.00	9.56	9.18	8.87	8.60	7.82	6.93	6.60	6.47	900
1000	13.28	12.40	11.69	11.11	10.62	10.20	9.85	9.55	8.68	7.69	7.34	7.19	1000
2000	26.56	24.80	23.38	22.21	21.23	20.40	19.70	19.09	17.36	15.38	14.67	14.38	2000
3000	39.84	37.20	35.06	33.31	31.84	30.60	29.55	28.64	26.04	23.07	22.00	21.57	3000
4000	53.12	49.60	46.75	44.41	42.45	40.80	39.39	38.18	34.72	30.76	29.33	28.75	4000
5000	66.40	62.00	58.44	55.51	53.06	51.00	49.24	47.73	43.40	38.45	36.66	35.94	5000
6000	79.68	74.40	70.12	66.61	63.68	61.20	59.09	57.27	52.07	46.14	43.99	43.13	6000
7000	92.96	86.79	81.81	77.71	74.29	71.40	68.94	66.82	60.75	53.83	51.32	50.32	7000
8000	106.24	99.19	93.50	88.81	84.90	81.60	78.78	76.36	69.43	61.52	58.65	57.50	8000
9000	119.52	111.59	105.18	99.91	95.51	91.80	88.63	85.91	78.11	69.21	65.98	64.69	9000
10000	132.80	123.99	116.87	111.01	106.12	102.00	98.48	95.45	86.79	76.90	73.31	71.88	10000
15000	199.20	185.98	175.30	166.51	159.18	152.99	147.72	143.18	130.18	115.34	109.97	107.82	15000
20000	265.59	247.98	233.73	222.02	212.24	203.99	196.95	190.90	173.57	153.79	146.62	143.75	20000
25000	331.99	309.97	292.16	277.52	265.30	254.98	246.19	238.63	216.96	192.23	183.28	179.69	25000
30000	398.39	371.96	350.60	333.02	318.36	305.98	295.43	286.35	260.35	230.68	219.93	215.63	30000
35000	464.78	433.95	409.03	388.52	371.42	356.98	344.66	334.08	303.74	269.12	256.59	251.56	35000
40000	531.18	495.95	467.46	444.03	424.48	407.97	393.90	381.80	347.13	307.57	293.24	287.50	40000
45000	597.58	557.94	525.89	499.53	477.54	458.97	443.14	429.53	390.53	346.02	329.90	323.44	45000
50000	663.97	619.93	584.32	555.03	530.59	509.96	492.37	477.25	433.92	384.46	366.55	359.38	50000
60000	796.77	743.92	701.19	666.04	636.71	611.96	590.85	572.70	520.70	461.35	439.86	431.25	60000
75000	995.96	929.90	876.48	832.55	795.89	764.94	738.56	715.87	650.87	576.69	549.83	539.06	75000
100000	1327.94	1239.86	1168.64	1110.06	1061.18	1019.92	984.74	954.50	867.83	768.92	733.10	718.75	100000
125000	1659.92	1549.83	1460.80	1387.57	1326.48	1274.90	1230.93	1193.12	1084.78	961.15	916.37	898.43	125000
150000	1991.91	1859.79	1752.96	1665.09	1591.77	1529.88	1477.11	1431.74	1301.74	1153.38	1099.65	1078.12	150000
175000	2323.89	2169.75	2045.12	1942.60	1857.07	1784.86	1723.30	1670.36	1518.70	1345.60	1282.92	1257.80	175000
200000	2655.88	2479.72	2337.28	2220.12	2122.36	2039.84	1969.48	1908.99	1735.65	1537.83	1466.19	1437.49	200000
250000	3319.84	3099.65	2921.60	2775.14	2652.95	2549.80	2461.85	2386.23	2169.56	1922.29	1832.74	1796.86	250000

Amount	1.0 Year	1.5 Years	2.0 Years	2.5 Years	3.0 Years	3.5 Years	4.0 Years	4.5 Years	5.0 Years	6.0 Years	7.0 Years	8.0 Years	Amount
100	8.74	5.95	4.56	3.73	3.17	2.78	2.48	2.25	2.07	1.80	1.60	1.46	100
200	17.47	11.90	9.12	7.45	6.34	5.55	4.96	4.50	4.13	3.59	3.20	2.91	200
300	26.21	17.85	13.68	11.17	9.51	8.32	7.43	6.75	6.20	5.38	4.79	4.36	300
400	34.94	23.80	18.23	14.90	12.68	11.10	9.91	8.99	8.26	7.17	6.39	5.81	400
500	43.67	29.75	22.79	18.62	15.85	13.87	12.39	11.24	10.32	8.96	7.99	7.27	500
600	52.41	35.69	27.35	22.34	19.02	16.64	14.86	13.49	12.39	10.75	9.58	8.72	600
700	61.14	41.64	31.90	26.07	22.18	19.41	17.34	15.73	14.45	12.54	11.18	10.17	700
800	69.87	47.59	36.46	29.79	25.35	22.19	19.82	17.98	16.51	14.33	12.77	11.62	800
900	78.61	53.54	41.02	33.51	28.52	24.96	22.29	20.23	18.58	16.12	14.37	13.07	900
1000	87.34	59.49	45.58	37.24	31.69	27.73	24.77	22.47	20.64	17.91	15.97	14.53	1000
2000	174.68	118.97	91.15	74.47	63.37	55.46	49.54	44.94	41.28	35.81	31.93	29.05	2000
3000	262.01	178.45	136.72	111.70	95.06	83.19	74.30	67.41	61.92	53.71	47.89	43.57	3000
4000	349.35	237.94	182.29	148.94	126.74	110.91	99.07	89.88	82.55	71.61	63.85	58.09	4000
5000	436.68	297.42	227.86	186.17	158.42	138.64	123.84	112.35	103.19	89.51	79.82	72.61	5000
6000	524.02	356.90	273.43	223.40	190.11	166.37	148.60	134.82	123.83	107.42	95.78	87.13	6000
7000	611.35	416.39	319.00	260.64	221.79	194.10	173.37	157.29	144.47	125.32	111.74	101.65	7000
8000	698.69	475.87	364.57	297.87	253.47	221.82	198.14	179.76	165.10	143.22	127.70	116.17	8000
9000	786.03	535.35	410.14	335.10	285.16	249.55	222.90	202.23	185.74	161.12	143.67	130.69	9000
10000	873.36	594.84	455.71	372.33	316.84	277.28	247.67	224.70	206.38	179.02	159.63	145.21	10000
15000	1310.04	892.25	683.56	558.50	475.26	415.91	371.50	337.05	309.56	268.53	239.44	217.82	15000
20000	1746.72	1189.67	911.41	744.66	633.68	554.55	495.34	449.40	412.75	358.04	319.25	290.42	20000
25000	2183.39	1487.08	1139.26	930.83	792.09	693.18	619.17	561.74	515.94	447.55	399.07	363.03	25000
30000	2620.07	1784.50	1367.11	1116.99	950.51	831.82	743.00	674.09	619.12	537.06	478.88	435.63	30000
35000	3056.75	2081.91	1594.96	1303.16	1108.93	970.46	866.83	786.44	722.31	626.56	558.69	508.23	35000
40000	3493.43	2379.33	1822.81	1489.32	1267.35	1109.09	990.67	898.79	825.49	716.07	638.50	580.84	40000
45000	3930.11	2676.75	2050.66	1675.48	1425.76	1247.73	1114.50	1011.14	928.68	805.58	718.32	653.44	45000
50000	4366.78	2974.16	2278.51	1861.65	1584.18	1386.36	1238.33	1123.48	1031.87	895.09	798.13	726.05	50000
60000	5240.14	3568.99	2734.21	2233.98	1901.02	1663.64	1486.00	1348.18	1238.24	1074.11	957.75	871.26	60000
75000	6550.17	4461.24	3417.76	2792.47	2376.27	2079.54	1857.49	1685.22	1547.80	1342.63	1197.19	1089.07	75000
100000	8733.56	5948.32	4557.02	3723.29	3168.36	2772.72	2476.66	2246.96	2063.73	1790.18	1596.25	1452.09	100000
125000	10916.95	7435.40	5696.27	4654.12	3960.44	3465.90	3095.82	2808.70	2579.66	2237.72	1995.32	1815.11	125000
150000	13100.34	8922.47	6835.52	5584.94	4752.53	4159.08	3714.98	3370.44	3095.59	2685.26	2394.38	2178.13	150000
175000	15283.73	10409.55	7974.78	6515.76	5544.62	4852.26	4334.14	3932.18	3611.52	3132.80	2793.44	2541.15	175000
200000	17467.10	11896.63	9114.03	7446.58	6336.71	5545.44	4953.31	4493.92	4127.45	3580.35	3192.50	2904.17	200000
250000	21833.90	14870.79	11392.54	9308.23	7920.88	6931.80	6191.63	5617.40	5159.31	4475.43	3990.63	3630.21	250000

Amount	9.0 Years	10.0 Years	11.0 Years	12.0 Years	13.0 Years	14.0 Years	15.0 Years	16.0 Years	20.0 Years	30.0 Years	40.0 Years	50.0 Years	Amount
100	1.35	1.26	1.19	1.13	1.08	1.04	1.00	0.97	0.89	0.79	0.76	0.74	100
200	2.69	2.51	2.37	2.25	2.16	2.07	2.00	1.94	1.77	1.58	1.51	1.48	200
300	4.03	3.76	3.55	3.38	3.23	3.11	3.00	2.91	2.66	2.37	2.26	2.22	300
400	5.37	5.02	4.73	4.50	4.31	4.14	4.00	3.88	3.54	3.15	3.01	2.96	400
500	6.71	6.27	5.92	5.62	5.38	5.18	5.00	4.85	4.42	3.94	3.77	3.70	500
600	8.05	7.52	7.10	6.75	6.46	6.21	6.00	5.82	5.31	4.73	4.52	4.44	600
700	9.39	8.78	8.28	7.87	7.53	7.25	7.00	6.79	6.19	5.51	5.27	5.18	700
800	10.73	10.03	9.46	9.00	8.61	8.28	8.00	7.76	7.07	6.30	6.02	5.91	800
900	12.07	11.28	10.65	10.12	9.68	9.31	9.00	8.73	7.96	7.09	6.77	6.65	900
1000	13.42	12.54	11.83	11.24	10.76	10.35	10.00	9.70	8.84	7.87	7.53	7.39	1000
2000	26.83	25.07	23.65	22.48	21.51	20.69	19.99	19.39	17.68	15.74	15.05	14.78	2000
3000	40.24	37.60	35.47	33.72	32.27	31.04	29.99	29.09	26.52	23.61	22.57	22.16	3000
4000	53.65	50.14	47.30	44.96	43.02	41.38	39.98	38.78	35.35	31.47	30.09	29.55	4000
5000	67.06	62.67	59.12	56.20	53.77	51.72	49.98	48.48	44.19	39.34	37.61	36.94	5000
6000	80.47	75.20	70.94	67.44	64.53	62.07	59.97	58.17	53.03	47.21	45.14	44.32	6000
7000	93.88	87.73	82.77	78.68	75.28	72.41	69.97	67.87	61.86	55.07	52.66	51.71	7000
8000	107.29	100.27	94.59	89.92	86.04	82.76	79.96	77.56	70.70	62.94	60.18	59.09	8000
9000	120.70	112.80	106.41	101.16	96.79	93.10	89.96	87.26	79.54	70.81	67.70	66.48	9000
10000	134.11	125.33	118.24	112.40	107.54	103.44	99.95	96.95	88.38	78.68	75.22	73.87	10000
15000	201.17	188.00	177.35	168.60	161.31	155.16	149.92	145.42	132.56	118.01	112.83	110.80	15000
20000	268.22	250.66	236.47	224.80	215.08	206.88	199.89	193.89	176.75	157.35	150.44	147.73	20000
25000	335.27	313.32	295.58	281.00	268.85	258.60	249.87	242.37	220.93	196.68	188.05	184.66	25000
30000	402.33	375.99	354.70	337.20	322.62	310.32	299.84	290.84	265.12	236.02	225.66	221.59	30000
35000	469.38	438.65	413.82	393.40	376.39	362.04	349.81	339.31	309.30	275.35	263.26	258.52	35000
40000	536.44	501.31	472.93	449.60	430.16	413.76	399.78	387.78	353.49	314.69	300.87	295.45	40000
45000	603.49	563.98	532.05	505.80	483.93	465.47	449.76	436.26	397.67	354.02	338.48	332.38	45000
50000	670.54	626.64	591.16	562.00	537.70	517.19	499.73	484.73	441.86	393.36	376.09	369.31	50000
60000	804.65	751.97	709.40	674.40	645.23	620.63	599.67	581.67	530.23	472.03	451.31	443.17	60000
75000	1005.81	939.96	886.74	843.00	806.54	775.79	749.59	727.09	662.79	590.03	564.13	553.96	75000
100000	1341.08	1253.27	1182.32	1124.00	1075.39	1034.38	999.45	969.45	883.72	786.71	752.18	738.62	100000
125000	1676.35	1566.59	1477.90	1405.00	1344.23	1292.98	1249.32	1211.81	1104.64	983.38	940.22	923.27	125000
150000	2011.62	1879.91	1773.48	1686.00	1613.08	1551.57	1499.18	1454.18	1325.57	1180.06	1128.26	1107.92	150000
175000	2346.89	2193.22	2069.06	1967.00	1881.92	1810.16	1749.04	1696.54	1546.50	1376.73	1316.30	1292.58	175000
200000	2682.16	2506.54	2364.64	2248.00	2150.77	2068.76	1998.90	1938.90	1767.43	1573.41	1504.35	1477.23	200000
250000	3352.70	3133.17	2955.80	2810.00	2688.46	2585.95	2498.63	2423.62	2209.28	1966.76	1880.43	1846.54	250000

Amount	1.0 Year	1.5 Years	2.0 Years	2.5 Years	3.0 Years	3.5 Years	4.0 Years	4.5 Years	5.0 Years	6.0 Years	7.0 Years	8.0 Years	Amount
100	8.75	5.96	4.57	3.74	3.18	2.79	2.49	2.26	2.08	1.81	1.61	1.47	100
200	17.50	11.92	9.14	7.47	6.36	5.57	4.98	4.52	4.16	3.61	3.22	2.94	200
300	26.24	17.88	13.71	11.21	9.54	8.36	7.47	6.78	6.23	5.41	4.83	4.40	300
400	34.99	23.84	18.28	14.94	12.72	11.14	9.96	9.04	8.31	7.22	6.44	5.87	400
500	43.73	29.80	22.85	18.68	15.90	13.93	12.45	11.30	10.38	9.02	8.05	7.33	500
600	52.48	35.76	27.42	22.41	19.08	16.71	14.94	13.56	12.46	10.82	9.66	8.80	600
700	61.22	41.72	31.98	26.15	22.26	19.50	17.42	15.82	14.54	12.62	11.27	10.26	700
800	69.97	47.68	36.55	29.88	25.44	22.28	19.91	18.08	16.61	14.43	12.88	11.73	800
900	78.71	53.64	41.12	33.62	28.62	25.07	22.40	20.34	18.69	16.23	14.49	13.19	900
1000	87.46	59.60	45.69	37.35	31.80	27.85	24.89	22.59	20.76	18.03	16.09	14.66	1000
2000	174.91	119.20	91.37	74.70	63.60	55.69	49.78	45.18	41.52	36.06	32.18	29.31	2000
3000	262.36	178.80	137.06	112.05	95.40	83.54	74.66	67.77	62.28	54.08	48.27	43.96	3000
4000	349.81	238.40	182.74	149.40	127.20	111.38	99.55	90.36	83.04	72.11	64.36	58.61	4000
5000	437.26	297.99	228.43	186.75	159.00	139.23	124.43	112.95	103.80	90.13	80.45	73.26	5000
6000	524.71	357.59	274.11	224.09	190.80	167.07	149.32	135.54	124.56	108.16	96.54	87.91	6000
7000	612.17	417.19	319.80	261.44	222.60	194.92	174.20	158.13	145.31	126.18	112.63	102.56	7000
8000	699.62	476.79	365.48	298.79	254.40	222.76	199.09	180.72	166.07	144.21	128.72	117.21	8000
9000	787.07	536.38	411.17	336.14	286.20	250.61	223.97	203.31	186.83	162.23	144.81	131.86	9000
10000	874.52	595.98	456.85	373.49	318.00	278.45	248.86	225.90	207.59	180.26	160.90	146.51	10000
15000	1311.78	893.97	685.28	560.23	477.00	417.67	373.28	338.85	311.38	270.39	241.34	219.76	15000
20000	1749.03	1191.96	913.70	746.97	636.00	556.90	497.71	451.79	415.17	360.52	321.79	293.01	20000
25000	2186.29	1489.95	1142.12	933.71	795.00	696.12	622.13	564.74	518.96	450.64	402.23	366.26	25000
30000	2623.55	1787.93	1370.55	1120.45	954.00	835.34	746.56	677.69	622.76	540.77	482.68	439.51	30000
35000	3060.81	2085.92	1598.97	1307.19	1113.00	974.56	870.98	790.63	726.55	630.90	563.12	512.76	35000
40000	3498.06	2383.91	1827.39	1493.93	1271.99	1113.79	995.41	903.58	830.34	721.03	643.57	586.01	40000
45000	3935.32	2681.90	2055.82	1680.67	1430.99	1253.01	1119.83	1016.53	934.13	811.15	724.01	659.26	45000
50000	4372.58	2979.89	2284.24	1867.41	1589.99	1392.23	1244.26	1129.47	1037.92	901.28	804.46	732.52	50000
60000	5247.09	3575.86	2741.09	2240.89	1907.99	1670.68	1493.11	1355.37	1245.51	1081.54	965.35	879.02	60000
75000	6558.87	4469.83	3426.36	2801.12	2384.98	2088.34	1866.38	1694.21	1556.88	1351.92	1206.69	1098.77	75000
100000	8745.15	5959.77	4568.48	3734.82	3179.98	2784.46	2488.51	2258.94	2075.84	1802.56	1608.91	1465.03	100000
125000	10931.44	7449.71	5710.60	4668.53	3974.97	3480.57	3110.64	2823.68	2594.80	2253.20	2011.14	1831.28	125000
150000	13117.73	8939.66	6852.72	5602.23	4769.96	4176.68	3732.76	3388.41	3113.76	2703.84	2413.37	2197.54	150000
175000	15304.01	10429.60	7994.83	6535.93	5564.96	4872.80	4354.89	3953.15	3632.72	3154.47	2815.59	2563.79	175000
200000	17490.30	11919.54	9136.95	7469.64	6359.95	5568.91	4977.01	4517.88	4151.68	3605.11	3217.82	2930.05	200000
250000	21862.87	14899.42	11421.19	9337.05	7949.94	6961.13	6221.27	5647.35	5189.59	4506.39	4022.27	3662.56	250000

Amount	9.0 Years	10.0 Years	11.0 Years	12.0 Years	13.0 Years	14.0 Years	15.0 Years	16.0 Years	20.0 Years	30.0 Years	40.0 Years	50.0 Years	Amount
100	1.36	1.27	1.20	1.14	1.09	1.05	1.02	0.99	0.90	0.81	0.78	0.76	100
200	2.71	2.54	2.40	2.28	2.18	2.10	2.03	1.97	1.80	1.61	1.55	1.52	200
300	4.07	3.81	3.59	3.42	3.27	3.15	3.05	2.96	2.70	2.42	2.32	2.28	300
400	5.42	5.07	4.79	4.56	4.36	4.20	4.06	3.94	3.60	3.22	3.09	3.04	400
500	6.78	6.34	5.99	5.70	5.45	5.25	5.08	4.93	4.50	4.03	3.86	3.80	500
600	8.13	7.61	7.18	6.83	6.54	6.30	6.09	5.91	5.40	4.83	4.63	4.56	600
700	9.49	8.87	8.38	7.97	7.63	7.35	7.10	6.90	6.30	5.64	5.40	5.31	700
800	10.84	10.14	9.57	9.11	8.72	8.40	8.12	7.88	7.20	6.44	6.18	6.07	800
900	12.19	11.41	10.77	10.25	9.81	9.45	9.13	8.87	8.10	7.25	6.95	6.83	900
1000	13.55	12.67	11.97	11.39	10.90	10.49	10.15	9.85	9.00	8.05	7.72	7.59	1000
2000	27.09	25.34	23.93	22.77	21.80	20.98	20.29	19.70	18.00	16.10	15.43	15.18	2000
3000	40.63	38.01	35.89	34.15	32.70	31.47	30.43	29.54	27.00	24.14	23.15	22.76	3000
4000	54.18	50.68	47.85	45.53	43.59	41.96	40.58	39.39	35.99	32.19	30.86	30.35	4000
5000	67.72	63.34	59.81	56.91	54.49	52.45	50.72	49.23	44.99	40.24	38.57	37.93	5000
6000	81.26	76.01	71.77	68.29	65.39	62.94	60.86	59.08	53.99	48.28	46.29	45.52	6000
7000	94.81	88.68	83.73	79.67	76.28	73.42	71.00	68.92	62.99	56.33	54.00	53.10	7000
8000	108.35	101.35	95.69	91.05	87.18	83.92	81.15	78.77	71.98	64.37	61.71	60.69	8000
9000	121.89	114.01	107.65	102.43	98.08	94.41	91.29	88.61	80.98	72.42	69.43	68.28	9000
10000	135.43	126.68	119.61	113.81	108.97	104.90	101.43	98.46	89.98	80.47	77.14	75.86	10000
15000	203.15	190.02	179.42	170.71	163.46	157.35	152.14	147.68	134.96	120.70	115.71	113.79	15000
20000	270.86	253.36	239.22	227.61	217.94	209.79	202.86	196.91	179.95	160.93	154.28	151.72	20000
25000	338.58	316.69	299.03	284.51	272.43	262.24	253.57	246.13	224.94	201.16	192.85	189.65	25000
30000	406.29	380.03	358.83	341.41	326.91	314.69	304.28	295.36	269.92	241.39	231.41	227.58	30000
35000	474.01	443.37	418.63	398.32	381.39	367.13	355.00	344.59	314.91	281.62	269.98	265.50	35000
40000	541.72	506.71	478.44	455.22	435.88	419.58	405.71	393.81	359.90	321.85	308.55	303.43	40000
45000	609.44	570.05	538.24	512.12	490.36	472.03	456.42	443.04	404.88	362.09	347.12	341.36	45000
50000	677.15	633.38	598.05	569.02	544.85	524.47	507.14	492.26	449.87	402.32	385.69	379.29	50000
60000	812.58	760.06	717.65	682.82	653.81	629.37	608.56	590.71	539.84	482.78	462.82	455.15	60000
75000	1015.72	950.07	897.07	853.53	817.27	786.71	760.70	738.39	674.80	603.47	578.53	568.93	75000
100000	1354.30	1266.76	1196.09	1138.04	1089.69	1048.94	1014.27	984.52	899.73	804.63	771.37	758.57	100000
125000	1692.87	1583.45	1495.11	1422.54	1362.11	1311.18	1267.84	1230.65	1124.66	1005.78	964.21	948.22	125000
150000	2031.44	1900.14	1794.13	1707.05	1634.53	1573.41	1521.40	1476.78	1349.59	1206.94	1157.05	1137.86	150000
175000	2370.01	2216.83	2093.15	1991.56	1906.95	1835.65	1774.97	1722.91	1574.53	1408.09	1349.89	1327.50	175000
200000	2708.59	2533.52	2392.17	2276.07	2179.37	2097.88	2028.54	1969.04	1799.46	1609.25	1542.73	1517.14	200000
250000	3385.73	3166.90	2990.21	2845.08	2724.21	2622.35	2535.67	2461.29	2249.32	2011.56	1928.41	1896.43	250000

Amount	1.0 Year	1.5 Years	2.0 Years	2.5 Years	3.0 Years	3.5 Years	4.0 Years	4.5 Years	5.0 Years	6.0 Years	7.0 Years	8.0 Years	Amount
100	8.76	5.98	4.58	3.75	3.20	2.80	2.51	2.28	2.09	1.82	1.63	1.48	100
200	17.52	11.95	9.16	7.50	6.39	5.60	5.01	4.55	4.18	3.63	3.25	2.96	200
300	26.28	17.92	13.74	11.24	9.58	8.39	7.51	6.82	6.27	5.45	4.87	4.44	300
400	35.03	23.89	18.32	14.99	12.77	11.19	10.01	9.09	8.36	7.26	6.49	5.92	400
500	43.79	29.86	22.90	18.74	15.96	13.99	12.51	11.36	10.44	9.08	8.11	7.40	500
600	52.55	35.83	27.48	22.48	19.15	16.78	15.01	13.63	12.53	10.89	9.73	8.87	600
700	61.30	41.80	32.06	26.23	22.35	19.58	17.51	15.90	14.62	12.71	11.36	10.35	700
800	70.06	47.77	36.64	29.98	25.54	22.37	20.01	18.17	16.71	14.52	12.98	11.83	800
900	78.82	53.75	41.22	33.72	28.73	25.17	22.51	20.44	18.80	16.34	14.60	13.31	900
1000	87.57	59.72	45.80	37.47	31.92	27.97	25.01	22.71	20.88	18.15	16.22	14.79	1000
2000	175.14	119.43	91.60	74.93	63.84	55.93	50.01	45.42	41.76	36.30	32.44	29.57	2000
3000	262.71	179.14	137.40	112.40	95.75	83.89	75.02	68.13	62.64	54.45	48.65	44.35	3000
4000	350.27	238.85	183.20	149.86	127.67	111.85	100.02	90.84	83.52	72.60	64.87	59.13	4000
5000	437.84	298.57	229.00	187.32	159.59	139.82	125.02	113.55	104.40	90.75	81.09	73.91	5000
6000	525.41	358.28	274.80	224.79	191.50	167.78	150.03	136.26	125.28	108.90	97.30	88.69	6000
7000	612.98	417.99	320.60	262.25	223.42	195.74	175.03	158.97	146.16	127.05	113.52	103.47	7000
8000	700.54	477.70	366.40	299.71	255.33	223.70	200.04	181.68	167.04	145.20	129.73	118.25	8000
9000	788.11	537.42	412.20	337.18	287.25	251.66	225.04	204.39	187.92	163.35	145.95	133.03	9000
10000	875.68	597.13	458.00	374.64	319.17	279.63	250.04	227.10	208.80	181.50	162.17	147.81	10000
15000	1313.52	895.69	687.00	561.96	478.75	419.44	375.06	340.65	313.20	272.25	243.25	221.71	15000
20000	1751.35	1194.25	916.00	749.28	638.33	559.25	500.08	454.20	417.60	363.00	324.33	295.61	20000
25000	2189.19	1492.81	1144.99	936.60	797.91	699.06	625.10	567.74	522.00	453.75	405.41	369.51	25000
30000	2627.03	1791.37	1373.99	1123.91	957.49	838.87	750.12	681.29	626.40	544.50	486.49	443.41	30000
35000	3064.87	2089.94	1602.99	1311.23	1117.07	978.68	875.14	794.84	730.80	635.25	567.57	517.31	35000
40000	3502.70	2388.50	1831.99	1498.55	1276.65	1118.49	1000.16	908.39	835.20	726.00	648.65	591.21	40000
45000	3940.54	2687.06	2060.98	1685.87	1436.23	1258.30	1125.18	1021.94	939.60	816.75	729.74	665.11	45000
50000	4378.38	2985.62	2289.98	1873.19	1595.82	1398.11	1250.20	1135.48	1044.00	907.50	810.82	739.02	50000
60000	5254.05	3582.74	2747.98	2247.82	1914.98	1677.73	1500.24	1362.58	1252.80	1089.00	972.98	886.82	60000
75000	6567.56	4478.43	3434.97	2809.78	2393.72	2097.17	1875.30	1703.22	1566.00	1361.24	1216.22	1108.52	75000
100000	8756.75	5971.24	4579.96	3746.37	3191.63	2796.22	2500.40	2270.96	2087.99	1814.99	1621.63	1478.03	100000
125000	10945.94	7464.05	5724.95	4682.96	3989.53	3495.27	3125.50	2838.70	2609.99	2268.74	2027.04	1847.53	125000
150000	13135.12	8956.85	6869.93	5619.55	4787.44	4194.33	3750.59	3406.44	3131.99	2722.48	2432.44	2217.04	150000
175000	15324.31	10449.66	8014.92	6556.14	5585.34	4893.38	4375.69	3974.18	3653.99	3176.23	2837.85	2586.54	175000
200000	17513.50	11942.47	9159.91	7492.74	6383.25	5592.43	5000.79	4541.92	4175.98	3629.98	3243.25	2956.05	200000
250000	21891.87	14928.09	11449.89	9365.92	7979.06	6990.54	6250.99	5677.40	5219.98	4537.47	4054.07	3695.06	250000

Amount	9.0 Years	10.0 Years	11.0 Years	12.0 Years	13.0 Years	14.0 Years	15.0 Years	16.0 Years	20.0 Years	30.0 Years	40.0 Years	50.0 Years	Amount
100	1.37	1.29	1.21	1.16	1.11	1.07	1.03	1.00	0.92	0.83	0.80	0.78	100
200	2.74	2.57	2.42	2.31	2.21	2.13	2.06	2.00	1.84	1.65	1.59	1.56	200
300	4.11	3.85	3.63	3.46	3.32	3.20	3.09	3.00	2.75	2.47	2.38	2.34	300
400	5.48	5.13	4.84	4.61	4.42	4.26	4.12	4.00	3.67	3.30	3.17	3.12	400
500	6.84	6.41	6.05	5.77	5.53	5.32	5.15	5.00	4.58	4.12	3.96	3.90	500
600	8.21	7.69	7.26	6.92	6.63	6.39	6.18	6.00	5.50	4.94	4.75	4.68	600
700	9.58	8.97	8.47	8.07	7.73	7.45	7.21	7.00	6.42	5.76	5.54	5.46	700
800	10.95	10.25	9.68	9.22	8.84	8.51	8.24	8.00	7.33	6.59	6.33	6.23	800
900	12.31	11.53	10.89	10.37	9.94	9.58	9.27	9.00	8.25	7.41	7.12	7.01	900
1000	13.68	12.81	12.10	11.53	11.05	10.64	10.30	10.00	9.16	8.23	7.91	7.79	1000
2000	27.36	25.61	24.20	23.05	22.09	21.28	20.59	20.00	18.32	16.46	15.82	15.58	2000
3000	41.03	38.41	36.30	34.57	33.13	31.91	30.88	30.00	27.48	24.69	23.72	23.36	3000
4000	54.71	51.22	48.40	46.09	44.17	42.55	41.17	39.99	36.64	32.91	31.63	31.15	4000
5000	68.38	64.02	60.50	57.61	55.21	53.19	51.46	49.99	45.80	41.14	39.54	38.94	5000
6000	82.06	76.82	72.60	69.13	66.25	63.82	61.76	59.99	54.96	49.37	47.44	46.72	6000
7000	95.74	89.63	84.70	80.66	77.29	74.46	72.05	69.98	64.12	57.59	55.35	54.51	7000
8000	109.41	102.43	96.80	92.18	88.33	85.09	82.34	79.98	73.27	65.82	63.26	62.29	8000
9000	123.09	115.23	108.90	103.70	99.37	95.73	92.63	89.98	82.43	74.05	71.16	70.08	9000
10000	136.76	128.04	121.00	115.22	110.41	106.37	102.92	99.97	91.59	82.27	79.07	77.87	10000
15000	205.14	192.05	181.49	172.83	165.62	159.55	154.38	149.96	137.39	123.41	118.60	116.80	15000
20000	273.52	256.07	241.99	230.44	220.82	212.73	205.84	199.94	183.18	164.54	158.14	155.73	20000
25000	341.90	320.09	302.49	288.04	276.02	265.91	257.30	249.93	228.97	205.67	197.67	194.66	25000
30000	410.28	384.10	362.98	345.65	331.23	319.09	308.76	299.91	274.77	246.81	237.20	233.59	30000
35000	478.07	448.12	423.48	403.26	386.43	372.27	360.22	349.90	320.56	287.94	276.74	272.52	35000
40000	547.04	512.14	483.98	460.87	441.64	425.45	411.68	399.88	366.35	329.08	316.27	311.45	40000
45000	615.41	576.15	544.47	518.48	496.84	478.63	463.14	449.87	412.15	370.21	355.80	350.38	45000
50000	683.79	640.17	604.97	576.08	552.04	531.81	514.60	499.85	457.94	411.34	395.34	389.31	50000
60000	820.55	768.20	725.96	691.30	662.45	638.17	617.52	599.82	549.53	493.61	474.40	467.17	60000
75000	1025.69	960.25	907.45	864.12	828.06	797.71	771.90	749.78	686.91	617.01	593.00	583.96	75000
100000	1367.58	1280.33	1209.93	1152.16	1104.08	1063.61	1029.20	999.70	915.87	822.68	790.67	778.61	100000
125000	1709.48	1600.41	1512.42	1440.20	1380.11	1329.51	1286.50	1249.63	1144.84	1028.35	988.33	973.26	125000
150000	2051.37	1920.50	1814.90	1728.24	1656.12	1595.41	1543.79	1499.55	1373.81	1234.02	1186.00	1167.91	150000
175000	2393.27	2240.58	2117.38	2016.28	1932.14	1861.31	1801.09	1749.48	1602.77	1439.69	1383.66	1362.56	175000
200000	2735.16	2560.66	2419.86	2304.32	2208.16	2127.21	2058.39	1999.40	1831.74	1645.36	1581.33	1557.21	200000
250000	3418.95	3200.82	3024.83	2880.40	2760.20	2659.01	2572.99	2499.25	2289.67	2056.69	1976.66	1946.51	250000

Amount	1.0 Year	1.5 Years	2.0 Years	2.5 Years	3.0 Years	3.5 Years	4.0 Years	4.5 Years	5.0 Years	6.0 Years	7.0 Years	8.0 Years	Amount
100	8.77	5.99	4.60	3.76	3.21	2.81	2.52	2.29	2.11	1.83	1.64	1.50	100
200	17.54	11.97	9.19	7.52	6.41	5.62	5.03	4.57	4.21	3.66	3.27	2.99	200
300	26.31	17.95	13.78	11.28	9.61	8.43	7.54	6.85	6.31	5.49	4.91	4.48	300
400	35.08	23.94	18.37	15.04	12.82	11.24	10.05	9.14	8.41	7.31	6.54	5.97	400
500	43.85	29.92	22.96	18.79	16.02	14.05	12.57	11.42	10.51	9.14	8.18	7.46	500
600	52.62	35.90	27.55	22.55	19.22	16.85	15.08	13.70	12.61	10.97	9.81	8.95	600
700	61.38	41.88	32.15	26.31	22.43	19.66	17.59	15.99	14.71	12.80	11.45	10.44	700
800	70.15	47.87	36.74	30.07	25.63	22.47	20.10	18.27	16.81	14.62	13.08	11.93	800
900	78.92	53.85	41.33	33.83	28.83	25.28	22.62	20.55	18.91	16.45	14.71	13.42	900
1000	87.69	59.83	45.92	37.58	32.04	28.09	25.13	22.84	21.01	18.28	16.35	14.92	1000
2000	175.37	119.66	91.83	75.16	64.07	56.17	50.25	45.67	42.01	36.55	32.69	29.83	2000
3000	263.06	179.49	137.75	112.74	96.10	84.25	75.37	68.50	63.01	54.83	49.04	44.74	3000
4000	350.74	239.31	183.66	150.32	128.14	112.33	100.50	91.33	84.01	73.10	65.38	59.65	4000
5000	438.42	299.14	229.58	187.90	160.17	140.41	125.62	114.16	105.01	91.38	81.72	74.56	5000
6000	526.11	358.97	275.49	225.48	192.20	168.49	150.74	136.99	126.02	109.65	98.07	89.47	6000
7000	613.79	418.79	321.41	263.06	224.24	196.57	175.87	159.82	147.02	127.93	114.41	104.38	7000
8000	701.47	478.62	367.32	300.64	256.27	224.65	200.99	182.65	168.02	146.20	130.76	119.29	8000
9000	789.16	538.45	413.24	338.22	288.30	252.73	226.11	205.48	189.02	164.48	147.10	134.20	9000
10000	876.84	598.28	459.15	375.80	320.33	280.81	251.24	228.31	210.02	182.75	163.44	149.11	10000
15000	1315.26	897.41	688.72	563.70	480.50	421.21	376.85	342.46	315.03	274.13	245.16	223.67	15000
20000	1753.68	1196.55	918.29	751.59	640.66	561.61	502.47	456.61	420.04	365.50	326.88	298.22	20000
25000	2192.09	1495.68	1147.87	939.49	800.83	702.01	628.08	570.76	525.05	456.87	408.60	372.78	25000
30000	2630.51	1794.82	1377.44	1127.39	960.99	842.41	753.70	684.91	630.06	548.25	490.32	447.33	30000
35000	3068.93	2093.95	1607.01	1315.28	1121.16	982.81	879.31	799.06	735.07	639.62	572.04	521.89	35000
40000	3507.35	2393.09	1836.58	1503.18	1281.32	1123.21	1004.93	913.21	840.08	730.99	653.76	596.44	40000
45000	3945.76	2692.23	2066.16	1691.08	1441.49	1263.61	1130.55	1027.36	945.09	822.37	735.48	670.99	45000
50000	4384.18	2991.36	2295.73	1878.97	1601.65	1404.01	1256.16	1141.51	1050.10	913.74	817.20	745.55	50000
60000	5261.02	3589.63	2754.87	2254.77	1921.98	1684.81	1507.39	1369.81	1260.12	1096.49	980.64	894.66	60000
75000	6576.27	4487.04	3443.59	2818.46	2402.48	2106.01	1884.24	1712.27	1575.14	1370.61	1225.80	1118.32	75000
100000	8768.36	5982.72	4591.45	3757.94	3203.30	2808.01	2512.32	2283.02	2100.19	1827.47	1634.40	1491.09	100000
125000	10960.44	7478.39	5739.32	4697.42	4004.12	3510.01	3140.40	2853.77	2625.24	2284.34	2043.00	1863.87	125000
150000	13152.53	8974.07	6887.18	5636.90	4804.95	4212.02	3768.48	3424.53	3150.28	2741.21	2451.60	2236.64	150000
175000	15344.62	10469.75	8035.04	6576.39	5605.77	4914.02	4396.55	3995.28	3675.33	3198.08	2860.20	2609.41	175000
200000	17536.71	11965.43	9182.90	7515.88	6406.59	5616.02	5024.63	4566.03	4200.38	3654.94	3268.80	2982.18	200000
250000	21920.88	14956.78	11478.63	9394.84	8008.24	7020.02	6280.79	5707.54	5250.47	4568.68	4086.00	3727.73	250000

Amount	9.0 Years	10.0 Years	11.0 Years	12.0 Years	13.0 Years	14.0 Years	15.0 Years	16.0 Years	20.0 Years	30.0 Years	40.0 Years	50.0 Years	Amount
100	1.39	1.30	1.23	1.17	1.12	1.08	1.05	1.02	0.94	0.85	0.82	0.80	100
200	2.77	2.59	2.45	2.34	2.24	2.16	2.09	2.03	1.87	1.69	1.63	1.60	200
300	4.15	3.89	3.68	3.50	3.36	3.24	3.14	3.05	2.80	2.53	2.44	2.40	300
400	5.53	5.18	4.90	4.67	4.48	4.32	4.18	4.06	3.73	3.37	3.25	3.20	400
500	6.91	6.47	6.12	5.84	5.60	5.40	5.23	5.08	4.67	4.21	4.06	4.00	500
600	8.29	7.77	7.35	7.00	6.72	6.48	6.27	6.09	5.60	5.05	4.87	4.80	600
700	9.67	9.06	8.57	8.17	7.84	7.55	7.31	7.11	6.53	5.89	5.68	5.60	700
800	11.05	10.36	9.80	9.34	8.95	8.63	8.36	8.12	7.46	6.73	6.49	6.39	800
900	12.43	11.65	11.02	10.50	10.07	9.71	9.40	9.14	8.39	7.57	7.30	7.19	900
1000	13.81	12.94	12.24	11.67	11.19	10.79	10.45	10.15	9.33	8.41	8.11	7.99	1000
2000	27.62	25.88	24.48	23.33	22.38	21.57	20.89	20.30	18.65	16.82	16.21	15.98	2000
3000	41.43	38.82	36.72	35.00	33.56	32.36	31.33	30.45	27.97	25.23	24.31	23.97	3000
4000	55.24	51.76	48.96	46.66	44.75	43.14	41.77	40.60	37.29	33.64	32.41	31.95	4000
5000	69.05	64.70	61.20	58.32	55.93	53.92	52.22	50.75	46.61	42.05	40.51	39.94	5000
6000	82.86	77.64	73.44	69.99	67.12	64.71	62.66	60.90	55.93	50.46	48.61	47.93	6000
7000	96.67	90.58	85.68	81.65	78.31	75.49	73.10	71.05	65.25	58.86	56.71	55.91	7000
8000	110.48	103.52	97.91	93.31	89.49	86.27	83.54	81.20	74.58	67.27	64.81	63.90	8000
9000	124.29	116.46	110.15	104.98	100.68	97.06	93.99	91.35	83.90	75.68	72.91	71.89	9000
10000	138.10	129.40	122.39	116.64	111.86	107.84	104.43	101.50	93.22	84.09	81.01	79.88	10000
15000	207.15	194.10	183.58	174.96	167.79	161.76	156.64	152.25	139.82	126.13	121.51	119.81	15000
20000	276.19	258.80	244.78	233.28	223.72	215.68	208.85	203.00	186.43	168.18	162.02	159.75	20000
25000	345.24	323.50	305.97	291.60	279.65	269.60	261.06	253.75	233.04	210.22	202.52	199.68	25000
30000	414.29	388.20	367.16	349.92	335.58	323.52	313.27	304.50	279.64	252.26	243.02	239.62	30000
35000	483.33	452.90	428.36	408.24	391.51	377.43	365.48	355.25	326.25	294.30	283.53	279.55	35000
40000	552.38	517.60	489.55	466.55	447.43	431.35	417.69	406.00	372.86	336.35	324.03	319.49	40000
45000	621.43	582.29	550.74	524.87	503.36	485.27	469.91	456.75	419.46	378.39	364.53	359.42	45000
50000	690.47	646.99	611.94	583.19	559.29	539.19	522.12	507.50	466.07	420.43	405.04	399.36	50000
60000	828.57	776.39	734.32	699.83	671.15	647.03	626.54	609.00	559.28	504.52	486.04	479.23	60000
75000	1035.71	970.49	917.90	874.78	838.93	808.78	783.17	761.25	699.10	630.65	607.55	599.04	75000
100000	1380.94	1293.98	1223.87	1166.38	1118.58	1078.37	1044.23	1014.99	932.14	840.86	810.07	798.71	100000
125000	1726.18	1617.47	1529.84	1457.97	1398.22	1347.97	1305.29	1268.74	1165.17	1051.07	1012.58	998.39	125000
150000	2071.41	1940.97	1835.80	1749.56	1677.86	1617.56	1566.34	1522.49	1398.20	1261.29	1215.10	1198.07	150000
175000	2416.64	2264.46	2141.77	2041.16	1957.51	1887.15	1827.40	1776.24	1631.23	1471.50	1417.61	1397.74	175000
200000	2761.88	2587.96	2447.73	2332.75	2237.15	2156.74	2088.45	2029.98	1864.27	1681.71	1620.13	1597.42	200000
250000	3452.35	3234.94	3059.67	2915.94	2796.44	2695.93	2610.57	2537.48	2330.33	2102.14	2025.16	1996.77	250000

Amount	1.0 Year	1.5 Years	2.0 Years	2.5 Years	3.0 Years	3.5 Years	4.0 Years	4.5 Years	5.0 Years	6.0 Years	7.0 Years	8.0 Years	Amount
100	8.78	6.00	4.61	3.77	3.22	2.82	2.53	2.30	2.12	1.85	1.65	1.51	100
200	17.56	11.99	9.21	7.54	6.43	5.64	5.05	4.60	4.23	3.69	3.30	3.01	200
300	26.34	17.99	13.81	11.31	9.65	8.46	7.58	6.89	6.34	5.53	4.95	4.52	300
400	35.12	23.98	18.42	15.08	12.86	11.28	10.10	9.19	8.45	7.37	6.59	6.02	400
500	43.90	29.98	23.02	18.85	16.08	14.10	12.63	11.48	10.57	9.21	8.24	7.53	500
600	52.68	35.97	27.62	22.62	19.29	16.92	15.15	13.78	12.68	11.05	9.89	9.03	600
700	61.46	41.96	32.23	26.39	22.51	19.74	17.67	16.07	14.79	12.89	11.54	10.53	700
800	70.24	47.96	36.83	30.16	25.72	22.56	20.20	18.37	16.90	14.73	13.18	12.04	800
900	79.02	53.95	41.43	33.93	28.94	25.38	22.72	20.66	19.02	16.57	14.83	13.54	900
1000	87.80	59.95	46.03	37.70	32.15	28.20	25.25	22.96	21.13	18.41	16.48	15.05	1000
2000	175.60	119.89	92.06	75.40	64.30	56.40	50.49	45.91	42.25	36.81	32.95	30.09	2000
3000	263.40	179.83	138.09	113.09	96.45	84.60	75.73	68.86	63.38	55.21	49.42	45.13	3000
4000	351.20	239.77	184.12	150.79	128.60	112.80	100.98	91.81	84.50	73.61	65.89	60.17	4000
5000	439.00	299.72	230.15	188.48	160.75	141.00	126.22	114.76	105.63	92.01	82.37	75.22	5000
6000	526.80	359.66	276.18	226.18	192.90	169.19	151.46	137.71	126.75	110.41	98.84	90.26	6000
7000	614.60	419.60	322.21	263.87	225.05	197.39	176.70	160.66	147.87	128.81	115.31	105.30	7000
8000	702.40	479.54	368.24	301.57	257.20	225.59	201.95	183.61	169.00	147.21	131.78	120.34	8000
9000	790.20	539.48	414.27	339.26	289.35	253.79	227.19	206.56	190.12	165.61	148.26	135.38	9000
10000	878.00	599.43	460.30	376.96	321.50	281.99	252.43	229.52	211.25	184.01	164.73	150.43	10000
15000	1317.00	899.14	690.45	565.43	482.25	422.98	378.65	344.27	316.87	276.01	247.09	225.64	15000
20000	1756.00	1198.85	920.60	753.91	643.00	563.97	504.86	459.03	422.49	368.01	329.45	300.85	20000
25000	2195.00	1498.56	1150.75	942.39	803.75	704.96	631.07	573.78	528.11	460.01	411.81	376.06	25000
30000	2633.99	1798.27	1380.89	1130.86	964.50	845.95	757.29	688.54	633.73	552.01	494.17	451.27	30000
35000	3072.99	2097.98	1611.04	1319.34	1125.25	986.95	883.50	803.29	739.35	644.01	576.54	526.48	35000
40000	3511.99	2397.69	1841.19	1507.82	1286.00	1127.94	1009.71	918.05	844.97	736.01	658.90	601.69	40000
45000	3950.99	2697.40	2071.34	1696.29	1446.75	1268.93	1135.93	1032.80	950.60	828.01	741.26	676.90	45000
50000	4389.99	2997.11	2301.49	1884.77	1607.50	1409.92	1262.14	1147.56	1056.22	920.01	823.62	752.12	50000
60000	5267.98	3596.53	2761.78	2261.72	1929.00	1691.90	1514.57	1377.07	1267.46	1104.01	988.34	902.54	60000
75000	6584.98	4495.66	3452.23	2827.15	2411.25	2114.88	1893.21	1721.34	1584.32	1380.01	1235.43	1128.17	75000
100000	8779.97	5994.21	4602.97	3769.53	3215.00	2819.83	2524.27	2295.11	2112.43	1840.01	1647.23	1504.23	100000
125000	10974.96	7492.76	5753.71	4711.91	4018.75	3524.79	3155.34	2868.89	2640.54	2300.01	2059.04	1880.28	125000
150000	13169.95	8991.31	6904.45	5654.30	4822.50	4229.75	3786.41	3442.67	3168.64	2760.01	2470.85	2256.34	150000
175000	15364.94	10489.86	8055.19	6596.68	5626.24	4934.71	4417.48	4016.44	3696.75	3220.01	2882.66	2632.39	175000
200000	17559.94	11988.41	9205.93	7539.06	6429.99	5639.66	5048.54	4590.22	4224.85	3680.01	3294.46	3008.45	200000
250000	21949.92	14985.51	11507.41	9423.82	8037.49	7049.58	6310.68	5737.78	5281.07	4600.01	4118.08	3760.56	250000

Amount	9.0 Years	10.0 Years	11.0 Years	12.0 Years	13.0 Years	14.0 Years	15.0 Years	16.0 Years	20.0 Years	30.0 Years	40.0 Years	50.0 Years	Amount
100	1.40	1.31	1.24	1.19	1.14	1.10	1.06	1.04	0.95	0.86	0.83	0.82	100
200	2.79	2.62	2.48	2.37	2.27	2.19	2.12	2.07	1.90	1.72	1.66	1.64	200
300	4.19	3.93	3.72	3.55	3.40	3.28	3.18	3.10	2.85	2.58	2.49	2.46	300
400	5.58	5.24	4.96	4.73	4.54	4.38	4.24	4.13	3.80	3.44	3.32	3.28	400
500	6.98	6.54	6.19	5.91	5.67	5.47	5.30	5.16	4.75	4.30	4.15	4.10	500
600	8.37	7.85	7.43	7.09	6.80	6.56	6.36	6.19	5.70	5.16	4.98	4.92	600
700	9.77	9.16	8.67	8.27	7.94	7.66	7.42	7.22	6.64	6.02	5.81	5.74	700
800	11.16	10.47	9.91	9.45	9.07	8.75	8.48	8.25	7.59	6.88	6.64	6.56	800
900	12.55	11.77	11.15	10.63	10.20	9.84	9.54	9.28	8.54	7.74	7.47	7.37	900
1000	13.95	13.08	12.38	11.81	11.34	10.94	10.60	10.31	9.49	8.60	8.30	8.19	1000
2000	27.89	26.16	24.76	23.62	22.67	21.87	21.19	20.61	18.98	17.19	16.60	16.38	2000
3000	41.84	39.24	37.14	35.43	34.00	32.80	31.79	30.92	28.46	25.78	24.89	24.57	3000
4000	55.78	52.31	49.52	47.23	45.33	43.73	42.38	41.22	37.95	34.37	33.19	32.76	4000
5000	69.72	65.39	61.90	59.04	56.66	54.67	52.97	51.52	47.43	42.96	41.48	40.95	5000
6000	83.67	78.47	74.28	70.85	67.99	65.60	63.57	61.83	56.92	51.55	49.78	49.14	6000
7000	97.61	91.54	86.66	82.65	79.33	76.53	74.16	72.13	66.40	60.15	58.07	57.33	7000
8000	111.55	104.62	99.04	94.46	90.66	87.46	84.75	82.44	75.89	68.74	66.37	65.52	8000
9000	125.50	117.70	111.41	106.27	101.99	98.40	95.35	92.74	85.37	77.33	74.67	73.70	9000
10000	139.44	130.78	123.79	118.07	113.32	109.33	105.94	103.04	94.86	85.92	82.96	81.89	10000
15000	209.16	196.16	185.69	177.11	169.98	163.99	158.91	154.56	142.28	128.88	124.44	122.84	15000
20000	278.88	261.55	247.58	236.14	226.64	218.65	211.88	206.08	189.71	171.84	165.92	163.78	20000
25000	348.60	326.93	309.48	295.18	283.30	273.31	264.85	257.60	237.13	214.79	207.39	204.72	25000
30000	418.31	392.32	371.37	354.21	339.95	327.98	317.81	309.12	284.56	257.75	248.87	245.67	30000
35000	488.03	457.70	433.26	413.24	396.61	382.64	370.78	360.64	331.99	300.71	290.35	286.61	35000
40000	557.75	523.09	495.16	472.28	453.27	437.30	423.75	412.16	379.41	343.67	331.83	327.56	40000
45000	627.47	588.47	557.05	531.31	509.93	491.96	476.72	463.68	426.84	386.62	373.31	368.50	45000
50000	697.19	653.86	618.95	590.35	566.59	546.62	529.69	515.20	474.26	429.58	414.78	409.44	50000
60000	836.62	784.63	742.74	708.41	679.90	655.95	635.62	618.24	569.12	515.50	497.74	491.33	60000
75000	1045.78	980.78	928.42	885.52	849.88	819.93	794.53	772.80	711.39	644.37	622.17	614.16	75000
100000	1394.37	1307.71	1237.89	1180.69	1133.17	1093.24	1059.37	1030.40	948.52	859.16	829.56	818.88	100000
125000	1742.96	1634.63	1547.36	1475.86	1416.46	1366.55	1324.21	1287.99	1185.65	1073.95	1036.95	1023.60	125000
150000	2091.55	1961.56	1856.83	1771.03	1699.75	1639.86	1589.05	1545.59	1422.78	1288.74	1244.34	1228.32	150000
175000	2440.15	2288.48	2166.30	2066.20	1983.04	1913.17	1853.89	1803.19	1659.91	1503.53	1451.73	1433.04	175000
200000	2788.74	2615.41	2475.77	2361.37	2266.33	2186.48	2118.73	2060.79	1897.04	1718.31	1659.12	1637.76	200000
250000	3485.92	3269.26	3094.72	2951.71	2832.91	2733.09	2648.41	2575.98	2371.30	2147.89	2073.90	2047.20	250000

Amount	1.0 Year	1.5 Years	2.0 Years	2.5 Years	3.0 Years	3.5 Years	4.0 Years	4.5 Years	5.0 Years	6.0 Years	7.0 Years	8.0 Years	Amount
100	8.80	6.01	4.62	3.79	3.23	2.84	2.54	2.31	2.13	1.86	1.67	1.52	100
200	17.59	12.02	9.23	7.57	6.46	5.67	5.08	4.62	4.25	3.71	3.33	3.04	200
300	26.38	18.02	13.85	11.35	9.69	8.50	7.61	6.93	6.38	5.56	4.99	4.56	300
400	35.17	24.03	18.46	15.13	12.91	11.33	10.15	9.23	8.50	7.42	6.65	6.07	400
500	43.96	30.03	23.08	18.91	16.14	14.16	12.69	11.54	10.63	9.27	8.31	7.59	500
600	52.75	36.04	27.69	22.69	19.37	17.00	15.22	13.85	12.75	11.12	9.97	9.11	600
700	61.55	42.04	32.31	26.47	22.59	19.83	17.76	16.16	14.88	12.97	11.63	10.63	700
800	70.34	48.05	36.92	30.25	25.82	22.66	20.30	18.46	17.00	14.83	13.29	12.14	800
900	79.13	54.06	41.54	34.04	29.05	25.49	22.83	20.77	19.13	16.68	14.95	13.66	900
1000	87.92	60.06	46.15	37.82	32.27	28.32	25.37	23.08	21.25	18.53	16.61	15.18	1000
2000	175.84	120.12	92.29	75.63	64.54	56.64	50.73	46.15	42.50	37.06	33.21	30.35	2000
3000	263.75	180.18	138.44	113.44	96.81	84.96	76.09	69.22	63.75	55.58	49.81	45.53	3000
4000	351.67	240.23	184.58	151.25	129.07	113.27	101.46	92.29	84.99	74.11	66.41	60.70	4000
5000	439.58	300.29	230.73	189.06	161.34	141.59	126.82	115.37	106.24	92.63	83.01	75.88	5000
6000	527.50	360.35	276.87	226.87	193.61	169.91	152.18	138.44	127.49	111.16	99.61	91.05	6000
7000	615.42	420.40	323.02	264.68	225.88	198.22	177.54	161.51	148.73	129.69	116.21	106.22	7000
8000	703.33	480.46	369.16	302.50	258.14	226.54	202.91	184.58	169.98	148.21	132.81	121.40	8000
9000	791.25	540.52	415.31	340.31	290.41	254.86	228.27	207.66	191.23	166.74	149.42	136.57	9000
10000	879.16	600.58	461.45	378.12	322.68	283.17	253.63	230.73	212.48	185.26	166.02	151.75	10000
15000	1318.74	900.86	692.18	567.18	484.01	424.76	380.44	346.09	318.71	277.89	249.02	227.62	15000
20000	1758.32	1201.15	922.90	756.23	645.35	566.34	507.26	461.45	424.95	370.52	332.03	303.49	20000
25000	2197.90	1501.43	1153.63	945.29	806.68	707.93	634.07	576.82	531.18	463.15	415.03	379.36	25000
30000	2637.48	1801.72	1384.35	1134.35	968.02	849.51	760.88	692.18	637.42	555.78	498.04	455.23	30000
35000	3077.06	2102.00	1615.08	1323.40	1129.36	991.09	887.70	807.54	743.65	648.41	581.05	531.10	35000
40000	3516.64	2402.29	1845.80	1512.46	1290.69	1132.68	1014.51	922.90	849.89	741.04	664.05	606.97	40000
45000	3956.22	2702.57	2076.53	1701.52	1452.03	1274.26	1141.32	1038.26	956.12	833.67	747.06	682.84	45000
50000	4395.80	3002.86	2307.25	1890.58	1613.36	1415.85	1268.13	1153.63	1062.36	926.30	830.06	758.71	50000
60000	5274.96	3603.43	2768.70	2268.69	1936.04	1699.01	1521.76	1384.35	1274.83	1111.56	996.08	910.45	60000
75000	6593.70	4504.29	3460.87	2835.86	2420.04	2123.77	1902.20	1730.44	1593.53	1389.44	1245.09	1138.07	75000
100000	8791.59	6005.71	4614.50	3781.15	3226.72	2831.69	2536.26	2307.25	2124.71	1852.59	1660.12	1517.42	100000
125000	10989.49	7507.14	5768.12	4726.43	4033.40	3539.61	3170.33	2884.06	2655.89	2315.73	2075.15	1896.78	125000
150000	13187.39	9008.57	6921.74	5671.72	4840.08	4247.53	3804.39	3460.87	3187.06	2778.88	2490.18	2276.13	150000
175000	15385.29	10509.99	8075.37	6617.00	5646.76	4955.45	4438.46	4037.68	3718.24	3242.03	2905.21	2655.48	175000
200000	17583.18	12011.42	9228.99	7562.29	6453.44	5663.37	5072.52	4614.49	4249.41	3705.17	3320.24	3034.84	200000
250000	21978.98	15014.28	11536.24	9452.86	8066.80	7079.21	6340.65	5768.11	5311.77	4631.46	4150.30	3793.55	250000

Amount	9.0 Years	10.0 Years	11.0 Years	12.0 Years	13.0 Years	14.0 Years	15.0 Years	16.0 Years	20.0 Years	30.0 Years	40.0 Years	50.0 Years	Amount
100	1.41	1.33	1.26	1.20	1.15	1.11	1.08	1.05	0.97	0.88	0.85	0.84	100
200	2.82	2.65	2.51	2.40	2.30	2.22	2.15	2.10	1.94	1.76	1.70	1.68	200
300	4.23	3.97	3.76	3.59	3.45	3.33	3.23	3.14	2.90	2.64	2.55	2.52	300
400	5.64	5.29	5.01	4.79	4.60	4.44	4.30	4.19	3.87	3.52	3.40	3.36	400
500	7.04	6.61	6.26	5.98	5.74	5.55	5.38	5.23	4.83	4.39	4.25	4.20	500
600	8.45	7.93	7.52	7.18	6.89	6.65	6.45	6.28	5.80	5.27	5.10	5.04	600
700	9.86	9.26	8.77	8.37	8.04	7.76	7.53	7.33	6.76	6.15	5.95	5.88	700
800	11.27	10.58	10.02	9.57	9.19	8.87	8.60	8.37	7.73	7.03	6.80	6.72	800
900	12.68	11.90	11.27	10.76	10.34	9.98	9.68	9.42	8.69	7.90	7.65	7.56	900
1000	14.08	13.22	12.52	11.96	11.48	11.09	10.75	10.46	9.66	8.78	8.50	8.40	1000
2000	28.16	26.44	25.04	23.91	22.96	22.17	21.50	20.92	19.31	17.56	16.99	16.79	2000
3000	42.24	39.65	37.56	35.86	34.44	33.25	32.24	31.38	28.96	26.33	25.48	25.18	3000
4000	56.32	52.87	50.08	47.81	45.92	44.33	42.99	41.84	38.61	35.11	33.97	33.57	4000
5000	70.40	66.08	62.60	59.76	57.40	55.42	53.74	52.30	48.26	43.88	42.46	41.96	5000
6000	84.48	79.30	75.12	71.71	68.88	66.50	64.48	62.76	57.91	52.66	50.95	50.35	6000
7000	98.56	92.51	87.64	83.66	80.35	77.58	75.23	73.22	67.56	61.44	59.45	58.74	7000
8000	112.63	105.73	100.16	95.61	91.83	88.66	85.97	83.68	77.21	70.21	67.94	67.13	8000
9000	126.71	118.94	112.68	107.56	103.31	99.74	96.72	94.14	86.86	78.99	76.43	75.52	9000
10000	140.79	132.16	125.20	119.51	114.79	110.83	107.47	104.60	96.51	87.76	84.92	83.92	10000
15000	211.19	198.23	187.80	179.27	172.18	166.24	161.20	156.89	144.76	131.64	127.38	125.87	15000
20000	281.58	264.31	250.40	239.02	229.57	221.65	214.93	209.19	193.01	175.52	169.83	167.83	20000
25000	351.97	330.38	313.00	298.77	286.97	277.06	268.66	261.48	241.26	219.40	212.29	209.78	25000
30000	422.37	396.46	375.60	358.53	344.36	332.47	322.39	313.78	289.51	263.28	254.75	251.74	30000
35000	492.76	462.53	438.20	418.28	401.75	387.88	376.12	366.07	337.76	307.16	297.21	293.69	35000
40000	563.15	528.61	500.80	478.04	459.14	443.29	429.85	418.37	386.01	351.03	339.66	335.65	40000
45000	633.55	594.68	563.40	537.79	516.54	498.70	483.58	470.66	434.26	394.91	382.12	377.60	45000
50000	703.94	660.76	626.00	597.54	573.93	554.11	537.31	522.96	482.52	438.79	424.58	419.56	50000
60000	844.73	792.91	751.20	717.05	688.71	664.93	644.77	627.55	579.02	526.55	509.49	503.47	60000
75000	1055.91	991.14	939.00	896.31	860.89	831.16	805.96	784.43	723.77	658.18	636.86	629.33	75000
100000	1407.87	1321.51	1251.99	1195.08	1147.85	1108.21	1074.61	1045.91	965.03	877.58	849.15	839.11	100000
125000	1759.84	1651.89	1564.99	1493.85	1434.82	1385.26	1343.26	1307.38	1206.28	1096.97	1061.44	1048.89	125000
150000	2111.81	1982.27	1877.99	1792.62	1721.78	1662.31	1611.91	1568.86	1447.54	1316.36	1273.72	1258.66	150000
175000	2463.78	2312.64	2190.98	2091.39	2008.74	1939.36	1880.56	1830.33	1688.79	1535.76	1486.01	1468.44	175000
200000	2815.74	2643.02	2503.98	2390.16	2295.70	2216.41	2149.22	2091.81	1930.05	1755.15	1698.30	1678.22	200000
250000	3519.68	3303.77	3129.97	2987.70	2869.63	2770.51	2686.52	2614.76	2412.56	2193.93	2122.87	2097.77	250000

Amount	1.0 Year	1.5 Years	2.0 Years	2.5 Years	3.0 Years	3.5 Years	4.0 Years	4.5 Years	5.0 Years	6.0 Years	7.0 Years	8.0 Years	Amount
100	8.81	6.02	4.63	3.80	3.24	2.85	2.55	2.32	2.14	1.87	1.68	1.54	100
200	17.61	12.04	9.26	7.59	6.48	5.69	5.10	4.64	4.28	3.74	3.35	3.07	200
300	26.41	18.06	13.88	11.38	9.72	8.54	7.65	6.96	6.42	5.60	5.02	4.60	300
400	35.22	24.07	18.51	15.18	12.96	11.38	10.20	9.28	8.55	7.47	6.70	6.13	400
500	44.02	30.09	23.14	18.97	16.20	14.22	12.75	11.60	10.69	9.33	8.37	7.66	500
600	52.82	36.11	27.76	22.76	19.44	17.07	15.29	13.92	12.83	11.20	10.04	9.19	600
700	61.63	42.13	32.39	26.55	22.67	19.91	17.84	16.24	14.96	13.06	11.72	10.72	700
800	70.43	48.14	37.01	30.35	25.91	22.75	20.39	18.56	17.10	14.93	13.39	12.25	800
900	79.23	54.16	41.64	34.14	29.15	25.60	22.94	20.88	19.24	16.79	15.06	13.78	900
1000	88.04	60.18	46.27	37.93	32.39	28.44	25.49	23.20	21.38	18.66	16.74	15.31	1000
2000	176.07	120.35	92.53	75.86	64.77	56.88	50.97	46.39	42.75	37.31	33.47	30.62	2000
3000	264.10	180.52	138.79	113.79	97.16	85.31	76.45	69.59	64.12	55.96	50.20	45.93	3000
4000	352.13	240.69	185.05	151.72	129.54	113.75	101.94	92.78	85.49	74.61	66.93	61.23	4000
5000	440.17	300.87	231.31	189.64	161.93	142.18	127.42	115.98	106.86	93.27	83.66	76.54	5000
6000	528.20	361.04	277.57	227.57	194.31	170.62	152.90	139.17	128.23	111.92	100.39	91.85	6000
7000	616.23	421.21	323.83	265.50	226.70	199.05	178.38	162.36	149.60	130.57	117.12	107.15	7000
8000	704.26	481.38	370.09	303.43	259.08	227.49	203.87	185.56	170.97	149.22	133.85	122.46	8000
9000	792.29	541.56	416.35	341.35	291.47	255.93	229.35	208.75	192.34	167.87	150.58	137.77	9000
10000	880.33	601.73	462.61	379.28	323.85	284.36	254.83	231.95	213.71	186.53	167.31	153.07	10000
15000	1320.49	902.59	693.91	568.92	485.78	426.54	382.25	347.92	320.56	279.79	250.96	229.61	15000
20000	1760.65	1203.45	925.21	758.56	647.70	568.72	509.66	463.89	427.41	373.05	334.62	306.14	20000
25000	2200.81	1504.31	1156.51	948.20	809.62	710.90	637.08	579.86	534.26	466.31	418.27	382.67	25000
30000	2640.97	1805.17	1387.82	1137.84	971.55	853.07	764.49	695.83	641.11	559.57	501.92	459.21	30000
35000	3081.13	2106.03	1619.12	1327.48	1133.47	995.25	891.90	811.80	747.96	652.83	585.58	535.74	35000
40000	3521.29	2406.90	1850.42	1517.12	1295.39	1137.43	1019.32	927.77	854.82	746.09	669.23	612.28	40000
45000	3961.45	2707.76	2081.72	1706.75	1457.32	1279.61	1146.73	1043.74	961.67	839.35	752.88	688.81	45000
50000	4401.62	3008.62	2313.02	1896.39	1619.24	1421.79	1274.15	1159.71	1068.52	932.61	836.54	765.34	50000
60000	5281.94	3610.34	2775.63	2275.67	1943.09	1706.14	1528.97	1391.65	1282.22	1119.13	1003.84	918.41	60000
75000	6602.42	4512.92	3469.53	2844.59	2428.86	2132.68	1911.22	1739.56	1602.77	1398.92	1254.80	1148.01	75000
100000	8803.23	6017.23	4626.04	3792.78	3238.47	2843.57	2548.29	2319.42	2137.03	1865.22	1673.07	1530.68	100000
125000	11004.03	7521.54	5782.55	4740.97	4048.09	3554.46	3185.36	2899.27	2671.29	2331.52	2091.34	1913.35	125000
150000	13204.84	9025.84	6939.06	5689.17	4857.71	4265.35	3822.43	3479.12	3205.54	2797.83	2509.60	2296.02	150000
175000	15405.64	10530.15	8095.57	6637.36	5667.33	4976.24	4459.50	4058.97	3739.80	3264.13	2927.87	2678.69	175000
200000	17606.45	12034.46	9252.08	7585.56	6476.94	5687.13	5096.57	4638.83	4274.06	3730.44	3346.13	3061.36	200000
250000	22008.06	15043.07	11565.10	9481.94	8096.18	7108.91	6370.71	5798.53	5342.57	4663.04	4182.67	3826.70	250000

Amount	9.0 Years	10.0 Years	11.0 Years	12.0 Years	13.0 Years	14.0 Years	15.0 Years	16.0 Years	20.0 Years	30.0 Years	40.0 Years	50.0 Years	Amount
100	1.43	1.34	1.27	1.21	1.17	1.13	1.09	1.07	0.99	0.90	0.87	0.86	100
200	2.85	2.68	2.54	2.42	2.33	2.25	2.18	2.13	1.97	1.80	1.74	1.72	200
300	4.27	4.01	3.80	3.63	3.49	3.37	3.27	3.19	2.95	2.69	2.61	2.58	300
400	5.69	5.35	5.07	4.84	4.66	4.50	4.36	4.25	3.93	3.59	3.48	3.44	400
500	7.11	6.68	6.34	6.05	5.82	5.62	5.45	5.31	4.91	4.49	4.35	4.30	500
600	8.53	8.02	7.60	7.26	6.98	6.74	6.54	6.37	5.89	5.38	5.22	5.16	600
700	9.96	9.35	8.87	8.47	8.14	7.87	7.63	7.44	6.88	6.28	6.09	6.02	700
800	11.38	10.69	10.13	9.68	9.31	8.99	8.72	8.50	7.86	7.17	6.96	6.88	800
900	12.80	12.02	11.40	10.89	10.47	10.11	9.81	9.56	8.84	8.07	7.82	7.74	900
1000	14.22	13.36	12.67	12.10	11.63	11.24	10.90	10.62	9.82	8.97	8.69	8.60	1000
2000	28.43	26.71	25.33	24.20	23.26	22.47	21.80	21.24	19.64	17.93	17.38	17.19	2000
3000	42.65	40.07	37.99	36.29	34.88	33.70	32.70	31.85	29.45	26.89	26.07	25.79	3000
4000	56.86	53.42	50.65	48.39	46.51	44.94	43.60	42.47	39.27	35.85	34.76	34.38	4000
5000	71.08	66.77	63.31	60.48	58.14	56.17	54.50	53.08	49.09	44.81	43.45	42.97	5000
6000	85.29	80.13	75.98	72.58	69.76	67.40	65.40	63.70	58.90	53.77	52.13	51.57	6000
7000	99.51	93.48	88.64	84.67	81.39	78.63	76.30	74.31	68.72	62.73	60.82	60.16	7000
8000	113.72	106.84	101.30	96.77	93.02	89.87	87.20	84.93	78.54	71.69	69.51	68.76	8000
9000	127.93	120.19	113.96	108.87	104.64	101.10	98.10	95.54	88.35	80.65	78.20	77.35	9000
10000	142.15	133.54	126.62	120.96	116.27	112.33	109.00	106.16	98.17	89.62	86.90	85.94	10000
15000	213.22	200.31	189.93	181.44	174.40	168.50	163.50	159.23	147.25	134.42	130.33	128.91	15000
20000	284.29	267.08	253.24	241.92	232.53	224.66	218.00	212.31	196.33	179.23	173.77	171.88	20000
25000	355.37	333.85	316.55	302.40	290.66	280.82	272.49	265.38	245.42	224.03	217.21	214.85	25000
30000	426.44	400.62	379.86	362.87	348.79	336.99	326.99	318.46	294.50	268.84	260.65	257.82	30000
35000	497.51	467.39	443.17	423.35	406.92	393.15	381.49	371.54	343.58	313.64	304.09	300.79	35000
40000	568.58	534.16	506.48	483.83	465.06	449.31	435.99	424.61	392.66	358.45	347.53	343.76	40000
45000	639.65	600.93	569.78	544.31	523.19	505.48	490.48	477.69	441.74	403.25	390.97	386.73	45000
50000	710.73	667.70	633.09	604.79	581.32	561.64	544.98	530.76	490.83	448.06	434.41	429.70	50000
60000	852.87	801.24	759.71	725.74	697.58	673.97	653.98	636.92	588.99	537.67	521.30	515.64	60000
75000	1066.09	1001.55	949.64	907.18	871.98	842.46	817.47	796.14	736.24	672.08	651.62	644.55	75000
100000	1421.45	1335.40	1266.18	1209.57	1162.63	1123.27	1089.96	1061.52	981.65	896.11	868.82	859.39	100000
125000	1776.81	1669.24	1582.72	1511.96	1453.29	1404.09	1362.44	1326.90	1227.06	1120.13	1086.03	1074.24	125000
150000	2132.17	2003.09	1899.27	1814.35	1743.95	1684.91	1634.93	1592.28	1472.47	1344.16	1303.23	1289.09	150000
175000	2487.53	2336.94	2215.81	2116.74	2034.60	1965.73	1907.42	1857.66	1717.88	1568.18	1520.44	1503.94	175000
200000	2842.89	2670.79	2532.36	2419.14	2325.26	2246.54	2179.91	2123.04	1963.29	1792.21	1737.64	1718.78	200000
250000	3553.61	3338.48	3165.44	3023.92	2906.58	2808.18	2724.88	2653.80	2454.11	2240.26	2172.05	2148.48	250000

Amount	1.0 Year	1.5 Years	2.0 Years	2.5 Years	3.0 Years	3.5 Years	4.0 Years	4.5 Years	5.0 Years	6.0 Years	7.0 Years	8.0 Years	Amount
100	8.82	6.03	4.64	3.81	3.26	2.86	2.57	2.34	2.15	1.88	1.69	1.55	100
200	17.63	12.06	9.28	7.61	6.51	5.72	5.13	4.67	4.30	3.76	3.38	3.09	200
300	26.45	18.09	13.92	11.42	9.76	8.57	7.69	7.00	6.45	5.64	5.06	4.64	300
400	35.26	24.12	18.56	15.22	13.01	11.43	10.25	9.33	8.60	7.52	6.75	6.18	400
500	44.08	30.15	23.19	19.03	16.26	14.28	12.81	11.66	10.75	9.39	8.44	7.73	500
600	52.89	36.18	27.83	22.83	19.51	17.14	15.37	13.99	12.90	11.27	10.12	9.27	600
700	61.71	42.21	32.47	26.64	22.76	19.99	17.93	16.33	15.05	13.15	11.81	10.81	700
800	70.52	48.24	37.11	30.44	26.01	22.85	20.49	18.66	17.20	15.03	13.49	12.36	800
900	79.34	54.26	41.74	34.24	29.26	25.70	23.05	20.99	19.35	16.91	15.18	13.90	900
1000	88.15	60.29	46.38	38.05	32.51	28.56	25.61	23.32	21.50	18.78	16.87	15.45	1000
2000	176.30	120.58	92.76	76.09	65.01	57.11	51.21	46.64	42.99	37.56	33.73	30.89	2000
3000	264.45	180.87	139.13	114.14	97.51	85.67	76.82	69.95	64.49	56.34	50.59	46.33	3000
4000	352.60	241.16	185.51	152.18	130.01	114.22	102.42	93.27	85.98	75.12	67.45	61.77	4000
5000	440.75	301.44	231.89	190.23	162.52	142.78	128.02	116.59	107.47	93.90	84.31	77.21	5000
6000	528.90	361.73	278.26	228.27	195.02	171.33	153.63	139.90	128.97	112.68	101.17	92.65	6000
7000	617.05	422.02	324.64	266.32	227.52	199.89	179.23	163.22	150.46	131.46	118.03	108.09	7000
8000	705.19	482.31	371.01	304.36	260.02	228.44	204.83	186.53	171.96	150.24	134.89	123.53	8000
9000	793.34	542.59	417.39	342.40	292.53	257.00	230.44	209.85	193.45	169.02	151.75	138.97	9000
10000	881.49	602.88	463.77	380.45	325.03	285.55	256.04	233.17	214.94	187.79	168.61	154.41	10000
15000	1322.23	904.32	695.65	570.67	487.54	428.33	384.06	349.75	322.41	281.69	252.92	231.61	15000
20000	1762.98	1205.76	927.53	760.89	650.05	571.10	512.07	466.33	429.88	375.58	337.22	308.81	20000
25000	2203.72	1507.19	1159.41	951.11	812.57	713.87	640.09	582.91	537.35	469.48	421.52	386.01	25000
30000	2644.46	1808.63	1391.29	1141.33	975.08	856.65	768.11	699.49	644.82	563.37	505.83	463.21	30000
35000	3085.21	2110.07	1623.17	1331.56	1137.59	999.42	896.12	816.07	752.29	657.27	590.13	540.41	35000
40000	3525.95	2411.51	1855.05	1521.78	1300.10	1142.19	1024.14	932.65	859.76	751.16	674.43	617.61	40000
45000	3966.69	2712.95	2086.93	1712.00	1462.61	1284.97	1152.16	1049.23	967.23	845.06	758.74	694.81	45000
50000	4407.44	3014.38	2318.81	1902.22	1625.13	1427.74	1280.17	1165.81	1074.70	938.95	843.04	772.01	50000
60000	5288.92	3617.26	2782.57	2282.66	1950.15	1713.29	1536.21	1398.98	1289.64	1126.74	1011.65	926.41	60000
75000	6611.15	4521.57	3478.21	2853.33	2437.69	2141.61	1920.26	1748.72	1612.05	1408.43	1264.56	1158.01	75000
100000	8814.87	6028.76	4637.61	3804.44	3250.25	2855.48	2560.34	2331.62	2149.40	1877.90	1686.07	1544.01	100000
125000	11018.58	7535.95	5797.01	4755.54	4062.81	3569.35	3200.43	2914.53	2686.74	2347.38	2107.59	1930.01	125000
150000	13222.30	9043.14	6956.41	5706.65	4875.37	4283.22	3840.51	3497.43	3224.09	2816.85	2529.11	2316.01	150000
175000	15426.01	10550.33	8115.81	6657.76	5687.93	4997.09	4480.60	4080.34	3761.44	3286.32	2950.62	2702.01	175000
200000	17629.73	12057.52	9275.21	7608.87	6500.49	5710.95	5120.68	4663.24	4298.79	3755.80	3372.14	3088.01	200000
250000	22037.16	15071.89	11594.02	9511.08	8125.62	7138.69	6400.85	5829.05	5373.48	4694.75	4215.17	3860.01	250000

Amount	9.0 Years	10.0 Years	11.0 Years	12.0 Years	13.0 Years	14.0 Years	15.0 Years	16.0 Years	20.0 Years	30.0 Years	40.0 Years	50.0 Years	Amount
100	1.44	1.35	1.29	1.23	1.18	1.14	1.11	1.08	1.00	0.92	0.89	0.88	100
200	2.88	2.70	2.57	2.45	2.36	2.28	2.22	2.16	2.00	1.83	1.78	1.76	200
300	4.31	4.05	3.85	3.68	3.54	3.42	3.32	3.24	3.00	2.75	2.67	2.64	300
400	5.75	5.40	5.13	4.90	4.72	4.56	4.43	4.31	4.00	3.66	3.56	3.52	400
500	7.18	6.75	6.41	6.13	5.89	5.70	5.53	5.39	5.00	4.58	4.45	4.40	500
600	8.62	8.10	7.69	7.35	7.07	6.84	6.64	6.47	6.00	5.49	5.34	5.28	600
700	10.05	9.45	8.97	8.57	8.25	7.97	7.74	7.55	6.99	6.41	6.22	6.16	700
800	11.49	10.80	10.25	9.80	9.43	9.11	8.85	8.62	7.99	7.32	7.11	7.04	800
900	12.92	12.15	11.53	11.02	10.60	10.25	9.95	9.70	8.99	8.24	8.00	7.92	900
1000	14.36	13.50	12.81	12.25	11.78	11.39	11.06	10.78	9.99	9.15	8.89	8.80	1000
2000	28.71	26.99	25.61	24.49	23.56	22.77	22.11	21.55	19.97	18.30	17.78	17.60	2000
3000	43.06	40.49	38.42	36.73	35.33	34.16	33.17	32.32	29.96	27.45	26.66	26.40	3000
4000	57.41	53.98	51.22	48.97	47.11	45.54	44.22	43.09	39.94	36.59	35.55	35.19	4000
5000	71.76	67.47	64.03	61.21	58.88	56.93	55.27	53.87	49.92	45.74	44.43	43.99	5000
6000	86.11	80.97	76.83	73.45	70.66	68.31	66.33	64.64	59.91	54.89	53.32	52.79	6000
7000	100.46	94.46	89.64	85.69	82.43	79.70	77.38	75.41	69.89	64.04	62.20	61.59	7000
8000	114.81	107.95	102.44	97.94	94.21	91.08	88.44	86.18	79.88	73.18	71.09	70.38	8000
9000	129.16	121.45	115.25	110.18	105.98	102.46	99.49	96.96	89.86	82.33	79.98	79.18	9000
10000	143.51	134.94	128.05	122.42	117.76	113.85	110.54	107.73	99.84	91.48	88.86	87.98	10000
15000	215.27	202.41	192.07	183.63	176.63	170.77	165.81	161.59	149.76	137.22	133.29	131.96	15000
20000	287.02	269.87	256.09	244.83	235.51	227.69	221.08	215.45	199.68	182.95	177.72	175.95	20000
25000	358.78	337.34	320.12	306.04	294.38	284.61	276.35	269.32	249.60	228.69	222.15	219.94	25000
30000	430.53	404.81	384.14	367.25	353.26	341.54	331.62	323.18	299.52	274.43	266.58	263.92	30000
35000	502.29	472.28	448.16	428.45	412.13	398.46	386.89	377.04	349.44	320.16	311.00	307.91	35000
40000	574.04	539.74	512.18	489.66	471.01	455.38	442.16	430.90	399.36	365.90	355.43	351.89	40000
45000	645.79	607.21	576.21	550.87	529.88	512.30	497.43	484.76	449.28	411.64	399.86	395.88	45000
50000	717.55	674.68	640.23	612.08	588.76	569.22	552.70	538.63	499.19	457.37	444.29	439.87	50000
60000	861.06	809.61	768.27	734.49	706.51	683.07	663.24	646.35	599.03	548.85	533.15	527.84	60000
75000	1076.32	1012.02	960.34	918.11	883.13	853.83	829.05	807.94	748.79	686.06	666.43	659.80	75000
100000	1435.09	1349.35	1280.45	1224.15	1177.51	1138.44	1105.40	1077.25	998.38	914.74	888.58	879.73	100000
125000	1793.86	1686.69	1600.56	1530.18	1471.88	1423.05	1381.75	1346.56	1247.98	1143.43	1110.72	1099.66	125000
150000	2152.63	2024.03	1920.67	1836.22	1766.26	1707.66	1658.10	1615.87	1497.57	1372.11	1332.86	1319.59	150000
175000	2511.41	2361.37	2240.79	2142.25	2060.63	1992.26	1934.45	1885.18	1747.17	1600.80	1555.00	1539.52	175000
200000	2870.18	2698.70	2560.90	2448.29	2355.01	2276.87	2210.80	2154.49	1996.76	1829.48	1777.15	1759.45	200000
250000	3587.72	3373.38	3201.12	3060.36	2943.76	2846.09	2763.50	2693.11	2495.95	2286.85	2221.43	2199.31	250000

Amount	1.0 Year	1.5 Years	2.0 Years	2.5 Years	3.0 Years	3.5 Years	4.0 Years	4.5 Years	5.0 Years	6.0 Years	7.0 Years	8.0 Years	Amount
100	8.83	6.05	4.65	3.82	3.27	2.87	2.58	2.35	2.17	1.90	1.70	1.56	100
200	17.66	12.09	9.30	7.64	6.53	5.74	5.15	4.69	4.33	3.79	3.40	3.12	200
300	26.48	18.13	13.95	11.45	9.79	8.61	7.72	7.04	6.49	5.68	5.10	4.68	300
400	35.31	24.17	18.60	15.27	13.05	11.47	10.29	9.38	8.65	7.57	6.80	6.23	400
500	44.14	30.21	23.25	19.09	16.32	14.34	12.87	11.72	10.81	9.46	8.50	7.79	500
600	52.96	36.25	27.90	22.90	19.58	17.21	15.44	14.07	12.98	11.35	10.20	9.35	600
700	61.79	42.29	32.55	26.72	22.84	20.08	18.01	16.41	15.14	13.24	11.90	10.91	700
800	70.62	48.33	37.20	30.53	26.10	22.94	20.58	18.76	17.30	15.13	13.60	12.46	800
900	79.44	54.37	41.85	34.35	29.36	25.81	23.16	21.10	19.46	17.02	15.30	14.02	900
1000	88.27	60.41	46.50	38.17	32.63	28.68	25.73	23.44	21.62	18.91	17.00	15.58	1000
2000	176.54	120.81	92.99	76.33	65.25	57.35	51.45	46.88	43.24	37.82	33.99	31.15	2000
3000	264.80	181.21	139.48	114.49	97.87	86.03	77.18	70.32	64.86	56.72	50.98	46.73	3000
4000	353.07	241.62	185.97	152.65	130.49	114.70	102.90	93.76	86.48	75.63	67.97	62.30	4000
5000	441.33	302.02	232.46	190.81	163.11	143.38	128.63	117.20	108.09	94.54	84.96	77.87	5000
6000	529.60	362.42	278.96	228.97	195.73	172.05	154.35	140.64	129.71	113.44	101.95	93.45	6000
7000	617.86	422.83	325.45	267.13	228.35	200.72	180.07	164.08	151.33	132.35	118.94	109.02	7000
8000	706.13	483.23	371.94	305.29	260.97	229.40	205.80	187.51	172.95	151.26	135.94	124.60	8000
9000	794.39	543.63	418.43	343.45	293.59	258.07	231.52	210.95	194.57	170.16	152.93	140.17	9000
10000	882.66	604.03	464.92	381.62	326.21	286.75	257.25	234.39	216.18	189.07	169.92	155.74	10000
15000	1323.98	906.05	697.38	572.42	489.31	430.12	385.87	351.58	324.27	283.60	254.87	233.61	15000
20000	1765.31	1208.06	929.84	763.23	652.41	573.49	514.49	468.78	432.36	378.13	339.83	311.48	20000
25000	2206.63	1510.08	1162.30	954.03	815.52	716.86	643.11	585.97	540.45	472.66	424.79	389.35	25000
30000	2647.96	1812.09	1394.76	1144.84	978.62	860.23	771.73	703.16	648.54	567.19	509.74	467.22	30000
35000	3089.28	2114.11	1627.22	1335.64	1141.72	1003.60	900.35	820.36	756.63	661.72	594.70	545.09	35000
40000	3530.61	2416.12	1859.68	1526.45	1304.82	1146.97	1028.98	937.55	864.72	756.26	679.66	622.96	40000
45000	3971.93	2718.14	2092.14	1717.25	1467.93	1290.34	1157.60	1054.74	972.81	850.79	764.61	700.83	45000
50000	4413.26	3020.15	2324.60	1908.06	1631.03	1433.71	1286.22	1171.94	1080.90	945.32	849.57	778.70	50000
60000	5295.91	3624.18	2789.52	2289.67	1957.23	1720.45	1543.46	1406.32	1297.08	1134.38	1019.48	934.44	60000
75000	6619.89	4530.23	3486.89	2862.09	2446.54	2150.57	1929.33	1757.90	1621.35	1417.98	1274.35	1168.05	75000
100000	8826.51	6040.30	4649.19	3816.11	3262.05	2867.42	2572.43	2343.87	2161.80	1890.63	1699.13	1557.40	100000
125000	11033.14	7550.38	5811.49	4770.14	4077.56	3584.27	3215.54	2929.84	2702.25	2363.29	2123.91	1946.74	125000
150000	13239.77	9060.45	6973.78	5724.17	4893.07	4301.13	3858.65	3515.80	3242.70	2835.95	2548.70	2336.09	150000
175000	15446.40	10570.53	8136.08	6678.19	5708.58	5017.98	4501.75	4101.77	3783.15	3308.60	2973.48	2725.44	175000
200000	17653.02	12080.60	9298.38	7632.22	6524.10	5734.84	5144.86	4687.74	4323.60	3781.26	3398.26	3114.79	200000
250000	22066.28	15100.75	11622.97	9540.28	8155.12	7168.54	6431.08	5859.67	5404.49	4726.57	4247.82	3893.48	250000

Amount	9.0 Years	10.0 Years	11.0 Years	12.0 Years	13.0 Years	14.0 Years	15.0 Years	16.0 Years	20.0 Years	30.0 Years	40.0 Years	50.0 Years	Amount
100	1.45	1.37	1.30	1.24	1.20	1.16	1.13	1.10	1.02	0.94	0.91	0.91	100
200	2.90	2.73	2.59	2.48	2.39	2.31	2.25	2.19	2.04	1.87	1.82	1.81	200
300	4.35	4.10	3.89	3.72	3.58	3.47	3.37	3.28	3.05	2.81	2.73	2.71	300
400	5.80	5.46	5.18	4.96	4.77	4.62	4.49	4.38	4.07	3.74	3.64	3.61	400
500	7.25	6.82	6.48	6.20	5.97	5.77	5.61	5.47	5.08	4.67	4.55	4.51	500
600	8.70	8.19	7.77	7.44	7.16	6.93	6.73	6.56	6.10	5.61	5.46	5.41	600
700	10.15	9.55	9.07	8.68	8.35	8.08	7.85	7.66	7.11	6.54	6.36	6.31	700
800	11.60	10.91	10.36	9.92	9.54	9.23	8.97	8.75	8.13	7.47	7.27	7.21	800
900	13.04	12.28	11.66	11.15	10.74	10.39	10.09	9.84	9.14	8.41	8.18	8.11	900
1000	14.49	13.64	12.95	12.39	11.93	11.54	11.21	10.94	10.16	9.34	9.09	9.01	1000
2000	28.98	27.27	25.90	24.78	23.85	23.08	22.42	21.87	20.31	18.67	18.17	18.01	2000
3000	43.47	40.91	38.85	37.17	35.78	34.62	33.63	32.80	30.46	28.01	27.26	27.01	3000
4000	57.96	54.54	51.80	49.56	47.70	46.15	44.84	43.73	40.61	37.34	36.34	36.01	4000
5000	72.45	68.17	64.74	61.95	59.63	57.69	56.05	54.66	50.77	46.68	45.42	45.01	5000
6000	86.93	81.81	77.69	74.33	71.55	69.23	67.26	65.59	60.92	56.01	54.51	54.01	6000
7000	101.42	95.44	90.64	86.72	83.48	80.76	78.47	76.52	71.07	65.35	63.59	63.01	7000
8000	115.91	109.08	103.59	99.11	95.40	92.30	89.68	87.45	81.22	74.68	72.68	72.01	8000
9000	130.40	122.71	116.54	111.50	107.33	103.84	100.89	98.38	91.38	84.02	81.76	81.01	9000
10000	144.89	136.34	129.48	123.89	119.25	115.37	112.10	109.31	101.53	93.35	90.84	90.02	10000
15000	217.33	204.51	194.22	185.83	178.88	173.06	168.15	163.97	152.29	140.03	136.26	135.02	15000
20000	289.77	272.68	258.96	247.77	238.50	230.74	224.19	218.62	203.05	186.70	181.68	180.03	20000
25000	362.21	340.85	323.70	309.71	298.12	288.43	280.24	273.27	253.81	233.38	227.10	225.03	25000
30000	434.65	409.02	388.44	371.65	357.75	346.11	336.29	327.93	304.57	280.05	272.52	270.04	30000
35000	507.09	477.19	453.18	433.59	417.37	403.80	392.34	382.58	355.34	326.72	317.94	315.04	35000
40000	579.53	545.36	517.92	495.53	476.99	461.48	448.38	437.23	406.10	373.40	363.36	360.05	40000
45000	651.97	613.53	582.66	557.47	536.62	519.17	504.43	491.89	456.86	420.07	408.78	405.05	45000
50000	724.41	681.70	647.40	619.41	596.24	576.85	560.48	546.54	507.62	466.75	454.20	450.06	50000
60000	869.29	818.04	776.88	743.29	715.49	692.22	672.57	655.85	609.14	560.09	545.04	540.07	60000
75000	1086.61	1022.55	971.10	929.11	894.36	865.28	840.72	819.81	761.43	700.12	681.30	675.08	75000
100000	1448.81	1363.39	1294.80	1238.81	1192.47	1153.70	1120.95	1093.07	1015.23	933.49	908.40	900.11	100000
125000	1811.01	1704.24	1618.50	1548.51	1490.59	1442.12	1401.19	1366.34	1269.04	1166.86	1135.50	1125.13	125000
150000	2173.21	2045.09	1942.20	1858.21	1788.71	1730.55	1681.43	1639.61	1522.85	1400.23	1362.60	1350.16	150000
175000	2535.41	2385.93	2265.90	2167.91	2086.83	2018.97	1961.66	1912.88	1776.66	1633.60	1589.70	1575.18	175000
200000	2897.61	2726.78	2589.60	2477.61	2384.94	2307.40	2241.90	2186.14	2030.46	1866.97	1816.80	1800.21	200000
250000	3622.01	3408.47	3237.00	3097.02	2981.18	2884.24	2802.37	2732.68	2538.08	2333.71	2271.00	2250.26	250000

Amount	1.0 Year	1.5 Years	2.0 Years	2.5 Years	3.0 Years	3.5 Years	4.0 Years	4.5 Years	5.0 Years	6.0 Years	7.0 Years	8.0 Years	Amount
100	8.84	6.06	4.67	3.83	3.28	2.88	2.59	2.36	2.18	1.91	1.72	1.58	100
200	17.68	12.11	9.33	7.66	6.55	5.76	5.17	4.72	4.35	3.81	3.43	3.15	200
300	26.52	18.16	13.99	11.49	9.83	8.64	7.76	7.07	6.53	5.72	5.14	4.72	300
400	35.36	24.21	18.65	15.32	13.10	11.52	10.34	9.43	8.70	7.62	6.85	6.29	400
500	44.20	30.26	23.31	19.14	16.37	14.40	12.93	11.79	10.88	9.52	8.57	7.86	500
600	53.03	36.32	27.97	22.97	19.65	17.28	15.51	14.14	13.05	11.43	10.28	9.43	600
700	61.87	42.37	32.63	26.80	22.92	20.16	18.10	16.50	15.22	13.33	11.99	11.00	700
800	70.71	48.42	37.29	30.63	26.20	23.04	20.68	18.85	17.40	15.23	13.70	12.57	800
900	79.55	54.47	41.95	34.46	29.47	25.92	23.27	21.21	19.57	17.14	15.42	14.14	900
1000	88.39	60.52	46.61	38.28	32.74	28.80	25.85	23.57	21.75	19.04	17.13	15.71	1000
2000	176.77	121.04	93.22	76.56	65.48	57.59	51.70	47.13	43.49	38.07	34.25	31.42	2000
3000	265.15	181.56	139.83	114.84	98.22	86.39	77.54	70.69	65.23	57.11	51.37	47.13	3000
4000	353.53	242.08	186.44	153.12	130.96	115.18	103.39	94.25	86.97	76.14	68.49	62.84	4000
5000	441.91	302.60	233.04	191.40	163.70	143.97	129.23	117.81	108.72	95.18	85.62	78.55	5000
6000	530.29	363.12	279.65	229.67	196.44	172.77	155.08	141.37	130.46	114.21	102.74	94.26	6000
7000	618.68	423.63	326.26	267.95	229.18	201.56	180.92	164.94	152.20	133.24	119.86	109.96	7000
8000	707.06	484.15	372.87	306.23	261.91	230.36	206.77	188.50	173.94	152.28	136.98	125.67	8000
9000	795.44	544.67	419.48	344.51	294.65	259.15	232.61	212.06	195.69	171.31	154.11	141.38	9000
10000	883.82	605.19	466.08	382.79	327.39	287.94	258.46	235.62	217.43	190.35	171.23	157.09	10000
15000	1325.73	907.78	699.12	574.18	491.09	431.91	387.69	353.43	326.14	285.52	256.84	235.63	15000
20000	1767.64	1210.38	932.16	765.57	654.78	575.88	516.92	471.23	434.85	380.69	342.45	314.17	20000
25000	2209.55	1512.97	1165.20	956.96	818.47	719.85	646.14	589.04	543.57	475.86	428.07	392.72	25000
30000	2651.45	1815.56	1398.24	1148.35	982.17	863.82	775.37	706.85	652.28	571.03	513.68	471.26	30000
35000	3093.36	2118.15	1631.28	1339.74	1145.86	1007.79	904.60	824.66	760.99	666.20	599.29	549.80	35000
40000	3535.27	2420.75	1864.32	1531.13	1309.55	1151.76	1033.83	942.46	869.70	761.37	684.90	628.34	40000
45000	3977.18	2723.34	2097.36	1722.52	1473.25	1295.73	1163.05	1060.27	978.41	856.54	770.51	706.88	45000
50000	4419.09	3025.93	2330.40	1913.91	1636.94	1439.70	1292.28	1178.08	1087.13	951.71	856.13	785.43	50000
60000	5302.90	3631.12	2796.48	2296.69	1964.33	1727.64	1550.74	1413.69	1304.55	1142.05	1027.35	942.51	60000
75000	6628.63	4538.90	3495.59	2870.86	2455.41	2159.54	1938.42	1767.12	1630.69	1427.56	1284.19	1178.14	75000
100000	8838.17	6051.86	4660.79	3827.81	3273.88	2879.39	2584.56	2356.15	2174.25	1903.41	1712.25	1570.85	100000
125000	11047.71	7564.82	5825.98	4784.76	4092.34	3599.24	3230.70	2945.19	2717.81	2379.26	2140.31	1963.56	125000
150000	13257.25	9077.79	6991.18	5741.71	4910.81	4319.08	3876.83	3534.23	3261.37	2855.12	2568.37	2356.27	150000
175000	15466.80	10590.75	8156.38	6698.67	5729.28	5038.93	4522.97	4123.27	3804.93	3330.97	2996.43	2748.98	175000
200000	17676.34	12103.71	9321.57	7655.62	6547.75	5758.78	5169.11	4712.30	4348.49	3806.82	3424.49	3141.69	200000
250000	22095.42	15129.64	11651.96	9569.52	8184.68	7198.47	6461.39	5890.38	5435.61	4758.52	4280.61	3927.11	250000

Amount	9.0 Years	10.0 Years	11.0 Years	12.0 Years	13.0 Years	14.0 Years	15.0 Years	16.0 Years	20.0 Years	30.0 Years	40.0 Years	50.0 Years	Amount
100	1.47	1.38	1.31	1.26	1.21	1.17	1.14	1.11	1.04	0.96	0.93	0.93	100
200	2.93	2.76	2.62	2.51	2.42	2.34	2.28	2.22	2.07	1.91	1.86	1.85	200
300	4.39	4.14	3.93	3.77	3.63	3.51	3.41	3.33	3.10	2.86	2.79	2.77	300
400	5.86	5.52	5.24	5.02	4.84	4.68	4.55	4.44	4.13	3.81	3.72	3.69	400
500	7.32	6.89	6.55	6.27	6.04	5.85	5.69	5.55	5.17	4.77	4.65	4.61	500
600	8.78	8.27	7.86	7.53	7.25	7.02	6.82	6.66	6.20	5.72	5.57	5.53	600
700	10.24	9.65	9.17	8.78	8.46	8.19	7.96	7.77	7.23	6.67	6.50	6.45	700
800	11.71	11.03	10.48	10.03	9.67	9.36	9.10	8.88	8.26	7.62	7.43	7.37	800
900	13.17	12.40	11.79	11.29	10.87	10.53	10.23	9.99	9.29	8.58	8.36	8.29	900
1000	14.63	13.78	13.10	12.54	12.08	11.70	11.37	11.10	10.33	9.53	9.29	9.21	1000
2000	29.26	27.56	26.19	25.08	24.16	23.39	22.74	22.19	20.65	19.05	18.57	18.42	2000
3000	43.88	41.33	39.28	37.61	36.23	35.08	34.10	33.28	30.97	28.57	27.85	27.62	3000
4000	58.51	55.11	52.37	50.15	48.31	46.77	45.47	44.37	41.29	38.10	37.14	36.83	4000
5000	73.13	68.88	65.47	62.68	60.38	58.46	56.83	55.46	51.61	47.62	46.42	46.03	5000
6000	87.76	82.66	78.56	75.22	72.46	70.15	68.20	66.55	61.94	57.14	55.70	55.24	6000
7000	102.39	96.43	91.65	87.75	84.53	81.84	79.57	77.64	72.26	66.67	64.99	64.44	7000
8000	117.01	110.21	104.74	100.29	96.61	93.53	90.93	88.73	82.58	76.19	74.27	73.65	8000
9000	131.64	123.98	117.84	112.82	108.68	105.22	102.30	99.82	92.90	85.71	83.55	82.85	9000
10000	146.26	137.76	130.93	125.36	120.76	116.91	113.66	110.91	103.22	95.24	92.83	92.06	10000
15000	219.39	206.63	196.39	188.04	181.13	175.36	170.49	166.36	154.83	142.85	139.25	138.08	15000
20000	292.52	275.51	261.85	250.72	241.51	233.82	227.32	221.81	206.44	190.47	185.66	184.11	20000
25000	365.65	344.38	327.31	313.39	301.89	292.27	284.15	277.26	258.05	238.09	232.08	230.14	25000
30000	438.78	413.26	392.78	376.07	362.26	350.72	340.98	332.71	309.66	285.70	278.49	276.16	30000
35000	511.91	482.13	458.24	438.75	422.64	409.17	397.81	388.16	361.27	333.32	324.91	322.19	35000
40000	585.04	551.01	523.70	501.43	483.02	467.63	454.64	443.61	412.88	380.93	371.32	368.21	40000
45000	658.17	619.88	589.16	564.10	543.39	526.08	511.47	499.06	464.49	428.55	417.74	414.24	45000
50000	731.30	688.76	654.62	626.78	603.77	584.53	568.30	554.51	516.10	476.17	464.15	460.27	50000
60000	877.56	826.51	785.55	752.14	724.52	701.44	681.96	665.41	619.32	571.40	556.98	552.32	60000
75000	1096.94	1033.13	981.93	940.17	905.65	876.80	852.45	831.76	774.15	714.25	696.23	690.40	75000
100000	1462.59	1377.51	1309.24	1253.56	1207.53	1169.06	1136.60	1109.01	1032.19	952.33	928.30	920.53	100000
125000	1828.24	1721.88	1636.55	1566.95	1509.41	1461.32	1420.75	1386.26	1290.24	1190.41	1160.37	1150.66	125000
150000	2193.88	2066.26	1963.86	1880.34	1811.30	1753.59	1704.90	1663.51	1548.29	1428.49	1392.45	1380.79	150000
175000	2559.53	2410.63	2291.17	2193.73	2113.18	2045.85	1989.05	1940.76	1806.33	1666.57	1624.52	1610.92	175000
200000	2925.18	2755.01	2618.47	2507.12	2415.06	2338.11	2273.20	2218.01	2064.38	1904.65	1856.59	1841.05	200000
250000	3656.47	3443.76	3273.09	3133.89	3018.82	2922.64	2841.50	2772.51	2580.48	2380.81	2320.74	2301.32	250000

Amount	1.0 Year	1.5 Years	2.0 Years	2.5 Years	3.0 Years	3.5 Years	4.0 Years	4.5 Years	5.0 Years	6.0 Years	7.0 Years	8.0 Years	Amount
100	8.85	6.07	4.68	3.84	3.29	2.90	2.60	2.37	2.19	1.92	1.73	1.59	100
200	17.70	12.13	9.35	7.68	6.58	5.79	5.20	4.74	4.38	3.84	3.46	3.17	200
300	26.55	18.20	14.02	11.52	9.86	8.68	7.80	7.11	6.57	5.75	5.18	4.76	300
400	35.40	24.26	18.69	15.36	13.15	11.57	10.39	9.48	8.75	7.67	6.91	6.34	400
500	44.25	30.32	23.37	19.20	16.43	14.46	12.99	11.85	10.94	9.59	8.63	7.93	500
600	53.10	36.39	28.04	23.04	19.72	17.35	15.59	14.22	13.13	11.50	10.36	9.51	600
700	61.95	42.45	32.71	26.88	23.01	20.24	18.18	16.58	15.31	13.42	12.08	11.10	700
800	70.80	48.51	37.38	30.72	26.29	23.14	20.78	18.95	17.50	15.33	13.81	12.68	800
900	79.65	54.58	42.06	34.56	29.58	26.03	23.38	21.32	19.69	17.25	15.53	14.26	900
1000	88.50	60.64	46.73	38.40	32.86	28.92	25.97	23.69	21.87	19.17	17.26	15.85	1000
2000	177.00	121.27	93.45	76.80	65.72	57.83	51.94	47.37	43.74	38.33	34.51	31.69	2000
3000	265.50	181.91	140.18	115.19	98.58	86.75	77.91	71.06	65.61	57.49	51.77	47.54	3000
4000	354.00	242.54	186.90	153.59	131.43	115.66	103.87	94.74	87.47	76.65	69.02	63.38	4000
5000	442.50	303.18	233.62	191.98	164.29	144.57	129.84	118.43	109.34	95.82	86.28	79.22	5000
6000	530.99	363.81	280.35	230.38	197.15	173.49	155.81	142.11	131.21	114.98	103.53	95.07	6000
7000	619.49	424.44	327.07	268.77	230.00	202.40	181.77	165.80	153.08	134.14	120.78	110.91	7000
8000	707.99	485.08	373.80	307.17	262.86	231.32	207.74	189.48	174.94	153.30	138.04	126.75	8000
9000	796.49	545.71	420.52	345.56	295.72	260.23	233.71	213.17	196.81	172.47	155.29	142.60	9000
10000	884.99	606.35	467.24	383.96	328.58	289.14	259.68	236.85	218.68	191.63	172.55	158.44	10000
15000	1327.48	909.52	700.86	575.93	492.86	433.71	389.51	355.28	328.01	287.44	258.82	237.66	15000
20000	1769.97	1212.69	934.48	767.91	657.15	578.28	519.35	473.70	437.35	383.25	345.09	316.88	20000
25000	2212.46	1515.86	1168.10	959.89	821.44	722.85	649.18	592.12	546.69	479.06	431.36	396.09	25000
30000	2654.95	1819.03	1401.72	1151.86	985.72	867.42	779.02	710.55	656.02	574.88	517.63	475.31	30000
35000	3097.45	2122.20	1635.34	1343.84	1150.01	1011.99	908.85	828.97	765.36	670.69	603.90	554.53	35000
40000	3539.94	2425.37	1868.96	1535.82	1314.29	1156.56	1038.69	947.39	874.70	766.50	690.17	633.75	40000
45000	3982.43	2728.55	2102.58	1727.79	1478.58	1301.13	1168.52	1065.82	984.03	862.31	776.44	712.97	45000
50000	4424.92	3031.72	2336.20	1919.77	1642.87	1445.70	1298.36	1184.24	1093.37	958.12	862.71	792.18	50000
60000	5309.90	3638.06	2803.44	2303.72	1971.44	1734.84	1558.03	1421.09	1312.04	1149.75	1035.26	950.62	60000
75000	6637.38	4547.57	3504.30	2879.65	2464.30	2168.54	1947.54	1776.36	1640.05	1437.18	1294.07	1188.27	75000
100000	8849.84	6063.43	4672.40	3839.53	3285.73	2891.39	2596.71	2368.47	2186.74	1916.24	1725.42	1584.36	100000
125000	11062.29	7579.28	5840.50	4799.41	4107.16	3614.24	3245.89	2960.59	2733.42	2395.30	2156.78	1980.45	125000
150000	13274.75	9095.14	7008.60	5759.29	4928.59	4337.08	3895.07	3552.71	3280.10	2874.36	2588.13	2376.54	150000
175000	15487.21	10610.99	8176.70	6719.18	5750.02	5059.93	4544.25	4144.83	3826.78	3353.42	3019.48	2772.63	175000
200000	17699.67	12126.85	9344.80	7679.06	6571.45	5782.78	5193.42	4736.94	4373.47	3832.48	3450.84	3168.72	200000
250000	22124.58	15158.56	11681.00	9598.82	8214.31	7228.47	6491.78	5921.18	5466.83	4790.60	4313.55	3960.90	250000

Amount	9.0 Years	10.0 Years	11.0 Years	12.0 Years	13.0 Years	14.0 Years	15.0 Years	16.0 Years	20.0 Years	30.0 Years	40.0 Years	50.0 Years	Amount
100	1.48	1.40	1.33	1.27	1.23	1.19	1.16	1.13	1.05	0.98	0.95	0.95	100
200	2.96	2.79	2.65	2.54	2.45	2.37	2.31	2.26	2.10	1.95	1.90	1.89	200
300	4.43	4.18	3.98	3.81	3.67	3.56	3.46	3.38	3.15	2.92	2.85	2.83	300
400	5.91	5.57	5.30	5.08	4.90	4.74	4.61	4.51	4.20	3.89	3.80	3.77	400
500	7.39	6.96	6.62	6.35	6.12	5.93	5.77	5.63	5.25	4.86	4.75	4.71	500
600	8.86	8.36	7.95	7.62	7.34	7.11	6.92	6.76	6.30	5.83	5.69	5.65	600
700	10.34	9.75	9.27	8.88	8.56	8.30	8.07	7.88	7.35	6.80	6.64	6.59	700
800	11.82	11.14	10.60	10.15	9.79	9.48	9.22	9.01	8.40	7.78	7.59	7.53	800
900	13.29	12.53	11.92	11.42	11.01	10.67	10.38	10.13	9.45	8.75	8.54	8.47	900
1000	14.77	13.92	13.24	12.69	12.23	11.85	11.53	11.26	10.50	9.72	9.49	9.41	1000
2000	29.53	27.84	26.48	25.37	24.46	23.70	23.05	22.51	20.99	19.43	18.97	18.82	2000
3000	44.30	41.76	39.72	38.06	36.69	35.54	34.58	33.76	31.48	29.14	28.45	28.23	3000
4000	59.06	55.67	52.96	50.74	48.91	47.39	46.10	45.01	41.98	38.86	37.94	37.64	4000
5000	73.83	69.59	66.19	63.42	61.14	59.23	57.62	56.26	52.47	48.57	47.42	47.05	5000
6000	88.59	83.51	79.43	76.11	73.37	71.08	69.15	67.51	62.96	58.28	56.90	56.46	6000
7000	103.36	97.42	92.67	88.79	85.59	82.92	80.67	78.76	73.45	67.99	66.38	65.87	7000
8000	118.12	111.34	105.91	101.48	97.82	94.77	92.19	90.01	83.95	77.71	75.87	75.28	8000
9000	132.88	125.26	119.14	114.16	110.05	106.61	103.72	101.26	94.44	87.42	85.35	84.69	9000
10000	147.65	139.17	132.38	126.84	122.27	118.46	115.24	112.51	104.93	97.13	94.83	94.10	10000
15000	221.47	208.76	198.57	190.26	183.41	177.68	172.86	168.76	157.39	145.69	142.24	141.15	15000
20000	295.29	278.34	264.76	253.68	244.54	236.91	230.47	225.01	209.86	194.26	189.66	188.20	20000
25000	369.12	347.93	330.94	317.10	305.67	296.13	288.09	281.26	262.32	242.82	237.07	235.25	25000
30000	442.94	417.51	397.13	380.52	366.81	355.36	345.71	337.51	314.78	291.38	284.48	282.30	30000
35000	516.76	487.10	463.32	443.94	427.94	414.58	403.33	393.77	367.24	339.95	331.90	329.35	35000
40000	590.58	556.68	529.51	507.36	489.08	473.81	460.94	450.02	419.71	388.51	379.31	376.40	40000
45000	664.40	626.27	595.69	570.78	550.21	533.03	518.56	506.27	472.17	437.07	426.72	423.45	45000
50000	738.23	695.85	661.88	634.20	611.34	592.26	576.18	562.52	524.63	485.64	474.13	470.50	50000
60000	885.87	835.02	794.26	761.04	733.61	710.71	691.41	675.02	629.56	582.76	568.96	564.60	60000
75000	1107.34	1043.77	992.82	951.30	917.01	888.39	864.26	843.78	786.95	728.45	711.20	705.74	75000
100000	1476.45	1391.69	1323.76	1268.40	1222.68	1184.51	1152.35	1125.04	1049.26	971.27	948.26	940.99	100000
125000	1845.56	1739.62	1654.70	1585.50	1528.35	1480.64	1440.44	1406.30	1311.58	1214.08	1185.33	1176.23	125000
150000	2214.67	2087.54	1985.63	1902.59	1834.02	1776.77	1728.52	1687.55	1573.89	1456.90	1422.39	1411.48	150000
175000	2583.78	2435.46	2316.57	2219.69	2139.69	2072.89	2016.61	1968.81	1836.20	1699.71	1659.46	1646.73	175000
200000	2952.89	2783.38	2647.51	2536.79	2445.36	2369.02	2304.69	2250.07	2098.52	1942.53	1896.52	1881.97	200000
250000	3691.11	3479.23	3309.39	3170.99	3056.70	2961.27	2880.87	2812.59	2623.15	2428.16	2370.65	2352.46	250000

Amount	1.0 Year	1.5 Years	2.0 Years	2.5 Years	3.0 Years	3.5 Years	4.0 Years	4.5 Years	5.0 Years	6.0 Years	7.0 Years	8.0 Years	Amount
100	8.87	6.08	4.69	3.86	3.30	2.91	2.61	2.39	2.20	1.93	1.74	1.60	100
200	17.73	12.16	9.37	7.71	6.60	5.81	5.22	4.77	4.40	3.86	3.48	3.20	200
300	26.59	18.23	14.06	11.56	9.90	8.72	7.83	7.15	6.60	5.79	5.22	4.80	300
400	35.45	24.31	18.74	15.41	13.20	11.62	10.44	9.53	8.80	7.72	6.96	6.40	400
500	44.31	30.38	23.43	19.26	16.49	14.52	13.05	11.91	11.00	9.65	8.70	7.99	500
600	53.17	36.46	28.11	23.11	19.79	17.43	15.66	14.29	13.20	11.58	10.44	9.59	600
700	62.04	42.53	32.79	26.96	23.09	20.33	18.27	16.67	15.40	13.51	12.18	11.19	700
800	70.90	48.61	37.48	30.82	26.39	23.23	20.88	19.05	17.60	15.44	13.91	12.79	800
900	79.76	54.68	42.16	34.67	29.68	26.14	23.49	21.43	19.80	17.37	15.65	14.39	900
1000	88.62	60.76	46.85	38.52	32.98	29.04	26.09	23.81	22.00	19.30	17.39	15.98	1000
2000	177.24	121.51	93.69	77.03	65.96	58.07	52.18	47.62	43.99	38.59	34.78	31.96	2000
3000	265.85	182.26	140.53	115.54	98.93	87.11	78.27	71.43	65.98	57.88	52.16	47.94	3000
4000	354.47	243.01	187.37	154.06	131.91	116.14	104.36	95.24	87.98	77.17	69.55	63.92	4000
5000	443.08	303.76	234.21	192.57	164.89	145.18	130.45	119.05	109.97	96.46	86.94	79.90	5000
6000	531.70	364.51	281.05	231.08	197.86	174.21	156.54	142.85	131.96	115.75	104.32	95.88	6000
7000	620.31	425.26	327.89	269.59	230.84	203.24	182.63	166.66	153.95	135.04	121.71	111.86	7000
8000	708.93	486.01	374.73	308.11	263.81	232.28	208.72	190.47	175.95	154.33	139.10	127.84	8000
9000	797.54	546.76	421.57	346.62	296.79	261.31	234.81	214.28	197.94	173.63	156.48	143.82	9000
10000	886.16	607.51	468.41	385.13	329.77	290.35	260.90	238.09	219.93	192.92	173.87	159.80	10000
15000	1329.23	911.26	702.61	577.69	494.65	435.52	391.34	357.13	329.89	289.37	260.80	239.70	15000
20000	1772.31	1215.01	936.81	770.26	659.53	580.69	521.79	476.17	439.86	385.83	347.73	319.59	20000
25000	2215.38	1518.76	1171.01	962.82	824.41	725.86	652.23	595.21	549.82	482.28	434.67	399.49	25000
30000	2658.46	1822.51	1405.21	1155.38	989.29	871.03	782.68	714.25	659.78	578.74	521.60	479.39	30000
35000	3101.53	2126.26	1639.42	1347.95	1154.17	1016.20	913.12	833.29	769.75	675.20	608.53	559.28	35000
40000	3544.61	2430.01	1873.62	1540.51	1319.05	1161.37	1043.57	952.34	879.71	771.65	695.46	639.18	40000
45000	3987.68	2733.76	2107.82	1733.07	1483.93	1306.54	1174.01	1071.38	989.67	868.11	782.40	719.08	45000
50000	4430.76	3037.51	2342.02	1925.64	1648.81	1451.71	1304.46	1190.42	1099.64	964.56	869.33	798.97	50000
60000	5316.91	3645.01	2810.42	2310.76	1978.57	1742.05	1565.35	1428.50	1319.56	1157.47	1043.19	958.77	60000
75000	6646.13	4556.26	3513.03	2888.45	2473.21	2177.57	1956.68	1785.63	1649.45	1446.84	1303.99	1198.46	75000
100000	8861.51	6075.01	4684.04	3851.27	3297.61	2903.42	2608.91	2380.83	2199.27	1929.12	1738.65	1597.94	100000
125000	11076.89	7593.76	5855.04	4814.09	4122.01	3629.27	3261.13	2976.04	2749.08	2411.40	2173.31	1997.43	125000
150000	13292.26	9112.51	7026.05	5776.90	4946.41	4355.13	3913.36	3571.25	3298.90	2893.68	2607.97	2396.91	150000
175000	15507.64	10631.26	8197.06	6739.72	5770.81	5080.98	4565.58	4166.45	3848.71	3375.96	3042.64	2796.40	175000
200000	17723.02	12150.01	9368.07	7702.54	6595.21	5806.84	5217.81	4761.66	4398.53	3858.24	3477.30	3195.88	200000
250000	22153.77	15187.51	11710.08	9628.17	8244.01	7258.54	6522.26	5952.08	5498.16	4822.79	4346.62	3994.85	250000

Amount	9.0 Years	10.0 Years	11.0 Years	12.0 Years	13.0 Years	14.0 Years	15.0 Years	16.0 Years	20.0 Years	30.0 Years	40.0 Years	50.0 Years	Amount
100	1.50	1.41	1.34	1.29	1.24	1.21	1.17	1.15	1.07	1.00	0.97	0.97	100
200	2.99	2.82	2.68	2.57	2.48	2.41	2.34	2.29	2.14	1.99	1.94	1.93	200
300	4.48	4.22	4.02	3.85	3.72	3.61	3.51	3.43	3.20	2.98	2.91	2.89	300
400	5.97	5.63	5.36	5.14	4.96	4.81	4.68	4.57	4.27	3.97	3.88	3.85	400
500	7.46	7.03	6.70	6.42	6.19	6.01	5.85	5.71	5.34	4.96	4.85	4.81	500
600	8.95	8.44	8.04	7.70	7.43	7.21	7.01	6.85	6.40	5.95	5.81	5.77	600
700	10.44	9.85	9.37	8.99	8.67	8.41	8.18	7.99	7.47	6.94	6.78	6.74	700
800	11.93	11.25	10.71	10.27	9.91	9.61	9.35	9.13	8.54	7.93	7.75	7.70	800
900	13.42	12.66	12.05	11.55	11.15	10.81	10.52	10.28	9.60	8.92	8.72	8.66	900
1000	14.91	14.06	13.39	12.84	12.38	12.01	11.69	11.42	10.67	9.91	9.69	9.62	1000
2000	29.81	28.12	26.77	25.67	24.76	24.01	23.37	22.83	21.33	19.81	19.37	19.23	2000
3000	44.72	42.18	40.16	38.50	37.14	36.01	35.05	34.24	32.00	29.71	29.05	28.85	3000
4000	59.62	56.24	53.54	51.34	49.52	48.01	46.73	45.65	42.66	39.62	38.74	38.46	4000
5000	74.52	70.30	66.92	64.17	61.90	60.01	58.41	57.06	53.33	49.52	48.42	48.08	5000
6000	89.43	84.36	80.31	77.00	74.28	72.01	70.10	68.47	63.99	59.42	58.10	57.69	6000
7000	104.33	98.42	93.69	89.84	86.66	84.01	81.78	79.89	74.66	69.33	67.78	67.31	7000
8000	119.23	112.48	107.07	102.67	99.04	96.01	93.46	91.30	85.32	79.23	77.47	76.92	8000
9000	134.14	126.54	120.46	115.50	111.42	108.01	105.14	102.71	95.98	89.13	87.15	86.54	9000
10000	149.04	140.60	133.84	128.34	123.80	120.01	116.82	114.12	106.65	99.03	96.83	96.15	10000
15000	223.56	210.90	200.76	192.50	185.69	180.01	175.23	171.18	159.97	148.55	145.25	144.23	15000
20000	298.08	281.20	267.68	256.67	247.59	240.02	233.64	228.24	213.29	198.06	193.66	192.30	20000
25000	372.60	351.49	334.59	320.83	309.48	300.02	292.05	285.30	266.61	247.58	242.08	240.37	25000
30000	447.11	421.79	401.51	385.00	371.38	360.02	350.46	342.35	319.93	297.09	290.49	288.45	30000
35000	521.63	492.09	468.43	449.17	433.28	420.02	408.87	399.41	373.26	346.61	338.90	336.52	35000
40000	596.15	562.39	535.35	513.33	495.17	480.03	467.28	456.47	426.58	396.12	387.32	384.60	40000
45000	670.67	632.68	602.26	577.50	557.07	540.03	525.69	513.53	479.90	445.64	435.73	432.67	45000
50000	745.19	702.98	669.18	641.66	618.96	600.03	584.10	570.59	533.22	495.15	484.15	480.74	50000
60000	894.22	843.58	803.02	769.99	742.76	720.04	700.92	684.70	639.86	594.18	580.97	576.89	60000
75000	1117.78	1054.47	1003.77	962.49	928.44	900.05	876.15	855.88	799.83	742.72	726.22	721.11	75000
100000	1490.37	1405.96	1338.36	1283.32	1237.92	1200.06	1168.19	1141.17	1066.43	990.30	968.29	961.48	100000
125000	1862.96	1757.45	1672.96	1604.15	1547.40	1500.07	1460.24	1426.46	1333.04	1237.87	1210.36	1201.85	125000
150000	2235.55	2108.94	2007.53	1924.98	1856.88	1800.09	1752.29	1711.75	1599.65	1485.44	1452.43	1442.22	150000
175000	2608.15	2460.43	2342.12	2245.81	2166.36	2100.10	2044.34	1997.04	1866.26	1733.02	1694.50	1682.59	175000
200000	2980.74	2811.93	2676.71	2566.64	2475.84	2400.12	2336.38	2282.33	2132.86	1980.59	1936.57	1922.96	200000
250000	3725.92	3514.89	3345.88	3208.30	3094.80	3000.14	2920.48	2852.92	2666.08	2475.73	2420.71	2403.70	250000

11.50% Page 54   Monthly Payment Required To Amortize A Loan   Page 54 **11.50%**

Amount	1.0 Year	1.5 Years	2.0 Years	2.5 Years	3.0 Years	3.5 Years	4.0 Years	4.5 Years	5.0 Years	6.0 Years	7.0 Years	8.0 Years	Amount
100	8.88	6.09	4.70	3.87	3.31	2.92	2.63	2.40	2.22	1.95	1.76	1.62	100
200	17.75	12.18	9.40	7.73	6.62	5.84	5.25	4.79	4.43	3.89	3.51	3.23	200
300	26.62	18.26	14.09	11.59	9.93	8.75	7.87	7.18	6.64	5.83	5.26	4.84	300
400	35.50	24.35	18.79	15.46	13.24	11.67	10.49	9.58	8.85	7.77	7.01	6.45	400
500	44.37	30.44	23.48	19.32	16.55	14.58	13.11	11.97	11.06	9.72	8.76	8.06	500
600	53.24	36.52	28.18	23.18	19.86	17.50	15.73	14.36	13.28	11.66	10.52	9.67	600
700	62.12	42.61	32.87	27.05	23.17	20.41	18.35	16.76	15.49	13.60	12.27	11.29	700
800	70.99	48.70	37.57	30.91	26.48	23.33	20.97	19.15	17.70	15.54	14.02	12.90	800
900	79.86	54.78	42.27	34.77	29.79	26.24	23.60	21.54	19.91	17.48	15.77	14.51	900
1000	88.74	60.87	46.96	38.64	33.10	29.16	26.22	23.94	22.12	19.43	17.52	16.12	1000
2000	177.47	121.74	93.92	77.27	66.20	58.31	52.43	47.87	44.24	38.85	35.04	32.24	2000
3000	266.20	182.60	140.88	115.90	99.29	87.47	78.64	71.80	66.36	58.27	52.56	48.35	3000
4000	354.93	243.47	187.83	154.53	132.39	116.62	104.85	95.73	88.48	77.69	70.08	64.47	4000
5000	443.66	304.33	234.79	193.16	165.48	145.78	131.06	119.67	110.60	97.11	87.60	80.58	5000
6000	532.40	365.20	281.75	231.79	198.58	174.93	157.27	143.60	132.71	116.53	105.12	96.70	6000
7000	621.13	426.07	328.70	270.42	231.67	204.09	183.48	167.53	154.83	135.95	122.64	112.82	7000
8000	709.86	486.93	375.66	309.05	264.77	233.24	209.70	191.46	176.95	155.37	140.16	128.93	8000
9000	798.59	547.80	422.62	347.68	297.86	262.40	235.91	215.40	199.07	174.79	157.68	145.05	9000
10000	887.32	608.66	469.57	386.31	330.96	291.55	262.12	239.33	221.19	194.21	175.20	161.16	10000
15000	1330.98	912.99	704.36	579.46	496.43	437.33	393.17	358.99	331.78	291.31	262.79	241.74	15000
20000	1774.64	1217.32	939.14	772.61	661.91	583.10	524.23	478.65	442.37	388.41	350.39	322.32	20000
25000	2218.30	1521.65	1173.93	965.76	827.38	728.87	655.29	598.31	552.96	485.52	437.99	402.90	25000
30000	2661.96	1825.98	1408.71	1158.91	992.86	874.65	786.34	717.97	663.55	582.62	525.58	483.48	30000
35000	3105.62	2130.31	1643.49	1352.06	1158.33	1020.42	917.40	837.63	774.15	679.72	613.18	564.06	35000
40000	3549.28	2434.64	1878.28	1545.22	1323.81	1166.19	1048.46	957.29	884.74	776.82	700.78	644.64	40000
45000	3992.94	2738.97	2113.06	1738.37	1489.28	1311.97	1179.51	1076.96	995.33	873.92	788.37	725.22	45000
50000	4436.60	3043.30	2347.85	1931.52	1654.76	1457.74	1310.57	1196.62	1105.92	971.03	875.97	805.79	50000
60000	5323.92	3651.96	2817.41	2317.82	1985.71	1749.29	1572.68	1435.94	1327.10	1165.23	1051.16	966.95	60000
75000	6654.90	4564.95	3521.77	2897.28	2482.13	2186.61	1965.85	1794.92	1658.88	1456.54	1313.95	1208.69	75000
100000	8873.19	6086.60	4695.69	3863.03	3309.51	2915.48	2621.13	2393.23	2211.84	1942.05	1751.94	1611.58	100000
125000	11091.49	7608.25	5869.61	4828.79	4136.88	3644.35	3276.41	2991.54	2764.80	2427.56	2189.92	2014.48	125000
150000	13309.79	9129.90	7043.53	5794.55	4964.26	4373.22	3931.69	3589.84	3317.75	2913.07	2627.90	2417.37	150000
175000	15528.08	10651.55	8217.45	6760.30	5791.64	5102.09	4586.97	4188.15	3870.71	3398.58	3065.89	2820.27	175000
200000	17746.38	12173.20	9391.37	7726.06	6619.01	5830.95	5242.26	4786.45	4423.67	3884.09	3503.87	3223.16	200000
250000	22182.97	15216.50	11739.21	9657.58	8273.76	7288.69	6552.82	5983.07	5529.59	4855.11	4379.83	4028.95	250000

Amount	9.0 Years	10.0 Years	11.0 Years	12.0 Years	13.0 Years	14.0 Years	15.0 Years	16.0 Years	20.0 Years	30.0 Years	40.0 Years	50.0 Years	Amount
100	1.51	1.43	1.36	1.30	1.26	1.22	1.19	1.16	1.09	1.01	0.99	0.99	100
200	3.01	2.85	2.71	2.60	2.51	2.44	2.37	2.32	2.17	2.02	1.98	1.97	200
300	4.52	4.27	4.06	3.90	3.76	3.65	3.56	3.48	3.26	3.03	2.97	2.95	300
400	6.02	5.69	5.42	5.20	5.02	4.87	4.74	4.63	4.34	4.04	3.96	3.93	400
500	7.53	7.11	6.77	6.50	6.27	6.08	5.93	5.79	5.42	5.05	4.95	4.92	500
600	9.03	8.53	8.12	7.79	7.52	7.30	7.11	6.95	6.51	6.06	5.94	5.90	600
700	10.54	9.95	9.48	9.09	8.78	8.51	8.29	8.11	7.59	7.07	6.92	6.88	700
800	12.04	11.37	10.83	10.39	10.03	9.73	9.48	9.26	8.67	8.08	7.91	7.86	800
900	13.54	12.79	12.18	11.69	11.28	10.95	10.66	10.42	9.76	9.09	8.90	8.84	900
1000	15.05	14.21	13.54	12.99	12.54	12.16	11.85	11.58	10.84	10.10	9.89	9.83	1000
2000	30.09	28.41	27.07	25.97	25.07	24.32	23.69	23.15	21.68	20.19	19.77	19.65	2000
3000	45.14	42.61	40.60	38.95	37.60	36.48	35.53	34.73	32.52	30.29	29.66	29.47	3000
4000	60.18	56.82	54.13	51.94	50.13	48.63	47.37	46.30	43.35	40.38	39.54	39.29	4000
5000	75.22	71.02	67.66	64.92	62.67	60.79	59.21	57.87	54.19	50.48	49.42	49.11	5000
6000	90.27	85.22	81.19	77.90	75.20	72.95	71.05	69.45	65.03	60.57	59.31	58.93	6000
7000	105.31	99.43	94.72	90.89	87.73	85.10	82.89	81.02	75.86	70.66	69.19	68.75	7000
8000	120.35	113.63	108.25	103.87	100.26	97.26	94.74	92.60	86.70	80.76	79.07	78.57	8000
9000	135.40	127.83	121.78	116.85	112.80	109.42	106.58	104.17	97.54	90.85	88.96	88.39	9000
10000	150.44	142.03	135.31	129.84	125.33	121.57	118.42	115.74	108.38	100.95	98.84	98.21	10000
15000	225.66	213.05	202.96	194.75	187.99	182.36	177.62	173.61	162.56	151.42	148.26	147.31	15000
20000	300.88	284.06	270.61	259.67	250.65	243.14	236.83	231.48	216.75	201.89	197.68	196.41	20000
25000	376.10	355.08	338.26	324.59	313.32	303.93	296.04	289.35	270.93	252.36	247.10	245.51	25000
30000	451.31	426.09	405.91	389.50	375.98	364.71	355.24	347.22	325.12	302.83	296.51	294.61	30000
35000	526.53	497.11	473.57	454.42	438.64	425.50	414.45	405.09	379.30	353.30	345.93	343.71	35000
40000	601.75	568.12	541.22	519.34	501.30	486.28	473.66	462.96	433.49	403.77	395.35	392.81	40000
45000	676.97	639.14	608.87	584.25	563.97	547.07	532.86	520.83	487.67	454.24	444.77	441.91	45000
50000	752.19	710.15	676.52	649.17	626.63	607.85	592.07	578.70	541.86	504.71	494.19	491.01	50000
60000	902.62	852.18	811.82	779.00	751.95	729.42	710.48	694.44	650.23	605.65	593.02	589.21	60000
75000	1128.28	1065.23	1014.78	973.75	939.94	911.78	888.10	868.05	812.79	757.06	741.28	736.51	75000
100000	1504.37	1420.30	1353.03	1298.33	1253.25	1215.70	1184.14	1157.40	1083.71	1009.41	988.37	982.01	100000
125000	1880.46	1775.37	1691.29	1622.91	1566.56	1519.63	1480.17	1446.75	1354.64	1261.77	1235.46	1227.51	125000
150000	2256.55	2130.45	2029.55	1947.49	1879.88	1823.55	1776.20	1736.10	1625.57	1514.12	1482.55	1473.01	150000
175000	2632.64	2485.52	2367.81	2272.07	2193.19	2127.47	2072.23	2025.45	1896.49	1766.47	1729.64	1718.51	175000
200000	3008.73	2840.59	2706.06	2596.66	2506.50	2431.40	2368.27	2314.80	2167.42	2018.82	1976.73	1964.01	200000
250000	3760.91	3550.74	3382.58	3245.82	3133.12	3039.25	2960.33	2893.50	2709.27	2523.53	2470.91	2455.02	250000

Amount	1.0 Year	1.5 Years	2.0 Years	2.5 Years	3.0 Years	3.5 Years	4.0 Years	4.5 Years	5.0 Years	6.0 Years	7.0 Years	8.0 Years	Amount
100	8.89	6.10	4.71	3.88	3.33	2.93	2.64	2.41	2.23	1.96	1.77	1.63	100
200	17.77	12.20	9.42	7.75	6.65	5.86	5.27	4.82	4.45	3.92	3.54	3.26	200
300	26.66	18.30	14.13	11.63	9.97	8.79	7.91	7.22	6.68	5.87	5.30	4.88	300
400	35.54	24.40	18.83	15.50	13.29	11.72	10.54	9.63	8.90	7.83	7.07	6.51	400
500	44.43	30.50	23.54	19.38	16.61	14.64	13.17	12.03	11.13	9.78	8.83	8.13	500
600	53.31	36.59	28.25	23.25	19.93	17.57	15.81	14.44	13.35	11.74	10.60	9.76	600
700	62.20	42.69	32.96	27.13	23.26	20.50	18.44	16.84	15.58	13.69	12.36	11.38	700
800	71.08	48.79	37.66	31.00	26.58	23.43	21.07	19.25	17.80	15.65	14.13	13.01	800
900	79.97	54.89	42.37	34.88	29.90	26.35	23.71	21.66	20.03	17.60	15.89	14.63	900
1000	88.85	60.99	47.08	38.75	33.22	29.28	26.34	24.06	22.25	19.56	17.66	16.26	1000
2000	177.70	121.97	94.15	77.50	66.43	58.56	52.67	48.12	44.49	39.11	35.31	32.51	2000
3000	266.55	182.95	141.23	116.25	99.65	87.83	79.01	72.17	66.74	58.66	52.96	48.76	3000
4000	355.40	243.93	188.30	155.00	132.86	117.11	105.34	96.23	88.98	78.21	70.62	65.02	4000
5000	444.25	304.92	235.37	193.75	166.08	146.38	131.67	120.29	111.23	97.76	88.27	81.27	5000
6000	533.10	365.90	282.45	232.49	199.29	175.66	158.01	144.34	133.47	117.31	105.92	97.52	6000
7000	621.95	426.88	329.52	271.24	232.51	204.93	184.34	168.40	155.72	136.86	123.57	113.77	7000
8000	710.80	487.86	376.59	309.99	265.72	234.21	210.68	192.46	177.96	156.41	141.23	130.03	8000
9000	799.64	548.84	423.67	348.74	298.93	263.49	237.01	216.51	200.21	175.96	158.88	146.28	9000
10000	888.49	609.83	470.74	387.49	332.15	292.76	263.34	240.57	222.45	195.51	176.53	162.53	10000
15000	1332.74	914.74	706.11	581.23	498.22	439.14	395.01	360.85	333.67	293.26	264.80	243.80	15000
20000	1776.98	1219.65	941.47	774.97	664.29	585.52	526.68	481.14	444.89	391.01	353.06	325.06	20000
25000	2221.22	1524.56	1176.84	968.71	830.36	731.90	658.35	601.42	556.12	488.76	441.32	406.33	25000
30000	2665.47	1829.47	1412.21	1162.45	996.43	878.27	790.02	721.70	667.34	586.51	529.59	487.59	30000
35000	3109.71	2134.38	1647.58	1356.19	1162.51	1024.65	921.69	841.99	778.56	684.26	617.85	568.85	35000
40000	3553.96	2439.29	1882.94	1549.93	1328.58	1171.03	1053.36	962.27	889.78	782.01	706.11	650.12	40000
45000	3998.20	2744.20	2118.31	1743.67	1494.65	1317.41	1185.03	1082.55	1001.01	879.76	794.38	731.38	45000
50000	4442.44	3049.11	2353.68	1937.41	1660.72	1463.79	1316.70	1202.83	1112.23	977.51	882.64	812.65	50000
60000	5330.93	3658.93	2824.41	2324.89	1992.86	1756.54	1580.04	1443.40	1334.67	1173.02	1059.17	975.18	60000
75000	6663.66	4573.66	3530.52	2906.11	2491.08	2195.68	1975.04	1804.25	1668.34	1466.27	1323.96	1218.97	75000
100000	8884.88	6098.21	4707.35	3874.82	3321.44	2927.57	2633.39	2405.66	2224.45	1955.02	1765.28	1625.29	100000
125000	11106.10	7622.76	5884.19	4843.52	4151.79	3659.46	3291.73	3007.08	2780.56	2443.78	2206.60	2031.61	125000
150000	13327.32	9147.31	7061.03	5812.23	4982.15	4391.35	3950.08	3608.49	3336.67	2932.53	2647.91	2437.93	150000
175000	15548.54	10671.86	8237.86	6780.92	5812.51	5123.24	4608.43	4209.91	3892.78	3421.29	3089.23	2844.25	175000
200000	17769.76	12196.41	9414.70	7749.63	6642.87	5855.13	5266.77	4811.32	4448.89	3910.04	3530.55	3250.57	200000
250000	22212.20	15245.52	11768.37	9687.03	8303.58	7318.91	6583.46	6014.15	5561.12	4887.55	4413.19	4063.22	250000

Amount	9.0 Years	10.0 Years	11.0 Years	12.0 Years	13.0 Years	14.0 Years	15.0 Years	16.0 Years	20.0 Years	30.0 Years	40.0 Years	50.0 Years	Amount
100	1.52	1.44	1.37	1.32	1.27	1.24	1.21	1.18	1.11	1.03	1.01	1.01	100
200	3.04	2.87	2.74	2.63	2.54	2.47	2.41	2.35	2.21	2.06	2.02	2.01	200
300	4.56	4.31	4.11	3.95	3.81	3.70	3.61	3.53	3.31	3.09	3.03	3.01	300
400	6.08	5.74	5.48	5.26	5.08	4.93	4.81	4.70	4.41	4.12	4.04	4.02	400
500	7.60	7.18	6.84	6.57	6.35	6.16	6.01	5.87	5.51	5.15	5.05	5.02	500
600	9.12	8.61	8.21	7.89	7.62	7.39	7.21	7.05	6.61	6.18	6.06	6.02	600
700	10.63	10.05	9.58	9.20	8.89	8.63	8.41	8.22	7.71	7.21	7.06	7.02	700
800	12.15	11.48	10.95	10.51	10.15	9.86	9.61	9.39	8.81	8.23	8.07	8.03	800
900	13.67	12.92	12.32	11.83	11.42	11.09	10.81	10.57	9.91	9.26	9.08	9.03	900
1000	15.19	14.35	13.68	13.14	12.69	12.32	12.01	11.74	11.02	10.29	10.09	10.03	1000
2000	30.37	28.70	27.36	26.27	25.38	24.63	24.01	23.48	22.03	20.58	20.17	20.06	2000
3000	45.56	43.05	41.04	39.41	38.05	36.95	36.01	35.22	33.04	30.86	30.26	30.09	3000
4000	60.74	57.39	54.72	52.54	50.75	49.26	48.01	46.95	44.05	41.15	40.34	40.11	4000
5000	75.93	71.74	68.39	65.68	63.44	61.58	60.01	58.69	55.06	51.44	50.43	50.13	5000
6000	91.11	86.09	82.07	78.81	76.12	73.89	72.02	70.43	66.07	61.72	60.51	60.16	6000
7000	106.29	100.43	95.75	91.94	88.81	86.21	84.02	82.17	77.08	72.01	70.60	70.18	7000
8000	121.48	114.78	109.43	105.08	101.50	98.52	96.02	93.90	88.09	82.29	80.68	80.21	8000
9000	136.66	129.13	123.11	118.21	114.18	110.83	108.02	105.64	99.10	92.58	90.77	90.24	9000
10000	151.85	143.48	136.78	131.35	126.87	123.15	120.02	117.38	110.11	102.87	100.85	100.26	10000
15000	227.77	215.21	205.17	197.02	190.30	184.72	180.03	176.06	165.17	154.30	151.28	150.39	15000
20000	303.69	286.95	273.56	262.69	253.74	246.29	240.04	234.75	220.22	205.73	201.70	200.52	20000
25000	379.61	358.68	341.95	328.36	317.17	307.86	300.05	293.44	275.28	257.16	252.13	250.65	25000
30000	455.53	430.42	410.34	394.03	380.60	369.43	360.06	352.12	330.33	308.59	302.55	300.77	30000
35000	531.45	502.15	478.73	459.70	444.04	431.01	420.06	410.81	385.39	360.02	352.98	350.90	35000
40000	607.37	573.89	547.12	525.37	507.47	492.58	480.07	469.50	440.44	411.45	403.40	401.03	40000
45000	683.30	645.62	615.51	591.04	570.90	554.15	540.08	528.18	495.49	462.88	453.83	451.16	45000
50000	759.22	717.36	683.90	656.71	634.34	615.72	600.09	586.87	550.55	514.31	504.25	501.29	50000
60000	911.06	860.83	820.68	788.06	761.20	738.86	720.11	704.24	660.66	617.17	605.10	601.54	60000
75000	1138.82	1076.04	1025.85	985.07	951.50	923.58	900.13	880.30	825.82	771.46	756.38	751.93	75000
100000	1518.43	1434.71	1367.79	1313.42	1268.67	1231.43	1200.17	1173.73	1101.09	1028.62	1008.50	1002.57	100000
125000	1898.03	1793.39	1709.74	1641.78	1585.84	1539.29	1500.22	1467.16	1376.36	1285.77	1260.63	1253.21	125000
150000	2277.64	2152.07	2051.69	1970.13	1903.00	1847.15	1800.26	1760.59	1651.63	1542.92	1512.75	1503.85	150000
175000	2657.25	2510.75	2393.63	2298.49	2220.17	2155.01	2100.30	2054.02	1926.91	1800.08	1764.88	1754.49	175000
200000	3036.85	2869.42	2735.58	2626.84	2537.34	2462.86	2400.34	2347.46	2202.18	2057.23	2017.00	2005.13	200000
250000	3796.06	3586.78	3419.47	3283.55	3171.67	3078.58	3000.43	2934.32	2752.72	2571.54	2521.25	2506.41	250000

Amount	1.0 Year	1.5 Years	2.0 Years	2.5 Years	3.0 Years	3.5 Years	4.0 Years	4.5 Years	5.0 Years	6.0 Years	7.0 Years	8.0 Years	Amount
100	8.90	6.11	4.72	3.89	3.34	2.94	2.65	2.42	2.24	1.97	1.78	1.64	100
200	17.80	12.22	9.44	7.78	6.67	5.88	5.30	4.84	4.48	3.94	3.56	3.28	200
300	26.69	18.33	14.16	11.66	10.01	8.82	7.94	7.26	6.72	5.91	5.34	4.92	300
400	35.59	24.44	18.88	15.55	13.34	11.76	10.59	9.68	8.95	7.88	7.12	6.56	400
500	44.49	30.55	23.60	19.44	16.67	14.70	13.23	12.10	11.19	9.85	8.90	8.20	500
600	53.38	36.66	28.32	23.32	20.01	17.64	15.88	14.51	13.43	11.81	10.68	9.84	600
700	62.28	42.77	33.04	27.21	23.34	20.58	18.52	16.93	15.66	13.78	12.46	11.48	700
800	71.18	48.88	37.76	31.10	26.67	23.52	21.17	19.35	17.90	15.75	14.23	13.12	800
900	80.07	54.99	42.48	34.98	30.01	26.46	23.82	21.77	20.14	17.72	16.01	14.76	900
1000	88.97	61.10	47.20	38.87	33.34	29.40	26.46	24.19	22.38	19.69	17.79	16.40	1000
2000	177.94	122.20	94.39	77.74	66.67	58.80	52.92	48.37	44.75	39.37	35.58	32.79	2000
3000	266.90	183.30	141.58	116.60	100.01	88.20	79.38	72.55	67.12	59.05	53.37	49.18	3000
4000	355.87	244.40	188.77	155.47	133.34	117.59	105.83	96.73	89.49	78.73	71.15	65.57	4000
5000	444.83	305.50	235.96	194.34	166.67	146.99	132.29	120.91	111.86	98.41	88.94	81.96	5000
6000	533.80	366.59	283.15	233.20	200.01	176.39	158.75	145.09	134.23	118.09	106.73	98.35	6000
7000	622.77	427.69	330.34	272.07	233.34	205.78	185.20	169.27	156.60	137.77	124.51	114.74	7000
8000	711.73	488.79	377.53	310.93	266.68	235.18	211.66	193.46	178.97	157.45	142.30	131.13	8000
9000	800.70	549.89	424.72	349.80	300.01	264.58	238.12	217.64	201.34	177.13	160.09	147.52	9000
10000	889.66	610.99	471.91	388.67	333.34	293.97	264.57	241.82	223.71	196.81	177.87	163.91	10000
15000	1334.49	916.48	707.86	583.00	500.01	440.96	396.86	362.72	335.57	295.21	266.81	245.86	15000
20000	1779.32	1221.97	943.81	777.33	666.68	587.94	529.14	483.63	447.42	393.61	355.74	327.82	20000
25000	2224.15	1527.46	1179.76	971.66	833.35	734.93	661.42	604.54	559.28	492.02	444.67	409.77	25000
30000	2668.98	1832.95	1415.71	1165.99	1000.02	881.91	793.71	725.44	671.13	590.42	533.61	491.72	30000
35000	3113.81	2138.44	1651.67	1360.32	1166.69	1028.89	925.99	846.35	782.99	688.82	622.54	573.67	35000
40000	3558.64	2443.93	1887.62	1554.65	1333.36	1175.88	1058.28	967.26	894.84	787.22	711.47	655.63	40000
45000	4003.47	2749.43	2123.57	1748.98	1500.03	1322.86	1190.56	1088.16	1006.70	885.62	800.41	737.58	45000
50000	4448.29	3054.92	2359.52	1943.31	1666.70	1469.85	1322.84	1209.07	1118.55	984.03	889.34	819.53	50000
60000	5337.95	3665.90	2831.42	2331.97	2000.04	1763.81	1587.41	1450.88	1342.26	1180.83	1067.21	983.44	60000
75000	6672.44	4582.37	3539.28	2914.97	2500.04	2204.77	1984.26	1813.60	1677.83	1476.04	1334.01	1229.29	75000
100000	8896.58	6109.83	4719.04	3886.62	3333.39	2939.69	2645.68	2418.13	2237.10	1968.05	1778.68	1639.06	100000
125000	11120.73	7637.29	5898.79	4858.27	4166.74	3674.61	3307.10	3022.67	2796.38	2460.06	2223.34	2048.82	125000
150000	13344.87	9164.74	7078.55	5829.93	5000.08	4409.53	3968.52	3627.20	3355.65	2952.07	2668.01	2458.58	150000
175000	15569.02	10692.20	8258.31	6801.58	5833.43	5144.45	4629.94	4231.73	3914.93	3444.08	3112.68	2868.34	175000
200000	17793.16	12219.65	9438.07	7773.24	6666.77	5879.37	5291.36	4836.26	4474.20	3936.09	3557.35	3278.11	200000
250000	22241.45	15274.57	11797.58	9716.54	8333.47	7349.21	6614.19	6045.33	5592.75	4920.12	4446.68	4097.63	250000

Amount	9.0 Years	10.0 Years	11.0 Years	12.0 Years	13.0 Years	14.0 Years	15.0 Years	16.0 Years	20.0 Years	30.0 Years	40.0 Years	50.0 Years	Amount
100	1.54	1.45	1.39	1.33	1.29	1.25	1.22	1.20	1.12	1.05	1.03	1.03	100
200	3.07	2.90	2.77	2.66	2.57	2.50	2.44	2.39	2.24	2.10	2.06	2.05	200
300	4.60	4.35	4.15	3.99	3.86	3.75	3.65	3.58	3.36	3.15	3.09	3.07	300
400	6.14	5.80	5.54	5.32	5.14	4.99	4.87	4.77	4.48	4.20	4.12	4.10	400
500	7.67	7.25	6.92	6.65	6.43	6.24	6.09	5.96	5.60	5.24	5.15	5.12	500
600	9.20	8.70	8.30	7.98	7.71	7.49	7.30	7.15	6.72	6.29	6.18	6.14	600
700	10.73	10.15	9.68	9.31	8.99	8.74	8.52	8.34	7.83	7.34	7.21	7.17	700
800	12.27	11.60	11.07	10.63	10.28	9.98	9.74	9.53	8.95	8.39	8.23	8.19	800
900	13.80	13.05	12.45	11.96	11.56	11.23	10.95	10.72	10.07	9.44	9.26	9.21	900
1000	15.33	14.50	13.83	13.29	12.85	12.48	12.17	11.91	11.19	10.48	10.29	10.24	1000
2000	30.66	28.99	27.66	26.58	25.69	24.95	24.33	23.81	22.38	20.96	20.58	20.47	2000
3000	45.98	43.48	41.48	39.86	38.53	37.42	36.49	35.71	33.56	31.44	30.87	30.70	3000
4000	61.31	57.97	55.31	53.15	51.37	49.90	48.66	47.61	44.75	41.92	41.15	40.93	4000
5000	76.63	72.46	69.14	66.43	64.21	62.37	60.82	59.51	55.93	52.40	51.44	51.16	5000
6000	91.96	86.96	82.96	79.72	77.06	74.84	72.98	71.41	67.12	62.88	61.73	61.39	6000
7000	107.28	101.45	96.79	93.01	89.90	87.31	85.15	83.32	78.30	73.36	72.01	71.62	7000
8000	122.61	115.94	110.62	106.29	102.74	99.79	97.31	95.22	89.49	83.84	82.30	81.86	8000
9000	137.93	130.43	124.44	119.58	115.58	112.26	109.47	107.12	100.68	94.32	92.59	92.09	9000
10000	153.26	144.92	138.27	132.86	128.42	124.73	121.63	119.02	111.86	104.79	102.87	102.32	10000
15000	229.89	217.38	207.40	199.29	192.63	187.09	182.45	178.53	167.79	157.19	154.31	153.48	15000
20000	306.52	289.84	276.53	265.72	256.84	249.46	243.26	238.04	223.72	209.58	205.74	204.63	20000
25000	383.14	362.30	345.66	332.15	321.05	311.82	304.08	297.54	279.65	261.98	257.18	255.79	25000
30000	459.77	434.76	414.79	398.58	385.26	374.18	364.89	357.05	335.57	314.37	308.61	306.95	30000
35000	536.40	507.22	483.92	465.01	449.47	436.54	425.71	416.56	391.50	366.77	360.05	358.10	35000
40000	613.03	579.68	553.06	531.44	513.67	498.91	486.52	476.07	447.43	419.16	411.48	409.26	40000
45000	689.65	652.14	622.19	597.87	577.88	561.27	547.34	535.57	503.36	471.56	462.91	460.42	45000
50000	766.28	724.60	691.32	664.30	642.09	623.63	608.15	595.08	559.29	523.95	514.35	511.58	50000
60000	919.54	869.52	829.58	797.16	770.51	748.36	729.78	714.10	671.14	628.74	617.22	613.89	60000
75000	1149.42	1086.90	1036.97	996.45	963.13	935.45	912.23	892.62	838.93	785.93	771.52	767.36	75000
100000	1532.56	1449.20	1382.63	1328.60	1284.18	1247.26	1216.30	1190.16	1118.57	1047.90	1028.69	1023.15	100000
125000	1915.70	1811.50	1728.29	1660.75	1605.22	1559.07	1520.38	1487.69	1398.21	1309.88	1285.86	1278.93	125000
150000	2298.84	2173.80	2073.94	1992.90	1926.26	1870.89	1824.45	1785.23	1677.85	1571.85	1543.03	1534.72	150000
175000	2681.98	2536.10	2419.60	2325.05	2247.31	2182.70	2128.53	2082.77	1957.49	1833.82	1800.21	1790.50	175000
200000	3065.12	2898.40	2765.26	2657.20	2568.35	2494.51	2432.60	2380.31	2237.13	2095.80	2057.38	2046.29	200000
250000	3831.39	3623.00	3456.57	3321.50	3210.44	3118.14	3040.75	2975.38	2796.42	2619.75	2571.72	2557.86	250000

Monthly Payment Required To Amortize A Loan

Amount	1.0 Year	1.5 Years	2.0 Years	2.5 Years	3.0 Years	3.5 Years	4.0 Years	4.5 Years	5.0 Years	6.0 Years	7.0 Years	8.0 Years	Amount
100	8.91	6.13	4.74	3.90	3.35	2.96	2.66	2.44	2.25	1.99	1.80	1.66	100
200	17.82	12.25	9.47	7.80	6.70	5.91	5.32	4.87	4.50	3.97	3.59	3.31	200
300	26.73	18.37	14.20	11.70	10.04	8.86	7.98	7.30	6.75	5.95	5.38	4.96	300
400	35.64	24.49	18.93	15.60	13.39	11.81	10.64	9.73	9.00	7.93	7.17	6.62	400
500	44.55	30.61	23.66	19.50	16.73	14.76	13.29	12.16	11.25	9.91	8.97	8.27	500
600	53.45	36.73	28.39	23.40	20.08	17.72	15.95	14.59	13.50	11.89	10.76	9.92	600
700	62.36	42.86	33.12	27.29	23.42	20.67	18.61	17.02	15.75	13.87	12.55	11.58	700
800	71.27	48.98	37.85	31.19	26.77	23.62	21.27	19.45	18.00	15.85	14.34	13.23	800
900	80.18	55.10	42.58	35.09	30.11	26.57	23.93	21.88	20.25	17.84	16.13	14.88	900
1000	89.09	61.22	47.31	38.99	33.46	29.52	26.58	24.31	22.50	19.82	17.93	16.53	1000
2000	178.17	122.43	94.62	77.97	66.91	59.04	53.16	48.62	45.00	39.63	35.85	33.06	2000
3000	267.25	183.65	141.93	116.96	100.37	88.56	79.74	72.92	67.50	59.44	53.77	49.59	3000
4000	356.34	244.86	189.23	155.94	133.82	118.08	106.32	97.23	90.00	79.25	71.69	66.12	4000
5000	445.42	306.08	236.54	194.93	167.27	147.60	132.90	121.54	112.49	99.06	89.61	82.65	5000
6000	534.50	367.29	283.85	233.91	200.73	177.11	159.48	145.84	134.99	118.87	107.53	99.18	6000
7000	623.59	428.51	331.16	272.90	234.18	206.63	186.06	170.15	157.49	138.68	125.45	115.71	7000
8000	712.67	489.72	378.46	311.88	267.63	236.15	212.64	194.46	179.99	158.49	143.37	132.24	8000
9000	801.75	550.94	425.77	350.86	301.09	265.67	239.22	218.76	202.49	178.31	161.30	148.76	9000
10000	890.83	612.15	473.08	389.85	334.54	295.19	265.80	243.07	224.98	198.12	179.22	165.29	10000
15000	1336.25	918.23	709.61	584.77	501.81	442.78	398.70	364.60	337.47	297.17	268.82	247.94	15000
20000	1781.66	1224.30	946.15	779.69	669.08	590.37	531.60	486.13	449.96	396.23	358.43	330.58	20000
25000	2227.08	1530.37	1182.69	974.62	836.35	737.96	664.50	607.66	562.45	495.28	448.04	413.23	25000
30000	2672.49	1836.44	1419.22	1169.54	1003.61	885.55	797.40	729.20	674.94	594.34	537.64	495.87	30000
35000	3117.91	2142.51	1655.76	1364.46	1170.88	1033.14	930.30	850.73	787.43	693.40	627.25	578.51	35000
40000	3563.32	2448.59	1892.30	1559.38	1338.15	1180.74	1063.20	972.26	899.92	792.45	716.85	661.16	40000
45000	4008.73	2754.66	2128.83	1754.30	1505.42	1328.33	1196.10	1093.79	1012.41	891.51	806.46	743.80	45000
50000	4454.15	3060.73	2365.37	1949.23	1672.69	1475.92	1329.00	1215.32	1124.90	990.56	896.07	826.45	50000
60000	5344.98	3672.88	2838.44	2339.07	2007.22	1771.10	1594.80	1458.39	1349.88	1188.68	1075.28	991.73	60000
75000	6681.22	4591.10	3548.05	2923.84	2509.03	2213.88	1993.50	1822.98	1687.35	1485.84	1344.10	1239.67	75000
100000	8908.29	6121.46	4730.74	3898.45	3345.37	2951.83	2658.00	2430.64	2249.80	1981.12	1792.13	1652.89	100000
125000	11135.36	7651.83	5913.42	4873.06	4181.71	3689.79	3322.50	3038.30	2812.25	2476.40	2240.16	2066.11	125000
150000	13362.43	9182.19	7096.10	5847.67	5018.05	4427.75	3987.00	3645.96	3374.70	2971.68	2688.19	2479.33	150000
175000	15589.51	10712.55	8278.78	6822.28	5854.39	5165.70	4651.50	4253.62	3937.14	3466.96	3136.22	2892.55	175000
200000	17816.58	12242.92	9461.47	7796.89	6690.73	5903.66	5316.00	4861.28	4499.59	3962.24	3584.25	3305.77	200000
250000	22270.72	15303.65	11826.83	9746.11	8363.41	7379.57	6645.00	6076.60	5624.49	4952.80	4480.31	4132.21	250000

Amount	9.0 Years	10.0 Years	11.0 Years	12.0 Years	13.0 Years	14.0 Years	15.0 Years	16.0 Years	20.0 Years	30.0 Years	40.0 Years	50.0 Years	Amount
100	1.55	1.47	1.40	1.35	1.30	1.27	1.24	1.21	1.14	1.07	1.05	1.05	100
200	3.10	2.93	2.80	2.69	2.60	2.53	2.47	2.42	2.28	2.14	2.10	2.09	200
300	4.65	4.40	4.20	4.04	3.90	3.79	3.70	3.63	3.41	3.21	3.15	3.14	300
400	6.19	5.86	5.60	5.38	5.20	5.06	4.94	4.83	4.55	4.27	4.20	4.18	400
500	7.74	7.32	6.99	6.72	6.50	6.32	6.17	6.04	5.69	5.34	5.25	5.22	500
600	9.29	8.79	8.39	8.07	7.80	7.58	7.40	7.25	6.82	6.41	6.30	6.27	600
700	10.83	10.25	9.79	9.41	9.10	8.85	8.63	8.45	7.96	7.48	7.35	7.31	700
800	12.38	11.72	11.19	10.76	10.40	10.11	9.87	9.66	9.09	8.54	8.40	8.35	800
900	13.93	13.18	12.58	12.10	11.70	11.37	11.10	10.87	10.23	9.61	9.45	9.40	900
1000	15.47	14.64	13.98	13.44	13.00	12.64	12.33	12.07	11.37	10.68	10.49	10.44	1000
2000	30.94	29.28	27.96	26.88	26.00	25.27	24.66	24.14	22.73	21.35	20.98	20.88	2000
3000	46.41	43.92	41.93	40.32	39.00	37.90	36.98	36.21	34.09	32.02	31.47	31.32	3000
4000	61.88	58.56	55.91	53.76	52.00	50.53	49.31	48.27	45.45	42.70	41.96	41.75	4000
5000	77.34	73.19	69.88	67.20	64.99	63.16	61.63	60.34	56.81	53.37	52.45	52.19	5000
6000	92.81	87.83	63.86	80.64	77.99	75.80	73.96	72.41	68.17	64.04	62.94	62.63	6000
7000	108.28	102.47	97.83	94.08	90.99	88.43	86.28	84.47	79.53	74.71	73.43	73.07	7000
8000	123.75	117.11	111.81	107.51	103.99	101.06	98.61	96.54	90.90	85.39	83.92	83.50	8000
9000	139.21	131.74	125.78	120.95	116.98	113.69	110.93	108.61	102.26	96.06	94.41	93.94	9000
10000	154.68	146.38	139.76	134.39	129.98	126.32	123.26	120.67	113.62	106.73	104.90	104.38	10000
15000	232.02	219.57	209.64	201.58	194.97	189.48	184.88	181.01	170.43	160.09	157.34	156.57	15000
20000	309.36	292.76	279.51	268.78	259.96	252.64	246.51	241.34	227.23	213.46	209.79	208.75	20000
25000	386.69	365.95	349.39	335.97	324.95	315.80	308.14	301.67	284.04	266.82	262.23	260.94	25000
30000	464.03	439.13	419.27	403.16	389.93	378.96	369.76	362.01	340.85	320.18	314.68	313.13	30000
35000	541.37	512.32	489.15	470.36	454.92	442.11	431.39	422.34	397.65	373.55	367.13	365.32	35000
40000	618.71	585.51	559.02	537.55	519.91	505.27	493.01	482.67	454.46	426.91	419.57	417.50	40000
45000	696.04	658.70	628.90	604.74	584.90	568.43	554.64	543.01	511.27	480.27	472.02	469.69	45000
50000	773.38	731.89	698.78	671.93	649.89	631.59	616.27	603.34	568.08	533.63	524.46	521.88	50000
60000	928.06	878.26	838.53	806.32	779.86	757.91	739.52	724.01	681.69	640.36	629.36	626.25	60000
75000	1160.07	1097.83	1048.16	1007.90	974.83	947.38	924.40	905.01	852.11	800.45	786.69	782.82	75000
100000	1546.76	1463.77	1397.55	1343.86	1299.77	1263.17	1232.53	1206.67	1136.15	1067.26	1048.92	1043.75	100000
125000	1933.45	1829.71	1746.93	1679.83	1624.71	1578.97	1540.66	1508.34	1420.18	1334.08	1311.15	1304.69	125000
150000	2320.14	2195.65	2096.32	2015.79	1949.65	1894.76	1848.79	1810.01	1704.22	1600.89	1573.38	1565.63	150000
175000	2706.83	2561.59	2445.71	2351.76	2274.60	2210.55	2156.92	2111.68	1988.25	1867.71	1835.61	1826.56	175000
200000	3093.52	2927.53	2795.09	2687.72	2599.54	2526.34	2465.05	2413.34	2272.29	2134.52	2097.84	2087.50	200000
250000	3866.89	3659.41	3493.86	3359.65	3249.42	3157.93	3081.31	3016.68	2840.36	2668.15	2622.30	2609.37	250000

Amount	1.0 Year	1.5 Years	2.0 Years	2.5 Years	3.0 Years	3.5 Years	4.0 Years	4.5 Years	5.0 Years	6.0 Years	7.0 Years	8.0 Years	Amount
100	8.93	6.14	4.75	3.92	3.36	2.97	2.68	2.45	2.27	2.00	1.81	1.67	100
200	17.85	12.27	9.49	7.83	6.72	5.93	5.35	4.89	4.53	3.99	3.62	3.34	200
300	26.77	18.40	14.23	11.74	10.08	8.90	8.02	7.33	6.79	5.99	5.42	5.01	300
400	35.69	24.54	18.97	15.65	13.43	11.86	10.69	9.78	9.06	7.98	7.23	6.67	400
500	44.61	30.67	23.72	19.56	16.79	14.83	13.36	12.22	11.32	9.98	9.03	8.34	500
600	53.53	36.80	28.46	23.47	20.15	17.79	16.03	14.66	13.58	11.97	10.84	10.01	600
700	62.45	42.94	33.20	27.38	23.51	20.75	18.70	17.11	15.84	13.96	12.64	11.67	700
800	71.37	49.07	37.94	31.29	26.86	23.72	21.37	19.55	18.11	15.96	14.45	13.34	800
900	80.29	55.20	42.69	35.20	30.22	26.68	24.04	21.99	20.37	17.95	16.26	15.01	900
1000	89.21	61.34	47.43	39.11	33.58	29.65	26.71	24.44	22.63	19.95	18.06	16.67	1000
2000	178.41	122.67	94.85	78.21	67.15	59.29	53.41	48.87	45.26	39.89	36.12	33.34	2000
3000	267.61	184.00	142.28	117.31	100.73	88.93	80.12	73.30	67.88	59.83	54.17	50.01	3000
4000	356.81	245.33	189.70	156.42	134.30	118.57	106.82	97.73	90.51	79.77	72.23	66.68	4000
5000	446.01	306.66	237.13	195.52	167.87	148.21	133.52	122.16	113.13	99.72	90.29	83.34	5000
6000	535.21	367.99	284.55	234.62	201.45	177.85	160.23	146.60	135.76	119.66	108.34	100.01	6000
7000	624.41	429.32	331.98	273.73	235.02	207.49	186.93	171.03	158.38	139.60	126.40	116.68	7000
8000	713.61	490.65	379.40	312.83	268.59	237.13	213.63	195.46	181.01	159.54	144.46	133.35	8000
9000	802.81	551.98	426.83	351.93	302.17	266.77	240.34	219.89	203.63	179.49	162.51	150.01	9000
10000	892.01	613.32	474.25	391.03	335.74	296.41	267.04	244.32	226.26	199.43	180.57	166.68	10000
15000	1338.01	919.97	711.37	586.55	503.61	444.61	400.56	366.48	339.38	299.14	270.85	250.02	15000
20000	1784.01	1226.63	948.49	782.06	671.48	592.81	534.08	488.64	452.51	398.85	361.13	333.36	20000
25000	2230.01	1533.28	1185.62	977.58	839.35	741.01	667.59	610.80	565.64	498.57	451.41	416.70	25000
30000	2676.01	1839.94	1422.74	1173.09	1007.21	889.21	801.11	732.96	678.76	598.28	541.69	500.04	30000
35000	3122.01	2146.59	1659.86	1368.61	1175.08	1037.41	934.63	855.12	791.89	697.99	631.98	583.38	35000
40000	3568.01	2453.25	1896.98	1564.12	1342.95	1185.61	1068.15	977.28	905.02	797.70	722.26	666.71	40000
45000	4014.01	2759.90	2134.11	1759.63	1510.82	1333.81	1201.67	1099.44	1018.14	897.41	812.54	750.05	45000
50000	4460.01	3066.56	2371.23	1955.15	1678.69	1482.01	1335.18	1221.60	1131.27	997.13	902.82	833.39	50000
60000	5352.01	3679.87	2845.47	2346.18	2014.42	1778.41	1602.22	1465.91	1357.52	1196.55	1083.38	1000.07	60000
75000	6690.01	4599.83	3556.84	2932.72	2518.03	2223.01	2002.77	1832.39	1696.90	1495.69	1354.23	1250.08	75000
100000	8920.01	6133.11	4742.45	3910.29	3357.37	2964.01	2670.36	2443.19	2262.54	1994.25	1805.64	1666.78	100000
125000	11150.01	7666.38	5928.07	4887.86	4196.71	3705.01	3337.95	3053.98	2828.17	2492.81	2257.05	2083.47	125000
150000	13380.01	9199.66	7113.68	5865.44	5036.05	4446.01	4005.54	3664.78	3393.80	2991.37	2708.45	2500.16	150000
175000	15610.01	10732.93	8299.29	6843.01	5875.40	5187.01	4673.13	4275.58	3959.43	3489.93	3159.86	2916.86	175000
200000	17840.01	12266.21	9484.90	7820.58	6714.74	5928.01	5340.72	4886.37	4525.07	3988.49	3611.27	3333.55	200000
250000	22300.01	15332.76	11856.13	9775.72	8393.42	7410.01	6675.90	6107.96	5656.33	4985.61	4514.09	4166.94	250000

Amount	9.0 Years	10.0 Years	11.0 Years	12.0 Years	13.0 Years	14.0 Years	15.0 Years	16.0 Years	20.0 Years	30.0 Years	40.0 Years	50.0 Years	Amount
100	1.57	1.48	1.42	1.36	1.32	1.28	1.25	1.23	1.16	1.09	1.07	1.07	100
200	3.13	2.96	2.83	2.72	2.64	2.56	2.50	2.45	2.31	2.18	2.14	2.13	200
300	4.69	4.44	4.24	4.08	3.95	3.84	3.75	3.67	3.47	3.27	3.21	3.20	300
400	6.25	5.92	5.66	5.44	5.27	5.12	5.00	4.90	4.62	4.35	4.28	4.26	400
500	7.81	7.40	7.07	6.80	6.58	6.40	6.25	6.12	5.77	5.44	5.35	5.33	500
600	9.37	8.88	8.48	8.16	7.90	7.68	7.50	7.34	6.93	6.53	6.42	6.39	600
700	10.93	10.35	9.89	9.52	9.21	8.96	8.75	8.57	8.08	7.61	7.49	7.46	700
800	12.49	11.83	11.31	10.88	10.53	10.24	10.00	9.79	9.24	8.70	8.56	8.52	800
900	14.05	13.31	12.72	12.24	11.84	11.52	11.24	11.01	10.39	9.79	9.63	9.58	900
1000	15.62	14.79	14.13	13.60	13.16	12.80	12.49	12.24	11.54	10.87	10.70	10.65	1000
2000	31.23	29.57	28.26	27.19	26.31	25.59	24.98	24.47	23.08	21.74	21.39	21.29	2000
3000	46.84	44.36	42.38	40.78	39.47	38.38	37.47	36.70	34.62	32.61	32.08	31.94	3000
4000	62.45	59.14	56.51	54.37	52.62	51.17	49.96	48.94	46.16	43.47	42.77	42.58	4000
5000	78.06	73.92	70.63	67.97	65.78	63.96	62.45	61.17	57.70	54.34	53.46	53.22	5000
6000	93.67	88.71	84.76	81.56	78.93	76.76	74.94	73.40	69.23	65.21	64.16	63.87	6000
7000	109.28	103.49	98.88	95.15	92.09	89.55	87.42	85.63	80.77	76.07	74.85	74.51	7000
8000	124.89	118.28	113.01	108.74	105.24	102.34	99.91	97.87	92.31	86.94	85.54	85.16	8000
9000	140.50	133.06	127.13	122.33	118.40	115.13	112.40	110.10	103.85	97.81	96.23	95.80	9000
10000	156.11	147.84	141.26	135.93	131.55	127.92	124.89	122.33	115.39	108.67	106.92	106.44	10000
15000	234.16	221.76	211.89	203.89	197.32	191.88	187.33	183.50	173.08	163.01	160.38	159.66	15000
20000	312.21	295.68	282.51	271.85	263.09	255.84	249.77	244.66	230.77	217.34	213.84	212.88	20000
25000	390.26	369.60	353.14	339.81	328.87	319.80	312.21	305.83	288.46	271.68	267.30	266.10	25000
30000	468.31	443.52	423.77	407.77	394.64	383.76	374.66	366.99	346.15	326.01	320.76	319.32	30000
35000	546.36	517.44	494.39	475.73	460.41	447.72	437.10	428.15	403.84	380.35	374.22	372.54	35000
40000	624.41	591.36	565.02	543.69	526.18	511.67	499.54	489.32	461.53	434.68	427.68	425.76	40000
45000	702.47	665.28	635.65	611.65	591.96	575.63	561.98	550.48	519.22	489.02	481.14	478.97	45000
50000	780.52	739.20	706.27	679.61	657.73	639.59	624.42	611.65	576.91	543.35	534.60	532.19	50000
60000	936.62	887.04	847.53	815.53	789.27	767.51	749.31	733.97	692.29	652.02	641.52	638.63	60000
75000	1170.77	1108.80	1059.41	1019.41	986.59	959.38	936.63	917.47	865.36	815.02	801.90	798.29	75000
100000	1561.03	1478.40	1412.54	1359.21	1315.45	1279.18	1248.84	1223.29	1153.82	1086.70	1069.20	1064.38	100000
125000	1951.28	1848.00	1765.68	1699.01	1644.31	1598.97	1561.05	1529.11	1442.27	1358.37	1336.50	1330.47	125000
150000	2341.54	2217.60	2118.81	2038.81	1973.17	1918.76	1873.26	1834.93	1730.72	1630.04	1603.80	1596.57	150000
175000	2731.80	2587.20	2471.95	2378.61	2302.03	2238.56	2185.47	2140.75	2019.18	1901.72	1871.10	1862.66	175000
200000	3122.05	2956.80	2825.08	2718.41	2630.90	2558.35	2497.68	2446.57	2307.63	2173.39	2138.40	2128.76	200000
250000	3902.56	3696.00	3531.35	3398.01	3288.62	3197.93	3122.10	3058.21	2884.53	2716.74	2673.00	2660.94	250000

Amount	1.0 Year	1.5 Years	2.0 Years	2.5 Years	3.0 Years	3.5 Years	4.0 Years	4.5 Years	5.0 Years	6.0 Years	7.0 Years	8.0 Years	Amount
100	8.94	6.15	4.76	3.93	3.37	2.98	2.69	2.46	2.28	2.01	1.82	1.69	100
200	17.87	12.29	9.51	7.85	6.74	5.96	5.37	4.92	4.56	4.02	3.64	3.37	200
300	26.80	18.44	14.27	11.77	10.11	8.93	8.05	7.37	6.83	6.03	5.46	5.05	300
400	35.73	24.58	19.02	15.69	13.48	11.91	10.74	9.83	9.11	8.03	7.28	6.73	400
500	44.66	30.73	23.78	19.62	16.85	14.89	13.42	12.28	11.38	10.04	9.10	8.41	500
600	53.60	36.87	28.53	23.54	20.22	17.86	16.10	14.74	13.66	12.05	10.92	10.09	600
700	62.53	43.02	33.28	27.46	23.59	20.84	18.78	17.20	15.93	14.06	12.74	11.77	700
800	71.46	49.16	38.04	31.38	26.96	23.81	21.47	19.65	18.21	16.06	14.56	13.45	800
900	80.39	55.31	42.79	35.30	30.33	26.79	24.15	22.11	20.48	18.07	16.38	15.13	900
1000	89.32	61.45	47.55	39.23	33.70	29.77	26.83	24.56	22.76	20.08	18.20	16.81	1000
2000	178.64	122.90	95.09	78.45	67.39	59.53	53.66	49.12	45.51	40.15	36.39	33.62	2000
3000	267.96	184.35	142.63	117.67	101.09	89.29	80.49	73.68	68.26	60.23	54.58	50.43	3000
4000	357.27	245.80	190.17	156.89	134.78	119.05	107.31	98.24	91.02	80.30	72.77	67.23	4000
5000	446.59	307.24	237.71	196.11	168.47	148.82	134.14	122.79	113.77	100.38	90.96	84.04	5000
6000	535.91	368.69	285.26	235.33	202.17	178.58	160.97	147.35	136.52	120.45	109.16	100.85	6000
7000	625.23	430.14	332.80	274.56	235.86	208.34	187.80	171.91	159.28	140.52	127.35	117.66	7000
8000	714.54	491.59	380.34	313.78	269.56	238.10	214.62	196.47	182.03	160.60	145.54	134.46	8000
9000	803.86	553.03	427.88	353.00	303.25	267.86	241.45	221.02	204.78	180.67	163.73	151.27	9000
10000	893.18	614.48	475.42	392.22	336.94	297.63	268.28	245.58	227.54	200.75	181.92	168.08	10000
15000	1339.76	921.72	713.13	588.33	505.41	446.44	402.42	368.37	341.30	301.12	272.88	252.11	15000
20000	1786.35	1228.96	950.84	784.44	673.88	595.25	536.55	491.16	455.07	401.49	363.84	336.15	20000
25000	2232.94	1536.19	1188.55	980.54	842.35	744.06	670.69	613.95	568.83	501.86	454.80	420.19	25000
30000	2679.52	1843.43	1426.26	1176.65	1010.82	892.87	804.83	736.73	682.60	602.23	545.76	504.22	30000
35000	3126.11	2150.67	1663.97	1372.76	1179.29	1041.68	938.97	859.52	796.36	702.60	636.72	588.26	35000
40000	3572.70	2457.91	1901.68	1568.87	1347.76	1190.49	1073.10	982.31	910.13	802.97	727.68	672.30	40000
45000	4019.28	2765.15	2139.39	1764.97	1516.23	1339.30	1207.24	1105.10	1023.89	903.34	818.64	756.33	45000
50000	4465.87	3072.38	2377.10	1961.08	1684.70	1488.11	1341.38	1227.89	1137.66	1003.71	909.60	840.37	50000
60000	5359.04	3686.86	2852.51	2353.30	2021.64	1785.73	1609.65	1473.46	1365.19	1204.45	1091.52	1008.44	60000
75000	6698.80	4608.57	3565.64	2941.62	2527.05	2232.16	2012.07	1841.83	1706.49	1505.56	1364.40	1260.55	75000
100000	8931.73	6144.76	4754.19	3922.16	3369.40	2976.21	2682.75	2455.77	2275.31	2007.42	1819.20	1680.73	100000
125000	11164.66	7680.95	5942.73	4902.70	4211.75	3720.27	3353.44	3069.71	2844.14	2509.27	2274.00	2100.91	125000
150000	13397.60	9217.14	7131.28	5883.24	5054.10	4464.32	4024.13	3683.65	3412.97	3011.12	2728.80	2521.09	150000
175000	15630.53	10753.33	8319.82	6863.78	5896.45	5208.37	4694.82	4297.60	3981.79	3512.97	3183.60	2941.27	175000
200000	17863.46	12289.52	9508.37	7844.31	6738.80	5952.42	5365.50	4911.54	4550.62	4014.83	3638.40	3361.46	200000
250000	22329.32	15361.90	11885.46	9805.39	8423.49	7440.53	6706.88	6139.42	5688.27	5018.53	4548.00	4201.82	250000

Amount	9.0 Years	10.0 Years	11.0 Years	12.0 Years	13.0 Years	14.0 Years	15.0 Years	16.0 Years	20.0 Years	30.0 Years	40.0 Years	50.0 Years	Amount
100	1.58	1.50	1.43	1.38	1.34	1.30	1.27	1.24	1.18	1.11	1.09	1.09	100
200	3.16	2.99	2.86	2.75	2.67	2.60	2.54	2.48	2.35	2.22	2.18	2.18	200
300	4.73	4.48	4.29	4.13	4.00	3.89	3.80	3.72	3.52	3.32	3.27	3.26	300
400	6.31	5.98	5.72	5.50	5.33	5.19	5.07	4.96	4.69	4.43	4.36	4.35	400
500	7.88	7.47	7.14	6.88	6.66	6.48	6.33	6.20	5.86	5.54	5.45	5.43	500
600	9.46	8.96	8.57	8.25	7.99	7.78	7.60	7.44	7.03	6.64	6.54	6.52	600
700	11.03	10.46	10.00	9.63	9.32	9.07	8.86	8.68	8.21	7.75	7.63	7.60	700
800	12.61	11.95	11.43	11.00	10.65	10.37	10.13	9.92	9.38	8.85	8.72	8.69	800
900	14.18	13.44	12.85	12.38	11.99	11.66	11.39	11.16	10.55	9.96	9.81	9.77	900
1000	15.76	14.94	14.28	13.75	13.32	12.96	12.66	12.40	11.72	11.07	10.90	10.86	1000
2000	31.51	29.87	28.56	27.50	26.63	25.91	25.31	24.80	23.44	22.13	21.80	21.71	2000
3000	47.27	44.80	42.83	41.24	39.94	38.86	37.96	37.20	35.15	33.19	32.69	32.56	3000
4000	63.02	59.73	57.11	54.99	53.25	51.82	50.61	49.60	46.87	44.25	43.59	43.41	4000
5000	78.77	74.66	71.39	68.74	66.57	64.77	63.27	62.00	58.58	55.31	54.48	54.26	5000
6000	94.53	89.59	85.66	82.48	79.88	77.72	75.92	74.40	70.30	66.38	65.38	65.11	6000
7000	110.28	104.52	99.94	96.23	93.19	90.67	88.57	86.80	82.02	77.44	76.27	75.96	7000
8000	126.03	119.45	114.21	109.98	106.50	103.63	101.22	99.20	93.73	88.50	87.17	86.81	8000
9000	141.79	134.38	128.49	123.72	119.81	116.58	113.88	111.60	105.45	99.56	98.06	97.66	9000
10000	157.54	149.32	142.77	137.47	133.13	129.53	126.53	124.00	117.16	110.62	108.96	108.51	10000
15000	236.31	223.97	214.15	206.20	199.69	194.29	189.79	186.00	175.74	165.93	163.43	162.76	15000
20000	315.08	298.63	285.53	274.93	266.25	259.06	253.05	248.00	234.32	221.24	217.91	217.01	20000
25000	393.84	373.28	356.91	343.66	332.81	323.82	316.32	310.00	292.90	276.55	272.38	271.26	25000
30000	472.61	447.94	428.29	412.39	399.37	388.58	379.58	372.00	351.48	331.86	326.86	325.51	30000
35000	551.38	522.59	499.67	481.12	465.93	453.35	442.84	434.00	410.06	387.17	381.33	379.76	35000
40000	630.15	597.25	571.05	549.86	532.49	518.11	506.10	496.00	468.64	442.48	435.81	434.01	40000
45000	708.92	671.90	642.43	618.59	599.05	582.87	569.36	558.00	527.21	497.79	490.29	488.27	45000
50000	787.68	746.56	713.81	687.32	665.61	647.64	632.63	620.00	585.79	553.10	544.76	542.52	50000
60000	945.22	895.87	856.57	824.78	798.73	777.16	759.15	744.00	702.95	663.72	653.71	651.02	60000
75000	1181.52	1119.84	1070.71	1030.97	998.41	971.45	948.94	930.00	878.69	829.65	817.14	813.77	75000
100000	1575.36	1493.11	1427.62	1374.63	1331.22	1295.27	1265.25	1239.99	1171.58	1106.20	1089.52	1085.03	100000
125000	1969.20	1866.39	1784.52	1718.29	1664.02	1619.08	1581.56	1549.99	1464.47	1382.75	1361.90	1356.28	125000
150000	2363.04	2239.67	2141.42	2061.94	1996.82	1942.90	1897.87	1859.99	1757.37	1659.30	1634.28	1627.54	150000
175000	2756.88	2612.94	2498.32	2405.60	2329.62	2266.72	2214.18	2169.98	2050.26	1935.85	1906.65	1898.79	175000
200000	3150.72	2986.22	2855.23	2749.26	2662.43	2590.53	2530.49	2479.98	2343.16	2212.40	2179.03	2170.05	200000
250000	3938.40	3732.77	3569.03	3436.57	3328.03	3238.16	3163.11	3099.97	2928.94	2765.50	2723.79	2712.56	250000

Amount	1.0 Year	1.5 Years	2.0 Years	2.5 Years	3.0 Years	3.5 Years	4.0 Years	4.5 Years	5.0 Years	6.0 Years	7.0 Years	8.0 Years	Amount
100	8.95	6.16	4.77	3.94	3.39	2.99	2.70	2.47	2.29	2.03	1.84	1.70	100
200	17.89	12.32	9.54	7.87	6.77	5.98	5.40	4.94	4.58	4.05	3.67	3.39	200
300	26.84	18.47	14.30	11.81	10.15	8.97	8.09	7.41	6.87	6.07	5.50	5.09	300
400	35.78	24.63	19.07	15.74	13.53	11.96	10.79	9.88	9.16	8.09	7.34	6.78	400
500	44.72	30.79	23.83	19.68	16.91	14.95	13.48	12.35	11.45	10.11	9.17	8.48	500
600	53.67	36.94	28.60	23.61	20.29	17.94	16.18	14.82	13.73	12.13	11.00	10.17	600
700	62.61	43.10	33.37	27.54	23.68	20.92	18.87	17.28	16.02	14.15	12.83	11.87	700
800	71.55	49.26	38.13	31.48	27.06	23.91	21.57	19.75	18.31	16.17	14.67	13.56	800
900	80.50	55.41	42.90	35.41	30.44	26.90	26.90	22.22	20.60	18.19	16.50	15.26	900
1000	89.44	61.57	47.66	39.35	33.82	29.89	26.96	24.69	22.89	20.21	18.33	16.95	1000
2000	178.87	123.13	95.32	78.69	67.63	59.77	53.91	49.37	45.77	40.42	36.66	33.90	2000
3000	268.31	184.70	142.98	118.03	101.45	89.66	80.86	74.06	68.65	60.62	54.99	50.85	3000
4000	357.74	246.26	190.64	157.37	135.26	119.54	107.81	98.74	91.53	80.83	73.32	67.79	4000
5000	447.18	307.83	238.30	196.71	169.08	149.43	134.76	123.42	114.41	101.04	91.65	84.74	5000
6000	536.61	369.39	285.96	236.05	202.89	179.31	161.72	148.11	137.29	121.24	109.97	101.69	6000
7000	626.05	430.96	333.62	275.39	236.71	209.20	188.67	172.79	160.17	141.45	128.30	118.64	7000
8000	715.48	492.52	381.28	314.73	270.52	239.08	215.62	197.48	183.06	161.66	146.63	135.58	8000
9000	804.92	554.08	428.94	354.07	304.34	268.96	242.57	222.16	205.94	181.86	164.96	152.53	9000
10000	894.35	615.65	476.60	393.41	338.15	298.85	269.52	246.84	228.82	202.07	183.29	169.48	10000
15000	1341.52	923.47	714.90	590.11	507.22	448.27	404.28	370.26	343.22	303.10	274.93	254.22	15000
20000	1788.70	1231.29	953.19	786.81	676.29	597.69	539.04	493.68	457.63	404.13	366.57	338.95	20000
25000	2235.87	1539.11	1191.49	983.52	845.37	747.12	673.80	617.10	572.04	505.16	458.21	423.69	25000
30000	2683.04	1846.93	1429.79	1180.22	1014.44	896.54	808.56	740.52	686.44	606.19	549.85	508.43	30000
35000	3130.22	2154.76	1668.08	1376.92	1183.51	1045.96	943.32	863.94	800.85	707.23	641.49	593.16	35000
40000	3577.39	2462.58	1906.38	1573.62	1352.58	1195.38	1078.07	987.36	915.26	808.26	733.13	677.90	40000
45000	4024.56	2770.40	2144.68	1770.33	1521.66	1344.80	1212.83	1110.78	1029.66	909.29	824.77	762.64	45000
50000	4471.74	3078.22	2382.97	1967.03	1690.73	1494.23	1347.59	1234.20	1144.07	1010.32	916.41	847.38	50000
60000	5366.08	3693.86	2859.57	2360.43	2028.87	1793.07	1617.11	1481.04	1372.88	1212.38	1099.69	1016.85	60000
75000	6707.60	4617.33	3574.46	2950.54	2536.09	2241.34	2021.39	1851.29	1716.10	1515.48	1374.62	1271.06	75000
100000	8943.47	6156.43	4765.94	3934.05	3381.45	2988.45	2695.18	2468.39	2288.13	2020.63	1832.82	1694.75	100000
125000	11179.34	7695.54	5957.42	4917.56	4226.82	3735.56	3368.97	3085.49	2860.16	2525.79	2291.02	2118.43	125000
150000	13415.20	9234.65	7148.91	5901.07	5072.18	4482.67	4042.77	3702.58	3432.19	3030.95	2749.23	2542.12	150000
175000	15651.06	10773.76	8340.39	6884.58	5917.54	5229.78	4716.56	4319.68	4004.22	3536.11	3207.43	2965.80	175000
200000	17886.93	12312.86	9531.87	7868.09	6762.90	5976.89	5390.35	4936.78	4576.26	4041.26	3665.64	3389.49	200000
250000	22358.66	15391.08	11914.84	9835.11	8453.63	7471.12	6737.94	6170.97	5720.32	5051.58	4582.04	4236.86	250000

Amount	9.0 Years	10.0 Years	11.0 Years	12.0 Years	13.0 Years	14.0 Years	15.0 Years	16.0 Years	20.0 Years	30.0 Years	40.0 Years	50.0 Years	Amount
100	1.59	1.51	1.45	1.40	1.35	1.32	1.29	1.26	1.19	1.13	1.11	1.11	100
200	3.18	3.02	2.89	2.79	2.70	2.63	2.57	2.52	2.38	2.26	2.22	2.22	200
300	4.77	4.53	4.33	4.18	4.05	3.94	3.85	3.78	3.57	3.38	3.33	3.32	300
400	6.36	6.04	5.78	5.57	5.39	5.25	5.13	5.03	4.76	4.51	4.44	4.43	400
500	7.95	7.54	7.22	6.96	6.74	6.56	6.41	6.29	5.95	5.63	5.55	5.53	500
600	9.54	9.05	8.66	8.35	8.09	7.87	7.70	7.55	7.14	6.76	6.66	6.64	600
700	11.13	10.56	10.10	9.74	9.43	9.19	8.98	8.80	8.33	7.89	7.77	7.74	700
800	12.72	12.07	11.55	11.13	10.78	10.50	10.26	10.06	9.52	9.01	8.88	8.85	800
900	14.31	13.58	12.99	12.52	12.13	11.81	11.54	11.32	10.71	10.14	9.99	9.96	900
1000	15.90	15.08	14.43	13.91	13.48	13.12	12.82	12.57	11.90	11.26	11.10	11.06	1000
2000	31.80	30.16	28.86	27.81	26.95	26.23	25.64	25.14	23.79	22.52	22.20	22.12	2000
3000	47.70	45.24	43.29	41.71	40.42	39.35	38.46	37.71	35.69	33.78	33.30	33.18	3000
4000	63.60	60.32	57.72	55.61	53.89	52.46	51.27	50.28	47.58	45.04	44.40	44.23	4000
5000	79.49	75.40	72.14	69.51	67.36	65.58	64.09	62.84	59.48	56.29	55.50	55.29	5000
6000	95.39	90.48	86.57	83.41	80.83	78.69	76.91	75.41	71.37	67.55	66.60	66.35	6000
7000	111.29	105.56	101.00	97.31	94.30	91.81	89.73	87.98	83.27	78.81	77.70	77.40	7000
8000	127.19	120.64	115.43	111.22	107.77	104.92	102.54	100.55	95.16	90.07	88.79	88.46	8000
9000	143.08	135.72	129.85	125.12	121.24	118.03	115.36	113.12	107.05	101.32	99.89	99.52	9000
10000	158.98	150.79	144.28	139.02	134.71	131.15	128.18	125.68	118.95	112.58	110.99	110.57	10000
15000	238.47	226.19	216.42	208.52	202.06	196.72	192.27	188.52	178.42	168.87	166.49	165.86	15000
20000	317.96	301.58	288.56	278.03	269.42	262.29	256.35	251.36	237.89	225.16	221.98	221.14	20000
25000	397.45	376.98	360.70	347.54	336.77	327.87	320.44	314.20	297.36	281.45	277.47	276.43	25000
30000	476.93	452.37	432.83	417.04	404.12	393.44	384.53	377.00	356.83	337.74	332.97	331.71	30000
35000	556.42	527.77	504.97	486.55	471.48	459.01	448.61	439.88	416.31	394.03	388.46	387.00	35000
40000	635.91	603.16	577.11	556.06	538.83	524.58	512.70	502.72	475.78	450.31	443.95	442.28	40000
45000	715.40	678.56	649.25	625.56	606.18	590.15	576.79	565.56	535.25	506.60	499.45	497.56	45000
50000	794.89	753.95	721.39	695.07	673.53	655.73	640.87	628.40	594.72	562.89	554.94	552.85	50000
60000	953.86	904.74	865.66	834.08	808.24	786.87	769.05	754.08	713.66	675.47	665.93	663.42	60000
75000	1192.33	1130.92	1082.08	1042.60	1010.30	983.59	961.31	942.59	892.08	844.34	832.41	829.27	75000
100000	1589.77	1507.89	1442.77	1390.14	1347.06	1311.45	1281.74	1256.79	1189.44	1125.78	1109.87	1105.69	100000
125000	1987.21	1884.87	1803.46	1737.67	1683.83	1639.31	1602.18	1570.98	1486.79	1407.22	1387.34	1382.11	125000
150000	2384.65	2261.84	2164.15	2085.20	2020.59	1967.17	1922.61	1885.18	1784.15	1688.67	1664.81	1658.54	150000
175000	2782.09	2638.81	2524.84	2432.73	2357.36	2295.03	2243.04	2199.38	2081.51	1970.11	1942.28	1934.96	175000
200000	3179.53	3015.78	2885.53	2780.27	2694.12	2622.89	2563.48	2513.57	2378.87	2251.55	2219.74	2211.38	200000
250000	3974.41	3769.73	3606.91	3475.33	3367.65	3278.61	3204.35	3141.96	2973.58	2814.44	2774.68	2764.22	250000

Amount	1.0 Year	1.5 Years	2.0 Years	2.5 Years	3.0 Years	3.5 Years	4.0 Years	4.5 Years	5.0 Years	6.0 Years	7.0 Years	8.0 Years	Amount
100	8.96	6.17	4.78	3.95	3.40	3.01	2.71	2.49	2.31	2.04	1.85	1.71	100
200	17.92	12.34	9.56	7.90	6.79	6.01	5.42	4.97	4.61	4.07	3.70	3.42	200
300	26.87	18.51	14.34	11.84	10.19	9.01	8.13	7.45	6.91	6.11	5.54	5.13	300
400	35.83	24.68	19.12	15.79	13.58	12.01	10.84	9.93	9.21	8.14	7.39	6.84	400
500	44.78	30.85	23.89	19.73	16.97	15.01	13.54	12.41	11.51	10.17	9.24	8.55	500
600	53.74	37.01	28.67	23.68	20.37	18.01	16.25	14.89	13.81	12.21	11.08	10.26	600
700	62.69	43.18	33.45	27.63	23.76	21.01	18.96	17.37	16.11	14.24	12.93	11.97	700
800	71.65	49.35	38.23	31.57	27.15	24.01	21.67	19.85	18.41	16.28	14.78	13.68	800
900	80.60	55.52	43.00	35.52	30.55	27.01	24.37	22.33	20.71	18.31	16.62	15.38	900
1000	89.56	61.69	47.78	39.46	33.94	30.01	27.08	24.82	23.01	20.34	18.47	17.09	1000
2000	179.11	123.37	95.56	78.92	67.88	60.02	54.16	49.63	46.02	40.68	36.93	34.18	2000
3000	268.66	185.05	143.34	118.38	101.81	90.03	81.23	74.44	69.03	61.02	55.40	51.27	3000
4000	358.21	246.73	191.11	157.84	135.75	120.03	108.31	99.25	92.04	81.36	73.86	68.36	4000
5000	447.77	308.41	238.89	197.30	169.68	150.04	135.39	124.06	115.05	101.70	92.33	85.45	5000
6000	537.32	370.09	286.67	236.76	203.62	180.05	162.46	148.87	138.06	122.04	110.79	102.53	6000
7000	626.87	431.77	334.44	276.22	237.55	210.05	189.54	173.68	161.07	142.38	129.26	119.62	7000
8000	716.42	493.45	382.22	315.68	271.49	240.06	216.62	198.49	184.08	162.72	147.72	136.71	8000
9000	805.97	555.14	430.00	355.14	305.42	270.07	243.69	223.30	207.09	183.06	166.19	153.80	9000
10000	895.53	616.82	477.78	394.60	339.36	300.08	270.77	248.11	230.10	203.39	184.65	170.89	10000
15000	1343.29	925.22	716.66	591.90	509.03	450.11	406.15	372.16	345.15	305.09	276.98	256.33	15000
20000	1791.05	1233.63	955.55	789.20	678.71	600.15	541.53	496.21	460.20	406.78	369.30	341.77	20000
25000	2238.81	1542.03	1194.43	986.49	848.39	750.18	676.91	620.27	575.25	508.48	461.63	427.21	25000
30000	2686.57	1850.44	1433.32	1183.79	1018.06	900.22	812.29	744.32	690.30	610.17	553.95	512.65	30000
35000	3134.33	2158.84	1672.20	1381.09	1187.74	1050.25	947.68	868.37	805.35	711.87	646.28	598.09	35000
40000	3582.09	2467.25	1911.09	1578.39	1357.42	1200.29	1083.06	992.42	920.40	813.56	738.60	683.53	40000
45000	4029.85	2775.66	2149.97	1775.68	1527.09	1350.32	1218.44	1116.47	1035.45	915.26	830.93	768.97	45000
50000	4477.61	3084.06	2388.86	1972.98	1696.77	1500.36	1353.82	1240.53	1150.50	1016.95	923.25	854.41	50000
60000	5373.13	3700.87	2866.63	2367.58	2036.12	1800.43	1624.58	1488.63	1380.60	1220.34	1107.90	1025.29	60000
75000	6716.41	4626.09	3583.28	2959.47	2545.15	2250.54	2030.73	1860.79	1725.74	1525.43	1384.87	1281.62	75000
100000	8955.21	6168.12	4777.71	3945.96	3393.53	3000.71	2707.64	2481.05	2300.99	2033.90	1846.49	1708.82	100000
125000	11194.01	7710.15	5972.13	4932.45	4241.92	3750.89	3384.55	3101.31	2876.24	2542.38	2308.12	2136.02	125000
150000	13432.81	9252.17	7166.56	5918.94	5090.30	4501.07	4061.45	3721.57	3451.48	3050.85	2769.74	2563.23	150000
175000	15671.61	10794.20	8360.98	6905.42	5938.68	5251.25	4738.36	4341.83	4026.73	3559.32	3231.36	2990.43	175000
200000	17910.41	12336.23	9555.41	7891.91	6787.06	6001.42	5415.27	4962.09	4601.97	4067.80	3692.98	3417.64	200000
250000	22388.01	15420.29	11944.26	9864.89	8483.83	7501.78	6769.09	6202.61	5752.47	5084.75	4616.23	4272.04	250000

Amount	9.0 Years	10.0 Years	11.0 Years	12.0 Years	13.0 Years	14.0 Years	15.0 Years	16.0 Years	20.0 Years	30.0 Years	40.0 Years	50.0 Years	Amount
100	1.61	1.53	1.46	1.41	1.37	1.33	1.30	1.28	1.21	1.15	1.14	1.13	100
200	3.21	3.05	2.92	2.82	2.73	2.66	2.60	2.55	2.42	2.30	2.27	2.26	200
300	4.82	4.57	4.38	4.22	4.09	3.99	3.90	3.83	3.63	3.44	3.40	3.38	300
400	6.42	6.10	5.84	5.63	5.46	5.32	5.20	5.10	4.83	4.59	4.53	4.51	400
500	8.03	7.62	7.29	7.03	6.82	6.64	6.50	6.37	6.04	5.73	5.66	5.64	500
600	9.63	9.14	8.75	8.44	8.18	7.97	7.79	7.65	7.25	6.88	6.79	6.76	600
700	11.23	10.66	10.21	9.85	9.55	9.30	9.09	8.92	8.46	8.02	7.92	7.89	700
800	12.84	12.19	11.67	11.25	10.91	10.63	10.39	10.19	9.66	9.17	9.05	9.02	800
900	14.44	13.71	13.13	12.66	12.27	11.95	11.69	11.47	10.87	10.31	10.18	10.14	900
1000	16.05	15.23	14.58	14.06	13.63	13.28	12.99	12.74	12.08	11.46	11.31	11.27	1000
2000	32.09	30.46	29.16	28.12	27.26	26.56	25.97	25.48	24.15	22.91	22.61	22.53	2000
3000	48.13	45.69	43.74	42.18	40.89	39.84	38.95	38.22	36.23	34.37	33.91	33.80	3000
4000	64.17	60.91	58.32	56.23	54.52	53.11	51.94	50.95	48.30	45.82	45.22	45.06	4000
5000	80.22	76.14	72.90	70.29	68.15	66.39	64.92	63.69	60.37	57.28	56.52	56.32	5000
6000	96.26	91.37	87.48	84.35	81.78	79.67	77.90	76.43	72.45	68.73	67.82	67.59	6000
7000	112.30	106.60	102.06	98.41	95.41	92.94	90.89	89.16	84.52	80.18	79.12	78.85	7000
8000	128.34	121.82	116.64	112.46	109.04	106.22	103.87	101.90	96.59	91.64	90.43	90.11	8000
9000	144.39	137.05	131.22	126.52	122.67	119.50	116.85	114.64	108.67	103.09	101.73	101.38	9000
10000	160.43	152.28	145.80	140.58	136.30	132.78	129.84	127.37	120.74	114.55	113.03	112.64	10000
15000	240.64	228.42	218.70	210.86	204.45	199.16	194.75	191.06	181.11	171.82	169.54	168.96	15000
20000	320.85	304.55	291.60	281.15	272.60	265.55	259.67	254.74	241.48	229.09	226.06	225.28	20000
25000	401.06	380.69	364.50	351.43	340.75	331.93	324.58	318.42	301.85	286.36	282.57	281.60	25000
30000	481.27	456.83	437.40	421.72	408.90	398.32	389.50	382.11	362.22	343.63	339.08	337.92	30000
35000	561.49	532.97	510.30	492.01	477.05	464.70	454.42	445.79	422.59	400.90	395.60	394.23	35000
40000	641.70	609.10	583.20	562.29	545.20	531.09	519.33	509.47	482.95	458.17	452.11	450.55	40000
45000	721.91	685.24	656.10	632.58	613.35	597.47	584.25	573.16	543.32	515.44	508.62	506.87	45000
50000	802.12	761.38	729.00	702.86	681.50	663.86	649.16	636.84	603.69	572.71	565.14	563.19	50000
60000	962.54	913.65	874.80	843.44	817.80	796.63	779.00	764.21	724.43	687.25	678.16	675.83	60000
75000	1203.18	1142.06	1093.50	1054.29	1022.25	995.79	973.74	955.26	905.54	859.06	847.70	844.78	75000
100000	1604.24	1522.75	1457.99	1405.72	1363.00	1327.71	1298.32	1273.67	1207.38	1145.42	1130.27	1126.37	100000
125000	2005.29	1903.43	1822.49	1757.15	1703.74	1659.64	1622.90	1592.09	1509.22	1431.77	1412.83	1407.97	125000
150000	2406.35	2284.12	2186.99	2108.58	2044.49	1991.57	1947.48	1910.51	1811.07	1718.12	1695.40	1689.56	150000
175000	2807.41	2664.81	2551.48	2460.01	2385.24	2323.49	2272.06	2228.92	2112.91	2004.48	1977.96	1971.15	175000
200000	3208.47	3045.49	2915.98	2811.44	2725.99	2655.42	2596.64	2547.34	2414.75	2290.83	2260.53	2252.74	200000
250000	4010.58	3806.86	3644.97	3514.30	3407.48	3319.27	3245.80	3184.18	3018.44	2863.54	2825.66	2815.93	250000

Amount	1.0 Year	1.5 Years	2.0 Years	2.5 Years	3.0 Years	3.5 Years	4.0 Years	4.5 Years	5.0 Years	6.0 Years	7.0 Years	8.0 Years	Amount
100	8.97	6.18	4.79	3.96	3.41	3.02	2.73	2.50	2.32	2.05	1.87	1.73	100
200	17.94	12.36	9.58	7.92	6.82	6.03	5.45	4.99	4.63	4.10	3.73	3.45	200
300	26.91	18.54	14.37	11.88	10.22	9.04	8.17	7.49	6.95	6.15	5.59	5.17	300
400	35.87	24.72	19.16	15.84	13.63	12.06	10.89	9.98	9.26	8.19	7.45	6.90	400
500	44.84	30.90	23.95	19.79	17.03	15.07	13.61	12.47	11.57	10.24	9.31	8.62	500
600	53.81	37.08	28.74	23.75	20.44	18.08	16.33	14.97	13.89	12.29	11.17	10.34	600
700	62.77	43.26	33.53	27.71	23.84	21.10	19.05	17.46	16.20	14.34	13.03	12.07	700
800	71.74	49.44	38.32	31.67	27.25	24.11	21.77	19.95	18.52	16.38	14.89	13.79	800
900	80.71	55.62	43.11	35.63	30.66	27.12	24.49	22.45	20.83	18.43	16.75	15.51	900
1000	89.67	61.80	47.90	39.58	34.06	30.14	27.21	24.94	23.14	20.48	18.61	17.23	1000
2000	179.34	123.60	95.79	79.16	68.12	60.27	54.41	49.88	46.28	40.95	37.21	34.46	2000
3000	269.01	185.40	143.69	118.74	102.17	90.40	81.61	74.82	69.42	61.42	55.81	51.69	3000
4000	358.68	247.20	191.58	158.32	136.23	120.53	108.81	99.75	92.56	81.89	74.41	68.92	4000
5000	448.35	309.00	239.48	197.90	170.29	150.66	136.01	124.69	115.70	102.37	93.02	86.15	5000
6000	538.02	370.79	287.37	237.48	204.34	180.79	163.21	149.63	138.84	122.84	111.62	103.38	6000
7000	627.69	432.59	335.27	277.06	238.40	210.92	190.41	174.57	161.98	143.31	130.22	120.61	7000
8000	717.36	494.39	383.16	316.64	272.46	241.05	217.61	199.50	185.12	163.78	148.82	137.84	8000
9000	807.03	556.19	431.06	356.21	306.51	271.18	244.82	224.44	208.25	184.25	167.42	155.07	9000
10000	896.70	617.99	478.95	395.79	340.57	301.31	272.02	249.38	231.39	204.73	186.03	172.30	10000
15000	1345.05	926.98	718.43	593.69	510.85	451.96	408.02	374.07	347.09	307.09	279.04	258.45	15000
20000	1793.40	1235.97	957.90	791.58	681.13	602.61	544.03	498.75	462.78	409.45	372.05	344.60	20000
25000	2241.74	1544.96	1197.38	989.48	851.41	753.26	680.04	623.44	578.48	511.81	465.06	430.74	25000
30000	2690.09	1853.95	1436.85	1187.37	1021.69	903.91	816.04	748.13	694.17	614.17	558.07	516.89	30000
35000	3138.44	2162.94	1676.33	1385.26	1191.98	1054.56	952.05	872.81	809.86	716.53	651.08	603.04	35000
40000	3586.79	2471.93	1915.80	1583.16	1362.26	1205.21	1088.05	997.50	925.56	818.89	744.09	689.19	40000
45000	4035.13	2780.92	2155.27	1781.05	1532.54	1355.86	1224.06	1122.19	1041.25	921.25	837.10	775.33	45000
50000	4483.48	3089.91	2394.75	1978.95	1702.82	1506.51	1360.07	1246.87	1156.95	1023.61	930.11	861.48	50000
60000	5380.18	3707.89	2873.70	2374.74	2043.38	1807.81	1632.08	1496.25	1388.34	1228.33	1116.14	1033.78	60000
75000	6725.22	4634.86	3592.12	2968.42	2554.23	2259.76	2040.10	1870.31	1735.42	1535.41	1395.17	1292.22	75000
100000	8966.96	6179.81	4789.49	3957.89	3405.64	3013.01	2720.13	2493.74	2313.89	2047.22	1860.22	1722.96	100000
125000	11208.70	7724.77	5986.86	4947.36	4257.05	3766.26	3400.16	3117.18	2892.36	2559.02	2325.28	2153.70	125000
150000	13450.43	9269.72	7184.23	5936.83	5108.45	4519.51	4080.19	3740.61	3470.83	3070.82	2790.33	2584.45	150000
175000	15692.17	10814.67	8381.61	6926.30	5959.86	5272.76	4760.22	4364.04	4049.30	3582.62	3255.39	3015.17	175000
200000	17933.91	12359.62	9578.98	7915.77	6811.27	6026.01	5440.25	4987.48	4627.77	4094.43	3720.44	3445.91	200000
250000	22417.39	15449.53	11973.72	9894.72	8514.09	7532.51	6800.31	6234.35	5784.72	5118.03	4650.55	4307.39	250000

Amount	9.0 Years	10.0 Years	11.0 Years	12.0 Years	13.0 Years	14.0 Years	15.0 Years	16.0 Years	20.0 Years	30.0 Years	40.0 Years	50.0 Years	Amount
100	1.62	1.54	1.48	1.43	1.38	1.35	1.32	1.30	1.23	1.17	1.16	1.15	100
200	3.24	3.08	2.95	2.85	2.76	2.69	2.63	2.59	2.46	2.34	2.31	2.30	200
300	4.86	4.62	4.42	4.27	4.14	4.04	3.95	3.88	3.68	3.50	3.46	3.45	300
400	6.48	6.16	5.90	5.69	5.52	5.38	5.26	5.17	4.91	4.67	4.61	4.59	400
500	8.10	7.69	7.37	7.11	6.90	6.73	6.58	6.46	6.13	5.83	5.76	5.74	500
600	9.72	9.23	8.84	8.53	8.28	8.07	7.89	7.75	7.36	7.00	6.91	6.89	600
700	11.34	10.77	10.32	9.95	9.66	9.41	9.21	9.04	8.58	8.16	8.06	8.03	700
800	12.96	12.31	11.79	11.38	11.04	10.76	10.52	10.33	9.81	9.33	9.21	9.18	800
900	14.57	13.84	13.26	12.80	12.42	12.10	11.84	11.62	11.03	10.49	10.36	10.33	900
1000	16.19	15.38	14.74	14.22	13.80	13.45	13.15	12.91	12.26	11.66	11.51	11.48	1000
2000	32.38	30.76	29.47	28.43	27.59	26.89	26.30	25.82	24.51	23.31	23.02	22.95	2000
3000	48.57	46.14	44.20	42.65	41.38	40.33	39.45	38.72	36.77	34.96	34.53	34.42	3000
4000	64.76	61.51	58.94	56.86	55.17	53.77	52.60	51.63	49.02	46.61	46.03	45.89	4000
5000	80.94	76.89	73.67	71.07	68.96	67.21	65.75	64.54	61.28	58.26	57.54	57.36	5000
6000	97.13	92.27	88.40	85.29	82.75	80.65	78.90	77.44	73.53	69.91	69.05	68.83	6000
7000	113.32	107.64	103.14	99.50	96.54	94.09	92.05	90.35	85.78	81.56	80.55	80.30	7000
8000	129.51	123.02	117.87	113.72	110.33	107.53	105.20	103.26	98.04	93.21	92.06	91.77	8000
9000	145.69	138.40	132.60	127.93	124.12	120.97	118.35	116.16	110.29	104.87	103.57	103.24	9000
10000	161.88	153.77	147.33	142.14	137.91	134.41	131.50	129.07	122.55	116.52	115.07	114.71	10000
15000	242.82	230.66	221.00	213.21	206.86	201.61	197.25	193.60	183.82	174.77	172.61	172.06	15000
20000	323.76	307.54	294.66	284.28	275.81	268.82	263.00	258.13	245.09	233.03	230.14	229.42	20000
25000	404.70	384.42	368.33	355.35	344.76	336.02	328.75	322.67	306.36	291.28	287.68	286.77	25000
30000	485.64	461.31	441.99	426.42	413.71	403.22	394.50	387.20	367.63	349.54	345.21	344.12	30000
35000	566.57	538.19	515.66	497.49	482.66	470.42	460.25	451.73	428.90	407.79	402.74	401.48	35000
40000	647.51	615.07	589.32	568.56	551.61	537.63	526.00	516.26	490.17	466.05	460.28	458.83	40000
45000	728.45	691.96	662.98	639.63	620.56	604.83	591.75	580.79	551.44	524.31	517.81	516.18	45000
50000	809.39	768.84	736.65	710.70	689.51	672.03	657.50	645.33	612.71	582.56	575.35	573.54	50000
60000	971.27	922.61	883.98	852.83	827.41	806.44	789.00	774.39	735.25	699.07	690.42	688.24	60000
75000	1214.08	1153.26	1104.97	1066.04	1034.26	1008.05	986.25	967.99	919.06	873.84	863.02	860.30	75000
100000	1618.77	1537.67	1473.29	1421.39	1379.01	1344.06	1314.99	1290.65	1225.41	1165.12	1150.69	1147.07	100000
125000	2023.46	1922.09	1841.62	1776.73	1723.76	1680.08	1643.74	1613.31	1531.76	1456.40	1438.36	1433.84	125000
150000	2428.16	2306.51	2209.94	2132.08	2068.51	2016.09	1972.49	1935.97	1838.11	1747.67	1726.03	1720.60	150000
175000	2832.85	2690.92	2578.26	2487.42	2413.27	2352.10	2301.23	2258.63	2144.46	2038.95	2013.70	2007.37	175000
200000	3237.54	3075.34	2946.58	2842.77	2758.02	2688.12	2629.98	2581.29	2450.82	2330.23	2301.38	2294.14	200000
250000	4046.92	3844.18	3683.23	3553.46	3447.52	3360.15	3287.47	3226.61	3063.52	2912.79	2876.72	2867.67	250000

Amount	1.0 Year	1.5 Years	2.0 Years	2.5 Years	3.0 Years	3.5 Years	4.0 Years	4.5 Years	5.0 Years	6.0 Years	7.0 Years	8.0 Years	Amount
100	8.98	6.20	4.81	3.97	3.42	3.03	2.74	2.51	2.33	2.07	1.88	1.74	100
200	17.96	12.39	9.61	7.94	6.84	6.06	5.47	5.02	4.66	4.13	3.75	3.48	200
300	26.94	18.58	14.41	11.91	10.26	9.08	8.20	7.52	6.99	6.19	5.63	5.22	300
400	35.92	24.77	19.21	15.88	13.68	12.11	10.94	10.03	9.31	8.25	7.50	6.95	400
500	44.90	30.96	24.01	19.85	17.09	15.13	13.67	12.54	11.64	10.31	9.38	8.69	500
600	53.88	37.15	28.81	23.82	20.51	18.16	16.40	15.04	13.97	12.37	11.25	10.43	600
700	62.86	43.35	33.61	27.79	23.93	21.18	19.13	17.55	16.29	14.43	13.12	12.17	700
800	71.83	49.54	38.42	31.76	27.35	24.21	21.87	20.06	18.62	16.49	15.00	13.90	800
900	80.81	55.73	43.22	35.73	30.76	27.23	24.60	22.56	20.95	18.55	16.87	15.64	900
1000	89.79	61.92	48.02	39.70	34.18	30.26	27.33	25.07	23.27	20.61	18.75	17.38	1000
2000	179.58	123.84	96.03	79.40	68.36	60.51	54.66	50.13	46.54	41.22	37.49	34.75	2000
3000	269.37	185.75	144.04	119.10	102.54	90.76	81.98	75.20	69.81	61.82	56.23	52.12	3000
4000	359.15	247.67	192.06	158.80	136.72	121.02	109.31	100.26	93.08	82.43	74.97	69.49	4000
5000	448.94	309.58	240.07	198.50	170.89	151.27	136.64	125.33	116.35	103.03	93.71	86.86	5000
6000	538.73	371.50	288.08	238.20	205.07	181.52	163.96	150.39	139.61	123.64	112.45	104.23	6000
7000	628.51	433.41	336.10	277.89	239.25	211.78	191.29	175.46	162.88	144.25	131.19	121.61	7000
8000	718.30	495.33	384.11	317.59	273.43	242.03	218.62	200.52	186.15	164.85	149.93	138.98	8000
9000	808.09	557.24	432.12	357.29	307.60	272.28	245.94	225.59	209.42	185.46	168.67	156.35	9000
10000	897.88	619.16	480.13	396.99	341.78	302.54	273.27	250.65	232.69	206.06	187.41	173.72	10000
15000	1346.81	928.73	720.20	595.48	512.67	453.80	409.90	375.98	349.03	309.09	281.11	260.58	15000
20000	1795.75	1238.31	960.26	793.97	683.56	605.07	546.53	501.30	465.37	412.12	374.81	347.44	20000
25000	2244.68	1547.88	1200.33	992.46	854.45	756.34	683.17	626.62	581.71	515.15	468.51	434.29	25000
30000	2693.62	1857.46	1440.39	1190.96	1025.33	907.60	819.80	751.95	698.05	618.18	562.21	521.15	30000
35000	3142.55	2167.04	1680.46	1389.45	1196.22	1058.87	956.43	877.27	814.39	721.21	655.91	608.01	35000
40000	3591.49	2476.61	1920.52	1587.94	1367.11	1210.13	1093.06	1002.59	930.74	824.23	749.61	694.87	40000
45000	4040.43	2786.19	2160.58	1786.43	1538.00	1361.40	1229.70	1127.92	1047.08	927.26	843.31	781.72	45000
50000	4489.36	3095.76	2400.65	1984.92	1708.89	1512.67	1366.33	1253.24	1163.42	1030.29	937.01	868.58	50000
60000	5387.23	3714.92	2880.78	2381.91	2050.66	1815.20	1639.59	1503.89	1396.10	1236.35	1124.41	1042.30	60000
75000	6734.04	4643.64	3600.97	2977.38	2563.33	2269.00	2049.49	1879.86	1745.12	1545.44	1405.51	1302.87	75000
100000	8978.72	6191.52	4801.29	3969.84	3417.77	3025.33	2732.65	2506.47	2326.83	2060.58	1874.01	1737.16	100000
125000	11223.39	7739.40	6001.62	4962.30	4272.21	3781.66	3415.81	3133.09	2908.54	2575.72	2342.51	2171.44	125000
150000	13468.07	9287.28	7201.94	5954.76	5126.65	4537.99	4098.98	3759.71	3490.24	3090.87	2811.01	2605.73	150000
175000	15712.75	10835.16	8402.26	6947.22	5981.09	5294.32	4782.14	4386.33	4071.95	3606.01	3279.51	3040.02	175000
200000	17957.43	12383.04	9602.58	7939.68	6835.53	6050.65	5465.30	5012.94	4653.66	4121.15	3748.01	3474.31	200000
250000	22446.78	15478.80	12003.23	9924.60	8544.41	7563.32	6831.62	6266.17	5817.07	5151.44	4685.01	4342.88	250000

Amount	9.0 Years	10.0 Years	11.0 Years	12.0 Years	13.0 Years	14.0 Years	15.0 Years	16.0 Years	20.0 Years	30.0 Years	40.0 Years	50.0 Years	Amount
100	1.64	1.56	1.49	1.44	1.40	1.37	1.34	1.31	1.25	1.19	1.18	1.17	100
200	3.27	3.11	2.98	2.88	2.80	2.73	2.67	2.62	2.49	2.37	2.35	2.34	200
300	4.91	4.66	4.47	4.32	4.19	4.09	4.00	3.93	3.74	3.56	3.52	3.51	300
400	6.54	6.22	5.96	5.75	5.59	5.45	5.33	5.24	4.98	4.74	4.69	4.68	400
500	8.17	7.77	7.45	7.19	6.98	6.81	6.66	6.54	6.22	5.93	5.86	5.84	500
600	9.81	9.32	8.94	8.63	8.38	8.17	8.00	7.85	7.47	7.11	7.03	7.01	600
700	11.44	10.87	10.43	10.06	9.77	9.53	9.33	9.16	8.71	8.30	8.20	8.18	700
800	13.07	12.43	11.91	11.50	11.17	10.89	10.66	10.47	9.95	9.48	9.37	9.35	800
900	14.71	13.98	13.40	12.94	12.56	12.25	11.99	11.77	11.20	10.67	10.55	10.51	900
1000	16.34	15.53	14.89	14.38	13.96	13.61	13.32	13.08	12.44	11.85	11.72	11.68	1000
2000	32.67	31.06	29.78	28.75	27.91	27.21	26.64	26.16	24.88	23.70	23.43	23.36	2000
3000	49.01	46.58	44.66	43.12	41.86	40.82	39.96	39.24	37.31	35.55	35.14	35.04	3000
4000	65.34	62.11	59.55	57.49	55.81	54.42	53.27	52.31	49.75	47.40	46.85	46.72	4000
5000	81.67	77.64	74.44	71.86	69.76	68.03	66.59	65.39	62.18	59.25	58.56	58.39	5000
6000	98.01	93.16	89.32	86.23	83.71	81.63	79.91	78.47	74.62	71.10	70.27	70.07	6000
7000	114.34	108.69	104.21	100.60	97.66	95.24	93.23	91.54	87.05	82.95	81.98	81.75	7000
8000	130.67	124.22	119.10	114.98	111.61	108.84	106.54	104.62	99.49	94.79	93.70	93.43	8000
9000	147.01	139.74	133.98	129.35	125.56	122.45	119.86	117.70	111.92	106.64	105.41	105.10	9000
10000	163.34	155.27	148.87	143.72	139.52	136.05	133.18	130.77	124.36	118.49	117.12	116.78	10000
15000	245.01	232.90	223.30	215.57	209.27	204.08	199.77	196.16	186.53	177.74	175.68	175.17	15000
20000	326.68	310.54	297.74	287.43	279.03	272.10	266.35	261.54	248.71	236.98	234.23	233.56	20000
25000	408.35	388.17	372.17	359.29	348.78	340.13	332.94	326.93	310.89	296.22	292.79	291.95	25000
30000	490.02	465.80	446.60	431.14	418.54	408.15	399.53	392.31	373.06	355.47	351.35	350.34	30000
35000	571.68	543.44	521.04	503.00	488.29	476.18	466.11	457.70	435.24	414.71	409.90	408.73	35000
40000	653.35	621.07	595.47	574.86	558.05	544.20	532.70	523.08	497.41	473.95	468.46	467.12	40000
45000	735.02	698.70	669.90	646.71	627.80	612.23	599.29	588.47	559.59	533.20	527.02	525.50	45000
50000	816.69	776.34	744.34	718.57	697.56	680.25	665.88	653.85	621.77	592.44	585.58	583.89	50000
60000	980.03	931.60	893.20	862.28	837.07	816.30	799.05	784.62	746.12	710.93	702.69	700.67	60000
75000	1225.03	1164.50	1116.50	1077.85	1046.33	1020.37	998.81	980.78	932.65	888.66	878.36	875.84	75000
100000	1633.38	1552.67	1488.67	1437.13	1395.11	1360.49	1331.75	1307.70	1243.53	1184.88	1171.15	1167.78	100000
125000	2041.72	1940.84	1860.84	1796.41	1743.88	1700.62	1664.68	1634.63	1554.41	1481.09	1463.93	1459.72	125000
150000	2450.06	2329.00	2233.00	2155.70	2092.66	2040.74	1997.62	1961.55	1865.29	1777.31	1756.72	1751.67	150000
175000	2858.40	2717.17	2605.17	2514.98	2441.44	2380.86	2330.55	2288.48	2176.17	2073.53	2049.50	2043.61	175000
200000	3266.75	3105.33	2977.34	2874.26	2790.21	2720.98	2663.49	2615.40	2487.05	2369.75	2342.29	2335.56	200000
250000	4083.43	3881.67	3721.67	3592.82	3487.76	3401.23	3329.36	3269.25	3108.81	2962.18	2927.86	2919.44	250000

Monthly Payment Required To Amortize A Loan

Amount	1.0 Year	1.5 Years	2.0 Years	2.5 Years	3.0 Years	3.5 Years	4.0 Years	4.5 Years	5.0 Years	6.0 Years	7.0 Years	8.0 Years	Amount
100	9.00	6.21	4.82	3.99	3.43	3.04	2.75	2.52	2.34	2.08	1.89	1.76	100
200	17.99	12.41	9.63	7.97	6.86	6.08	5.50	5.04	4.68	4.15	3.78	3.51	200
300	26.98	18.61	14.44	11.95	10.29	9.12	8.24	7.56	7.02	6.23	5.67	5.26	300
400	35.97	24.82	19.26	15.93	13.72	12.16	10.99	10.08	9.36	8.30	7.56	7.01	400
500	44.96	31.02	24.07	19.91	17.15	15.19	13.73	12.60	11.70	10.37	9.44	8.76	500
600	53.95	37.22	28.88	23.90	20.58	18.23	16.48	15.12	14.04	12.45	11.33	10.51	600
700	62.94	43.43	33.70	27.88	24.01	21.27	19.22	17.64	16.38	14.52	13.22	12.26	700
800	71.93	49.63	38.51	31.86	27.44	24.31	21.97	20.16	18.72	16.60	15.11	14.02	800
900	80.92	55.83	43.32	35.84	30.87	27.34	24.71	22.68	21.06	18.67	17.00	15.77	900
1000	89.91	62.04	48.14	39.82	34.30	30.38	27.46	25.20	23.40	20.74	18.88	17.52	1000
2000	179.81	124.07	96.27	79.64	68.60	60.76	54.91	50.39	46.80	41.48	37.76	35.03	2000
3000	269.72	186.10	144.40	119.46	102.90	91.14	82.36	75.58	70.20	62.22	56.64	52.55	3000
4000	359.62	248.13	192.53	159.28	137.20	121.51	109.81	100.77	93.60	82.96	75.52	70.06	4000
5000	449.53	310.17	240.66	199.10	171.50	151.89	137.27	125.97	117.00	103.70	94.40	87.58	5000
6000	539.43	372.20	288.79	238.91	205.80	182.27	164.72	151.16	140.39	124.44	113.28	105.09	6000
7000	629.34	434.23	336.92	278.73	240.10	212.64	192.17	176.35	163.79	145.18	132.15	122.60	7000
8000	719.24	496.26	385.05	318.55	274.40	243.02	219.62	201.54	187.19	165.92	151.03	140.12	8000
9000	809.15	558.30	433.18	358.37	308.70	273.40	247.07	226.74	210.59	186.66	169.91	157.63	9000
10000	899.05	620.33	481.32	398.19	343.00	303.77	274.53	251.93	233.99	207.40	188.79	175.15	10000
15000	1348.58	930.49	721.97	597.28	514.49	455.66	411.79	377.89	350.98	311.10	283.18	262.72	15000
20000	1798.10	1240.65	962.63	796.37	685.99	607.54	549.05	503.85	467.97	414.80	377.57	350.29	20000
25000	2247.62	1550.81	1203.28	995.46	857.48	759.42	686.31	629.81	584.96	518.50	471.96	437.86	25000
30000	2697.15	1860.98	1443.94	1194.55	1028.98	911.31	823.57	755.78	701.95	622.20	566.36	525.43	30000
35000	3146.67	2171.14	1684.59	1393.64	1200.48	1063.19	960.83	881.74	818.94	725.90	660.75	613.00	35000
40000	3596.20	2481.30	1925.25	1592.73	1371.97	1215.08	1098.09	1007.70	935.93	829.60	755.14	700.57	40000
45000	4045.72	2791.46	2165.90	1791.82	1543.47	1366.96	1235.35	1133.66	1052.92	933.30	849.53	788.14	45000
50000	4495.24	3101.62	2406.56	1990.91	1714.96	1518.84	1372.61	1259.62	1169.91	1037.00	943.92	875.71	50000
60000	5394.29	3721.95	2887.87	2389.09	2057.96	1822.61	1647.13	1511.55	1403.89	1244.40	1132.71	1050.85	60000
75000	6742.86	4652.43	3609.84	2986.36	2572.44	2278.26	2058.91	1889.43	1754.86	1555.49	1415.88	1313.56	75000
100000	8990.48	6203.24	4813.11	3981.81	3429.92	3037.68	2745.21	2519.24	2339.81	2073.99	1887.84	1751.41	100000
125000	11238.10	7754.05	6016.39	4977.27	4287.40	3797.10	3431.51	3149.05	2924.76	2592.49	2359.80	2189.26	125000
150000	13485.72	9304.86	7219.67	5972.72	5144.88	4556.52	4117.81	3778.86	3509.71	3110.98	2831.76	2627.12	150000
175000	15733.34	10855.67	8422.94	6968.17	6002.36	5315.94	4804.11	4408.67	4094.67	3629.48	3303.72	3064.97	175000
200000	17980.96	12406.48	9626.22	7963.62	6859.84	6075.36	5490.41	5038.48	4679.62	4147.97	3775.68	3502.82	200000
250000	22476.20	15508.10	12032.77	9954.53	8574.80	7594.20	6863.02	6298.09	5849.52	5184.97	4719.60	4378.52	250000

Amount	9.0 Years	10.0 Years	11.0 Years	12.0 Years	13.0 Years	14.0 Years	15.0 Years	16.0 Years	20.0 Years	30.0 Years	40.0 Years	50.0 Years	Amount
100	1.65	1.57	1.51	1.46	1.42	1.38	1.35	1.33	1.27	1.21	1.20	1.19	100
200	3.30	3.14	3.01	2.91	2.83	2.76	2.70	2.65	2.53	2.41	2.39	2.38	200
300	4.95	4.71	4.52	4.36	4.24	4.14	4.05	3.98	3.79	3.62	3.58	3.57	300
400	6.60	6.28	6.02	5.82	5.65	5.51	5.40	5.30	5.05	4.82	4.77	4.76	400
500	8.25	7.84	7.53	7.27	7.06	6.89	6.75	6.63	6.31	6.03	5.96	5.95	500
600	9.89	9.41	9.03	8.72	8.47	8.27	8.10	7.95	7.58	7.23	7.15	7.14	600
700	11.54	10.98	10.53	10.18	9.88	9.64	9.45	9.28	8.84	8.44	8.35	8.32	700
800	13.19	12.55	12.04	11.63	11.30	11.02	10.79	10.60	10.10	9.64	9.54	9.51	800
900	14.84	14.11	13.54	13.08	12.71	12.40	12.14	11.93	11.36	10.85	10.73	10.70	900
1000	16.49	15.68	15.05	14.53	14.12	13.78	13.49	13.25	12.62	12.05	11.92	11.89	1000
2000	32.97	31.36	30.09	29.06	28.23	27.55	26.98	26.50	25.24	24.10	23.84	23.77	2000
3000	49.45	47.04	45.13	43.59	42.34	41.32	40.46	39.75	37.86	36.15	35.75	35.66	3000
4000	65.93	62.71	60.17	58.12	56.46	55.09	53.95	53.00	50.47	48.19	47.67	47.54	4000
5000	82.41	78.39	75.21	72.65	70.57	68.86	67.43	66.25	63.09	60.24	59.59	59.43	5000
6000	98.89	94.07	90.25	87.18	84.68	82.63	80.92	79.50	75.71	72.29	71.50	71.31	6000
7000	115.37	109.75	105.29	101.71	98.79	96.40	94.41	92.74	88.33	84.33	83.42	83.20	7000
8000	131.85	125.42	120.33	116.24	112.91	110.17	107.89	105.99	100.94	96.38	95.33	95.08	8000
9000	148.33	141.10	135.38	130.77	127.02	123.94	121.38	119.24	113.56	108.43	107.25	106.97	9000
10000	164.81	156.78	150.42	145.30	141.13	137.71	134.86	132.49	126.18	120.47	119.17	118.85	10000
15000	247.21	235.16	225.62	217.95	211.70	206.56	202.29	198.73	189.26	180.71	178.75	178.28	15000
20000	329.61	313.55	300.83	290.59	282.26	275.41	269.72	264.97	252.35	240.94	238.33	237.70	20000
25000	412.01	391.94	376.03	363.24	352.83	344.26	337.15	331.22	315.43	301.18	297.91	297.13	25000
30000	494.42	470.32	451.24	435.89	423.39	413.11	404.58	397.46	378.52	361.41	357.49	356.55	30000
35000	576.82	548.71	526.45	508.54	493.95	481.96	472.01	463.70	441.61	421.65	417.07	415.98	35000
40000	659.22	627.10	601.65	581.18	564.52	550.81	539.44	529.94	504.69	481.88	476.65	475.40	40000
45000	741.62	705.48	676.86	653.83	635.08	619.66	606.87	596.18	567.78	542.11	536.24	534.83	45000
50000	824.02	783.87	752.06	726.48	705.65	688.51	674.29	662.43	630.86	602.35	595.82	594.25	50000
60000	988.83	940.64	902.48	871.77	846.77	826.21	809.15	794.91	757.04	722.82	714.98	713.10	60000
75000	1236.03	1175.80	1128.09	1089.72	1058.47	1032.76	1011.44	993.64	946.29	903.52	893.72	891.38	75000
100000	1648.04	1567.74	1504.12	1452.95	1411.29	1377.01	1348.58	1324.85	1261.72	1204.69	1191.63	1188.50	100000
125000	2060.05	1959.67	1880.15	1816.19	1764.11	1721.26	1685.73	1656.06	1577.15	1505.86	1489.53	1485.63	125000
150000	2472.05	2351.60	2256.18	2179.43	2116.93	2065.51	2022.87	1987.27	1892.58	1807.04	1787.44	1782.75	150000
175000	2884.07	2743.53	2632.21	2542.67	2469.75	2409.76	2360.02	2318.48	2208.01	2108.21	2085.35	2079.88	175000
200000	3296.08	3135.47	3008.24	2905.90	2822.57	2754.02	2697.16	2649.69	2523.44	2409.38	2383.25	2377.00	200000
250000	4120.10	3919.33	3760.30	3632.38	3528.21	3442.52	3371.45	3312.11	3154.30	3011.72	2979.06	2971.25	250000

Amount	1.0 Year	1.5 Years	2.0 Years	2.5 Years	3.0 Years	3.5 Years	4.0 Years	4.5 Years	5.0 Years	6.0 Years	7.0 Years	8.0 Years	Amount
100	9.01	6.22	4.83	4.00	3.45	3.06	2.76	2.54	2.36	2.09	1.91	1.77	100
200	18.01	12.43	9.65	7.99	6.89	6.11	5.52	5.07	4.71	4.18	3.81	3.54	200
300	27.01	18.65	14.48	11.99	10.33	9.16	8.28	7.60	7.06	6.27	5.71	5.30	300
400	36.01	24.86	19.30	15.98	13.77	12.21	11.04	10.13	9.42	8.35	7.61	7.07	400
500	45.02	31.08	24.13	19.97	17.22	15.26	13.79	12.67	11.77	10.44	9.51	8.83	500
600	54.02	37.29	28.95	23.97	20.66	18.31	16.55	15.20	14.12	12.53	11.42	10.60	600
700	63.02	43.51	33.78	27.96	24.10	21.36	19.31	17.73	16.47	14.62	13.32	12.37	700
800	72.02	49.72	38.60	31.96	27.54	24.41	22.07	20.26	18.83	16.70	15.22	14.13	800
900	81.03	55.94	43.43	35.95	30.98	27.46	24.83	22.79	21.18	18.79	17.12	15.90	900
1000	90.03	62.15	48.25	39.94	34.43	30.51	27.58	25.33	23.53	20.88	19.02	17.66	1000
2000	180.05	124.30	96.50	79.88	68.85	61.01	55.16	50.65	47.06	41.75	38.04	35.32	2000
3000	270.07	186.45	144.75	119.82	103.27	91.51	82.74	75.97	70.59	62.63	57.06	52.98	3000
4000	360.10	248.60	193.00	159.76	137.69	122.01	110.32	101.29	94.12	83.50	76.07	70.63	4000
5000	450.12	310.75	241.25	199.70	172.11	152.51	137.89	126.61	117.65	104.38	95.09	88.29	5000
6000	540.14	372.90	289.50	239.63	206.53	183.01	165.47	151.93	141.17	125.25	114.11	105.95	6000
7000	630.16	435.05	337.75	279.57	240.95	213.51	193.05	177.25	164.70	146.13	133.13	123.61	7000
8000	720.19	497.20	386.00	319.51	275.37	244.01	220.63	202.57	188.23	167.00	152.14	141.26	8000
9000	810.21	559.35	434.25	359.45	309.79	274.51	248.21	227.89	211.76	187.87	171.16	158.92	9000
10000	900.23	621.50	482.50	399.39	344.21	305.01	275.78	253.21	235.29	208.75	190.18	176.58	10000
15000	1350.34	932.25	723.75	599.08	516.32	457.51	413.67	379.81	352.93	313.12	285.26	264.86	15000
20000	1800.46	1243.00	964.99	798.77	688.42	610.02	551.56	506.41	470.57	417.49	380.35	353.15	20000
25000	2250.57	1553.75	1206.24	998.46	860.53	762.52	689.45	633.02	588.21	521.87	475.44	441.44	25000
30000	2700.68	1864.50	1447.49	1198.15	1032.63	915.02	827.34	759.62	705.85	626.24	570.52	529.72	30000
35000	3150.79	2175.25	1688.73	1397.84	1204.74	1067.53	965.23	886.22	823.49	730.61	665.61	618.01	35000
40000	3600.91	2485.99	1929.98	1597.53	1376.84	1220.03	1103.12	1012.82	941.14	834.98	760.70	706.30	40000
45000	4051.02	2796.74	2171.23	1797.22	1548.95	1372.53	1241.01	1139.42	1058.78	939.35	855.78	794.58	45000
50000	4501.13	3107.49	2412.48	1996.91	1721.05	1525.03	1378.90	1266.03	1176.42	1043.73	950.87	882.87	50000
60000	5401.36	3728.99	2894.97	2396.29	2065.26	1830.04	1654.68	1519.23	1411.70	1252.47	1141.04	1059.44	60000
75000	6751.70	4661.23	3618.71	2995.36	2581.58	2287.55	2068.35	1899.04	1764.63	1565.59	1426.30	1324.30	75000
100000	9002.26	6214.98	4824.95	3993.81	3442.10	3050.06	2757.80	2532.05	2352.83	2087.45	1901.74	1765.73	100000
125000	11252.82	7768.72	6031.18	4992.26	4302.63	3812.58	3447.25	3165.06	2941.04	2609.31	2377.17	2207.16	125000
150000	13503.39	9322.46	7237.42	5990.71	5163.15	4575.09	4136.70	3798.07	3529.25	3131.17	2852.60	2648.59	150000
175000	15753.95	10876.21	8443.65	6989.16	6023.68	5337.61	4826.15	4431.08	4117.45	3653.03	3328.03	3090.02	175000
200000	18004.51	12429.95	9649.89	7987.61	6884.20	6100.12	5515.60	5064.09	4705.66	4174.89	3803.47	3531.46	200000
250000	22505.64	15537.44	12062.36	9984.51	8605.25	7625.15	6894.49	6330.11	5882.08	5218.61	4754.33	4414.32	250000

Amount	9.0 Years	10.0 Years	11.0 Years	12.0 Years	13.0 Years	14.0 Years	15.0 Years	16.0 Years	20.0 Years	30.0 Years	40.0 Years	50.0 Years	Amount
100	1.67	1.59	1.52	1.47	1.43	1.40	1.37	1.35	1.28	1.23	1.22	1.21	100
200	3.33	3.17	3.04	2.94	2.86	2.79	2.74	2.69	2.56	2.45	2.43	2.42	200
300	4.99	4.75	4.56	4.41	4.29	4.19	4.10	4.03	3.84	3.68	3.64	3.63	300
400	6.66	6.34	6.08	5.88	5.72	5.58	5.47	5.37	5.12	4.90	4.85	4.84	400
500	8.32	7.92	7.60	7.35	7.14	6.97	6.83	6.72	6.40	6.13	6.07	6.05	500
600	9.98	9.50	9.12	8.82	8.57	8.37	8.20	8.06	7.68	7.35	7.28	7.26	600
700	11.64	11.09	10.64	10.29	10.00	9.76	9.56	9.40	8.96	8.58	8.49	8.47	700
800	13.31	12.67	12.16	11.76	11.43	11.15	10.93	10.74	10.24	9.80	9.70	9.68	800
900	14.97	14.25	13.68	13.22	12.85	12.55	12.29	12.08	11.52	11.03	10.91	10.89	900
1000	16.63	15.83	15.20	14.69	14.28	13.94	13.66	13.43	12.80	12.25	12.13	12.10	1000
2000	33.26	31.66	30.40	29.38	28.56	27.88	27.32	26.85	25.60	24.50	24.25	24.19	2000
3000	49.89	47.49	45.59	44.07	42.83	41.81	40.97	40.27	38.40	36.74	36.37	36.28	3000
4000	66.52	63.32	60.79	58.76	57.11	55.75	54.63	53.69	51.20	48.99	48.49	48.37	4000
5000	83.14	79.15	75.99	73.45	71.38	69.69	68.28	67.11	64.00	61.23	60.61	60.47	5000
6000	99.77	94.98	91.18	88.14	85.66	83.62	81.94	80.53	76.80	73.48	72.73	72.56	6000
7000	116.40	110.81	106.38	102.82	99.93	97.56	95.59	93.95	89.60	85.72	84.85	84.65	7000
8000	133.03	126.63	121.58	117.51	114.21	111.49	109.25	107.37	102.40	97.97	96.98	96.74	8000
9000	149.65	142.46	136.77	132.20	128.48	125.43	122.90	120.79	115.20	110.22	109.10	108.84	9000
10000	166.28	158.29	151.97	146.89	142.76	139.37	136.56	134.21	128.00	122.46	121.22	120.93	10000
15000	249.42	237.44	227.95	220.33	214.14	209.05	204.83	201.32	192.00	183.69	181.82	181.39	15000
20000	332.56	316.58	303.93	293.77	285.51	278.73	273.11	268.42	256.00	244.92	242.43	241.85	20000
25000	415.70	395.72	379.92	367.22	356.89	348.41	341.38	335.52	320.00	306.14	303.04	302.31	25000
30000	498.84	474.87	455.90	440.66	428.27	418.09	409.66	402.63	384.00	367.37	363.64	362.77	30000
35000	581.98	554.01	531.88	514.10	499.64	487.77	477.93	469.73	448.00	428.60	424.25	423.24	35000
40000	665.11	633.15	607.86	587.54	571.02	557.45	546.21	536.83	512.00	489.83	484.86	483.70	40000
45000	748.25	712.30	683.84	660.99	642.40	627.13	614.48	603.94	576.00	551.06	545.46	544.16	45000
50000	831.39	791.44	759.83	734.43	713.77	696.81	682.76	671.04	640.00	612.28	606.07	604.62	50000
60000	997.67	949.73	911.79	881.31	856.53	836.17	819.31	805.25	768.00	734.74	727.28	725.54	60000
75000	1247.08	1187.16	1139.74	1101.64	1070.66	1045.21	1024.13	1006.56	960.00	918.42	909.10	906.93	75000
100000	1662.78	1582.87	1519.65	1468.85	1427.54	1393.61	1365.51	1342.08	1280.00	1224.56	1212.14	1209.24	100000
125000	2078.47	1978.59	1899.56	1836.07	1784.43	1742.01	1706.88	1677.59	1600.00	1530.70	1515.17	1511.54	125000
150000	2494.16	2374.31	2279.47	2203.28	2141.31	2090.41	2048.26	2013.11	1920.00	1836.84	1818.20	1813.85	150000
175000	2909.86	2770.02	2659.38	2570.49	2498.20	2438.81	2389.63	2348.63	2240.00	2142.98	2121.24	2116.16	175000
200000	3325.55	3165.74	3039.29	2937.70	2855.08	2787.21	2731.01	2684.15	2560.00	2449.12	2424.27	2418.47	200000
250000	4156.93	3957.17	3799.11	3672.13	3568.85	3484.01	3413.76	3355.18	3200.00	3061.39	3030.34	3023.08	250000

Amount	1.0 Year	1.5 Years	2.0 Years	2.5 Years	3.0 Years	3.5 Years	4.0 Years	4.5 Years	5.0 Years	6.0 Years	7.0 Years	8.0 Years	Amount
100	9.02	6.23	4.84	4.01	3.46	3.07	2.78	2.55	2.37	2.11	1.92	1.79	100
200	18.03	12.46	9.68	8.02	6.91	6.13	5.55	5.09	4.74	4.21	3.84	3.57	200
300	27.05	18.69	14.52	12.02	10.37	9.19	8.32	7.64	7.10	6.31	5.75	5.35	300
400	36.06	24.91	19.35	16.03	13.82	12.25	11.09	10.18	9.47	8.41	7.67	7.13	400
500	45.08	31.14	24.19	20.03	17.28	15.32	13.86	12.73	11.83	10.51	9.58	8.91	500
600	54.09	37.37	29.03	24.04	20.73	18.38	16.63	15.27	14.20	12.61	11.50	10.69	600
700	63.10	43.59	33.86	28.05	24.19	21.44	19.40	17.82	16.57	14.71	13.41	12.47	700
800	72.12	49.82	38.70	32.05	27.64	24.50	22.17	20.36	18.93	16.81	15.33	14.25	800
900	81.13	56.05	43.54	36.06	31.09	27.57	24.94	22.91	21.30	18.91	17.25	16.03	900
1000	90.15	62.27	48.37	40.06	34.55	30.63	27.71	25.45	23.66	21.01	19.16	17.81	1000
2000	180.29	124.54	96.74	80.12	69.09	61.25	55.41	50.90	47.32	42.02	38.32	35.61	2000
3000	270.43	186.81	145.11	120.18	103.63	91.88	83.12	76.35	70.98	63.03	57.48	53.41	3000
4000	360.57	249.07	193.48	160.24	138.18	122.50	110.82	101.80	94.64	84.04	76.63	71.21	4000
5000	450.71	311.34	241.84	200.30	172.72	153.13	138.53	127.25	118.30	105.05	95.79	89.01	5000
6000	540.85	373.61	290.21	240.35	207.26	183.75	166.23	152.70	141.96	126.06	114.95	106.81	6000
7000	630.99	435.88	338.58	280.41	241.81	214.38	193.93	178.15	165.62	147.07	134.10	124.61	7000
8000	721.13	498.14	386.95	320.47	276.35	245.00	221.64	203.60	189.28	168.08	153.26	142.41	8000
9000	811.27	560.41	435.32	360.53	310.89	275.63	249.34	229.04	212.94	189.09	172.42	160.21	9000
10000	901.41	622.68	483.68	400.59	345.44	306.25	277.05	254.49	236.59	210.10	191.57	178.02	10000
15000	1352.11	934.01	725.52	600.88	518.15	459.38	415.57	381.74	354.89	315.15	287.36	267.02	15000
20000	1802.81	1245.35	967.36	801.17	690.87	612.50	554.09	508.98	473.18	420.19	383.14	356.03	20000
25000	2253.51	1556.68	1209.20	1001.46	863.58	765.62	692.61	636.23	591.48	525.24	478.92	445.03	25000
30000	2704.22	1868.02	1451.04	1201.75	1036.30	918.75	831.13	763.47	709.77	630.29	574.71	534.04	30000
35000	3154.92	2179.36	1692.88	1402.04	1209.01	1071.87	969.65	890.71	828.07	735.34	670.49	623.04	35000
40000	3605.62	2490.69	1934.72	1602.33	1381.73	1224.99	1108.17	1017.96	946.36	840.38	766.28	712.05	40000
45000	4056.32	2802.03	2176.56	1802.62	1554.44	1378.12	1246.69	1145.20	1064.66	945.43	862.06	801.05	45000
50000	4507.02	3113.36	2418.40	2002.91	1727.16	1531.24	1385.21	1272.45	1182.95	1050.48	957.84	890.06	50000
60000	5408.43	3736.04	2902.08	2403.50	2072.59	1837.49	1662.26	1526.93	1419.54	1260.57	1149.41	1068.07	60000
75000	6760.53	4670.04	3627.60	3004.37	2590.73	2296.86	2077.82	1908.67	1774.42	1575.72	1436.76	1335.08	75000
100000	9014.04	6226.72	4836.80	4005.82	3454.31	3062.47	2770.42	2544.89	2365.90	2100.95	1915.68	1780.11	100000
125000	11267.55	7783.40	6046.00	5007.28	4317.88	3828.09	3463.03	3181.11	2957.37	2626.19	2394.60	2225.13	125000
150000	13521.06	9340.08	7255.20	6008.73	5181.46	4593.71	4155.63	3817.33	3548.84	3151.43	2873.52	2670.16	150000
175000	15774.57	10896.76	8464.40	7010.19	6045.03	5359.32	4848.24	4453.55	4140.31	3676.66	3352.44	3115.19	175000
200000	18028.08	12453.44	9673.60	8011.64	6908.61	6124.94	5540.84	5089.77	4731.79	4201.90	3831.36	3560.21	200000
250000	22535.10	15566.80	12091.99	10014.55	8635.76	7656.17	6926.05	6362.21	5914.73	5252.38	4789.20	4450.26	250000

Amount	9.0 Years	10.0 Years	11.0 Years	12.0 Years	13.0 Years	14.0 Years	15.0 Years	16.0 Years	20.0 Years	30.0 Years	40.0 Years	50.0 Years	Amount
100	1.68	1.60	1.54	1.49	1.45	1.42	1.39	1.36	1.30	1.25	1.24	1.23	100
200	3.36	3.20	3.08	2.97	2.89	2.83	2.77	2.72	2.60	2.49	2.47	2.46	200
300	5.04	4.80	4.61	4.46	4.34	4.24	4.15	4.08	3.90	3.74	3.70	3.69	300
400	6.72	6.40	6.15	5.94	5.78	5.65	5.54	5.44	5.20	4.98	4.94	4.92	400
500	8.39	8.00	7.68	7.43	7.22	7.06	6.92	6.80	6.50	6.23	6.17	6.15	500
600	10.07	9.59	9.22	8.91	8.67	8.47	8.30	8.16	7.80	7.47	7.40	7.38	600
700	11.75	11.19	10.75	10.40	10.11	9.88	9.68	9.52	9.09	8.72	8.63	8.61	700
800	13.43	12.79	12.29	11.88	11.56	11.29	11.07	10.88	10.39	9.96	9.87	9.84	800
900	15.10	14.39	13.82	13.37	13.00	12.70	12.45	12.24	11.69	11.21	11.10	11.07	900
1000	16.78	15.99	15.36	14.85	14.44	14.11	13.83	13.60	12.99	12.45	12.33	12.30	1000
2000	33.56	31.97	30.71	29.70	28.88	28.21	27.66	27.19	25.97	24.89	24.66	24.60	2000
3000	50.33	47.95	46.06	44.55	43.32	42.31	41.48	40.79	38.96	37.34	36.99	36.90	3000
4000	67.11	63.93	61.41	59.40	57.76	56.42	55.31	54.38	51.94	49.78	49.31	49.20	4000
5000	83.88	79.91	76.77	74.25	72.20	70.52	69.13	67.97	64.92	62.23	61.64	61.50	5000
6000	100.66	95.89	92.12	89.09	86.64	84.62	82.96	81.57	77.91	74.67	73.97	73.80	6000
7000	117.43	111.87	107.47	103.94	101.08	98.72	96.78	95.16	90.89	87.12	86.29	86.10	7000
8000	134.21	127.85	122.82	118.79	115.51	112.83	110.61	108.76	103.87	99.56	98.62	98.40	8000
9000	150.99	143.83	138.18	133.64	129.95	126.93	124.43	122.35	116.86	112.01	110.95	110.70	9000
10000	167.76	159.81	153.53	148.49	144.39	141.03	138.26	135.94	129.84	124.45	123.27	123.00	10000
15000	251.64	239.72	230.29	222.73	216.59	211.55	207.38	203.91	194.76	186.68	184.91	184.50	15000
20000	335.52	319.62	307.05	296.97	288.78	282.06	276.51	271.88	259.68	248.90	246.54	246.00	20000
25000	419.40	399.52	383.82	371.21	360.97	352.58	345.63	339.85	324.59	311.12	308.17	307.50	25000
30000	503.28	479.43	460.58	445.45	433.17	423.09	414.76	407.82	389.51	373.35	369.81	369.00	30000
35000	587.15	559.33	537.34	519.69	505.36	493.60	483.88	475.79	454.43	435.57	431.44	430.50	35000
40000	671.03	639.23	614.10	593.94	577.55	564.12	553.01	543.76	519.35	497.80	493.07	491.99	40000
45000	754.91	719.14	690.86	668.18	649.75	634.63	622.13	611.73	584.26	560.02	554.71	553.49	45000
50000	838.79	799.04	767.63	742.42	721.94	705.15	691.26	679.69	649.18	622.24	616.34	614.99	50000
60000	1006.55	958.85	921.15	890.90	866.33	846.17	829.51	815.63	779.02	746.69	739.61	737.99	60000
75000	1258.18	1198.56	1151.44	1113.62	1082.91	1057.72	1036.88	1019.54	973.77	933.36	924.51	922.48	75000
100000	1677.58	1598.08	1535.25	1484.83	1443.88	1410.29	1382.51	1359.38	1298.36	1244.46	1232.67	1229.98	100000
125000	2096.97	1997.60	1919.06	1856.04	1804.85	1762.86	1728.13	1699.23	1622.95	1555.60	1540.84	1537.47	125000
150000	2516.36	2397.12	2302.87	2227.24	2165.82	2115.43	2073.76	2039.07	1947.54	1866.72	1849.01	1844.96	150000
175000	2935.75	2796.63	2686.69	2598.45	2526.78	2468.00	2419.39	2378.92	2272.13	2177.84	2157.17	2152.46	175000
200000	3355.15	3196.15	3070.49	2969.66	2887.75	2820.57	2765.01	2718.76	2596.72	2488.96	2465.34	2459.95	200000
250000	4193.93	3995.19	3838.11	3712.07	3609.69	3525.71	3456.26	3398.45	3245.89	3111.19	3081.67	3074.94	250000

Amount	1.0 Year	1.5 Years	2.0 Years	2.5 Years	3.0 Years	3.5 Years	4.0 Years	4.5 Years	5.0 Years	6.0 Years	7.0 Years	8.0 Years	Amount
100	9.03	6.24	4.85	4.02	3.47	3.08	2.79	2.56	2.38	2.12	1.93	1.80	100
200	18.06	12.48	9.70	8.04	6.94	6.15	5.57	5.12	4.76	4.23	3.86	3.59	200
300	27.08	18.72	14.55	12.06	10.40	9.23	8.35	7.68	7.14	6.35	5.79	5.39	300
400	36.11	24.96	19.40	16.08	13.87	12.30	11.14	10.24	9.52	8.46	7.72	7.18	400
500	45.13	31.20	24.25	20.09	17.34	15.38	13.92	12.79	11.90	10.58	9.65	8.98	500
600	54.16	37.44	29.10	24.11	20.80	18.45	16.70	15.35	14.28	12.69	11.58	10.77	600
700	63.19	43.67	33.95	28.13	24.27	21.53	19.49	17.91	16.66	14.81	13.51	12.57	700
800	72.21	49.91	38.79	32.15	27.74	24.60	22.27	20.47	19.04	16.92	15.44	14.36	800
900	81.24	56.15	43.64	36.17	31.20	27.68	25.05	23.02	21.42	19.04	17.37	16.16	900
1000	90.26	62.39	48.49	40.18	34.67	30.75	27.84	25.58	23.79	21.15	19.30	17.95	1000
2000	180.52	124.77	96.98	80.36	69.34	61.50	55.67	51.16	47.58	42.30	38.60	35.90	2000
3000	270.78	187.16	145.46	120.54	104.00	92.25	83.50	76.74	71.37	63.44	57.90	53.84	3000
4000	361.04	249.54	193.95	160.72	138.67	123.00	111.33	102.32	95.16	84.59	77.19	71.79	4000
5000	451.30	311.93	242.44	200.90	173.33	153.75	139.16	127.89	118.95	105.73	96.49	89.73	5000
6000	541.55	374.31	290.92	241.08	208.00	184.50	166.99	153.47	142.74	126.88	115.79	107.68	6000
7000	631.81	436.70	339.41	281.25	242.66	215.25	194.82	179.05	166.53	148.02	135.08	125.62	7000
8000	722.07	499.08	387.90	321.43	277.33	246.00	222.65	204.63	190.32	169.17	154.38	143.57	8000
9000	812.33	561.47	436.38	361.61	311.99	276.75	250.48	230.20	214.11	190.31	173.68	161.51	9000
10000	902.59	623.85	484.87	401.79	346.66	307.50	278.31	255.78	237.90	211.46	192.97	179.46	10000
15000	1353.88	935.78	727.30	602.68	519.98	461.24	417.47	383.67	356.85	317.18	289.46	269.19	15000
20000	1805.17	1247.70	969.74	803.58	693.31	614.99	556.62	511.56	475.80	422.91	385.94	358.91	20000
25000	2256.46	1559.62	1212.17	1004.47	866.64	768.73	695.77	639.45	594.75	528.63	482.42	448.64	25000
30000	2707.75	1871.55	1454.60	1205.36	1039.96	922.48	834.93	767.33	713.70	634.36	578.91	538.37	30000
35000	3159.05	2183.47	1697.04	1406.25	1213.29	1076.22	974.08	895.22	832.65	740.08	675.39	628.09	35000
40000	3610.34	2495.40	1939.47	1607.15	1386.62	1229.97	1113.23	1023.11	951.60	845.81	771.88	717.82	40000
45000	4061.63	2807.32	2181.90	1808.04	1559.94	1383.71	1252.39	1151.00	1070.55	951.53	868.36	807.55	45000
50000	4512.92	3119.24	2424.34	2008.93	1733.27	1537.46	1391.54	1278.89	1189.50	1057.26	964.84	897.28	50000
60000	5415.50	3743.09	2909.20	2410.72	2079.92	1844.95	1669.85	1534.66	1427.40	1268.71	1157.81	1076.73	60000
75000	6769.38	4678.86	3636.50	3013.40	2599.90	2306.18	2087.31	1918.33	1784.25	1585.88	1447.26	1345.91	75000
100000	9025.84	6238.48	4848.67	4017.86	3466.54	3074.91	2783.08	2557.77	2379.00	2114.51	1929.68	1794.55	100000
125000	11282.29	7798.10	6060.84	5022.32	4333.17	3843.64	3478.85	3197.21	2973.75	2643.13	2412.10	2243.18	125000
150000	13538.75	9357.72	7273.00	6026.79	5199.80	4612.36	4174.62	3836.65	3568.49	3171.76	2894.52	2691.82	150000
175000	15795.21	10917.34	8485.17	7031.25	6066.44	5381.09	4870.39	4476.09	4163.24	3700.38	3376.94	3140.45	175000
200000	18051.67	12476.96	9697.33	8035.71	6933.07	6149.82	5566.15	5115.53	4757.99	4229.01	3859.36	3589.09	200000
250000	22564.58	15596.20	12121.67	10044.64	8666.34	7687.27	6957.69	6394.41	5947.49	5286.26	4824.19	4486.36	250000

Amount	9.0 Years	10.0 Years	11.0 Years	12.0 Years	13.0 Years	14.0 Years	15.0 Years	16.0 Years	20.0 Years	30.0 Years	40.0 Years	50.0 Years	Amount
100	1.70	1.62	1.56	1.51	1.47	1.43	1.40	1.38	1.32	1.27	1.26	1.26	100
200	3.39	3.23	3.11	3.01	2.93	2.86	2.80	2.76	2.64	2.53	2.51	2.51	200
300	5.08	4.85	4.66	4.51	4.39	4.29	4.20	4.14	3.96	3.80	3.76	3.76	300
400	6.77	6.46	6.21	6.01	5.85	5.71	5.60	5.51	5.27	5.06	5.02	5.01	400
500	8.47	8.07	7.76	7.51	7.31	7.14	7.00	6.89	6.59	6.33	6.27	6.26	500
600	10.16	9.69	9.31	9.01	8.77	8.57	8.40	8.27	7.91	7.59	7.52	7.51	600
700	11.85	11.30	10.86	10.51	10.23	9.99	9.80	9.64	9.22	8.86	8.78	8.76	700
800	13.54	12.91	12.41	12.01	11.69	11.42	11.20	11.02	10.54	10.12	10.03	10.01	800
900	15.24	14.53	13.96	13.51	13.15	12.85	12.60	12.40	11.86	11.38	11.28	11.26	900
1000	16.93	16.14	15.51	15.01	14.61	14.28	14.00	13.77	13.17	12.65	12.54	12.51	1000
2000	33.85	32.27	31.02	30.02	29.21	28.55	28.00	27.54	26.34	25.29	25.07	25.02	2000
3000	50.78	48.41	46.53	45.03	43.81	42.82	41.99	41.31	39.51	37.94	37.60	37.53	3000
4000	67.70	64.54	62.04	60.04	58.42	57.09	55.99	55.08	52.68	50.58	50.13	50.03	4000
5000	84.63	80.67	77.55	75.05	73.02	71.36	69.98	68.84	65.84	63.23	62.67	62.54	5000
6000	101.55	96.81	93.06	90.06	87.62	85.63	83.98	82.61	79.01	75.87	75.20	75.05	6000
7000	118.48	112.94	108.57	105.07	102.23	99.90	97.98	96.38	92.18	88.52	87.73	87.56	7000
8000	135.40	129.07	124.08	120.08	116.83	114.17	111.97	110.15	105.35	101.16	100.26	100.06	8000
9000	152.32	145.21	139.59	135.08	131.43	128.44	125.97	123.91	118.52	113.80	112.80	112.57	9000
10000	169.25	161.34	155.10	150.09	146.03	142.71	139.96	137.68	131.68	126.45	125.33	125.08	10000
15000	253.87	242.01	232.64	225.14	219.05	214.06	209.94	206.52	197.52	189.67	187.99	187.61	15000
20000	338.49	322.67	310.19	300.18	292.06	285.41	279.92	275.36	263.36	252.89	250.65	250.15	20000
25000	423.11	403.34	387.73	375.22	365.08	356.76	349.90	344.20	329.20	316.12	313.31	312.69	25000
30000	507.74	484.01	465.28	450.27	438.09	428.12	419.88	413.04	395.04	379.34	375.97	375.22	30000
35000	592.36	564.68	542.83	525.31	511.11	499.47	489.86	481.87	460.88	442.56	438.63	437.76	35000
40000	676.98	645.34	620.37	600.36	584.12	570.82	559.84	550.71	526.72	505.78	501.29	500.29	40000
45000	761.60	726.01	697.92	675.40	657.13	642.17	629.82	619.55	592.56	569.00	563.96	562.83	45000
50000	846.22	806.68	775.46	750.44	730.15	713.52	699.80	688.39	658.40	632.23	626.62	625.37	50000
60000	1015.47	968.01	930.55	900.53	876.18	856.23	839.76	826.07	790.08	758.67	751.94	750.44	60000
75000	1269.33	1210.02	1163.19	1125.66	1095.22	1070.28	1049.70	1032.58	987.60	948.34	939.92	938.05	75000
100000	1692.44	1613.35	1550.92	1500.88	1460.29	1427.04	1399.59	1376.77	1316.79	1264.45	1253.23	1250.73	100000
125000	2115.55	2016.69	1938.65	1876.10	1825.36	1783.80	1749.49	1720.97	1645.99	1580.56	1566.54	1563.41	125000
150000	2538.66	2420.03	2326.38	2251.32	2190.44	2140.56	2099.39	2065.16	1975.19	1896.67	1879.84	1876.09	150000
175000	2961.76	2823.37	2714.11	2626.54	2555.51	2497.32	2449.28	2409.35	2304.39	2212.78	2193.15	2188.77	175000
200000	3384.87	3226.70	3101.83	3001.76	2920.58	2854.08	2799.18	2753.54	2633.58	2528.89	2506.45	2501.45	200000
250000	4231.09	4033.38	3877.29	3752.20	3650.72	3567.60	3498.97	3441.93	3291.98	3161.12	3133.07	3126.82	250000

Amount	1.0 Year	1.5 Years	2.0 Years	2.5 Years	3.0 Years	3.5 Years	4.0 Years	4.5 Years	5.0 Years	6.0 Years	7.0 Years	8.0 Years	Amount
100	9.04	6.26	4.87	4.03	3.48	3.09	2.80	2.58	2.40	2.13	1.95	1.81	100
200	18.08	12.51	9.73	8.06	6.96	6.18	5.60	5.15	4.79	4.26	3.89	3.62	200
300	27.12	18.76	14.59	12.09	10.44	9.27	8.39	7.72	7.18	6.39	5.84	5.43	300
400	36.16	25.01	19.45	16.12	13.92	12.35	11.19	10.29	9.57	8.52	7.78	7.24	400
500	45.19	31.26	24.31	20.15	17.40	15.44	13.98	12.86	11.97	10.65	9.72	9.05	500
600	54.23	37.51	29.17	24.18	20.88	18.53	16.78	15.43	14.36	12.77	11.67	10.86	600
700	63.27	43.76	34.03	28.21	24.36	21.62	19.58	18.00	16.75	14.90	13.61	12.67	700
800	72.31	50.01	38.89	32.24	27.84	24.70	22.37	20.57	19.14	17.03	15.55	14.48	800
900	81.34	56.26	43.75	36.27	31.31	27.79	25.17	23.14	21.53	19.16	17.50	16.29	900
1000	90.38	62.51	48.61	40.30	34.79	30.88	27.96	25.71	23.93	21.29	19.44	18.10	1000
2000	180.76	125.01	97.22	80.60	69.58	61.75	55.92	51.42	47.85	42.57	38.88	36.19	2000
3000	271.13	187.51	145.82	120.90	104.37	92.63	83.88	77.13	71.77	63.85	58.32	54.28	3000
4000	361.51	250.02	194.43	161.20	139.16	123.50	111.84	102.83	95.69	85.13	77.75	72.37	4000
5000	451.89	312.52	243.03	201.50	173.94	154.37	139.79	128.54	119.61	106.41	97.19	90.46	5000
6000	542.26	375.02	291.64	241.80	208.73	185.25	167.75	154.25	143.53	127.69	116.63	108.55	6000
7000	632.64	437.52	340.24	282.10	243.52	216.12	195.71	179.95	167.45	148.97	136.07	126.64	7000
8000	723.02	500.03	388.85	322.40	278.31	246.99	223.67	205.66	191.38	170.25	155.50	144.73	8000
9000	813.39	562.53	437.45	362.70	313.10	277.87	251.62	231.37	215.30	191.53	174.94	162.82	9000
10000	903.77	625.03	486.06	403.00	347.88	308.74	279.58	257.07	239.22	212.82	194.38	180.91	10000
15000	1355.65	937.54	729.09	604.49	521.82	463.11	419.37	385.61	358.83	319.22	291.56	271.36	15000
20000	1807.53	1250.06	972.12	805.99	695.76	617.48	559.16	514.14	478.43	425.63	388.75	361.81	20000
25000	2259.41	1562.57	1215.14	1007.48	869.70	771.85	698.95	642.67	598.04	532.03	485.94	452.26	25000
30000	2711.29	1875.08	1458.17	1208.98	1043.64	926.22	838.73	771.21	717.65	638.44	583.12	542.72	30000
35000	3163.18	2187.59	1701.20	1410.47	1217.58	1080.59	978.52	899.74	837.25	744.84	680.31	633.17	35000
40000	3615.06	2500.11	1944.23	1611.97	1391.52	1234.95	1118.31	1028.28	956.86	851.25	777.50	723.62	40000
45000	4066.94	2812.62	2187.25	1813.47	1565.46	1389.32	1258.10	1156.81	1076.47	957.65	874.68	814.07	45000
50000	4518.82	3125.13	2430.28	2014.96	1739.40	1543.69	1397.89	1285.34	1196.07	1064.06	971.87	904.52	50000
60000	5422.58	3750.16	2916.34	2417.95	2087.28	1852.43	1677.46	1542.41	1435.29	1276.87	1166.24	1085.43	60000
75000	6778.23	4687.69	3645.42	3022.44	2609.10	2315.54	2096.83	1928.01	1794.11	1596.08	1457.80	1356.78	75000
100000	9037.64	6250.26	4860.56	4029.92	3478.79	3087.38	2795.77	2570.68	2392.14	2128.11	1943.73	1809.04	100000
125000	11297.05	7812.82	6075.69	5037.39	4348.49	3859.22	3494.71	3213.35	2990.17	2660.13	2429.67	2261.30	125000
150000	13556.45	9375.38	7290.83	6044.87	5218.19	4631.07	4193.65	3856.02	3588.21	3192.16	2915.60	2713.56	150000
175000	15815.86	10937.94	8505.97	7052.35	6087.88	5402.91	4892.59	4498.69	4186.24	3724.18	3401.53	3165.82	175000
200000	18075.27	12500.51	9721.11	8059.83	6957.58	6174.75	5591.53	5141.36	4784.28	4256.21	3887.46	3618.08	200000
250000	22594.09	15625.63	12151.38	10074.78	8696.97	7718.44	6989.41	6426.69	5980.34	5320.26	4859.33	4522.60	250000

Amount	9.0 Years	10.0 Years	11.0 Years	12.0 Years	13.0 Years	14.0 Years	15.0 Years	16.0 Years	20.0 Years	30.0 Years	40.0 Years	50.0 Years	Amount
100	1.71	1.63	1.57	1.52	1.48	1.45	1.42	1.40	1.34	1.29	1.28	1.28	100
200	3.42	3.26	3.14	3.04	2.96	2.89	2.84	2.79	2.68	2.57	2.55	2.55	200
300	5.13	4.89	4.70	4.56	4.44	4.34	4.26	4.19	4.01	3.86	3.83	3.82	300
400	6.83	6.52	6.27	6.07	5.91	5.78	5.67	5.58	5.35	5.14	5.10	5.09	400
500	8.54	8.15	7.84	7.59	7.39	7.22	7.09	6.98	6.68	6.43	6.37	6.36	500
600	10.25	9.78	9.40	9.11	8.87	8.67	8.51	8.37	8.02	7.71	7.65	7.63	600
700	11.96	11.41	10.97	10.62	10.34	10.11	9.92	9.76	9.35	9.00	8.92	8.91	700
800	13.66	13.03	12.54	12.14	11.82	11.56	11.34	11.16	10.69	10.28	10.20	10.18	800
900	15.37	14.66	14.10	13.66	13.30	13.00	12.76	12.55	12.02	11.57	11.47	11.45	900
1000	17.08	16.29	15.67	15.18	14.77	14.44	14.17	13.95	13.36	12.85	12.74	12.72	1000
2000	34.15	32.58	31.34	30.35	29.54	28.88	28.34	27.89	26.71	25.69	25.48	25.43	2000
3000	51.23	48.87	47.00	45.52	44.31	43.32	42.51	41.83	40.06	38.54	38.22	38.15	3000
4000	68.30	65.15	62.67	60.69	59.08	57.76	56.67	55.77	53.42	51.38	50.96	50.86	4000
5000	85.37	81.44	78.34	75.86	73.84	72.20	70.84	69.72	66.77	64.23	63.70	63.58	5000
6000	102.45	97.73	94.00	91.03	88.61	86.64	85.01	83.66	80.12	77.07	76.43	76.29	6000
7000	119.52	114.01	109.67	106.20	103.38	101.08	99.18	97.60	93.48	89.92	89.17	89.01	7000
8000	136.59	130.30	125.34	121.37	118.15	115.52	113.34	111.54	106.83	102.76	101.91	101.72	8000
9000	153.67	146.59	141.00	136.54	132.92	129.95	127.51	125.49	120.18	115.61	114.65	114.44	9000
10000	170.74	162.87	156.67	151.71	147.68	144.39	141.68	139.43	133.53	128.45	127.39	127.15	10000
15000	256.11	244.31	235.00	227.56	221.52	216.59	212.52	209.14	200.30	192.67	191.08	190.73	15000
20000	341.48	325.74	313.34	303.41	295.36	288.78	283.35	278.85	267.06	256.90	254.77	254.30	20000
25000	426.85	407.18	391.67	379.26	369.20	360.97	354.19	348.56	333.83	321.12	318.46	317.88	25000
30000	512.21	488.61	470.00	455.11	443.04	433.17	425.03	418.28	400.59	385.34	382.15	381.45	30000
35000	597.58	570.05	548.34	530.96	516.88	505.36	495.87	487.99	467.36	449.57	445.84	445.02	35000
40000	682.95	651.48	626.67	606.81	590.72	577.56	566.70	557.70	534.12	513.79	509.53	508.60	40000
45000	768.32	732.92	705.00	682.66	664.56	649.75	637.54	627.41	600.89	578.01	573.22	572.17	45000
50000	853.69	814.35	783.33	758.51	738.39	721.94	708.38	697.12	667.65	642.23	636.91	635.75	50000
60000	1024.42	977.22	940.00	910.21	886.07	866.33	850.05	836.55	801.18	770.68	764.29	762.90	60000
75000	1280.53	1221.53	1175.00	1137.76	1107.59	1082.91	1062.57	1045.68	1001.48	963.35	955.36	953.62	75000
100000	1707.37	1628.70	1566.66	1517.01	1476.78	1443.88	1416.75	1394.24	1335.30	1284.46	1273.81	1271.49	100000
125000	2134.21	2035.87	1958.33	1896.26	1845.98	1804.85	1770.94	1742.80	1669.13	1605.58	1592.26	1589.36	125000
150000	2561.05	2443.05	2349.99	2275.51	2215.17	2165.82	2125.13	2091.36	2002.95	1926.69	1910.71	1907.23	150000
175000	2987.89	2850.22	2741.66	2654.76	2584.37	2526.79	2479.32	2439.92	2336.78	2247.81	2229.16	2225.10	175000
200000	3414.73	3257.39	3133.32	3034.01	2953.56	2887.76	2833.50	2788.48	2670.60	2568.92	2547.61	2542.97	200000
250000	4268.41	4071.74	3916.65	3792.51	3691.95	3609.70	3541.88	3485.60	3338.25	3211.15	3184.51	3178.72	250000

Amount	1.0 Year	1.5 Years	2.0 Years	2.5 Years	3.0 Years	3.5 Years	4.0 Years	4.5 Years	5.0 Years	6.0 Years	7.0 Years	8.0 Years	Amount
100	9.05	6.27	4.88	4.05	3.50	3.10	2.81	2.59	2.41	2.15	1.96	1.83	100
200	18.10	12.53	9.75	8.09	6.99	6.20	5.62	5.17	4.82	4.29	3.92	3.65	200
300	27.15	18.79	14.62	12.13	10.48	9.30	8.43	7.76	7.22	6.43	5.88	5.48	300
400	36.20	25.05	19.49	16.17	13.97	12.40	11.24	10.34	9.63	8.57	7.84	7.30	400
500	45.25	31.32	24.37	20.21	17.46	15.50	14.05	12.92	12.03	10.71	9.79	9.12	500
600	54.30	37.58	29.24	24.26	20.95	18.60	16.86	15.51	14.44	12.86	11.75	10.95	600
700	63.35	43.84	34.11	28.30	24.44	21.70	19.66	18.09	16.84	15.00	13.71	12.77	700
800	72.40	50.10	38.98	32.34	27.93	24.80	22.47	20.67	19.25	17.14	15.67	14.59	800
900	81.45	56.36	43.86	36.38	31.42	27.90	25.28	23.26	21.65	19.28	17.63	16.42	900
1000	90.50	62.63	48.73	40.42	34.92	31.00	28.09	25.84	24.06	21.42	19.58	18.24	1000
2000	180.99	125.25	97.45	80.84	69.83	62.00	56.17	51.68	48.11	42.84	39.16	36.48	2000
3000	271.49	187.87	146.18	121.26	104.74	93.00	84.26	77.51	72.16	64.26	58.74	54.71	3000
4000	361.98	250.49	194.90	161.68	139.65	124.00	112.34	103.35	96.22	85.67	78.32	72.95	4000
5000	452.48	313.11	243.63	202.10	174.56	155.00	140.43	129.19	120.27	107.09	97.90	91.18	5000
6000	542.97	375.73	292.35	242.52	209.47	186.00	168.51	155.02	144.32	128.51	117.48	109.42	6000
7000	633.47	438.35	341.08	282.94	244.38	217.00	196.60	180.86	168.38	149.93	137.05	127.66	7000
8000	723.96	500.97	389.80	323.36	279.29	247.99	224.68	206.70	192.43	171.34	156.63	145.89	8000
9000	814.45	563.59	438.53	363.78	314.20	278.99	252.77	232.53	216.48	192.76	176.21	164.13	9000
10000	904.95	626.21	487.25	404.20	349.11	309.99	280.85	258.37	240.54	214.18	195.79	182.36	10000
15000	1357.42	939.31	730.87	606.30	523.67	464.99	421.28	387.55	360.80	321.27	293.68	273.54	15000
20000	1809.89	1252.41	974.50	808.40	698.22	619.98	561.70	516.73	481.07	428.35	391.57	364.72	20000
25000	2262.37	1565.51	1218.12	1010.50	872.77	774.97	702.13	645.91	601.33	535.44	489.46	455.90	25000
30000	2714.84	1878.62	1461.74	1212.60	1047.33	929.97	842.55	775.09	721.60	642.53	587.36	547.08	30000
35000	3167.31	2191.72	1705.36	1414.70	1221.88	1084.96	982.98	904.27	841.87	749.62	685.25	638.26	35000
40000	3619.78	2504.82	1948.99	1616.80	1396.43	1239.95	1123.40	1033.46	962.13	856.70	783.14	729.44	40000
45000	4072.25	2817.92	2192.61	1818.90	1570.99	1394.95	1263.82	1162.64	1082.40	963.79	881.03	820.62	45000
50000	4524.73	3131.02	2436.23	2021.00	1745.54	1549.94	1404.25	1291.82	1202.66	1070.88	978.92	911.80	50000
60000	5429.67	3757.23	2923.48	2425.20	2094.65	1859.93	1685.10	1550.18	1443.20	1285.05	1174.71	1094.16	60000
75000	6787.09	4696.53	3654.35	3031.50	2618.31	2324.91	2106.37	1937.72	1803.99	1606.32	1468.38	1367.70	75000
100000	9049.45	6262.04	4872.46	4041.99	3491.09	3099.88	2808.49	2583.63	2405.32	2141.75	1957.84	1823.60	100000
125000	11311.81	7827.55	6090.57	5052.49	4363.84	3874.84	3510.61	3229.54	3006.65	2677.19	2447.30	2279.50	125000
150000	13574.17	9393.06	7308.69	6062.99	5236.61	4649.81	4212.73	3875.44	3607.98	3212.63	2936.76	2735.39	150000
175000	15836.53	10958.57	8526.80	7073.49	6109.37	5424.78	4914.86	4521.35	4209.31	3748.07	3426.22	3191.29	175000
200000	18098.89	12524.08	9744.91	8083.98	6982.14	6199.75	5616.98	5167.26	4810.64	4283.50	3915.67	3647.19	200000
250000	22623.61	15655.09	12181.14	10104.98	8727.68	7749.68	7021.22	6459.07	6013.30	5354.38	4894.59	4558.99	250000

Amount	9.0 Years	10.0 Years	11.0 Years	12.0 Years	13.0 Years	14.0 Years	15.0 Years	16.0 Years	20.0 Years	30.0 Years	40.0 Years	50.0 Years	Amount
100	1.73	1.65	1.59	1.54	1.50	1.47	1.44	1.42	1.36	1.31	1.30	1.30	100
200	3.45	3.29	3.17	3.07	2.99	2.93	2.87	2.83	2.71	2.61	2.59	2.59	200
300	5.17	4.94	4.75	4.60	4.49	4.39	4.31	4.24	4.07	3.92	3.89	3.88	300
400	6.89	6.58	6.33	6.14	5.98	5.85	5.74	5.65	5.42	5.22	5.18	5.17	400
500	8.62	8.23	7.92	7.67	7.47	7.31	7.17	7.06	6.77	6.53	6.48	6.47	500
600	10.34	9.87	9.50	9.20	8.97	8.77	8.61	8.48	8.13	7.83	7.77	7.76	600
700	12.06	11.51	11.08	10.74	10.46	10.23	10.04	9.89	9.48	9.14	9.07	9.05	700
800	13.78	13.16	12.66	12.27	11.95	11.69	11.48	11.30	10.84	10.44	10.36	10.34	800
900	15.51	14.80	14.25	13.80	13.45	13.15	12.91	12.71	12.19	11.75	11.65	11.64	900
1000	17.23	16.45	15.83	15.34	14.94	14.61	14.34	14.12	13.54	13.05	12.95	12.93	1000
2000	34.45	32.89	31.65	30.67	29.87	29.22	28.68	28.24	27.08	26.10	25.89	25.85	2000
3000	51.68	49.33	47.48	46.00	44.81	43.83	43.02	42.36	40.62	39.14	38.84	38.77	3000
4000	68.90	65.77	63.30	61.33	59.74	58.44	57.36	56.48	54.16	52.19	51.78	51.70	4000
5000	86.12	82.21	79.13	76.67	74.67	73.04	71.70	70.59	67.70	65.23	64.72	64.62	5000
6000	103.35	98.65	94.95	92.00	89.61	87.65	86.04	84.71	81.24	78.28	77.67	77.54	6000
7000	120.57	115.09	110.78	107.33	104.54	102.26	100.38	98.83	94.78	91.32	90.61	90.46	7000
8000	137.79	131.53	126.60	122.66	119.47	116.87	114.72	112.95	108.32	104.37	103.56	103.39	8000
9000	155.02	147.97	142.43	137.99	134.41	131.48	129.06	127.07	121.85	117.41	116.50	116.31	9000
10000	172.24	164.42	158.25	153.33	149.34	146.08	143.40	141.18	135.39	130.46	129.44	129.23	10000
15000	258.36	246.62	237.38	229.99	224.01	219.12	215.10	211.77	203.09	195.68	194.16	193.84	15000
20000	344.48	328.83	316.50	306.65	298.67	292.16	286.80	282.36	270.78	260.91	258.88	258.46	20000
25000	430.59	411.03	395.62	383.31	373.34	365.20	358.50	352.95	338.48	326.13	323.60	323.07	25000
30000	516.71	493.24	474.75	459.97	448.01	438.24	430.20	423.54	406.17	391.36	388.32	387.68	30000
35000	602.83	575.44	553.87	536.63	522.68	511.28	501.90	494.13	473.86	456.59	453.04	452.29	35000
40000	688.95	657.65	632.99	613.29	597.34	584.32	573.60	564.72	541.56	521.81	517.76	516.91	40000
45000	775.06	739.85	712.12	689.95	672.01	657.36	645.30	635.31	609.25	587.04	582.48	581.52	45000
50000	861.18	822.06	791.24	766.61	746.68	730.40	717.00	705.90	676.95	652.26	647.20	646.13	50000
60000	1033.42	986.47	949.49	919.93	896.01	876.48	860.40	847.08	812.33	782.72	776.64	775.36	60000
75000	1291.77	1233.08	1186.86	1149.91	1120.01	1095.60	1075.50	1058.85	1015.42	978.39	970.80	969.19	75000
100000	1722.36	1644.11	1582.48	1533.21	1493.35	1460.79	1434.00	1411.79	1353.89	1304.52	1294.40	1292.26	100000
125000	2152.95	2055.14	1978.10	1916.51	1866.69	1825.99	1792.49	1764.74	1692.36	1630.65	1618.00	1615.32	125000
150000	2583.53	2466.16	2373.72	2299.81	2240.02	2191.19	2150.99	2117.69	2030.83	1956.78	1941.60	1938.38	150000
175000	3014.12	2877.19	2769.34	2683.11	2613.36	2556.39	2509.49	2470.63	2369.30	2282.91	2265.20	2261.45	175000
200000	3444.71	3288.22	3164.95	3066.41	2986.70	2921.58	2867.99	2823.58	2707.77	2609.04	2588.80	2584.51	200000
250000	4305.89	4110.27	3956.19	3833.02	3733.37	3651.98	3584.98	3529.47	3384.71	3261.30	3236.00	3230.63	250000

Amount	1.0 Year	1.5 Years	2.0 Years	2.5 Years	3.0 Years	3.5 Years	4.0 Years	4.5 Years	5.0 Years	6.0 Years	7.0 Years	8.0 Years	Amount
100	9.07	6.28	4.89	4.06	3.51	3.12	2.83	2.60	2.42	2.16	1.98	1.84	100
200	18.13	12.55	9.77	8.11	7.01	6.23	5.65	5.20	4.84	4.32	3.95	3.68	200
300	27.19	18.83	14.66	12.17	10.52	9.34	8.47	7.79	7.26	6.47	5.92	5.52	300
400	36.25	25.10	19.54	16.22	14.02	12.45	11.29	10.39	9.68	8.63	7.89	7.36	400
500	45.31	31.37	24.43	20.28	17.52	15.57	14.11	12.99	12.10	10.78	9.86	9.20	500
600	54.37	37.65	29.31	24.33	21.03	18.68	16.93	15.58	14.52	12.94	11.84	11.03	600
700	63.43	43.92	34.20	28.38	24.53	21.79	19.75	18.18	16.93	15.09	13.81	12.87	700
800	72.50	50.20	39.08	32.44	28.03	24.90	22.57	20.78	19.35	17.25	15.78	14.71	800
900	81.56	56.47	43.96	36.49	31.54	28.02	25.40	23.37	21.77	19.40	17.75	16.55	900
1000	90.62	62.74	48.85	40.55	35.04	31.13	28.22	25.97	24.19	21.56	19.72	18.39	1000
2000	181.23	125.48	97.69	81.09	70.07	62.25	56.43	51.94	48.38	43.11	39.44	36.77	2000
3000	271.84	188.22	146.54	121.63	105.11	93.38	84.64	77.90	72.56	64.67	59.16	55.15	3000
4000	362.46	250.96	195.38	162.17	140.14	124.50	112.85	103.87	96.75	86.22	78.88	73.53	4000
5000	453.07	313.70	244.22	202.71	175.17	155.62	141.07	129.84	120.93	107.78	98.60	91.92	5000
6000	543.68	376.43	293.07	243.25	210.21	186.75	169.28	155.80	145.12	129.33	118.32	110.30	6000
7000	634.29	439.17	341.91	283.79	245.24	217.87	197.49	181.77	169.30	150.89	138.04	128.68	7000
8000	724.91	501.91	390.75	324.33	280.27	249.00	225.70	207.73	193.49	172.44	157.76	147.06	8000
9000	815.52	564.65	439.60	364.87	315.31	280.12	253.92	233.70	217.67	193.99	177.48	165.44	9000
10000	906.13	627.39	488.44	405.41	350.34	311.24	282.13	259.67	241.86	215.55	197.20	183.83	10000
15000	1359.19	941.08	732.66	608.12	525.51	466.86	423.19	389.50	362.79	323.32	295.80	275.74	15000
20000	1812.26	1254.77	976.88	810.82	700.68	622.48	564.25	519.33	483.71	431.09	394.40	367.65	20000
25000	2265.32	1568.46	1221.10	1013.53	875.85	778.10	705.32	649.16	604.64	538.87	493.00	459.56	25000
30000	2718.38	1882.15	1465.32	1216.23	1051.02	933.72	846.38	778.99	725.57	646.64	591.60	551.47	30000
35000	3171.45	2195.85	1709.54	1418.94	1226.19	1089.34	987.44	908.82	846.49	754.41	690.20	643.38	35000
40000	3624.51	2509.54	1953.75	1621.64	1401.35	1244.96	1128.50	1038.65	967.42	862.18	788.80	735.29	40000
45000	4077.57	2823.23	2197.97	1824.34	1576.52	1400.58	1269.56	1168.48	1088.35	969.95	887.40	827.20	45000
50000	4530.63	3136.92	2442.19	2027.05	1751.69	1556.20	1410.63	1298.31	1209.28	1077.73	986.00	919.11	50000
60000	5436.76	3764.30	2930.63	2432.46	2102.03	1867.44	1692.75	1557.97	1451.13	1293.27	1183.20	1102.93	60000
75000	6795.95	4705.38	3663.29	3040.57	2627.53	2334.30	2115.94	1947.47	1813.91	1616.59	1479.00	1378.66	75000
100000	9061.26	6273.84	4884.38	4054.09	3503.38	3112.40	2821.25	2596.62	2418.55	2155.45	1972.00	1838.21	100000
125000	11326.58	7842.30	6105.47	5067.62	4379.22	3890.50	3526.56	3245.77	3023.18	2694.31	2465.00	2297.76	125000
150000	13591.89	9410.75	7326.57	6081.14	5255.06	4668.60	4231.87	3894.93	3627.82	3233.17	2958.00	2757.31	150000
175000	15857.21	10979.21	8547.66	7094.66	6130.91	5446.70	4937.18	4544.08	4232.45	3772.03	3450.99	3216.87	175000
200000	18122.52	12547.67	9768.75	8108.18	7006.75	6224.80	5642.49	5193.23	4837.09	4310.89	3943.99	3676.42	200000
250000	22653.15	15684.59	12210.94	10135.23	8758.44	7781.00	7053.11	6491.54	6046.36	5388.61	4929.99	4595.52	250000

Amount	9.0 Years	10.0 Years	11.0 Years	12.0 Years	13.0 Years	14.0 Years	15.0 Years	16.0 Years	20.0 Years	30.0 Years	40.0 Years	50.0 Years	Amount
100	1.74	1.66	1.60	1.55	1.51	1.48	1.46	1.43	1.38	1.33	1.32	1.32	100
200	3.48	3.32	3.20	3.10	3.02	2.96	2.91	2.86	2.75	2.65	2.64	2.63	200
300	5.22	4.98	4.80	4.65	4.53	4.44	4.36	4.29	4.12	3.98	3.95	3.94	300
400	6.95	6.64	6.40	6.20	6.04	5.92	5.81	5.72	5.50	5.30	5.27	5.26	400
500	8.69	8.30	8.00	7.75	7.55	7.39	7.26	7.15	6.87	6.63	6.58	6.57	500
600	10.43	9.96	9.60	9.30	9.06	8.87	8.71	8.58	8.24	7.95	7.90	7.88	600
700	12.17	11.62	11.19	10.85	10.57	10.35	10.16	10.01	9.61	9.28	9.21	9.20	700
800	13.90	13.28	12.79	12.40	12.08	11.83	11.62	11.44	10.99	10.60	10.53	10.51	800
900	15.64	14.94	14.39	13.95	13.59	13.31	13.07	12.87	12.36	11.93	11.84	11.82	900
1000	17.38	16.60	15.99	15.50	15.10	14.78	14.52	14.30	13.73	13.25	13.16	13.14	1000
2000	34.75	33.20	31.97	30.99	30.20	29.56	29.03	28.59	27.46	26.50	26.31	26.27	2000
3000	52.13	49.79	47.96	46.49	45.30	44.34	43.54	42.89	41.18	39.74	39.46	39.40	3000
4000	69.50	66.39	63.94	61.98	60.40	59.12	58.06	57.18	54.91	52.99	52.61	52.53	4000
5000	86.88	82.98	79.92	77.48	75.50	73.89	72.57	71.48	68.63	66.24	65.76	65.66	5000
6000	104.25	99.58	95.91	92.97	90.60	88.67	87.08	85.77	82.36	79.48	78.91	78.79	6000
7000	121.62	116.18	111.89	108.47	105.70	103.45	101.60	100.06	96.08	92.73	92.06	91.92	7000
8000	139.00	132.77	127.87	123.96	120.80	118.23	116.11	114.36	109.81	105.97	105.21	105.05	8000
9000	156.37	149.37	143.86	139.46	135.90	133.01	130.62	128.65	123.53	119.22	118.36	118.18	9000
10000	173.75	165.96	159.84	154.95	151.00	147.78	145.14	142.95	137.26	132.47	131.51	131.31	10000
15000	260.62	248.94	239.76	232.43	226.50	221.67	217.70	214.42	205.89	198.70	197.26	196.96	15000
20000	347.49	331.92	319.68	309.90	302.00	295.56	290.27	285.89	274.51	264.93	263.01	262.61	20000
25000	434.36	414.90	399.60	387.37	377.50	369.45	362.83	357.36	343.14	331.16	328.76	328.26	25000
30000	521.23	497.88	479.51	464.85	453.00	443.34	435.40	428.83	411.77	397.39	394.51	393.91	30000
35000	608.10	580.86	559.43	542.32	528.50	517.23	507.96	500.30	480.39	463.62	460.26	459.56	35000
40000	694.97	663.84	639.35	619.80	604.00	591.12	580.53	571.77	549.02	529.85	526.01	525.22	40000
45000	781.84	746.82	719.27	697.27	679.50	665.01	653.09	643.24	617.65	596.08	591.76	590.87	45000
50000	868.71	829.80	799.19	774.74	755.00	738.90	725.66	714.71	686.27	662.31	657.51	656.52	50000
60000	1042.45	995.76	959.02	929.69	906.00	886.67	870.79	857.65	823.53	794.78	789.01	787.82	60000
75000	1303.06	1244.69	1198.78	1162.11	1132.50	1108.34	1088.49	1072.06	1029.41	993.47	986.27	984.77	75000
100000	1737.41	1659.59	1598.37	1549.48	1509.99	1477.79	1451.31	1429.42	1372.54	1324.62	1315.02	1313.03	100000
125000	2171.76	2074.49	1997.96	1936.85	1887.49	1847.23	1814.14	1786.77	1715.67	1655.78	1643.77	1641.29	125000
150000	2606.12	2489.38	2397.55	2324.22	2264.99	2216.68	2176.97	2144.12	2058.81	1986.93	1972.53	1969.54	150000
175000	3040.47	2904.28	2797.14	2711.59	2642.48	2586.12	2539.79	2501.47	2401.94	2318.08	2301.28	2297.80	175000
200000	3474.82	3319.17	3196.73	3098.96	3019.98	2955.57	2902.62	2858.83	2745.07	2649.24	2630.04	2626.05	200000
250000	4343.52	4148.97	3995.91	3873.70	3774.97	3694.46	3628.27	3573.53	3431.34	3311.55	3287.54	3282.57	250000

Amount	1.0 Year	1.5 Years	2.0 Years	2.5 Years	3.0 Years	3.5 Years	4.0 Years	4.5 Years	5.0 Years	6.0 Years	7.0 Years	8.0 Years	Amount
100	9.08	6.29	4.90	4.07	3.52	3.13	2.84	2.61	2.44	2.17	1.99	1.86	100
200	18.15	12.58	9.80	8.14	7.04	6.25	5.67	5.22	4.87	4.34	3.98	3.71	200
300	27.22	18.86	14.69	12.20	10.55	9.38	8.51	7.83	7.30	6.51	5.96	5.56	300
400	36.30	25.15	19.59	16.27	14.07	12.50	11.34	10.44	9.73	8.68	7.95	7.42	400
500	45.37	31.43	24.49	20.34	17.58	15.63	14.18	13.05	12.16	10.85	9.94	9.27	500
600	54.44	37.72	29.38	24.40	21.10	18.75	17.01	15.66	14.60	13.02	11.92	11.12	600
700	63.52	44.00	34.28	28.47	24.61	21.88	19.84	18.27	17.03	15.19	13.91	12.98	700
800	72.59	50.29	39.18	32.53	28.13	25.00	22.68	20.88	19.46	17.36	15.89	14.83	800
900	81.66	56.58	44.07	36.60	31.65	28.13	25.51	23.49	21.89	19.53	17.88	16.68	900
1000	90.74	62.86	48.97	40.67	35.16	31.25	28.35	26.10	24.32	21.70	19.87	18.53	1000
2000	181.47	125.72	97.93	81.33	70.32	62.50	56.69	52.20	48.64	43.39	39.73	37.06	2000
3000	272.20	188.57	146.89	121.99	105.48	93.75	85.03	78.29	72.96	65.08	59.59	55.59	3000
4000	362.93	251.43	195.86	162.65	140.63	125.00	113.37	104.39	97.28	86.77	79.45	74.12	4000
5000	453.66	314.29	244.82	203.32	175.79	156.25	141.71	130.49	121.60	108.46	99.32	92.65	5000
6000	544.39	377.14	293.78	243.98	210.95	187.50	170.05	156.58	145.91	130.16	119.18	111.18	6000
7000	635.12	440.00	342.75	284.64	246.10	218.75	198.39	182.68	170.23	151.85	139.04	129.71	7000
8000	725.85	502.86	391.71	325.30	281.26	250.00	226.73	208.78	194.55	173.54	158.90	148.24	8000
9000	816.58	565.71	440.67	365.96	316.42	281.25	255.07	234.87	218.87	195.23	178.76	166.76	9000
10000	907.31	628.57	489.64	406.63	351.58	312.50	283.41	260.97	243.19	216.92	198.63	185.29	10000
15000	1360.97	942.85	734.45	609.94	527.36	468.75	425.11	391.45	364.78	325.38	297.94	277.94	15000
20000	1814.62	1257.13	979.27	813.25	703.15	625.00	566.81	521.93	486.37	433.84	397.25	370.58	20000
25000	2268.28	1571.42	1224.08	1016.56	878.93	781.24	708.51	652.41	607.96	542.30	496.56	463.22	25000
30000	2721.93	1885.70	1468.90	1219.87	1054.72	937.49	850.21	782.90	729.55	650.76	595.87	555.87	30000
35000	3175.59	2199.98	1713.71	1423.18	1230.50	1093.74	991.91	913.38	851.14	759.22	695.18	648.51	35000
40000	3629.24	2514.26	1958.53	1626.49	1406.29	1249.99	1133.62	1043.86	972.73	867.68	794.49	741.16	40000
45000	4082.89	2828.54	2203.34	1829.80	1582.07	1406.23	1275.32	1174.34	1094.32	976.14	893.80	833.80	45000
50000	4536.55	3142.83	2448.16	2033.11	1757.86	1562.48	1417.02	1304.83	1215.91	1084.60	993.11	926.44	50000
60000	5443.86	3771.39	2937.79	2439.73	2109.43	1874.98	1700.42	1565.79	1459.09	1301.52	1191.73	1111.73	60000
75000	6804.82	4714.24	3672.24	3049.66	2636.78	2343.72	2125.53	1957.23	1823.86	1626.89	1489.66	1389.66	75000
100000	9073.09	6285.65	4896.32	4066.21	3515.71	3124.96	2834.03	2609.64	2431.81	2169.19	1986.21	1852.88	100000
125000	11341.36	7857.06	6120.39	5082.77	4394.63	3906.19	3542.54	3262.05	3039.76	2711.49	2482.76	2316.10	125000
150000	13609.63	9428.47	7344.47	6099.32	5273.56	4687.43	4251.05	3914.46	3647.71	3253.78	2979.31	2779.32	150000
175000	15877.91	10999.88	8568.55	7115.87	6152.49	5468.67	4959.55	4566.87	4255.66	3796.08	3475.87	3242.54	175000
200000	18146.18	12571.29	9792.63	8132.42	7031.41	6249.91	5668.06	5219.28	4863.62	4338.37	3972.42	3705.76	200000
250000	22682.72	15714.11	12240.78	10165.53	8789.26	7812.38	7085.08	6524.10	6079.52	5422.97	4965.52	4632.20	250000

Amount	9.0 Years	10.0 Years	11.0 Years	12.0 Years	13.0 Years	14.0 Years	15.0 Years	16.0 Years	20.0 Years	30.0 Years	40.0 Years	50.0 Years	Amount
100	1.76	1.68	1.62	1.57	1.53	1.50	1.47	1.45	1.40	1.35	1.34	1.34	100
200	3.51	3.36	3.23	3.14	3.06	2.99	2.94	2.90	2.79	2.69	2.68	2.67	200
300	5.26	5.03	4.85	4.70	4.59	4.49	4.41	4.35	4.18	4.04	4.01	4.01	300
400	7.02	6.71	6.46	6.27	6.11	5.98	5.88	5.79	5.57	5.38	5.35	5.34	400
500	8.77	8.38	8.08	7.83	7.64	7.48	7.35	7.24	6.96	6.73	6.68	6.67	500
600	10.52	10.06	9.69	9.40	9.17	8.97	8.82	8.69	8.35	8.07	8.02	8.01	600
700	12.27	11.73	11.31	10.97	10.69	10.47	10.29	10.13	9.74	9.42	9.35	9.34	700
800	14.03	13.41	12.92	12.53	12.22	11.96	11.75	11.58	11.14	10.76	10.69	10.68	800
900	15.78	15.08	14.53	14.10	13.75	13.46	13.22	13.03	12.53	12.11	12.03	12.01	900
1000	17.53	16.76	16.15	15.66	15.27	14.95	14.69	14.48	13.92	13.45	13.36	13.34	1000
2000	35.06	33.51	32.29	31.32	30.54	29.90	29.38	28.95	27.83	26.90	26.72	26.68	2000
3000	52.58	50.26	48.43	46.98	45.81	44.85	44.07	43.42	41.74	40.35	40.07	40.02	3000
4000	70.11	67.01	64.58	62.64	61.07	59.80	58.75	57.89	55.66	53.80	53.43	53.36	4000
5000	87.63	83.76	80.72	78.30	76.34	74.75	73.44	72.36	69.57	67.24	66.79	66.70	5000
6000	105.16	100.51	96.86	93.95	91.61	89.70	88.13	86.83	83.48	80.69	80.14	80.03	6000
7000	122.68	117.26	113.01	109.61	106.87	104.64	102.81	101.30	97.39	94.14	93.50	93.37	7000
8000	140.21	134.02	129.15	125.27	122.14	119.59	117.50	115.77	111.31	107.59	106.86	106.71	8000
9000	157.73	150.77	145.29	140.93	137.41	134.54	132.19	130.24	125.22	121.03	120.21	120.05	9000
10000	175.26	167.52	161.44	156.59	152.68	149.49	146.88	144.72	139.13	134.48	133.57	133.39	10000
15000	262.88	251.27	242.15	234.88	229.01	224.23	220.31	217.07	208.69	201.72	200.35	200.08	15000
20000	350.51	335.03	322.87	313.17	305.35	298.97	293.75	289.43	278.26	268.96	267.13	266.77	20000
25000	438.14	418.79	403.58	391.46	381.68	373.72	367.18	361.78	347.82	336.19	333.92	333.46	25000
30000	525.76	502.54	484.30	469.75	458.02	448.46	440.62	434.14	417.38	403.43	400.70	400.15	30000
35000	613.39	586.30	565.02	548.04	534.35	523.20	514.05	506.49	486.94	470.67	467.48	466.84	35000
40000	701.02	670.06	645.73	626.34	610.69	597.94	587.49	578.85	556.51	537.91	534.26	533.53	40000
45000	788.64	753.81	726.45	704.63	687.02	672.69	660.92	651.20	626.07	605.15	601.05	600.22	45000
50000	876.27	837.57	807.16	782.92	763.36	747.43	734.36	723.56	695.63	672.38	667.83	666.91	50000
60000	1051.52	1005.08	968.60	939.50	916.03	896.91	881.23	868.27	834.76	806.86	801.39	800.29	60000
75000	1314.40	1256.35	1210.74	1174.37	1145.03	1121.14	1101.53	1085.34	1043.45	1008.57	1001.74	1000.36	75000
100000	1752.53	1675.14	1614.32	1565.83	1526.71	1494.85	1468.71	1447.12	1391.26	1344.76	1335.65	1333.81	100000
125000	2190.66	2093.92	2017.90	1957.29	1908.39	1868.56	1835.88	1808.89	1739.07	1680.95	1669.57	1667.26	125000
150000	2628.79	2512.70	2421.48	2348.74	2290.06	2242.27	2203.06	2170.67	2086.89	2017.14	2003.48	2000.71	150000
175000	3066.92	2931.48	2825.06	2740.20	2671.74	2615.98	2570.23	2532.45	2434.70	2353.33	2337.39	2334.16	175000
200000	3505.06	3350.27	3228.64	3131.66	3053.41	2989.70	2937.41	2894.23	2782.52	2689.52	2671.30	2667.62	200000
250000	4381.32	4187.83	4035.80	3914.57	3816.77	3737.12	3671.76	3617.78	3478.14	3361.90	3339.13	3334.52	250000

Amount	1.0 Year	1.5 Years	2.0 Years	2.5 Years	3.0 Years	3.5 Years	4.0 Years	4.5 Years	5.0 Years	6.0 Years	7.0 Years	8.0 Years	Amount
100	9.09	6.30	4.91	4.08	3.53	3.14	2.85	2.63	2.45	2.19	2.01	1.87	100
200	18.17	12.60	9.82	8.16	7.06	6.28	5.70	5.25	4.90	4.37	4.01	3.74	200
300	27.26	18.90	14.73	12.24	10.59	9.42	8.55	7.87	7.34	6.55	6.01	5.61	300
400	36.34	25.19	19.64	16.32	14.12	12.56	11.39	10.50	9.79	8.74	8.01	7.48	400
500	45.43	31.49	24.55	20.40	17.65	15.69	14.24	13.12	12.23	10.92	10.01	9.34	500
600	54.51	37.79	29.45	24.48	21.17	18.83	17.09	15.74	14.68	13.10	12.01	11.21	600
700	63.60	44.09	34.36	28.55	24.70	21.97	19.93	18.36	17.12	15.29	14.01	13.08	700
800	72.68	50.38	39.27	32.63	28.23	25.11	22.78	20.99	19.57	17.47	16.01	14.95	800
900	81.77	56.68	44.18	36.71	31.76	28.24	25.63	23.61	22.01	19.65	18.01	16.81	900
1000	90.85	62.98	49.09	40.79	35.29	31.38	28.47	26.23	24.46	21.83	20.01	18.68	1000
2000	181.70	125.95	98.17	81.57	70.57	62.76	56.94	52.46	48.91	43.66	40.01	37.36	2000
3000	272.55	188.93	147.25	122.36	105.85	94.13	85.41	78.69	73.36	65.49	60.02	56.03	3000
4000	363.40	251.90	196.34	163.14	141.13	125.51	113.88	104.91	97.81	87.32	80.02	74.71	4000
5000	454.25	314.88	245.42	203.92	176.41	156.88	142.35	131.14	122.26	109.15	100.03	93.39	5000
6000	545.10	377.85	294.50	244.71	211.69	188.26	170.82	157.37	146.71	130.98	120.03	112.06	6000
7000	635.95	440.83	343.58	285.49	246.97	219.63	199.28	183.59	171.16	152.81	140.04	130.74	7000
8000	726.80	503.80	392.67	326.27	282.25	251.01	227.75	209.82	195.61	174.64	160.04	149.41	8000
9000	817.65	566.78	441.75	367.06	317.53	282.38	256.22	236.05	220.06	196.47	180.05	168.09	9000
10000	908.50	629.75	490.83	407.84	352.81	313.76	284.69	262.27	244.52	218.30	200.05	186.77	10000
15000	1362.74	944.62	736.24	611.76	529.21	470.64	427.03	393.41	366.77	327.45	300.08	280.15	15000
20000	1816.99	1259.50	981.66	815.67	705.62	627.51	569.37	524.54	489.03	436.60	400.10	373.53	20000
25000	2271.24	1574.37	1227.07	1019.59	882.02	784.39	711.72	655.68	611.28	545.75	500.12	466.91	25000
30000	2725.48	1889.24	1472.48	1223.51	1058.42	941.27	854.06	786.81	733.54	654.90	600.15	560.29	30000
35000	3179.73	2204.12	1717.90	1427.43	1234.83	1098.14	996.40	917.95	855.79	764.05	700.17	653.67	35000
40000	3633.97	2518.99	1963.31	1631.34	1411.23	1255.02	1138.74	1049.08	978.05	873.19	800.19	747.05	40000
45000	4088.22	2833.86	2208.72	1835.26	1587.63	1411.90	1281.09	1180.22	1100.30	982.34	900.22	840.43	45000
50000	4542.47	3148.74	2454.14	2039.18	1764.03	1568.77	1423.43	1311.35	1222.56	1091.49	1000.24	933.81	50000
60000	5450.96	3778.48	2944.96	2447.01	2116.84	1882.53	1708.11	1573.62	1467.07	1309.79	1200.29	1120.57	60000
75000	6813.70	4723.10	3681.20	3058.77	2646.05	2353.16	2135.14	1967.03	1833.84	1637.23	1500.36	1400.71	75000
100000	9084.93	6297.47	4908.27	4078.35	3528.06	3137.54	2846.85	2622.70	2445.11	2182.98	2000.48	1867.61	100000
125000	11356.16	7871.84	6135.34	5097.94	4410.08	3921.92	3558.57	3278.38	3056.39	2728.72	2500.59	2334.52	125000
150000	13627.39	9446.20	7362.40	6117.53	5292.09	4706.31	4270.28	3934.05	3667.67	3274.46	3000.71	2801.42	150000
175000	15898.62	11020.57	8589.47	7137.12	6174.11	5490.69	4981.99	4589.73	4278.95	3820.21	3500.83	3268.32	175000
200000	18169.85	12594.94	9816.53	8156.70	7056.12	6275.08	5693.70	5245.40	4890.22	4365.95	4000.95	3735.22	200000
250000	22712.31	15743.67	12270.67	10195.88	8820.15	7843.84	7117.13	6556.75	6112.78	5457.43	5001.18	4669.03	250000

Amount	9.0 Years	10.0 Years	11.0 Years	12.0 Years	13.0 Years	14.0 Years	15.0 Years	16.0 Years	20.0 Years	30.0 Years	40.0 Years	50.0 Years	Amount
100	1.77	1.70	1.64	1.59	1.55	1.52	1.49	1.47	1.42	1.37	1.36	1.36	100
200	3.54	3.39	3.27	3.17	3.09	3.03	2.98	2.93	2.83	2.73	2.72	2.71	200
300	5.31	5.08	4.90	4.75	4.64	4.54	4.46	4.40	4.24	4.10	4.07	4.07	300
400	7.08	6.77	6.53	6.33	6.18	6.05	5.95	5.86	5.65	5.46	5.43	5.42	400
500	8.84	8.46	8.16	7.92	7.72	7.56	7.44	7.33	7.06	6.83	6.79	6.78	500
600	10.61	10.15	9.79	9.50	9.27	9.08	8.92	8.79	8.47	8.19	8.14	8.13	600
700	12.38	11.84	11.42	11.08	10.81	10.59	10.41	10.26	9.88	9.56	9.50	9.49	700
800	14.15	13.53	13.05	12.66	12.35	12.10	11.89	11.72	11.29	10.92	10.86	10.84	800
900	15.91	15.22	14.68	14.25	13.90	13.61	13.38	13.19	12.70	12.29	12.21	12.20	900
1000	17.68	16.91	16.31	15.83	15.44	15.12	14.87	14.65	14.11	13.65	13.57	13.55	1000
2000	35.36	33.82	32.61	31.65	30.87	30.24	29.73	29.30	28.21	27.30	27.13	27.10	2000
3000	53.04	50.73	48.92	47.47	46.31	45.36	44.59	43.95	42.31	40.95	40.69	40.64	3000
4000	70.71	67.63	65.22	63.29	61.74	60.48	59.45	58.60	56.41	54.60	54.26	54.19	4000
5000	88.39	84.54	81.52	79.12	77.18	75.60	74.31	73.25	70.51	68.25	67.82	67.73	5000
6000	106.07	101.45	97.83	94.94	92.61	90.72	89.18	87.90	84.61	81.90	81.38	81.28	6000
7000	123.74	118.36	114.13	110.76	108.05	105.84	104.04	102.55	98.71	95.55	94.95	94.83	7000
8000	141.42	135.26	130.43	126.58	123.48	120.96	118.90	117.20	112.81	109.20	108.51	108.37	8000
9000	159.10	152.17	146.74	142.41	138.92	136.08	133.76	131.84	126.91	122.85	122.07	121.92	9000
10000	176.78	169.08	163.04	158.23	154.35	151.20	148.62	146.49	141.01	136.50	135.63	135.46	10000
15000	265.16	253.62	244.56	237.34	231.53	226.80	222.93	219.74	211.51	204.75	203.45	203.19	15000
20000	353.55	338.15	326.07	316.45	308.70	302.40	297.24	292.98	282.01	272.99	271.26	270.92	20000
25000	441.93	422.69	407.59	395.57	385.88	378.00	371.55	366.23	352.52	341.24	339.08	338.65	25000
30000	530.32	507.23	489.11	474.68	463.05	453.60	445.86	439.47	423.02	409.49	406.89	406.38	30000
35000	618.70	591.77	570.63	553.79	540.23	529.20	520.16	512.71	493.52	477.73	474.71	474.11	35000
40000	707.09	676.30	652.14	632.90	617.40	604.80	594.47	585.96	564.02	545.98	542.52	541.84	40000
45000	795.47	760.84	733.66	712.01	694.58	680.40	668.78	659.20	634.53	614.23	610.34	609.57	45000
50000	883.86	845.38	815.18	791.13	771.75	756.00	743.09	732.45	705.03	682.47	678.15	677.30	50000
60000	1060.63	1014.45	978.21	949.35	926.10	907.20	891.71	878.94	846.03	818.97	813.78	812.76	60000
75000	1325.78	1268.06	1222.76	1186.69	1157.63	1133.99	1114.63	1098.67	1057.54	1023.71	1017.23	1015.95	75000
100000	1767.71	1690.75	1630.35	1582.25	1543.50	1511.99	1486.17	1464.89	1410.05	1364.94	1356.30	1354.60	100000
125000	2209.64	2113.44	2037.93	1977.81	1929.37	1889.99	1857.72	1831.11	1762.56	1706.17	1695.38	1693.24	125000
150000	2651.56	2536.12	2445.52	2373.37	2315.25	2267.98	2229.26	2197.33	2115.07	2047.41	2034.45	2031.89	150000
175000	3093.49	2958.81	2853.11	2768.93	2701.12	2645.98	2600.80	2563.55	2467.58	2388.64	2373.52	2370.54	175000
200000	3535.42	3381.49	3260.69	3164.49	3086.99	3023.98	2972.34	2929.77	2820.10	2729.87	2712.60	2709.19	200000
250000	4419.27	4226.87	4075.86	3955.61	3858.74	3779.97	3715.43	3662.21	3525.12	3412.34	3390.75	3386.48	250000

Amount	1.0 Year	1.5 Years	2.0 Years	2.5 Years	3.0 Years	3.5 Years	4.0 Years	4.5 Years	5.0 Years	6.0 Years	7.0 Years	8.0 Years	Amount
100	9.10	6.31	4.93	4.10	3.55	3.16	2.86	2.64	2.46	2.20	2.02	1.89	100
200	18.20	12.62	9.85	8.19	7.09	6.31	5.72	5.28	4.92	4.40	4.03	3.77	200
300	27.30	18.93	14.77	12.28	10.63	9.46	8.58	7.91	7.38	6.60	6.05	5.65	300
400	36.39	25.24	19.69	16.37	14.17	12.61	11.44	10.55	9.84	8.79	8.06	7.53	400
500	45.49	31.55	24.61	20.46	17.71	15.76	14.30	13.18	12.30	10.99	10.08	9.42	500
600	54.59	37.86	29.53	24.55	21.25	18.91	17.16	15.82	14.76	13.19	12.09	11.30	600
700	63.68	44.17	34.45	28.64	24.79	22.06	20.02	18.46	17.21	15.38	14.11	13.18	700
800	72.78	50.48	39.37	32.73	28.33	25.21	22.88	21.09	19.67	17.58	16.12	15.06	800
900	81.88	56.79	44.29	36.82	31.87	28.36	25.74	23.73	22.13	19.78	18.14	16.95	900
1000	90.97	63.10	49.21	40.91	35.41	31.51	28.60	26.36	24.59	21.97	20.15	18.83	1000
2000	181.94	126.19	98.41	81.82	70.81	63.01	57.20	52.72	49.17	43.94	40.30	37.65	2000
3000	272.91	189.28	147.61	122.72	106.22	94.51	85.80	79.08	73.76	65.91	60.45	56.48	3000
4000	363.88	252.38	196.81	163.63	141.62	126.01	114.39	105.44	98.34	87.88	80.60	75.30	4000
5000	454.84	315.47	246.02	204.53	177.03	157.51	142.99	131.79	122.93	109.85	100.74	94.12	5000
6000	545.81	378.56	295.22	245.44	212.43	189.01	171.59	158.15	147.51	131.81	120.89	112.95	6000
7000	636.78	441.66	344.42	286.34	247.84	220.52	200.18	184.51	172.10	153.78	141.04	131.77	7000
8000	727.75	504.75	393.62	327.25	283.24	252.02	228.78	210.87	196.68	175.75	161.19	150.60	8000
9000	818.71	567.84	442.83	368.15	318.64	283.52	257.38	237.23	221.27	197.72	181.34	169.42	9000
10000	909.68	630.94	492.03	409.06	354.05	315.02	285.98	263.58	245.85	219.69	201.48	188.24	10000
15000	1364.52	946.40	738.04	613.58	531.07	472.53	428.96	395.37	368.77	329.53	302.22	282.36	15000
20000	1819.36	1261.87	984.05	818.11	708.09	630.03	571.95	527.16	491.70	439.37	402.96	376.48	20000
25000	2274.20	1577.33	1230.06	1022.63	885.11	787.54	714.93	658.95	614.62	549.21	503.70	470.60	25000
30000	2729.03	1892.80	1476.08	1227.16	1062.14	945.05	857.92	790.74	737.54	659.05	604.44	564.72	30000
35000	3183.87	2208.26	1722.09	1431.68	1239.16	1102.56	1000.90	922.53	860.46	768.89	705.18	658.84	35000
40000	3638.71	2523.73	1968.10	1636.21	1416.18	1260.06	1143.89	1054.32	983.39	878.73	805.92	752.96	40000
45000	4093.55	2839.19	2214.11	1840.73	1593.20	1417.57	1286.87	1186.11	1106.31	988.57	906.66	847.08	45000
50000	4548.39	3154.66	2460.12	2045.26	1770.22	1575.08	1429.86	1317.90	1229.23	1098.41	1007.40	941.20	50000
60000	5458.06	3785.59	2952.15	2454.31	2124.27	1890.09	1715.83	1581.48	1475.08	1318.09	1208.88	1129.44	60000
75000	6822.58	4731.98	3690.18	3067.89	2655.33	2362.62	2144.78	1976.85	1843.84	1647.61	1511.10	1411.80	75000
100000	9096.77	6309.31	4920.24	4090.52	3540.44	3150.15	2859.71	2635.80	2458.46	2196.81	2014.79	1882.40	100000
125000	11370.96	7886.63	6150.30	5113.14	4425.55	3937.69	3574.63	3294.75	3073.07	2746.01	2518.49	2353.00	125000
150000	13645.15	9463.96	7380.36	6135.77	5310.66	4725.23	4289.56	3953.70	3687.68	3295.21	3022.19	2823.60	150000
175000	15919.34	11041.28	8610.42	7158.40	6195.77	5512.76	5004.48	4612.65	4302.30	3844.42	3525.89	3294.20	175000
200000	18193.53	12618.61	9840.48	8181.03	7080.88	6300.30	5719.41	5271.60	4916.91	4393.62	4029.58	3764.80	200000
250000	22741.91	15773.26	12300.59	10226.28	8851.10	7875.37	7149.26	6589.50	6146.14	5492.02	5036.98	4706.00	250000

Amount	9.0 Years	10.0 Years	11.0 Years	12.0 Years	13.0 Years	14.0 Years	15.0 Years	16.0 Years	20.0 Years	30.0 Years	40.0 Years	50.0 Years	Amount
100	1.79	1.71	1.65	1.60	1.57	1.53	1.51	1.49	1.43	1.39	1.38	1.38	100
200	3.57	3.42	3.30	3.20	3.13	3.06	3.01	2.97	2.86	2.78	2.76	2.76	200
300	5.35	5.12	4.94	4.80	4.69	4.59	4.52	4.45	4.29	4.16	4.14	4.13	300
400	7.14	6.83	6.59	6.40	6.25	6.12	6.02	5.94	5.72	5.55	5.51	5.51	400
500	8.92	8.54	8.24	8.00	7.81	7.65	7.52	7.42	7.15	6.93	6.89	6.88	500
600	10.70	10.24	9.88	9.60	9.37	9.18	9.03	8.90	8.58	8.32	8.27	8.26	600
700	12.49	11.95	11.53	11.20	10.93	10.71	10.53	10.38	10.01	9.70	9.64	9.63	700
800	14.27	13.66	13.18	12.79	12.49	12.24	12.03	11.87	11.44	11.09	11.02	11.01	800
900	16.05	15.36	14.82	14.39	14.05	13.77	13.54	13.35	12.87	12.47	12.40	12.38	900
1000	17.83	17.07	16.47	15.99	15.61	15.30	15.04	14.83	14.29	13.86	13.77	13.76	1000
2000	35.66	34.13	32.93	31.98	31.21	30.59	30.08	29.66	28.58	27.71	27.54	27.51	2000
3000	53.49	51.20	49.40	47.97	46.82	45.88	45.12	44.49	42.87	41.56	41.31	41.27	3000
4000	71.32	68.26	65.86	63.95	62.42	61.17	60.15	59.31	57.16	55.41	55.08	55.02	4000
5000	89.15	85.33	82.33	79.94	78.02	76.46	75.19	74.14	71.45	69.26	68.85	68.77	5000
6000	106.98	102.39	98.79	95.93	93.63	91.76	90.23	88.97	85.74	83.11	82.62	82.53	6000
7000	124.81	119.45	115.26	111.92	109.23	107.05	105.26	103.80	100.03	96.97	96.39	96.28	7000
8000	142.64	136.52	131.72	127.90	124.83	122.34	120.30	118.62	114.32	110.82	110.16	110.04	8000
9000	160.47	153.58	148.18	143.89	140.44	137.63	135.34	133.45	128.61	124.67	123.93	123.79	9000
10000	178.30	170.65	164.65	159.88	156.04	152.92	150.38	148.28	142.90	138.52	137.70	137.54	10000
15000	267.45	255.97	246.97	239.82	234.06	229.38	225.56	222.41	214.34	207.78	206.55	206.31	15000
20000	356.59	341.29	329.29	319.75	312.08	305.84	300.75	296.55	285.79	277.03	275.40	275.08	20000
25000	445.74	426.61	411.61	399.69	390.09	382.30	375.93	370.69	357.23	346.29	344.24	343.85	25000
30000	534.89	511.93	493.94	479.63	468.11	458.76	451.12	444.82	428.68	415.55	413.09	412.62	30000
35000	624.04	597.25	576.26	559.56	546.13	535.22	526.30	518.96	500.12	484.81	481.94	481.39	35000
40000	713.18	682.57	658.58	639.50	624.15	611.68	601.49	593.10	571.57	554.06	550.79	550.16	40000
45000	802.33	767.90	740.90	719.44	702.17	688.14	676.67	667.23	643.01	623.32	619.64	618.93	45000
50000	891.48	853.22	823.22	799.37	780.18	764.60	751.86	741.37	714.46	692.58	688.48	687.70	50000
60000	1069.77	1023.86	987.87	959.25	936.22	917.52	902.23	889.64	857.35	831.09	826.18	825.23	60000
75000	1337.22	1279.82	1234.83	1199.06	1170.27	1146.90	1127.79	1112.05	1071.68	1038.87	1032.72	1031.54	75000
100000	1782.95	1706.43	1646.44	1598.74	1560.36	1529.20	1503.71	1482.73	1428.91	1385.15	1376.96	1375.39	100000
125000	2228.69	2133.03	2058.05	1998.42	1950.45	1911.50	1879.64	1853.42	1786.13	1731.44	1721.20	1719.23	125000
150000	2674.43	2559.64	2469.66	2398.11	2340.54	2293.80	2255.57	2224.10	2143.36	2077.73	2065.44	2063.08	150000
175000	3120.16	2986.25	2881.27	2797.79	2730.63	2676.10	2631.50	2594.78	2500.58	2424.01	2409.68	2406.92	175000
200000	3565.90	3412.85	3292.88	3197.47	3120.72	3058.40	3007.42	2965.46	2857.81	2770.30	2753.92	2750.77	200000
250000	4457.38	4266.06	4116.10	3996.84	3900.90	3823.00	3759.28	3706.83	3572.26	3462.88	3442.40	3438.46	250000

Amount	1.0 Year	1.5 Years	2.0 Years	2.5 Years	3.0 Years	3.5 Years	4.0 Years	4.5 Years	5.0 Years	6.0 Years	7.0 Years	8.0 Years	Amount
100	9.11	6.33	4.94	4.11	3.56	3.17	2.88	2.65	2.48	2.22	2.03	1.90	100
200	18.22	12.65	9.87	8.21	7.11	6.33	5.75	5.30	4.95	4.43	4.06	3.80	200
300	27.33	18.97	14.80	12.31	10.66	9.49	8.62	7.95	7.42	6.64	6.09	5.70	300
400	36.44	25.29	19.73	16.42	14.22	12.66	11.50	10.60	9.89	8.85	8.12	7.59	400
500	45.55	31.61	24.67	20.52	17.77	15.82	14.37	13.25	12.36	11.06	10.15	9.49	500
600	54.66	37.93	29.60	24.62	21.32	18.98	17.24	15.90	14.84	13.27	12.18	11.39	600
700	63.77	44.25	34.53	28.72	24.87	22.14	20.11	18.55	17.31	15.48	14.21	13.29	700
800	72.87	50.57	39.46	32.83	28.43	25.31	22.99	21.20	19.78	17.69	16.24	15.18	800
900	81.98	56.90	44.40	36.93	31.98	28.47	25.86	23.85	22.25	19.90	18.27	17.08	900
1000	91.09	63.22	49.33	41.03	35.53	31.63	28.73	26.49	24.72	22.11	20.30	18.98	1000
2000	182.18	126.43	98.65	82.06	71.06	63.26	57.46	52.98	49.44	44.22	40.59	37.95	2000
3000	273.26	189.64	147.97	123.09	106.59	94.89	86.18	79.47	74.16	66.33	60.88	56.92	3000
4000	364.35	252.85	197.29	164.11	142.12	126.52	114.91	105.96	98.88	88.43	81.17	75.89	4000
5000	455.44	316.06	246.62	205.14	177.65	158.14	143.63	132.45	123.60	110.54	101.46	94.87	5000
6000	546.52	379.27	295.94	246.17	213.18	189.77	172.36	158.94	148.32	132.65	121.75	113.84	6000
7000	637.61	442.49	345.26	287.19	248.70	221.40	201.09	185.43	173.03	154.75	142.05	132.81	7000
8000	728.69	505.70	394.58	328.22	284.23	253.03	229.81	211.92	197.75	176.86	162.34	151.78	8000
9000	819.78	568.91	443.91	369.25	319.76	284.66	258.54	238.41	222.47	198.97	182.63	170.76	9000
10000	910.87	632.12	493.23	410.27	355.29	316.28	287.26	264.90	247.19	221.07	202.92	189.73	10000
15000	1366.30	948.18	739.84	615.41	532.93	474.42	430.89	397.34	370.78	331.61	304.38	284.59	15000
20000	1821.73	1264.23	986.45	820.54	710.57	632.56	574.52	529.79	494.37	442.14	405.84	379.45	20000
25000	2277.16	1580.29	1233.06	1025.68	888.22	790.70	718.15	662.24	617.96	552.68	507.29	474.32	25000
30000	2732.59	1896.35	1479.67	1230.81	1065.86	948.84	861.78	794.68	741.56	663.21	608.75	569.18	30000
35000	3188.02	2212.41	1726.28	1435.95	1243.50	1106.98	1005.41	927.13	865.15	773.75	710.21	664.04	35000
40000	3643.45	2528.46	1972.89	1641.08	1421.14	1265.12	1149.04	1059.58	988.74	884.28	811.67	758.90	40000
45000	4098.88	2844.52	2219.51	1846.22	1598.78	1423.26	1292.67	1192.02	1112.33	994.81	913.13	853.76	45000
50000	4554.31	3160.58	2466.12	2051.35	1776.43	1581.40	1436.30	1324.47	1235.92	1105.35	1014.58	948.63	50000
60000	5465.17	3792.69	2959.34	2461.62	2131.71	1897.68	1723.56	1589.36	1483.11	1326.42	1217.50	1138.35	60000
75000	6831.47	4740.87	3699.17	3077.02	2664.64	2372.10	2154.44	1986.70	1853.88	1658.02	1521.87	1422.94	75000
100000	9108.62	6321.15	4932.23	4102.70	3553.25	3162.79	2872.59	2648.90	2471.84	2210.69	2029.16	1897.25	100000
125000	11385.77	7901.44	6165.28	5128.37	4441.06	3953.49	3590.74	3311.17	3089.80	2763.36	2536.45	2371.56	125000
150000	13662.93	9481.73	7398.34	6154.04	5329.27	4744.19	4308.88	3973.40	3707.76	3316.03	3043.74	2845.87	150000
175000	15940.08	11062.02	8631.39	7179.72	6217.48	5534.89	5027.03	4635.63	4325.72	3868.71	3551.03	3320.18	175000
200000	18217.24	12642.30	9864.45	8205.39	7105.69	6325.58	5745.18	5297.87	4943.68	4421.38	4058.32	3794.49	200000
250000	22771.54	15802.88	12330.56	10256.74	8882.11	7906.98	7181.47	6622.33	6179.59	5526.72	5072.90	4743.11	250000

Amount	9.0 Years	10.0 Years	11.0 Years	12.0 Years	13.0 Years	14.0 Years	15.0 Years	16.0 Years	20.0 Years	30.0 Years	40.0 Years	50.0 Years	Amount
100	1.80	1.73	1.67	1.62	1.58	1.55	1.53	1.51	1.45	1.41	1.40	1.40	100
200	3.60	3.45	3.33	3.24	3.16	3.10	3.05	3.01	2.90	2.82	2.80	2.80	200
300	5.40	5.17	4.99	4.85	4.74	4.64	4.57	4.51	4.35	4.22	4.20	4.19	300
400	7.20	6.89	6.66	6.47	6.31	6.19	6.09	6.01	5.80	5.63	5.60	5.59	400
500	9.00	8.62	8.32	8.08	7.89	7.74	7.61	7.51	7.24	7.03	6.99	6.99	500
600	10.79	10.34	9.98	9.70	9.47	9.28	9.13	9.01	8.69	8.44	8.39	8.38	600
700	12.59	12.06	11.64	11.31	11.05	10.83	10.65	10.51	10.14	9.84	9.79	9.78	700
800	14.39	13.78	13.31	12.93	12.62	12.38	12.18	12.01	11.59	11.25	11.19	11.17	800
900	16.19	15.50	14.97	14.54	14.20	13.92	13.70	13.51	13.04	12.65	12.58	12.57	900
1000	17.99	17.23	16.63	16.16	15.78	15.47	15.22	15.01	14.48	14.06	13.98	13.97	1000
2000	35.97	34.45	33.26	32.31	31.55	30.93	30.43	30.02	28.96	28.11	27.96	27.93	2000
3000	53.95	51.67	49.88	48.46	47.32	46.40	45.64	45.02	43.44	42.17	41.93	41.89	3000
4000	71.94	68.89	66.51	64.62	63.10	61.86	60.86	60.03	57.92	56.22	55.91	55.85	4000
5000	89.92	86.11	83.14	80.77	78.87	77.33	76.07	75.04	72.40	70.27	69.89	69.81	5000
6000	107.90	103.34	99.76	96.92	94.64	92.79	91.28	90.04	86.87	84.33	83.86	83.78	6000
7000	125.88	120.56	116.39	113.08	110.42	108.26	106.50	105.05	101.35	98.38	97.84	97.74	7000
8000	143.87	137.78	133.01	129.23	126.19	123.72	121.71	120.06	115.83	112.44	111.82	111.70	8000
9000	161.85	155.00	149.64	145.38	141.96	139.19	136.92	135.06	130.31	126.49	125.79	125.66	9000
10000	179.83	172.22	166.27	161.53	157.73	154.65	152.14	150.07	144.79	140.54	139.77	139.62	10000
15000	269.74	258.33	249.40	242.30	236.60	231.98	228.20	225.10	217.18	210.81	209.65	209.43	15000
20000	359.66	344.44	332.53	323.06	315.46	309.30	304.27	300.13	289.57	281.08	279.53	279.24	20000
25000	449.57	430.55	415.66	403.83	394.33	386.63	380.34	375.17	361.96	351.35	349.41	349.05	25000
30000	539.48	516.66	498.79	484.59	473.19	463.95	456.40	450.20	434.35	421.62	419.30	418.86	30000
35000	629.39	602.76	581.92	565.36	552.06	541.27	532.47	525.23	506.74	491.89	489.18	488.67	35000
40000	719.31	688.87	665.05	646.12	630.92	618.60	608.53	600.26	579.13	562.16	559.06	558.47	40000
45000	809.22	774.98	748.18	726.89	709.79	695.92	684.60	675.30	651.52	632.43	628.94	628.28	45000
50000	899.13	861.09	831.31	807.65	788.65	773.25	760.67	750.33	723.91	702.70	698.82	698.09	50000
60000	1078.96	1033.31	997.57	969.18	946.38	927.89	912.80	900.39	868.70	843.24	838.59	837.71	60000
75000	1348.69	1291.63	1246.96	1211.48	1182.97	1159.87	1141.00	1125.49	1085.87	1054.05	1048.23	1047.14	75000
100000	1798.26	1722.17	1662.61	1615.30	1577.30	1546.49	1521.33	1500.65	1447.82	1405.40	1397.64	1396.18	100000
125000	2247.82	2152.71	2078.26	2019.12	1971.62	1933.11	1901.66	1875.81	1809.78	1756.75	1747.05	1745.22	125000
150000	2697.38	2583.26	2493.91	2422.95	2365.94	2319.73	2281.99	2250.98	2171.73	2108.10	2096.46	2094.27	150000
175000	3146.95	3013.80	2909.56	2826.77	2760.26	2706.35	2662.32	2626.14	2533.69	2459.45	2445.87	2443.31	175000
200000	3596.51	3444.34	3325.21	3230.59	3154.59	3092.97	3042.65	3001.30	2895.64	2810.80	2795.28	2792.35	200000
250000	4495.64	4305.42	4156.51	4038.24	3943.23	3866.21	3803.31	3751.62	3619.55	3513.49	3494.09	3490.44	250000

Amount	1.0 Year	1.5 Years	2.0 Years	2.5 Years	3.0 Years	3.5 Years	4.0 Years	4.5 Years	5.0 Years	6.0 Years	7.0 Years	8.0 Years	Amount
100	9.13	6.34	4.95	4.12	3.57	3.18	2.89	2.67	2.49	2.23	2.05	1.92	100
200	18.25	12.67	9.89	8.23	7.14	6.36	5.78	5.33	4.98	4.45	4.09	3.83	200
300	27.37	19.00	14.84	12.35	10.70	9.53	8.66	7.99	7.46	6.68	6.14	5.74	300
400	36.49	25.34	19.78	16.46	14.27	12.71	11.55	10.65	9.95	8.90	8.18	7.65	400
500	45.61	31.67	24.73	20.58	17.83	15.88	14.43	13.32	12.43	11.13	10.22	9.57	500
600	54.73	38.00	29.67	24.69	21.40	19.06	17.32	15.98	14.92	13.35	12.27	11.48	600
700	63.85	44.34	34.61	28.81	24.96	22.23	20.20	18.64	17.40	15.58	14.31	13.39	700
800	72.97	50.67	39.56	32.92	28.53	25.41	23.09	21.30	19.89	17.80	16.35	15.30	800
900	82.09	57.00	44.50	37.04	32.09	28.58	25.97	23.96	22.37	20.03	18.40	17.21	900
1000	91.21	63.34	49.45	41.15	35.66	31.76	28.86	26.63	24.86	22.25	20.44	19.13	1000
2000	182.41	126.67	98.89	82.30	71.31	63.51	57.72	53.25	49.71	44.50	40.88	38.25	2000
3000	273.62	190.00	148.33	123.45	106.96	95.27	86.57	79.87	74.56	66.74	61.31	57.37	3000
4000	364.82	253.33	197.77	164.60	142.62	127.02	115.43	106.49	99.42	88.99	81.75	76.49	4000
5000	456.03	316.66	247.22	205.75	178.27	158.78	144.28	133.11	124.27	111.24	102.18	95.61	5000
6000	547.23	379.99	296.66	246.90	213.92	190.53	173.14	159.73	149.12	133.48	122.62	114.73	6000
7000	638.44	443.32	346.10	288.05	249.57	222.29	201.99	186.35	173.97	155.73	143.06	133.86	7000
8000	729.64	506.65	395.54	329.20	285.23	254.04	230.85	212.97	198.83	177.97	163.49	152.98	8000
9000	820.85	569.98	444.99	370.35	320.88	285.80	259.70	239.59	223.68	200.22	183.93	172.10	9000
10000	912.05	633.31	494.43	411.49	356.53	317.55	288.56	266.21	248.53	222.47	204.36	191.22	10000
15000	1368.08	949.96	741.64	617.24	534.80	476.32	432.83	399.32	372.79	333.70	306.54	286.83	15000
20000	1824.10	1266.61	988.85	822.98	713.06	635.10	577.11	532.42	497.06	444.93	408.72	382.43	20000
25000	2280.12	1583.26	1236.06	1028.73	891.32	793.87	721.38	665.53	621.32	556.16	510.90	478.04	25000
30000	2736.15	1899.91	1483.27	1234.47	1069.59	952.64	865.66	798.63	745.58	667.39	613.08	573.65	30000
35000	3192.17	2216.56	1730.48	1440.22	1247.85	1111.42	1009.93	931.74	869.85	778.62	715.26	669.26	35000
40000	3648.20	2533.21	1977.70	1645.96	1426.11	1270.19	1154.21	1064.84	994.11	889.85	817.44	764.86	40000
45000	4104.22	2849.86	2224.91	1851.71	1604.38	1428.96	1298.48	1197.95	1118.37	1001.08	919.62	860.47	45000
50000	4560.24	3166.51	2472.12	2057.45	1782.64	1587.73	1442.76	1331.05	1242.63	1112.31	1021.80	956.08	50000
60000	5472.29	3799.81	2966.54	2468.94	2139.17	1905.28	1731.31	1597.26	1491.16	1334.77	1226.15	1147.29	60000
75000	6840.36	4749.76	3708.17	3086.18	2673.96	2381.60	2164.13	1996.58	1863.95	1668.46	1532.69	1434.11	75000
100000	9120.48	6333.01	4944.23	4114.90	3565.28	3175.46	2885.51	2662.10	2485.26	2224.62	2043.59	1912.15	100000
125000	11400.60	7916.27	6180.29	5143.63	4456.60	3969.33	3606.89	3327.63	3106.58	2780.77	2554.48	2390.19	125000
150000	13680.72	9499.52	7416.36	6172.35	5347.91	4763.19	4328.26	3993.15	3727.89	3336.92	3065.38	2868.22	150000
175000	15960.84	11082.77	8652.40	7201.07	6239.23	5557.06	5049.64	4658.68	4349.21	3893.08	3576.27	3346.26	175000
200000	18240.96	12666.02	9888.46	8229.80	7130.55	6350.92	5771.01	5324.20	4970.52	4449.23	4087.17	3824.30	200000
250000	22801.19	15832.53	12360.57	10287.25	8913.19	7938.65	7213.77	6655.25	6213.15	5561.54	5108.96	4780.37	250000

Amount	9.0 Years	10.0 Years	11.0 Years	12.0 Years	13.0 Years	14.0 Years	15.0 Years	16.0 Years	20.0 Years	30.0 Years	40.0 Years	50.0 Years	Amount
100	1.82	1.74	1.68	1.64	1.60	1.57	1.54	1.52	1.47	1.43	1.42	1.42	100
200	3.63	3.48	3.36	3.27	3.19	3.13	3.08	3.04	2.94	2.86	2.84	2.84	200
300	5.45	5.22	5.04	4.90	4.79	4.70	4.62	4.56	4.41	4.28	4.26	4.26	300
400	7.26	6.96	6.72	6.53	6.38	6.26	6.16	6.08	5.87	5.71	5.68	5.67	400
500	9.07	8.69	8.40	8.16	7.98	7.82	7.70	7.60	7.34	7.13	7.10	7.09	500
600	10.89	10.43	10.08	9.80	9.57	9.39	9.24	9.12	8.81	8.56	8.51	8.51	600
700	12.70	12.17	11.76	11.43	11.17	10.95	10.78	10.64	10.27	9.98	9.93	9.92	700
800	14.51	13.91	13.44	13.06	12.76	12.52	12.32	12.15	11.74	11.41	11.35	11.34	800
900	16.33	15.65	15.11	14.69	14.35	14.08	13.86	13.67	13.21	12.84	12.77	12.76	900
1000	18.14	17.38	16.79	16.32	15.95	15.64	15.40	15.19	14.67	14.26	14.19	14.17	1000
2000	36.28	34.76	33.58	32.64	31.89	31.28	30.79	30.38	29.34	28.52	28.37	28.34	2000
3000	54.41	52.14	50.37	48.96	47.83	46.92	46.18	45.56	44.01	42.78	42.55	42.51	3000
4000	72.55	69.52	67.16	65.28	63.78	62.56	61.57	60.75	58.68	57.03	56.74	56.68	4000
5000	90.69	86.90	83.95	81.60	79.72	78.20	76.96	75.94	73.35	71.29	70.92	70.85	5000
6000	108.82	104.28	100.73	97.92	95.66	93.84	92.35	91.12	88.01	85.55	85.10	85.02	6000
7000	126.96	121.66	117.52	114.24	111.61	109.47	107.74	106.31	102.68	99.80	99.29	99.19	7000
8000	145.09	139.04	134.31	130.56	127.55	125.11	123.13	121.50	117.35	114.06	113.47	113.36	8000
9000	163.23	156.42	151.10	146.88	143.49	140.75	138.52	136.68	132.02	128.32	127.65	127.53	9000
10000	181.37	173.80	167.89	163.20	159.43	156.39	153.91	151.87	146.69	142.57	141.84	141.70	10000
15000	272.05	260.70	251.83	244.79	239.15	234.58	230.86	227.80	220.03	213.86	212.75	212.55	15000
20000	362.73	347.60	335.77	326.39	318.86	312.77	307.81	303.73	293.37	285.14	283.67	283.40	20000
25000	453.41	434.50	419.71	407.99	398.58	390.96	384.76	379.66	366.71	356.42	354.59	354.25	25000
30000	544.09	521.40	503.65	489.58	478.29	469.16	461.71	455.60	440.05	427.71	425.50	425.10	30000
35000	634.77	608.30	587.60	571.18	558.01	547.35	538.66	531.53	513.39	498.99	496.42	495.95	35000
40000	725.45	695.20	671.54	652.77	637.72	625.54	615.61	607.46	586.73	570.28	567.33	566.79	40000
45000	816.13	782.09	755.48	734.37	717.44	703.73	692.56	683.39	660.07	641.56	638.25	637.64	45000
50000	906.81	868.99	839.42	815.97	797.15	781.92	769.51	759.32	733.41	712.84	709.17	708.49	50000
60000	1088.18	1042.79	1007.30	979.16	956.58	938.31	923.41	911.19	880.09	855.41	851.00	850.19	60000
75000	1360.22	1303.49	1259.13	1223.95	1195.73	1172.88	1154.26	1138.98	1100.11	1069.26	1063.75	1062.73	75000
100000	1813.62	1737.98	1678.84	1631.93	1594.30	1563.84	1539.01	1518.64	1466.81	1425.68	1418.33	1416.98	100000
125000	2267.03	2172.48	2098.55	2039.91	1992.87	1954.80	1923.76	1898.30	1833.51	1782.10	1772.91	1771.22	125000
150000	2720.43	2606.97	2518.25	2447.89	2391.45	2345.76	2308.51	2277.96	2200.21	2138.52	2127.49	2125.46	150000
175000	3173.84	3041.46	2937.96	2855.87	2790.02	2736.72	2693.26	2657.61	2566.91	2494.94	2482.07	2479.71	175000
200000	3627.24	3475.96	3357.67	3263.85	3188.60	3127.68	3078.01	3037.27	2933.61	2851.36	2836.65	2833.96	200000
250000	4534.05	4344.95	4197.09	4079.81	3985.74	3909.60	3847.52	3796.59	3667.01	3564.19	3545.81	3542.44	250000

Amount	1.0 Year	1.5 Years	2.0 Years	2.5 Years	3.0 Years	3.5 Years	4.0 Years	4.5 Years	5.0 Years	6.0 Years	7.0 Years	8.0 Years	Amount
100	9.14	6.35	4.96	4.13	3.58	3.19	2.90	2.68	2.50	2.24	2.06	1.93	100
200	18.27	12.69	9.92	8.26	7.16	6.38	5.80	5.36	5.00	4.48	4.12	3.86	200
300	27.40	19.04	14.87	12.39	10.74	9.57	8.70	8.03	7.50	6.72	6.18	5.79	300
400	36.53	25.38	19.83	16.51	14.32	12.76	11.60	10.71	10.00	8.96	8.24	7.71	400
500	45.67	31.73	24.79	20.64	17.89	15.95	14.50	13.38	12.50	11.20	10.30	9.64	500
600	54.80	38.07	29.74	24.77	21.47	19.13	17.40	16.06	15.00	13.44	12.35	11.57	600
700	63.93	44.42	34.70	28.89	25.05	22.32	20.29	18.73	17.50	15.68	14.41	13.49	700
800	73.06	50.76	39.65	33.02	28.63	25.51	23.19	21.41	19.99	17.91	16.47	15.42	800
900	82.20	57.11	44.61	37.15	32.20	28.70	26.09	24.08	22.49	20.15	18.53	17.35	900
1000	91.33	63.45	49.57	41.28	35.78	31.89	28.99	26.76	24.99	22.39	20.59	19.28	1000
2000	182.65	126.90	99.13	82.55	71.56	63.77	57.97	53.51	49.98	44.78	41.17	38.55	2000
3000	273.98	190.35	148.69	123.82	107.34	95.65	86.96	80.26	74.97	67.16	61.75	57.82	3000
4000	365.30	253.80	198.25	165.09	143.11	127.53	115.94	107.02	99.95	89.55	82.33	77.09	4000
5000	456.62	317.25	247.82	206.36	178.89	159.41	144.93	133.77	124.94	111.93	102.91	96.36	5000
6000	547.95	380.70	297.38	247.63	214.67	191.29	173.91	160.52	149.93	134.32	123.49	115.63	6000
7000	639.27	444.15	346.94	288.90	250.45	223.18	202.90	187.28	174.92	156.71	144.07	134.90	7000
8000	730.59	507.60	396.50	330.17	286.22	255.06	231.88	214.03	199.90	179.09	164.65	154.17	8000
9000	821.92	571.04	446.07	371.45	322.00	286.94	260.87	240.78	224.89	201.48	185.23	173.44	9000
10000	913.24	634.49	495.63	412.72	357.78	318.82	289.85	267.54	249.88	223.86	205.81	192.72	10000
15000	1369.86	951.74	743.44	619.07	536.66	478.23	434.77	401.30	374.81	335.79	308.71	289.07	15000
20000	1826.47	1268.98	991.25	825.43	715.55	637.64	579.70	535.07	499.75	447.72	411.62	385.43	20000
25000	2283.09	1586.23	1239.07	1031.79	894.44	797.04	724.62	668.83	624.68	559.65	514.52	481.78	25000
30000	2739.71	1903.47	1486.88	1238.14	1073.32	956.45	869.54	802.60	749.62	671.58	617.42	578.14	30000
35000	3196.33	2220.71	1734.69	1444.50	1252.21	1115.86	1014.46	936.36	874.56	783.51	720.32	674.49	35000
40000	3652.94	2537.96	1982.50	1650.85	1431.10	1275.27	1159.39	1070.13	999.49	895.44	823.23	770.85	40000
45000	4109.56	2855.20	2230.32	1857.21	1609.98	1434.68	1304.31	1203.89	1124.43	1007.37	926.13	867.20	45000
50000	4566.18	3172.45	2478.13	2063.57	1788.87	1594.08	1449.23	1337.66	1249.36	1119.30	1029.03	963.56	50000
60000	5479.41	3806.93	2973.75	2476.28	2146.64	1912.90	1739.08	1605.19	1499.24	1343.16	1234.84	1156.27	60000
75000	6849.26	4758.67	3717.19	3095.35	2683.30	2391.12	2173.85	2006.48	1874.04	1678.94	1543.55	1445.33	75000
100000	9132.35	6344.89	4956.25	4127.13	3577.73	3188.16	2898.46	2675.31	2498.72	2238.59	2058.06	1927.11	100000
125000	11415.43	7931.11	6195.31	5158.91	4472.16	3985.20	3623.07	3344.14	3123.40	2798.24	2572.57	2408.89	125000
150000	13698.52	9517.33	7434.38	6190.69	5366.60	4782.24	4347.69	4012.96	3748.08	3357.88	3087.09	2890.66	150000
175000	15981.61	11103.55	8673.44	7222.47	6261.03	5579.28	5072.30	4681.79	4372.76	3917.53	3601.60	3372.44	175000
200000	18264.69	12689.77	9912.50	8254.25	7155.46	6376.32	5796.91	5350.62	4997.44	4477.18	4116.11	3854.21	200000
250000	22830.86	15862.21	12390.62	10317.81	8944.32	7970.40	7246.14	6688.27	6246.80	5596.47	5145.14	4817.77	250000

Amount	9.0 Years	10.0 Years	11.0 Years	12.0 Years	13.0 Years	14.0 Years	15.0 Years	16.0 Years	20.0 Years	30.0 Years	40.0 Years	50.0 Years	Amount
100	1.83	1.76	1.70	1.65	1.62	1.59	1.56	1.54	1.49	1.45	1.44	1.44	100
200	3.66	3.51	3.40	3.30	3.23	3.17	3.12	3.08	2.98	2.90	2.88	2.88	200
300	5.49	5.27	5.09	4.95	4.84	4.75	4.68	4.62	4.46	4.34	4.32	4.32	300
400	7.32	7.02	6.79	6.60	6.45	6.33	6.23	6.15	5.95	5.79	5.76	5.76	400
500	9.15	8.77	8.48	8.25	8.06	7.91	7.79	7.69	7.43	7.23	7.20	7.19	500
600	10.98	10.53	10.18	9.90	9.67	9.49	9.35	9.23	8.92	8.68	8.64	8.63	600
700	12.81	12.28	11.87	11.55	11.28	11.07	10.90	10.76	10.41	10.13	10.08	10.07	700
800	14.64	14.04	13.57	13.19	12.90	12.66	12.46	12.30	11.89	11.57	11.52	11.51	800
900	16.47	15.79	15.26	14.84	14.51	14.24	14.02	13.84	13.38	13.02	12.96	12.94	900
1000	18.30	17.54	16.96	16.49	16.12	15.82	15.57	15.37	14.86	14.46	14.40	14.38	1000
2000	36.59	35.08	33.91	32.98	32.23	31.63	31.14	30.74	29.72	28.92	28.79	28.76	2000
3000	54.88	52.62	50.86	49.46	48.35	47.44	46.71	46.11	44.58	43.38	43.18	43.14	3000
4000	73.17	70.16	67.81	65.95	64.46	63.26	62.28	61.47	59.44	57.84	57.57	57.52	4000
5000	91.46	87.70	84.76	82.44	80.57	79.07	77.84	76.84	74.30	72.30	71.96	71.89	5000
6000	109.75	105.24	101.71	98.92	96.69	94.88	93.41	92.21	89.16	86.76	86.35	86.27	6000
7000	128.04	122.77	118.66	115.41	112.80	110.69	108.98	107.57	104.01	101.22	100.74	100.65	7000
8000	146.33	140.31	135.62	131.89	128.91	126.51	124.55	122.94	118.87	115.68	115.13	115.03	8000
9000	164.62	157.85	152.57	148.38	145.03	142.32	140.11	138.31	133.73	130.14	129.52	129.40	9000
10000	182.91	175.39	169.52	164.87	161.14	158.13	155.68	153.67	148.59	144.60	143.91	143.78	10000
15000	274.36	263.08	254.27	247.30	241.71	237.19	233.52	230.51	222.88	216.90	215.86	215.67	15000
20000	365.81	350.78	339.03	329.73	322.28	316.26	311.36	307.34	297.17	289.20	287.81	287.56	20000
25000	457.27	438.47	423.79	412.16	402.85	395.32	389.19	384.18	371.47	361.50	359.76	359.45	25000
30000	548.72	526.16	508.54	494.59	483.42	474.38	467.03	461.01	445.76	433.80	431.71	431.34	30000
35000	640.17	613.85	593.30	577.02	563.98	553.45	544.87	537.85	520.05	506.10	503.66	503.23	35000
40000	731.62	701.55	678.06	659.45	644.55	632.51	622.71	614.68	594.34	578.40	575.61	575.11	40000
45000	823.08	789.24	762.81	741.88	725.12	711.57	700.55	691.52	668.63	650.70	647.57	647.00	45000
50000	914.53	876.93	847.57	824.32	805.69	790.64	778.38	768.35	742.93	723.00	719.52	718.89	50000
60000	1097.43	1052.32	1017.08	989.18	966.83	948.76	934.06	922.02	891.51	867.60	863.42	862.67	60000
75000	1371.79	1315.39	1271.35	1236.47	1208.53	1185.95	1167.57	1152.52	1114.39	1084.49	1079.27	1078.34	75000
100000	1829.05	1753.86	1695.13	1648.63	1611.37	1581.27	1556.76	1536.69	1485.85	1445.99	1439.03	1437.78	100000
125000	2286.31	2192.32	2118.92	2060.78	2014.22	1976.58	1945.95	1920.87	1857.31	1807.49	1798.78	1797.22	125000
150000	2743.57	2630.78	2542.70	2472.94	2417.06	2371.90	2335.14	2305.04	2228.77	2168.98	2158.54	2156.67	150000
175000	3200.84	3069.24	2966.48	2885.09	2819.90	2767.22	2724.33	2689.21	2600.23	2530.48	2518.30	2516.11	175000
200000	3658.10	3507.71	3390.26	3297.25	3222.74	3162.53	3113.52	3073.38	2971.69	2891.98	2878.05	2875.55	200000
250000	4572.62	4384.63	4237.83	4121.56	4028.43	3953.16	3891.90	3841.73	3714.61	3614.97	3597.56	3594.44	250000

Amount	1.0 Year	1.5 Years	2.0 Years	2.5 Years	3.0 Years	3.5 Years	4.0 Years	4.5 Years	5.0 Years	6.0 Years	7.0 Years	8.0 Years	Amount
100	9.15	6.36	4.97	4.14	3.60	3.21	2.92	2.69	2.52	2.26	2.08	1.95	100
200	18.29	12.72	9.94	8.28	7.19	6.41	5.83	5.38	5.03	4.51	4.15	3.89	200
300	27.44	19.08	14.91	12.42	10.78	9.61	8.74	8.07	7.54	6.76	6.22	5.83	300
400	36.58	25.43	19.88	16.56	14.37	12.81	11.65	10.76	10.05	9.02	8.30	7.77	400
500	45.73	31.79	24.85	20.70	17.96	16.01	14.56	13.45	12.57	11.27	10.37	9.72	500
600	54.87	38.15	29.81	24.84	21.55	19.21	17.47	16.14	15.08	13.52	12.44	11.66	600
700	64.01	44.50	34.78	28.98	25.14	22.41	20.39	18.82	17.59	15.77	14.51	13.60	700
800	73.16	50.86	39.75	33.12	28.73	25.61	23.30	21.51	20.10	18.03	16.59	15.54	800
900	82.30	57.22	44.72	37.26	32.32	28.81	26.21	24.20	22.61	20.28	18.66	17.48	900
1000	91.45	63.57	49.69	41.40	35.91	32.01	29.12	26.89	25.13	22.53	20.73	19.43	1000
2000	182.89	127.14	99.37	82.79	71.81	64.02	58.23	53.78	50.25	45.06	41.46	38.85	2000
3000	274.33	190.71	149.05	124.19	107.71	96.03	87.35	80.66	75.37	67.58	62.18	58.27	3000
4000	365.77	254.28	198.74	165.58	143.61	128.04	116.46	107.55	100.49	90.11	82.91	77.69	4000
5000	457.22	317.84	248.42	206.97	179.52	160.05	145.58	134.43	125.62	112.64	103.63	97.11	5000
6000	548.66	381.41	298.10	248.37	215.42	192.06	174.69	161.32	150.74	135.16	124.36	116.53	6000
7000	640.10	444.98	347.78	289.76	251.32	224.07	203.81	188.20	175.86	157.69	145.09	135.95	7000
8000	731.54	508.55	397.47	331.15	287.22	256.08	232.92	215.09	200.98	180.21	165.81	155.37	8000
9000	822.98	572.11	447.15	372.55	323.12	288.08	262.03	241.97	226.10	202.74	186.54	174.80	9000
10000	914.43	635.68	496.83	413.94	359.03	320.09	291.15	268.86	251.23	225.27	207.26	194.22	10000
15000	1371.64	953.52	745.25	620.91	538.54	480.14	436.72	403.29	376.84	337.90	310.89	291.32	15000
20000	1828.85	1271.36	993.66	827.88	718.05	640.18	582.29	537.71	502.45	450.53	414.52	388.43	20000
25000	2286.06	1589.20	1242.08	1034.85	897.56	800.23	727.86	672.14	628.06	563.16	518.15	485.54	25000
30000	2743.27	1907.04	1490.49	1241.81	1077.07	960.27	873.44	806.57	753.67	675.79	621.78	582.64	30000
35000	3200.48	2224.87	1738.90	1448.78	1256.58	1120.31	1019.01	941.00	879.28	788.42	725.41	679.75	35000
40000	3657.69	2542.71	1987.32	1655.75	1436.09	1280.36	1164.58	1075.42	1004.89	901.05	829.04	776.85	40000
45000	4114.90	2860.55	2235.73	1862.72	1615.60	1440.40	1310.15	1209.85	1130.50	1013.68	932.67	873.96	45000
50000	4572.12	3178.39	2484.15	2069.69	1795.11	1600.45	1455.72	1344.28	1256.12	1126.31	1036.29	971.07	50000
60000	5486.54	3814.07	2980.98	2483.62	2154.13	1920.54	1746.87	1613.13	1507.34	1351.57	1243.55	1165.28	60000
75000	6858.17	4767.58	3726.22	3104.53	2692.66	2400.67	2183.58	2016.42	1884.17	1689.46	1554.44	1456.60	75000
100000	9144.23	6356.77	4968.29	4139.37	3590.21	3200.89	2911.44	2688.55	2512.23	2252.61	2072.58	1942.13	100000
125000	11430.28	7945.97	6210.36	5174.21	4487.76	4001.11	3639.30	3360.69	3140.28	2815.76	2590.73	2427.66	125000
150000	13716.34	9535.16	7452.43	6209.05	5385.31	4801.33	4367.16	4032.83	3768.34	3378.91	3108.87	2913.19	150000
175000	16002.39	11124.35	8694.50	7243.90	6282.87	5601.55	5095.02	4704.96	4396.39	3942.06	3627.02	3398.72	175000
200000	18288.45	12713.54	9936.57	8278.74	7180.42	6401.78	5822.88	5377.10	5024.45	4505.21	4145.16	3884.25	200000
250000	22860.56	15891.93	12420.72	10348.42	8975.52	8002.22	7278.60	6721.37	6280.56	5631.52	5181.45	4855.31	250000

Amount	9.0 Years	10.0 Years	11.0 Years	12.0 Years	13.0 Years	14.0 Years	15.0 Years	16.0 Years	20.0 Years	30.0 Years	40.0 Years	50.0 Years	Amount
100	1.85	1.77	1.72	1.67	1.63	1.60	1.58	1.56	1.51	1.47	1.46	1.46	100
200	3.69	3.54	3.43	3.34	3.26	3.20	3.15	3.11	3.01	2.94	2.92	2.92	200
300	5.54	5.31	5.14	5.00	4.89	4.80	4.73	4.67	4.52	4.40	4.38	4.38	300
400	7.38	7.08	6.85	6.67	6.52	6.40	6.30	6.22	6.02	5.87	5.84	5.84	400
500	9.23	8.85	8.56	8.33	8.15	8.00	7.88	7.78	7.53	7.34	7.30	7.30	500
600	11.07	10.62	10.27	10.00	9.78	9.60	9.45	9.33	9.03	8.80	8.76	8.76	600
700	12.92	12.39	11.99	11.66	11.40	11.20	11.03	10.89	10.54	10.27	10.22	10.22	700
800	14.76	14.16	13.70	13.33	13.03	12.80	12.60	12.44	12.04	11.74	11.68	11.67	800
900	16.61	15.93	15.41	14.99	14.66	14.39	14.18	14.00	13.55	13.20	13.14	13.13	900
1000	18.45	17.70	17.12	16.66	16.29	15.99	15.75	15.55	15.05	14.67	14.60	14.59	1000
2000	36.90	35.40	34.23	33.31	32.58	31.98	31.50	31.10	30.10	29.33	29.20	29.18	2000
3000	55.34	53.10	51.35	49.97	48.86	47.97	47.24	46.65	45.15	43.99	43.80	43.76	3000
4000	73.79	70.80	68.46	66.62	65.15	63.96	62.99	62.20	60.20	58.66	58.39	58.35	4000
5000	92.23	88.49	85.58	83.27	81.43	79.94	78.73	77.75	75.25	73.32	72.99	72.93	5000
6000	110.68	106.19	102.69	99.93	97.72	95.93	94.48	93.29	90.30	87.98	87.59	87.52	6000
7000	129.12	123.89	119.81	116.58	114.00	111.92	110.23	108.84	105.35	102.65	102.19	102.11	7000
8000	147.57	141.59	136.92	133.24	130.29	127.91	125.97	124.39	120.40	117.31	116.78	116.69	8000
9000	166.01	159.29	154.04	149.89	146.57	143.89	141.72	139.94	135.45	131.97	131.38	131.28	9000
10000	184.46	176.98	171.15	166.54	162.86	159.88	157.46	155.49	150.50	146.64	145.98	145.86	10000
15000	276.69	265.47	256.73	249.81	244.28	239.82	236.19	233.23	225.75	219.95	218.97	218.79	15000
20000	368.91	353.96	342.30	333.08	325.71	319.76	314.92	310.97	300.99	293.27	291.95	291.72	20000
25000	461.14	442.45	427.88	416.35	407.13	399.69	393.65	388.71	376.24	366.59	364.94	364.65	25000
30000	553.37	530.94	513.45	499.62	488.56	479.63	472.38	466.45	451.49	439.90	437.93	437.58	30000
35000	645.59	619.43	599.03	582.89	569.98	559.57	551.11	544.19	526.73	513.22	510.91	510.51	35000
40000	737.82	707.92	684.60	666.16	651.41	639.51	629.84	621.93	601.98	586.54	583.90	583.44	40000
45000	830.05	796.41	770.18	749.43	732.84	719.45	708.57	699.67	677.23	659.85	656.89	656.37	45000
50000	922.27	884.90	855.75	832.70	814.26	799.38	787.29	777.41	752.48	733.17	729.87	729.29	50000
60000	1106.73	1061.88	1026.90	999.24	977.11	959.26	944.75	932.89	902.97	879.80	875.85	875.15	60000
75000	1383.41	1327.35	1283.63	1249.05	1221.39	1199.07	1180.94	1166.11	1128.71	1099.75	1094.81	1093.94	75000
100000	1844.54	1769.79	1711.50	1665.39	1628.52	1598.76	1574.58	1554.82	1504.95	1466.33	1459.74	1458.58	100000
125000	2305.67	2212.24	2139.37	2081.74	2035.65	1998.45	1968.23	1943.52	1881.18	1832.91	1824.67	1823.23	125000
150000	2766.81	2654.69	2567.25	2498.09	2442.77	2398.14	2361.87	2332.22	2257.42	2199.49	2189.61	2187.87	150000
175000	3227.94	3097.13	2995.12	2914.43	2849.90	2797.83	2755.52	2720.93	2633.65	2566.07	2554.54	2552.52	175000
200000	3689.07	3539.58	3423.00	3330.78	3257.03	3197.52	3149.16	3109.63	3009.89	2932.66	2919.47	2917.16	200000
250000	4611.34	4424.47	4278.74	4163.47	4071.29	3996.90	3936.45	3887.04	3762.36	3665.82	3649.34	3646.45	250000

Amount	1.0 Year	1.5 Years	2.0 Years	2.5 Years	3.0 Years	3.5 Years	4.0 Years	4.5 Years	5.0 Years	6.0 Years	7.0 Years	8.0 Years	Amount
100	9.16	6.37	4.99	4.16	3.61	3.22	2.93	2.71	2.53	2.27	2.09	1.96	100
200	18.32	12.74	9.97	8.31	7.21	6.43	5.85	5.41	5.06	4.54	4.18	3.92	200
300	27.47	19.11	14.95	12.46	10.81	9.65	8.78	8.11	7.58	6.81	6.27	5.88	300
400	36.63	25.48	19.93	16.61	14.42	12.86	11.70	10.81	10.11	9.07	8.35	7.83	400
500	45.79	31.85	24.91	20.76	18.02	16.07	14.63	13.51	12.63	11.34	10.44	9.79	500
600	54.94	38.22	29.89	24.91	21.62	19.29	17.55	16.22	15.16	13.61	12.53	11.75	600
700	64.10	44.59	34.87	29.07	25.22	22.50	20.48	18.92	17.69	15.87	14.62	13.71	700
800	73.25	50.95	39.85	33.22	28.83	25.71	23.40	21.62	20.21	18.14	16.70	15.66	800
900	82.41	57.32	44.83	37.37	32.43	28.93	26.33	24.32	22.74	20.41	18.79	17.62	900
1000	91.57	63.69	49.81	41.52	36.03	32.14	29.25	27.02	25.26	22.67	20.88	19.58	1000
2000	183.13	127.38	99.61	83.04	72.06	64.28	58.49	54.04	50.52	45.34	41.75	39.15	2000
3000	274.69	191.07	149.42	124.55	108.09	96.41	87.74	81.06	75.78	68.01	62.62	58.72	3000
4000	366.25	254.75	199.22	166.07	144.11	128.55	116.98	108.08	101.04	90.67	83.49	78.29	4000
5000	457.81	318.44	249.02	207.59	180.14	160.69	146.23	135.10	126.29	113.34	104.36	97.86	5000
6000	549.37	382.13	298.83	249.10	216.17	192.82	175.47	162.11	151.55	136.01	125.23	117.44	6000
7000	640.93	445.81	348.63	290.62	252.19	224.96	204.72	189.13	176.81	158.67	146.11	137.01	7000
8000	732.49	509.50	398.43	332.14	288.22	257.10	233.96	216.15	202.07	181.34	166.98	156.58	8000
9000	824.05	573.19	448.24	373.65	324.25	289.23	263.21	243.17	227.32	204.01	187.85	176.15	9000
10000	915.62	636.87	498.04	415.17	360.28	321.37	292.45	270.19	252.58	226.67	208.72	195.72	10000
15000	1373.42	955.31	747.06	622.75	540.41	482.05	438.67	405.28	378.87	340.01	313.08	293.58	15000
20000	1831.23	1273.74	996.07	830.33	720.55	642.73	584.90	540.37	505.16	453.34	417.44	391.44	20000
25000	2289.03	1592.17	1245.09	1037.91	900.68	803.42	731.12	675.46	631.45	566.67	521.79	489.30	25000
30000	2746.84	1910.61	1494.11	1245.49	1080.82	964.10	877.34	810.55	757.73	680.01	626.15	587.16	30000
35000	3204.64	2229.04	1743.12	1453.08	1260.95	1124.78	1023.56	945.64	884.02	793.34	730.51	685.02	35000
40000	3662.45	2547.47	1992.14	1660.66	1441.09	1285.46	1169.79	1080.73	1010.31	906.67	834.87	782.88	40000
45000	4120.25	2865.91	2241.16	1868.24	1621.22	1446.14	1316.01	1215.83	1136.60	1020.01	939.23	880.74	45000
50000	4578.06	3184.34	2490.17	2075.82	1801.36	1606.83	1462.23	1350.92	1262.89	1133.34	1043.58	978.60	50000
60000	5493.67	3821.21	2988.21	2490.98	2161.63	1928.19	1754.68	1621.10	1515.46	1360.01	1252.30	1174.32	60000
75000	6867.08	4776.51	3735.26	3113.73	2702.04	2410.24	2193.34	2026.37	1894.33	1700.01	1565.37	1467.90	75000
100000	9156.11	6368.67	4980.34	4151.64	3602.72	3213.65	2924.46	2701.83	2525.77	2266.67	2087.16	1957.20	100000
125000	11445.14	7960.84	6225.43	5189.55	4503.39	4017.06	3655.57	3377.29	3157.21	2833.34	2608.95	2446.50	125000
150000	13734.16	9553.01	7470.51	6227.45	5404.07	4820.47	4386.68	4052.74	3788.65	3400.01	3130.74	2935.79	150000
175000	16023.19	11145.17	8715.60	7265.36	6304.75	5623.88	5117.80	4728.20	4420.09	3966.68	3652.53	3425.09	175000
200000	18312.22	12737.34	9960.68	8303.27	7205.43	6427.29	5848.91	5403.65	5051.53	4533.34	4174.32	3914.39	200000
250000	22890.27	15921.67	12450.85	10379.09	9006.78	8034.11	7311.14	6754.57	6314.41	5666.68	5217.90	4892.99	250000

Amount	9.0 Years	10.0 Years	11.0 Years	12.0 Years	13.0 Years	14.0 Years	15.0 Years	16.0 Years	20.0 Years	30.0 Years	40.0 Years	50.0 Years	Amount
100	1.87	1.79	1.73	1.69	1.65	1.62	1.60	1.58	1.53	1.49	1.49	1.48	100
200	3.73	3.58	3.46	3.37	3.30	3.24	3.19	3.15	3.05	2.98	2.97	2.96	200
300	5.59	5.36	5.19	5.05	4.94	4.85	4.78	4.72	4.58	4.47	4.45	4.44	300
400	7.45	7.15	6.92	6.73	6.59	6.47	6.37	6.30	6.10	5.95	5.93	5.92	400
500	9.31	8.93	8.64	8.42	8.23	8.09	7.97	7.87	7.63	7.44	7.41	7.40	500
600	11.17	10.72	10.37	10.10	9.88	9.70	9.56	9.44	9.15	8.93	8.89	8.88	600
700	13.03	12.51	12.10	11.78	11.53	11.32	11.15	11.02	10.67	10.41	10.37	10.36	700
800	14.89	14.29	13.83	13.46	13.17	12.94	12.74	12.59	12.20	11.90	11.85	11.84	800
900	16.75	16.08	15.56	15.14	14.82	14.55	14.34	14.16	13.72	13.39	13.33	13.32	900
1000	18.61	17.86	17.28	16.83	16.46	16.17	15.93	15.74	15.25	14.87	14.81	14.80	1000
2000	37.21	35.72	34.56	33.65	32.92	32.33	31.85	31.47	30.49	29.74	29.61	29.59	2000
3000	55.81	53.58	51.84	50.47	49.38	48.49	47.78	47.20	45.73	44.61	44.42	44.39	3000
4000	74.41	71.44	69.12	67.29	65.83	64.66	63.70	62.93	60.97	59.47	59.22	59.18	4000
5000	93.01	89.29	86.40	84.12	82.29	80.82	79.63	78.66	76.21	74.34	74.03	73.97	5000
6000	111.61	107.15	103.68	100.94	98.75	96.98	95.55	94.39	91.45	89.21	88.83	88.77	6000
7000	130.21	125.00	120.96	117.76	115.21	113.15	111.48	110.12	106.69	104.07	103.64	103.56	7000
8000	148.81	142.87	138.24	134.58	131.66	129.31	127.40	125.85	121.93	118.94	118.44	118.36	8000
9000	167.41	160.73	155.52	151.40	148.12	145.47	143.33	141.58	137.17	133.81	133.25	133.15	9000
10000	186.01	178.58	172.80	168.23	164.58	161.64	159.25	157.31	152.41	148.67	148.05	147.94	10000
15000	279.02	267.87	259.19	252.34	246.86	242.45	238.87	235.96	228.62	223.01	222.07	221.91	15000
20000	372.02	357.16	345.59	336.45	329.15	323.27	318.50	314.61	304.82	297.34	296.10	295.88	20000
25000	465.03	446.45	431.99	420.56	411.44	404.09	398.12	393.26	381.03	371.68	370.12	369.85	25000
30000	558.03	535.74	518.38	504.67	493.72	484.90	477.74	471.91	457.23	446.01	444.14	443.82	30000
35000	651.03	625.03	604.78	588.78	576.01	565.72	557.37	550.56	533.44	520.35	518.16	517.79	35000
40000	744.04	714.32	691.17	672.89	658.29	646.53	636.99	629.21	609.64	594.68	592.19	591.76	40000
45000	837.04	803.61	777.57	757.00	740.58	727.35	716.61	707.86	685.85	669.02	666.21	665.73	45000
50000	930.05	892.90	863.97	841.12	822.87	808.17	796.24	786.51	762.05	743.35	740.23	739.70	50000
60000	1116.05	1071.48	1036.76	1009.34	987.44	969.80	955.48	943.81	914.46	892.02	888.28	887.64	60000
75000	1395.07	1339.35	1295.95	1261.67	1234.30	1212.25	1194.35	1179.76	1143.08	1115.02	1110.35	1109.55	75000
100000	1860.09	1785.79	1727.93	1682.23	1645.73	1616.33	1592.47	1573.01	1524.10	1486.70	1480.46	1479.39	100000
125000	2325.11	2232.24	2159.91	2102.78	2057.16	2020.41	1990.59	1966.26	1905.13	1858.37	1850.57	1849.24	125000
150000	2790.13	2678.69	2591.89	2523.34	2468.59	2424.49	2388.70	2359.51	2286.15	2230.04	2220.69	2219.09	150000
175000	3255.15	3125.13	3023.87	2943.89	2880.02	2828.57	2786.82	2752.76	2667.18	2601.72	2590.80	2588.93	175000
200000	3720.17	3571.58	3455.85	3364.45	3291.45	3232.65	3184.94	3146.01	3048.20	2973.39	2960.91	2958.78	200000
250000	4650.21	4464.48	4319.81	4205.56	4114.31	4040.81	3981.17	3932.51	3810.25	3716.74	3701.14	3698.47	250000

Amount	1.0 Year	1.5 Years	2.0 Years	2.5 Years	3.0 Years	3.5 Years	4.0 Years	4.5 Years	5.0 Years	6.0 Years	7.0 Years	8.0 Years	Amount
100	9.17	6.39	5.00	4.17	3.62	3.23	2.94	2.72	2.54	2.29	2.11	1.98	100
200	18.34	12.77	9.99	8.33	7.24	6.46	5.88	5.44	5.08	4.57	4.21	3.95	200
300	27.51	19.15	14.98	12.50	10.85	9.68	8.82	8.15	7.62	6.85	6.31	5.92	300
400	36.68	25.53	19.97	16.66	14.47	12.91	11.75	10.87	10.16	9.13	8.41	7.89	400
500	45.84	31.91	24.97	20.82	18.08	16.14	14.69	13.58	12.70	11.41	10.51	9.87	500
600	55.01	38.29	29.96	24.99	21.70	19.36	17.63	16.30	15.24	13.69	12.62	11.84	600
700	64.18	44.67	34.95	29.15	25.31	22.59	20.57	19.01	17.78	15.97	14.72	13.81	700
800	73.35	51.05	39.94	33.32	28.93	25.82	23.50	21.73	20.32	18.25	16.82	15.78	800
900	82.52	57.43	44.94	37.48	32.54	29.04	26.44	24.44	22.86	20.53	18.92	17.76	900
1000	91.68	63.81	49.93	41.64	36.16	32.27	29.38	27.16	25.40	22.81	21.02	19.73	1000
2000	183.36	127.62	99.85	83.28	72.31	64.53	58.75	54.31	50.79	45.62	42.04	39.45	2000
3000	275.04	191.42	149.78	124.92	108.46	96.80	88.13	81.46	76.19	68.43	63.06	59.17	3000
4000	366.72	255.23	199.70	166.56	144.61	129.06	117.50	108.61	101.58	91.24	84.08	78.90	4000
5000	458.40	319.03	249.63	208.20	180.77	161.33	146.88	135.76	126.97	114.04	105.09	98.62	5000
6000	550.08	382.84	299.55	249.84	216.92	193.59	176.25	162.91	152.37	136.85	126.11	118.34	6000
7000	641.76	446.65	349.47	291.48	253.07	225.85	205.63	190.06	177.76	159.66	147.13	138.07	7000
8000	733.44	510.45	399.40	333.12	289.22	258.12	235.00	217.22	203.15	182.47	168.15	157.79	8000
9000	825.12	574.26	449.32	374.76	325.38	290.38	264.38	244.37	228.55	205.28	189.17	177.51	9000
10000	916.80	638.06	499.25	416.40	361.53	322.65	293.75	271.52	253.94	228.08	210.18	197.24	10000
15000	1375.20	957.09	748.87	624.59	542.29	483.97	440.63	407.28	380.91	342.12	315.27	295.85	15000
20000	1833.60	1276.12	998.49	832.79	723.05	645.29	587.50	543.03	507.87	456.16	420.36	394.47	20000
25000	2292.00	1595.15	1248.11	1040.98	903.81	806.61	734.38	678.79	634.84	570.20	525.45	493.09	25000
30000	2750.40	1914.18	1497.73	1249.18	1084.58	967.93	881.25	814.55	761.81	684.24	630.54	591.70	30000
35000	3208.80	2233.21	1747.35	1457.38	1265.34	1129.25	1028.13	950.30	888.77	798.28	735.63	690.32	35000
40000	3667.20	2552.24	1996.97	1665.57	1446.10	1290.58	1175.00	1086.06	1015.74	912.32	840.72	788.93	40000
45000	4125.60	2871.27	2246.59	1873.77	1626.86	1451.90	1321.88	1221.82	1142.71	1026.36	945.81	887.55	45000
50000	4584.00	3190.29	2496.21	2081.96	1807.62	1613.22	1468.75	1357.57	1269.68	1140.39	1050.90	986.17	50000
60000	5500.80	3828.35	2995.45	2498.36	2169.15	1935.86	1762.50	1629.09	1523.61	1368.47	1261.08	1183.40	60000
75000	6876.00	4785.44	3744.31	3122.94	2711.43	2419.82	2203.13	2036.36	1904.51	1710.59	1576.34	1479.25	75000
100000	9168.00	6380.58	4992.42	4163.92	3615.24	3226.43	2937.50	2715.14	2539.35	2280.78	2101.79	1972.33	100000
125000	11460.00	7975.73	6240.52	5204.90	4519.05	4033.04	3671.88	3393.93	3174.18	2850.98	2627.23	2465.41	125000
150000	13752.00	9570.87	7488.62	6245.88	5422.86	4839.64	4406.25	4072.71	3809.02	3421.17	3152.68	2958.49	150000
175000	16044.00	11166.02	8736.72	7286.86	6326.67	5646.25	5140.63	4751.50	4443.85	3991.37	3678.13	3451.57	175000
200000	18336.00	12761.16	9984.83	8327.84	7230.48	6452.86	5875.00	5430.28	5078.69	4561.56	4203.57	3944.65	200000
250000	22920.00	15951.45	12481.03	10409.80	9038.10	8066.07	7343.75	6787.85	6348.36	5701.95	5254.46	4930.81	250000

Amount	9.0 Years	10.0 Years	11.0 Years	12.0 Years	13.0 Years	14.0 Years	15.0 Years	16.0 Years	20.0 Years	30.0 Years	40.0 Years	50.0 Years	Amount
100	1.88	1.81	1.75	1.70	1.67	1.64	1.62	1.60	1.55	1.51	1.51	1.51	100
200	3.76	3.61	3.49	3.40	3.33	3.27	3.23	3.19	3.09	3.02	3.01	3.01	200
300	5.63	5.41	5.24	5.10	4.99	4.91	4.84	4.78	4.63	4.53	4.51	4.51	300
400	7.51	7.21	6.98	6.80	6.66	6.54	6.45	6.37	6.18	6.03	6.01	6.01	400
500	9.38	9.01	8.73	8.50	8.32	8.17	8.06	7.96	7.72	7.54	7.51	7.51	500
600	11.26	10.82	10.47	10.20	9.98	9.81	9.67	9.55	9.26	9.05	9.01	9.01	600
700	13.13	12.62	12.22	11.90	11.65	11.44	11.28	11.14	10.81	10.55	10.51	10.51	700
800	15.01	14.42	13.96	13.60	13.31	13.08	12.89	12.74	12.35	12.06	12.01	12.01	800
900	16.89	16.22	15.70	15.30	14.97	14.71	14.50	14.33	13.89	13.57	13.52	13.51	900
1000	18.76	18.02	17.45	17.00	16.64	16.34	16.11	15.92	15.44	15.08	15.02	15.01	1000
2000	37.52	36.04	34.89	33.99	33.27	32.68	32.21	31.83	30.87	30.15	30.03	30.01	2000
3000	56.28	54.06	52.34	50.98	49.90	49.02	48.32	47.74	46.30	45.22	45.04	45.01	3000
4000	75.03	72.08	69.78	67.97	66.53	65.36	64.42	63.66	61.74	60.29	60.05	60.01	4000
5000	93.79	90.10	87.23	84.96	83.16	81.70	80.53	79.57	77.17	75.36	75.06	75.01	5000
6000	112.55	108.12	104.67	101.95	99.79	98.04	96.63	95.48	92.60	90.43	90.08	90.02	6000
7000	131.30	126.13	122.11	118.94	116.42	114.38	112.73	111.39	108.04	105.50	105.09	105.02	7000
8000	150.06	144.15	139.56	135.93	133.05	130.72	128.84	127.31	123.47	120.57	120.10	120.02	8000
9000	168.82	162.17	157.00	152.93	149.68	147.06	144.94	143.22	138.90	135.64	135.11	135.02	9000
10000	187.57	180.19	174.45	169.92	166.31	163.40	161.05	159.13	154.34	150.71	150.12	150.02	10000
15000	281.36	270.28	261.67	254.87	249.46	245.10	241.57	238.69	231.50	226.07	225.18	225.03	15000
20000	375.14	360.38	348.89	339.83	332.61	326.80	322.09	318.26	308.67	301.42	300.24	300.04	20000
25000	468.93	450.47	436.11	424.78	415.76	408.49	402.61	397.82	385.83	376.78	375.30	375.05	25000
30000	562.71	540.56	523.33	509.74	498.91	490.19	483.13	477.38	463.00	452.13	450.36	450.06	30000
35000	656.50	630.65	610.55	594.70	582.06	571.89	563.65	556.94	540.16	527.48	525.42	525.07	35000
40000	750.28	720.75	697.77	679.65	665.21	653.59	644.17	636.51	617.33	602.84	600.48	600.08	40000
45000	844.06	810.84	784.99	764.61	748.36	735.28	724.69	716.07	694.50	678.19	675.54	675.09	45000
50000	937.85	900.93	872.21	849.56	831.51	816.98	805.22	795.63	771.66	753.55	750.60	750.10	50000
60000	1125.42	1081.12	1046.66	1019.48	997.81	980.38	966.26	954.76	925.99	904.26	900.71	900.12	60000
75000	1406.77	1351.39	1308.32	1274.34	1247.26	1225.47	1207.82	1193.45	1157.49	1130.32	1125.89	1125.15	75000
100000	1875.69	1801.86	1744.42	1699.12	1663.01	1633.96	1610.43	1591.26	1543.32	1507.09	1501.19	1500.20	100000
125000	2344.62	2252.32	2180.53	2123.90	2078.76	2042.44	2013.03	1989.07	1929.14	1883.86	1876.48	1875.25	125000
150000	2813.54	2702.78	2616.63	2548.68	2494.51	2450.93	2415.64	2386.89	2314.97	2260.63	2251.78	2250.30	150000
175000	3282.46	3153.25	3052.74	2973.46	2910.26	2859.42	2818.24	2784.70	2700.80	2637.40	2627.07	2625.35	175000
200000	3751.38	3603.71	3488.84	3398.24	3326.01	3267.91	3220.85	3182.52	3086.63	3014.18	3002.37	3000.40	200000
250000	4689.23	4504.63	4361.05	4247.80	4157.51	4084.88	4026.06	3978.14	3858.28	3767.72	3752.96	3750.50	250000

Amount	1.0 Year	1.5 Years	2.0 Years	2.5 Years	3.0 Years	3.5 Years	4.0 Years	4.5 Years	5.0 Years	6.0 Years	7.0 Years	8.0 Years	Amount
100	9.18	6.40	5.01	4.18	3.63	3.24	2.96	2.73	2.56	2.30	2.12	1.99	100
200	18.36	12.79	10.01	8.36	7.26	6.48	5.91	5.46	5.11	4.59	4.24	3.98	200
300	27.54	19.18	15.02	12.53	10.89	9.72	8.86	8.19	7.66	6.89	6.35	5.97	300
400	36.72	25.58	20.02	16.71	14.52	12.96	11.81	10.92	10.22	9.18	8.47	7.96	400
500	45.90	31.97	25.03	20.89	18.14	16.20	14.76	13.65	12.77	11.48	10.59	9.94	500
600	55.08	38.36	30.03	25.06	21.77	19.44	17.71	16.38	15.32	13.77	12.70	11.93	600
700	64.26	44.75	35.04	29.24	25.40	22.68	20.66	19.10	17.88	16.07	14.82	13.92	700
800	73.44	51.15	40.04	33.41	29.03	25.92	23.61	21.83	20.43	18.36	16.94	15.91	800
900	82.62	57.54	45.05	37.59	32.66	29.16	26.56	24.56	22.98	20.66	19.05	17.89	900
1000	91.80	63.93	50.05	41.77	36.28	32.40	29.51	27.29	25.53	22.95	21.17	19.88	1000
2000	183.60	127.86	100.09	83.53	72.56	64.79	59.02	54.57	51.06	45.90	42.33	39.76	2000
3000	275.40	191.78	150.14	125.29	108.84	97.18	88.52	81.86	76.59	68.85	63.50	59.63	3000
4000	367.20	255.71	200.18	167.05	145.12	129.57	118.03	109.14	102.12	91.80	84.66	79.51	4000
5000	459.00	319.63	250.23	208.82	181.39	161.97	147.53	136.43	127.65	114.75	105.83	99.38	5000
6000	550.80	383.56	300.27	250.58	217.67	194.36	177.04	163.71	153.18	137.70	126.99	119.26	6000
7000	642.60	447.48	350.32	292.34	253.95	226.75	206.55	191.00	178.71	160.65	148.16	139.13	7000
8000	734.40	511.41	400.36	334.10	290.23	259.14	236.05	218.28	204.24	183.60	169.32	159.01	8000
9000	826.20	575.33	450.41	375.87	326.51	291.54	265.56	245.57	229.77	206.55	190.49	178.88	9000
10000	918.00	639.26	500.45	417.63	362.78	323.93	295.06	272.85	255.30	229.50	211.65	198.76	10000
15000	1376.99	958.88	750.68	626.44	544.17	485.89	442.59	409.28	382.95	344.25	317.47	298.13	15000
20000	1835.99	1278.51	1000.90	835.25	725.56	647.85	590.12	545.70	510.60	458.99	423.30	397.51	20000
25000	2294.98	1598.13	1251.13	1044.06	906.95	809.81	737.65	682.13	638.25	573.74	529.12	496.88	25000
30000	2753.98	1917.76	1501.35	1252.87	1088.34	971.78	885.18	818.55	765.89	688.49	634.94	596.26	30000
35000	3212.97	2237.38	1751.58	1461.68	1269.73	1133.74	1032.71	954.98	893.54	803.23	740.77	695.63	35000
40000	3671.97	2557.01	2001.80	1670.50	1451.12	1295.70	1180.24	1091.40	1021.19	917.98	846.59	795.01	40000
45000	4130.96	2876.63	2252.03	1879.31	1632.51	1457.66	1327.77	1227.82	1148.84	1032.73	952.41	894.38	45000
50000	4589.96	3196.26	2502.25	2088.12	1813.90	1619.62	1475.29	1364.25	1276.49	1147.47	1058.24	993.76	50000
60000	5507.95	3835.51	3002.70	2505.74	2176.68	1943.55	1770.35	1637.10	1531.78	1376.97	1269.88	1192.51	60000
75000	6884.93	4794.38	3753.38	3132.17	2720.85	2429.43	2212.94	2046.37	1914.73	1721.21	1587.35	1490.63	75000
100000	9179.91	6392.51	5004.50	4176.23	3627.80	3239.24	2950.58	2728.49	2552.97	2294.94	2116.47	1987.51	100000
125000	11474.88	7990.63	6255.63	5220.29	4534.75	4049.05	3688.23	3410.61	3191.21	2868.67	2645.58	2484.39	125000
150000	13769.86	9588.76	7506.75	6264.34	5441.69	4858.86	4425.87	4092.74	3829.45	3442.41	3174.70	2981.26	150000
175000	16064.83	11186.88	8757.88	7308.40	6348.64	5668.67	5163.52	4774.86	4467.69	4016.14	3703.81	3478.14	175000
200000	18359.81	12785.01	10009.00	8352.46	7255.59	6478.48	5901.16	5456.98	5105.93	4589.87	4232.93	3975.02	200000
250000	22949.76	15981.26	12511.25	10440.57	9069.49	8098.10	7376.45	6821.22	6382.41	5737.34	5291.16	4968.77	250000

Amount	9.0 Years	10.0 Years	11.0 Years	12.0 Years	13.0 Years	14.0 Years	15.0 Years	16.0 Years	20.0 Years	30.0 Years	40.0 Years	50.0 Years	Amount
100	1.90	1.82	1.77	1.72	1.69	1.66	1.63	1.61	1.57	1.53	1.53	1.53	100
200	3.79	3.64	3.53	3.44	3.37	3.31	3.26	3.22	3.13	3.06	3.05	3.05	200
300	5.68	5.46	5.29	5.15	5.05	4.96	4.89	4.83	4.69	4.59	4.57	4.57	300
400	7.57	7.28	7.05	6.87	6.73	6.61	6.52	6.44	6.26	6.12	6.09	6.09	400
500	9.46	9.09	8.81	8.59	8.41	8.26	8.15	8.05	7.82	7.64	7.61	7.61	500
600	11.35	10.91	10.57	10.30	10.09	9.91	9.78	9.66	9.38	9.17	9.14	9.13	600
700	13.24	12.73	12.33	12.02	11.77	11.57	11.40	11.27	10.94	10.70	10.66	10.65	700
800	15.14	14.55	14.09	13.73	13.45	13.22	13.03	12.88	12.51	12.23	12.18	12.17	800
900	17.03	16.37	15.85	15.45	15.13	14.87	14.66	14.49	14.07	13.75	13.70	13.69	900
1000	18.92	18.18	17.61	17.17	16.81	16.52	16.29	16.10	15.63	15.28	15.22	15.22	1000
2000	37.83	36.36	35.22	34.33	33.61	33.04	32.57	32.20	31.26	30.56	30.44	30.43	2000
3000	56.75	54.54	52.83	51.49	50.42	49.55	48.86	48.29	46.88	45.83	45.66	45.64	3000
4000	75.66	72.72	70.44	68.65	67.22	66.07	65.14	64.39	62.51	61.11	60.88	60.85	4000
5000	94.57	90.90	88.05	85.81	84.02	82.59	81.43	80.48	78.13	76.38	76.10	76.06	5000
6000	113.49	109.08	105.66	102.97	100.83	99.10	97.71	96.58	93.76	91.66	91.32	91.27	6000
7000	132.40	127.26	123.27	120.13	117.63	115.62	114.00	112.68	109.39	106.93	106.54	106.48	7000
8000	151.31	145.44	140.88	137.29	134.43	132.14	130.28	128.77	125.01	122.21	121.76	121.69	8000
9000	170.23	163.62	158.49	154.45	151.24	148.65	146.56	144.87	140.64	137.48	136.98	136.90	9000
10000	189.14	181.80	176.10	171.61	168.04	165.17	162.85	160.96	156.26	152.76	152.20	152.11	10000
15000	283.71	272.70	264.15	257.42	252.06	247.75	244.27	241.44	234.39	229.13	228.29	228.16	15000
20000	378.28	363.60	352.20	343.22	336.07	330.33	325.69	321.92	312.52	305.51	304.39	304.21	20000
25000	472.84	454.50	440.25	429.03	420.09	412.92	407.12	402.40	390.65	381.88	380.48	380.26	25000
30000	567.41	545.40	528.30	514.83	504.11	495.50	488.54	482.88	468.78	458.26	456.58	456.31	30000
35000	661.98	636.30	616.35	600.63	588.13	578.08	569.96	563.36	546.91	534.63	532.68	532.36	35000
40000	756.55	727.20	704.40	686.44	672.14	660.66	651.38	643.83	625.04	611.01	608.77	608.41	40000
45000	851.12	818.10	792.44	772.24	756.16	743.25	732.80	724.31	703.17	687.38	684.87	684.46	45000
50000	945.68	908.99	880.49	858.05	840.18	825.83	814.23	804.79	781.29	763.76	760.96	760.51	50000
60000	1134.82	1090.79	1056.59	1029.66	1008.21	990.99	977.07	965.75	937.55	916.51	913.16	912.61	60000
75000	1418.52	1363.49	1320.74	1287.07	1260.26	1238.74	1221.34	1207.18	1171.94	1145.63	1141.44	1140.76	75000
100000	1891.36	1817.98	1760.98	1716.09	1680.35	1651.65	1628.45	1609.58	1562.58	1527.51	1521.92	1521.02	100000
125000	2364.20	2272.48	2201.23	2145.11	2100.44	2064.56	2035.56	2011.97	1953.23	1909.38	1902.40	1901.27	125000
150000	2837.04	2726.97	2641.47	2574.13	2520.52	2477.47	2442.67	2414.36	2343.87	2291.26	2282.88	2281.52	150000
175000	3309.88	3181.47	3081.71	3003.15	2940.61	2890.38	2849.78	2816.76	2734.52	2673.14	2663.36	2661.77	175000
200000	3782.72	3635.96	3521.96	3432.17	3360.69	3303.30	3256.89	3219.15	3125.16	3055.01	3043.84	3042.03	200000
250000	4728.39	4544.95	4402.45	4290.22	4200.87	4129.12	4071.11	4023.94	3906.45	3818.76	3804.80	3802.53	250000

Amount	1.0 Year	1.5 Years	2.0 Years	2.5 Years	3.0 Years	3.5 Years	4.0 Years	4.5 Years	5.0 Years	6.0 Years	7.0 Years	8.0 Years	Amount
100	9.20	6.41	5.02	4.19	3.65	3.26	2.97	2.75	2.57	2.31	2.14	2.01	100
200	18.39	12.81	10.04	8.38	7.29	6.51	5.93	5.49	5.14	4.62	4.27	4.01	200
300	27.58	19.22	15.05	12.57	10.93	9.76	8.90	8.23	7.70	6.93	6.40	6.01	300
400	36.77	25.62	20.07	16.76	14.57	13.01	11.86	10.97	10.27	9.24	8.53	8.02	400
500	45.96	32.03	25.09	20.95	18.21	16.27	14.82	13.71	12.84	11.55	10.66	10.02	500
600	55.16	38.43	30.10	25.14	21.85	19.52	17.79	16.46	15.40	13.86	12.79	12.02	600
700	64.35	44.84	35.12	29.32	25.49	22.77	20.75	19.20	17.97	16.17	14.92	14.02	700
800	73.54	51.24	40.14	33.51	29.13	26.02	23.71	21.94	20.54	18.48	17.05	16.03	800
900	82.73	57.64	45.15	37.70	32.77	29.27	26.68	24.68	23.10	20.79	19.19	18.03	900
1000	91.92	64.05	50.17	41.89	36.41	32.53	29.64	27.42	25.67	23.10	21.32	20.03	1000
2000	183.84	128.09	100.34	83.78	72.81	65.05	59.28	54.84	51.34	46.19	42.63	40.06	2000
3000	275.76	192.14	150.50	125.66	109.22	97.57	88.92	82.26	77.00	69.28	63.94	60.09	3000
4000	367.68	256.18	200.67	167.55	145.62	130.09	118.55	109.68	102.67	92.37	85.25	80.11	4000
5000	459.60	320.23	250.84	209.43	182.02	162.61	148.19	137.10	128.34	115.46	106.56	100.14	5000
6000	551.51	384.27	301.00	251.32	218.43	195.13	177.83	164.52	154.00	138.55	127.88	120.17	6000
7000	643.43	448.32	351.17	293.20	254.83	227.65	207.46	191.94	179.67	161.64	149.19	140.20	7000
8000	735.35	512.36	401.33	335.09	291.23	260.17	237.10	219.35	205.33	184.74	170.50	160.22	8000
9000	827.27	576.40	451.50	376.97	327.64	292.69	266.74	246.77	231.00	207.83	191.81	180.25	9000
10000	919.19	640.45	501.67	418.86	364.04	325.21	296.37	274.19	256.67	230.92	213.12	200.28	10000
15000	1378.78	960.67	752.50	628.29	546.06	487.82	444.56	411.29	385.00	346.38	319.68	300.42	15000
20000	1838.37	1280.89	1003.33	837.72	728.08	650.42	592.74	548.38	513.33	461.83	426.24	400.55	20000
25000	2297.96	1601.11	1254.16	1047.14	910.10	813.03	740.93	685.47	641.66	577.29	532.80	500.69	25000
30000	2757.55	1921.34	1504.99	1256.57	1092.12	975.63	889.11	822.57	769.99	692.75	639.36	600.83	30000
35000	3217.14	2241.56	1755.82	1466.00	1274.14	1138.23	1037.30	959.66	898.32	808.20	745.92	700.97	35000
40000	3676.73	2561.78	2006.65	1675.43	1456.15	1300.84	1185.48	1096.75	1026.65	923.66	852.48	801.10	40000
45000	4136.32	2882.00	2257.48	1884.85	1638.17	1463.44	1333.67	1233.85	1154.98	1039.12	959.04	901.24	45000
50000	4595.91	3202.22	2508.31	2094.28	1820.19	1626.05	1481.85	1370.94	1283.32	1154.57	1065.60	1001.38	50000
60000	5515.09	3842.67	3009.97	2513.14	2184.23	1951.25	1778.22	1645.13	1539.98	1385.49	1278.72	1201.65	60000
75000	6893.86	4803.33	3762.46	3141.42	2730.28	2439.07	2222.77	2056.41	1924.97	1731.86	1598.40	1502.06	75000
100000	9191.82	6404.44	5016.61	4188.56	3640.38	3252.09	2963.70	2741.88	2566.63	2309.14	2131.20	2002.75	100000
125000	11489.77	8005.55	6270.76	5235.70	4550.47	4065.11	3704.62	3427.35	3208.28	2886.42	2663.99	2503.44	125000
150000	13787.72	9606.66	7524.91	6282.84	5460.56	4878.13	4445.54	4112.81	3849.94	3463.71	3196.79	3004.12	150000
175000	16085.68	11207.77	8779.06	7329.98	6370.66	5691.15	5186.47	4798.28	4491.59	4040.99	3729.59	3504.81	175000
200000	18383.63	12808.88	10033.21	8377.11	7280.75	6504.17	5927.39	5483.75	5133.25	4618.28	4262.39	4005.49	200000
250000	22979.53	16011.10	12541.51	10471.39	9100.93	8130.21	7409.23	6854.69	6416.56	5772.84	5327.98	5006.87	250000

Amount	9.0 Years	10.0 Years	11.0 Years	12.0 Years	13.0 Years	14.0 Years	15.0 Years	16.0 Years	20.0 Years	30.0 Years	40.0 Years	50.0 Years	Amount
100	1.91	1.84	1.78	1.74	1.70	1.67	1.65	1.63	1.59	1.55	1.55	1.55	100
200	3.82	3.67	3.56	3.47	3.40	3.34	3.30	3.26	3.17	3.10	3.09	3.09	200
300	5.73	5.51	5.34	5.20	5.10	5.01	4.94	4.89	4.75	4.65	4.63	4.63	300
400	7.63	7.34	7.12	6.94	6.80	6.68	6.59	6.52	6.33	6.20	6.18	6.17	400
500	9.54	9.18	8.89	8.67	8.49	8.35	8.24	8.14	7.91	7.74	7.72	7.71	500
600	11.45	11.01	10.67	10.40	10.19	10.02	9.88	9.77	9.50	9.29	9.26	9.26	600
700	13.35	12.84	12.45	12.14	11.89	11.69	11.53	11.40	11.08	10.84	10.80	10.80	700
800	15.26	14.68	14.23	13.87	13.59	13.36	13.18	13.03	12.66	12.39	12.35	12.34	800
900	17.17	16.51	16.00	15.60	15.28	15.03	14.82	14.66	14.24	13.94	13.89	13.88	900
1000	19.08	18.35	17.78	17.34	16.98	16.70	16.47	16.28	15.82	15.48	15.43	15.42	1000
2000	38.15	36.69	35.56	34.67	33.96	33.39	32.94	32.56	31.64	30.96	30.86	30.84	2000
3000	57.22	55.03	53.33	52.00	50.94	50.09	49.40	48.84	47.46	46.44	46.28	46.26	3000
4000	76.29	73.37	71.11	69.33	67.92	66.78	65.87	65.12	63.28	61.92	61.71	61.68	4000
5000	95.36	91.71	88.88	86.66	84.89	83.48	82.33	81.40	79.10	77.40	77.14	77.10	5000
6000	114.43	110.05	106.66	103.99	101.87	100.17	98.80	97.68	94.92	92.88	92.56	92.51	6000
7000	133.50	128.40	124.44	121.32	118.85	116.86	115.26	113.96	110.74	108.36	107.99	107.93	7000
8000	152.57	146.74	142.21	138.65	135.83	133.56	131.73	130.24	126.56	123.84	123.42	123.35	8000
9000	171.64	165.08	159.99	155.99	152.80	150.25	148.19	146.52	142.38	139.32	138.84	138.77	9000
10000	190.71	183.42	177.76	173.32	169.78	166.95	164.66	162.80	158.19	154.80	154.27	154.19	10000
15000	286.07	275.13	266.64	259.97	254.67	250.42	246.98	244.20	237.29	232.20	231.40	231.28	15000
20000	381.42	366.84	355.52	346.63	339.56	333.89	329.31	325.60	316.38	309.59	308.54	308.37	20000
25000	476.78	458.55	444.40	433.28	424.44	417.36	411.64	406.99	395.48	386.99	385.67	385.46	25000
30000	572.13	550.25	533.28	519.94	509.33	500.83	493.96	488.39	474.57	464.39	462.80	462.55	30000
35000	667.48	641.96	622.16	606.59	594.22	584.30	576.29	569.79	553.67	541.79	539.94	539.64	35000
40000	762.84	733.67	711.04	693.25	679.11	667.77	658.61	651.19	632.76	619.18	617.07	616.74	40000
45000	858.19	825.38	799.92	779.91	763.99	751.24	740.94	732.58	711.86	696.58	694.20	693.83	45000
50000	953.55	917.09	888.80	866.56	848.88	834.71	823.27	813.98	790.95	773.98	771.34	770.92	50000
60000	1144.25	1100.50	1066.56	1039.87	1018.65	1001.65	987.92	976.78	949.14	928.77	925.60	925.10	60000
75000	1430.32	1375.63	1333.20	1299.84	1273.32	1252.06	1234.90	1220.97	1186.43	1160.96	1157.00	1156.37	75000
100000	1907.09	1834.17	1777.60	1733.12	1697.76	1669.41	1646.53	1627.96	1581.90	1547.95	1542.67	1541.83	100000
125000	2383.86	2292.71	2222.00	2166.40	2122.20	2086.76	2058.16	2034.95	1977.38	1934.94	1928.34	1927.29	125000
150000	2860.63	2751.25	2666.40	2599.68	2546.63	2504.11	2469.79	2441.93	2372.85	2321.92	2314.00	2312.74	150000
175000	3337.40	3209.79	3110.80	3032.95	2971.07	2921.46	2881.42	2848.92	2768.32	2708.91	2699.67	2698.20	175000
200000	3814.17	3668.34	3555.20	3466.23	3395.51	3338.82	3293.05	3255.91	3163.80	3095.89	3085.33	3083.66	200000
250000	4767.71	4585.42	4444.00	4332.79	4244.39	4173.52	4116.31	4069.89	3954.75	3869.87	3856.67	3854.57	250000

Amount	1.0 Year	1.5 Years	2.0 Years	2.5 Years	3.0 Years	3.5 Years	4.0 Years	4.5 Years	5.0 Years	6.0 Years	7.0 Years	8.0 Years	Amount
100	9.21	6.42	5.03	4.21	3.66	3.27	2.98	2.76	2.59	2.33	2.15	2.02	100
200	18.41	12.84	10.06	8.41	7.31	6.53	5.96	5.52	5.17	4.65	4.30	4.04	200
300	27.62	19.25	15.09	12.61	10.96	9.80	8.94	8.27	7.75	6.98	6.44	6.06	300
400	36.82	25.67	20.12	16.81	14.62	13.06	11.91	11.03	10.33	9.30	8.59	8.08	400
500	46.02	32.09	25.15	21.01	18.27	16.33	14.89	13.78	12.91	11.62	10.73	10.10	500
600	55.23	38.50	30.18	25.21	21.92	19.59	17.87	16.54	15.49	13.95	12.88	12.11	600
700	64.43	44.92	35.21	29.41	25.58	22.86	20.84	19.29	18.07	16.27	15.03	14.13	700
800	73.63	51.34	40.23	33.61	29.23	26.12	23.82	22.05	20.65	18.59	17.17	16.15	800
900	82.84	57.75	45.26	37.81	32.88	29.39	26.80	24.80	23.23	20.92	19.32	18.17	900
1000	92.04	64.17	50.29	42.01	36.53	32.65	29.77	27.56	25.81	23.24	21.46	20.19	1000
2000	184.08	128.33	100.58	84.02	73.06	65.30	59.54	55.11	51.61	46.47	42.92	40.37	2000
3000	276.12	192.50	150.87	126.03	109.59	97.95	89.31	82.66	77.41	69.71	64.38	60.55	3000
4000	368.15	256.66	201.15	168.04	146.12	130.60	119.08	110.22	103.22	92.94	85.84	80.73	4000
5000	460.19	320.82	251.44	210.05	182.65	163.25	148.85	137.77	129.02	116.17	107.30	100.91	5000
6000	552.23	384.99	301.73	252.06	219.18	195.90	178.62	165.32	154.82	139.41	128.76	121.09	6000
7000	644.27	449.15	352.02	294.07	255.71	228.55	208.38	192.88	180.63	162.64	150.22	141.27	7000
8000	736.30	513.32	402.30	336.08	292.24	261.20	238.15	220.43	206.43	185.88	171.68	161.45	8000
9000	828.34	577.48	452.59	378.09	328.77	293.85	267.92	247.98	232.23	209.11	193.14	181.63	9000
10000	920.38	641.64	502.88	420.10	365.30	326.50	297.69	275.53	258.04	232.34	214.60	201.81	10000
15000	1380.56	962.46	754.31	630.14	547.95	489.75	446.53	413.30	387.05	348.51	321.90	302.71	15000
20000	1840.75	1283.28	1005.75	840.19	730.60	653.00	595.37	551.06	516.07	464.68	429.20	403.61	20000
25000	2300.94	1604.10	1257.19	1050.23	913.25	816.24	744.21	688.83	645.08	580.85	536.50	504.51	25000
30000	2761.12	1924.92	1508.62	1260.28	1095.90	979.49	893.06	826.59	774.10	697.02	643.80	605.42	30000
35000	3221.31	2245.74	1760.06	1470.32	1278.55	1142.74	1041.90	964.36	903.12	813.19	751.10	706.32	35000
40000	3681.50	2566.56	2011.49	1680.37	1461.19	1305.99	1190.74	1102.12	1032.13	929.36	858.39	807.22	40000
45000	4141.68	2887.38	2262.93	1890.41	1643.84	1469.23	1339.58	1239.89	1161.15	1045.53	965.69	908.12	45000
50000	4601.87	3208.20	2514.37	2100.46	1826.49	1632.48	1488.42	1377.65	1290.16	1161.70	1072.99	1009.02	50000
60000	5522.24	3849.84	3017.24	2520.55	2191.79	1958.98	1786.11	1653.18	1548.20	1394.03	1287.59	1210.83	60000
75000	6902.80	4812.30	3771.55	3150.68	2739.74	2448.72	2232.63	2066.47	1935.24	1742.54	1609.48	1513.53	75000
100000	9203.74	6416.39	5028.73	4200.91	3652.98	3264.96	2976.84	2755.30	2580.32	2323.39	2145.98	2018.04	100000
125000	11504.67	8020.49	6285.91	5251.13	4566.22	4081.19	3721.05	3444.12	3225.40	2904.23	2682.47	2522.55	125000
150000	13805.60	9624.59	7543.09	6301.36	5479.47	4897.43	4465.26	4132.94	3870.48	3485.08	3218.96	3027.06	150000
175000	16106.53	11228.68	8800.27	7351.59	6392.71	5713.67	5209.47	4821.77	4515.56	4065.92	3755.46	3531.57	175000
200000	18407.47	12832.78	10057.45	8401.81	7305.95	6529.91	5953.68	5510.59	5160.64	4646.77	4291.95	4036.08	200000
250000	23009.33	16040.97	12571.81	10502.26	9132.44	8162.38	7442.09	6888.24	6450.80	5808.46	5364.93	5045.10	250000

Amount	9.0 Years	10.0 Years	11.0 Years	12.0 Years	13.0 Years	14.0 Years	15.0 Years	16.0 Years	20.0 Years	30.0 Years	40.0 Years	50.0 Years	Amount
100	1.93	1.86	1.80	1.76	1.72	1.69	1.67	1.65	1.61	1.57	1.57	1.57	100
200	3.85	3.71	3.59	3.51	3.44	3.38	3.33	3.30	3.21	3.14	3.13	3.13	200
300	5.77	5.56	5.39	5.26	5.15	5.07	4.94	4.94	4.81	4.71	4.70	4.69	300
400	7.70	7.41	7.18	7.01	6.87	6.75	6.66	6.59	6.41	6.28	6.26	6.26	400
500	9.62	9.26	8.98	8.76	8.58	8.44	8.33	8.24	8.01	7.85	7.82	7.82	500
600	11.54	11.11	10.77	10.51	10.30	10.13	9.99	9.88	9.61	9.42	9.39	9.38	600
700	13.47	12.96	12.56	12.26	12.01	11.82	11.66	11.53	11.21	10.98	10.95	10.94	700
800	15.39	14.81	14.36	14.01	13.73	13.50	13.32	13.18	12.82	12.55	12.51	12.51	800
900	17.31	16.66	16.15	15.76	15.44	15.19	14.99	14.82	14.42	14.12	14.08	14.07	900
1000	19.23	18.51	17.95	17.51	17.16	16.88	16.65	16.47	16.02	15.69	15.64	15.63	1000
2000	38.46	37.01	35.89	35.01	34.31	33.75	33.30	32.93	32.03	31.37	31.27	31.26	2000
3000	57.69	55.52	53.83	52.51	51.46	50.62	49.95	49.40	48.04	47.06	46.91	46.88	3000
4000	76.92	74.02	71.78	70.01	68.61	67.49	66.59	65.86	64.06	62.74	62.54	62.51	4000
5000	96.15	92.53	89.72	87.52	85.77	84.37	83.24	82.32	80.07	78.43	78.18	78.14	5000
6000	115.38	111.03	107.66	105.02	102.92	101.24	99.89	98.79	96.08	94.11	93.81	93.76	6000
7000	134.61	129.53	125.60	122.52	120.07	118.11	116.53	115.25	112.09	109.79	109.44	109.39	7000
8000	153.83	148.04	143.55	140.02	137.22	134.98	133.18	131.72	128.11	125.48	125.08	125.02	8000
9000	173.06	166.54	161.49	157.52	154.38	151.86	149.83	148.18	144.12	141.16	140.71	140.64	9000
10000	192.29	185.05	179.43	175.03	171.53	168.73	166.47	164.64	160.13	156.85	156.35	156.27	10000
15000	288.43	277.57	269.15	262.54	257.29	253.09	249.71	246.96	240.19	235.27	234.52	234.40	15000
20000	384.58	370.09	358.86	350.05	343.05	337.45	332.94	329.28	320.26	313.69	312.69	312.53	20000
25000	480.72	462.61	448.58	437.56	428.81	421.81	416.17	411.60	400.32	392.11	390.86	390.67	25000
30000	576.86	555.13	538.29	525.07	514.57	506.17	499.41	493.92	480.38	470.53	469.03	468.80	30000
35000	673.01	647.65	628.00	612.58	600.33	590.53	582.64	576.24	560.45	548.95	547.20	546.93	35000
40000	769.15	740.17	717.72	700.09	686.10	674.90	665.87	658.56	640.51	627.37	625.37	625.06	40000
45000	865.29	832.69	807.43	787.60	771.86	759.26	749.11	740.88	720.57	705.79	703.54	703.19	45000
50000	961.44	925.21	897.15	875.11	857.62	843.62	832.34	823.20	800.64	784.21	781.71	781.33	50000
60000	1153.72	1110.25	1076.58	1050.13	1029.14	1012.34	998.81	987.84	960.76	941.05	938.05	937.59	60000
75000	1442.15	1387.82	1345.72	1312.66	1286.42	1265.43	1248.51	1234.80	1200.95	1176.31	1172.57	1171.99	75000
100000	1922.87	1850.42	1794.29	1750.21	1715.23	1687.23	1664.67	1646.40	1601.27	1568.41	1563.42	1562.65	100000
125000	2403.59	2313.02	2242.86	2187.76	2144.04	2109.04	2080.84	2058.00	2001.59	1960.52	1954.28	1953.31	125000
150000	2884.30	2775.63	2691.43	2625.32	2572.84	2530.85	2497.01	2469.59	2401.90	2352.62	2345.13	2343.97	150000
175000	3365.02	3238.23	3140.00	3062.87	3001.65	2952.65	2913.18	2881.19	2802.22	2744.72	2735.98	2734.63	175000
200000	3845.74	3700.83	3588.57	3500.42	3430.46	3374.46	3329.34	3292.79	3202.54	3136.82	3126.84	3125.29	200000
250000	4807.17	4626.04	4485.72	4375.52	4288.07	4218.08	4161.68	4115.99	4003.17	3921.03	3908.55	3906.61	250000

Amount	1.0 Year	1.5 Years	2.0 Years	2.5 Years	3.0 Years	3.5 Years	4.0 Years	4.5 Years	5.0 Years	6.0 Years	7.0 Years	8.0 Years	Amount
100	9.22	6.43	5.05	4.22	3.67	3.28	3.00	2.77	2.60	2.34	2.17	2.04	100
200	18.44	12.86	10.09	8.43	7.34	6.56	5.99	5.54	5.19	4.68	4.33	4.07	200
300	27.65	19.29	15.13	12.64	11.00	9.84	8.98	8.31	7.79	7.02	6.49	6.11	300
400	36.87	25.72	20.17	16.86	14.67	13.12	11.97	11.08	10.38	9.36	8.65	8.14	400
500	46.08	32.15	25.21	21.07	18.33	16.39	14.96	13.85	12.98	11.69	10.81	10.17	500
600	55.30	38.58	30.25	25.28	22.00	19.67	17.95	16.62	15.57	14.03	12.97	12.21	600
700	64.51	45.00	35.29	29.50	25.66	22.95	20.94	19.39	18.16	16.37	15.13	14.24	700
800	73.73	51.43	40.33	33.71	29.33	26.23	23.93	22.15	20.76	18.71	17.29	16.27	800
900	82.95	57.86	45.37	37.92	33.00	29.51	26.92	24.92	23.35	21.04	19.45	18.31	900
1000	92.16	64.29	50.41	42.14	36.66	32.78	29.91	27.69	25.95	23.38	21.61	20.34	1000
2000	184.32	128.57	100.82	84.27	73.32	65.56	59.81	55.38	51.89	46.76	43.22	40.67	2000
3000	276.47	192.86	151.23	126.40	109.97	98.34	89.71	83.07	77.83	70.14	64.83	61.01	3000
4000	368.63	257.14	201.64	168.54	146.63	131.12	119.61	110.75	103.77	93.51	86.44	81.34	4000
5000	460.79	321.42	252.05	210.67	183.29	163.90	149.51	138.44	129.71	116.89	108.05	101.67	5000
6000	552.94	385.71	302.46	252.80	219.94	196.68	179.41	166.13	155.65	140.27	129.65	122.01	6000
7000	645.10	449.99	352.87	294.93	256.60	229.45	209.31	193.82	181.59	163.64	151.26	142.34	7000
8000	737.26	514.27	403.27	337.07	293.25	262.23	239.21	221.50	207.53	187.02	172.87	162.68	8000
9000	829.41	578.56	453.68	379.20	329.91	295.01	269.11	249.19	233.47	210.40	194.48	183.01	9000
10000	921.57	642.84	504.09	421.33	366.57	327.79	299.01	276.88	259.41	233.77	216.09	203.34	10000
15000	1382.35	964.26	756.13	632.00	549.85	491.68	448.51	415.32	389.11	350.66	324.13	305.01	15000
20000	1843.14	1285.67	1008.18	842.66	733.13	655.57	598.01	553.75	518.82	467.54	432.17	406.68	20000
25000	2303.92	1607.09	1260.22	1053.32	916.41	819.47	747.51	692.19	648.52	584.42	540.21	508.35	25000
30000	2764.70	1928.51	1512.26	1263.99	1099.69	983.36	897.01	830.63	778.22	701.31	648.25	610.02	30000
35000	3225.49	2249.93	1764.31	1474.65	1282.97	1147.25	1046.51	969.07	907.92	818.19	756.29	711.69	35000
40000	3686.27	2571.34	2016.35	1685.31	1466.25	1311.14	1196.01	1107.50	1037.63	935.07	864.33	813.36	40000
45000	4147.05	2892.76	2268.39	1895.98	1649.53	1475.04	1345.51	1245.94	1167.33	1051.96	972.37	915.03	45000
50000	4607.83	3214.18	2520.44	2106.64	1832.81	1638.93	1495.01	1384.38	1297.03	1168.84	1080.41	1016.70	50000
60000	5529.40	3857.01	3024.52	2527.97	2199.37	1966.71	1794.01	1661.25	1556.44	1402.61	1296.49	1220.04	60000
75000	6911.75	4821.27	3780.65	3159.96	2749.21	2458.39	2242.51	2076.57	1945.55	1753.26	1620.61	1525.04	75000
100000	9215.66	6428.35	5040.87	4213.28	3665.61	3277.85	2990.02	2768.75	2594.06	2337.68	2160.81	2033.39	100000
125000	11519.58	8035.44	6301.08	5266.60	4582.01	4097.32	3737.52	3460.94	3242.57	2922.10	2701.01	2541.74	125000
150000	13823.49	9642.53	7561.30	6319.92	5498.41	4916.78	4485.02	4153.13	3891.09	3506.51	3241.21	3050.08	150000
175000	16127.41	11249.61	8821.51	7373.23	6414.81	5736.24	5232.53	4845.32	4539.60	4090.93	3781.41	3558.43	175000
200000	18431.32	12856.70	10081.73	8426.55	7331.21	6555.70	5980.03	5537.50	5188.12	4675.35	4321.61	4066.78	200000
250000	23039.15	16070.88	12602.16	10533.19	9164.01	8194.63	7475.03	6921.88	6485.14	5844.19	5402.01	5083.47	250000

Amount	9.0 Years	10.0 Years	11.0 Years	12.0 Years	13.0 Years	14.0 Years	15.0 Years	16.0 Years	20.0 Years	30.0 Years	40.0 Years	50.0 Years	Amount
100	1.94	1.87	1.82	1.77	1.74	1.71	1.69	1.67	1.63	1.59	1.59	1.59	100
200	3.88	3.74	3.63	3.54	3.47	3.42	3.37	3.33	3.25	3.18	3.17	3.17	200
300	5.82	5.61	5.44	5.31	5.20	5.12	5.05	5.00	4.87	4.77	4.76	4.76	300
400	7.76	7.47	7.25	7.07	6.94	6.83	6.74	6.66	6.49	6.36	6.34	6.34	400
500	9.70	9.34	9.06	8.84	8.67	8.53	8.42	8.33	8.11	7.95	7.93	7.92	500
600	11.64	11.21	10.87	10.61	10.40	10.24	10.10	9.99	9.73	9.54	9.51	9.51	600
700	13.58	13.07	12.68	12.38	12.13	11.94	11.79	11.66	11.35	11.13	11.09	11.09	700
800	15.51	14.94	14.49	14.14	13.87	13.65	13.47	13.32	12.97	12.72	12.68	12.67	800
900	17.45	16.81	16.30	15.91	15.60	15.35	15.15	14.99	14.59	14.31	14.26	14.26	900
1000	19.39	18.67	18.12	17.68	17.33	17.06	16.83	16.65	16.21	15.89	15.85	15.84	1000
2000	38.78	37.34	36.23	35.35	34.66	34.11	33.66	33.30	32.42	31.78	31.69	31.67	2000
3000	58.17	56.01	54.34	53.03	51.99	51.16	50.49	49.95	48.63	47.67	47.53	47.51	3000
4000	77.55	74.67	72.45	70.70	69.32	68.21	67.32	66.60	64.83	63.56	63.37	63.34	4000
5000	96.94	93.34	90.56	88.37	86.64	85.26	84.15	83.25	81.04	79.45	79.21	79.18	5000
6000	116.33	112.01	108.67	106.05	103.97	102.31	100.98	99.90	97.25	95.34	95.06	95.01	6000
7000	135.71	130.68	126.78	123.72	121.30	119.36	117.81	116.55	113.45	111.23	110.90	110.85	7000
8000	155.10	149.34	144.89	141.39	138.63	136.41	134.64	133.20	129.66	127.12	126.74	126.68	8000
9000	174.49	168.01	163.00	159.07	155.95	153.47	151.46	149.85	145.87	143.01	142.58	142.52	9000
10000	193.88	186.68	181.11	176.74	173.28	170.52	168.29	166.49	162.07	158.89	158.42	158.35	10000
15000	290.81	280.01	271.66	265.11	259.92	255.77	252.44	249.74	243.11	238.34	237.63	237.52	15000
20000	387.75	373.35	362.21	353.48	346.56	341.03	336.58	332.98	324.14	317.78	316.84	316.70	20000
25000	484.68	466.69	452.76	441.85	433.20	426.28	420.72	416.23	405.18	397.23	396.05	395.87	25000
30000	581.62	560.02	543.31	530.21	519.83	511.54	504.87	499.47	486.21	476.67	475.26	475.04	30000
35000	678.55	653.36	633.87	618.58	606.47	596.80	589.01	582.72	567.24	556.12	554.47	554.22	35000
40000	775.49	746.69	724.42	706.95	693.11	682.05	673.16	665.96	648.28	635.56	633.67	633.39	40000
45000	872.42	840.03	814.97	795.32	779.75	767.31	757.30	749.21	729.31	715.01	712.88	712.56	45000
50000	969.36	933.37	905.52	883.69	866.39	852.56	841.44	832.45	810.35	794.45	792.09	791.74	50000
60000	1163.23	1120.04	1086.62	1060.42	1039.66	1023.07	1009.73	998.94	972.42	953.34	950.51	950.08	60000
75000	1454.04	1400.05	1358.28	1325.53	1299.58	1278.84	1262.16	1248.67	1215.52	1191.67	1188.14	1187.60	75000
100000	1938.71	1866.73	1811.04	1767.37	1732.77	1705.12	1682.88	1664.90	1620.69	1588.90	1584.18	1583.47	100000
125000	2423.39	2333.41	2263.80	2209.21	2165.96	2131.40	2103.60	2081.12	2025.86	1986.12	1980.22	1979.33	125000
150000	2908.07	2800.09	2716.55	2651.05	2599.15	2557.68	2524.32	2497.34	2431.03	2383.34	2376.27	2375.20	150000
175000	3392.74	3266.77	3169.31	3092.89	3032.34	2983.96	2945.04	2913.57	2836.20	2780.57	2772.31	2771.06	175000
200000	3877.42	3733.45	3622.07	3534.73	3465.53	3410.23	3365.76	3329.79	3241.37	3177.79	3168.35	3166.93	200000
250000	4846.78	4666.81	4527.59	4418.42	4331.91	4262.79	4207.20	4162.24	4051.72	3972.24	3960.44	3958.66	250000

Amount	1.0 Year	1.5 Years	2.0 Years	2.5 Years	3.0 Years	3.5 Years	4.0 Years	4.5 Years	5.0 Years	6.0 Years	7.0 Years	8.0 Years	Amount
100	9.23	6.45	5.06	4.23	3.68	3.30	3.01	2.79	2.61	2.36	2.18	2.05	100
200	18.46	12.89	10.11	8.46	7.36	6.59	6.01	5.57	5.22	4.71	4.36	4.10	200
300	27.69	19.33	15.16	12.68	11.04	9.88	9.01	8.35	7.83	7.06	6.53	6.15	300
400	36.92	25.77	20.22	16.91	14.72	13.17	12.02	11.13	10.44	9.41	8.71	8.20	400
500	46.14	32.21	25.27	21.13	18.40	16.46	15.02	13.92	13.04	11.77	10.88	10.25	500
600	55.37	38.65	30.32	25.36	22.07	19.75	18.02	16.70	15.65	14.12	13.06	12.30	600
700	64.60	45.09	35.38	29.58	25.75	23.04	21.03	19.48	18.26	16.47	15.23	14.35	700
800	73.83	51.53	40.43	33.81	29.43	26.33	24.03	22.26	20.87	18.82	17.41	16.40	800
900	83.05	57.97	45.48	38.04	33.11	29.62	27.03	25.05	23.48	21.17	19.59	18.44	900
1000	92.28	64.41	50.54	42.26	36.79	32.91	30.04	27.83	26.08	23.53	21.76	20.49	1000
2000	184.56	128.81	101.07	84.52	73.57	65.82	60.07	55.65	52.16	47.05	43.52	40.98	2000
3000	276.83	193.21	151.60	126.77	110.35	98.73	90.10	83.47	78.24	70.57	65.28	61.47	3000
4000	369.11	257.62	202.13	169.03	147.14	131.64	120.13	111.29	104.32	94.09	87.03	81.96	4000
5000	461.38	322.02	252.66	211.29	183.92	164.54	150.17	139.12	130.40	117.61	108.79	102.44	5000
6000	553.66	386.42	303.19	253.54	220.70	197.45	180.20	166.94	156.47	141.13	130.55	122.93	6000
7000	645.94	450.83	353.72	295.80	257.48	230.36	210.23	194.76	182.55	164.65	152.30	143.42	7000
8000	738.21	515.23	404.25	338.06	294.27	263.27	240.26	222.58	208.63	188.17	174.06	163.91	8000
9000	830.49	579.63	454.78	380.31	331.05	296.17	270.29	250.41	234.71	211.69	195.82	184.40	9000
10000	922.76	644.04	505.31	422.57	367.83	329.08	300.33	278.23	260.79	235.21	217.57	204.88	10000
15000	1384.14	966.05	757.96	633.85	551.74	493.62	450.49	417.34	391.18	352.81	326.36	307.32	15000
20000	1845.52	1288.07	1010.61	845.14	735.66	658.16	600.65	556.45	521.57	470.41	435.14	409.76	20000
25000	2306.90	1610.09	1263.26	1056.42	919.57	822.70	750.81	695.57	651.96	588.01	543.93	512.20	25000
30000	2768.28	1932.10	1515.91	1267.70	1103.48	987.24	900.97	834.68	782.35	705.61	652.71	614.64	30000
35000	3229.66	2254.12	1768.56	1478.99	1287.39	1151.78	1051.13	973.79	912.75	823.21	761.49	717.08	35000
40000	3691.04	2576.13	2021.21	1690.27	1471.31	1316.32	1201.29	1112.90	1043.14	940.81	870.28	819.52	40000
45000	4152.42	2898.15	2273.86	1901.55	1655.22	1480.85	1351.45	1252.01	1173.53	1058.41	979.06	921.96	45000
50000	4613.80	3220.17	2526.51	2112.84	1839.13	1645.39	1501.62	1391.13	1303.92	1176.01	1087.85	1024.40	50000
60000	5536.56	3864.20	3031.81	2535.40	2206.96	1974.47	1801.94	1669.35	1564.70	1411.21	1305.41	1229.28	60000
75000	6920.70	4830.25	3789.77	3169.25	2758.70	2468.09	2252.42	2086.69	1955.88	1764.01	1631.77	1536.60	75000
100000	9227.60	6440.33	5053.02	4225.67	3678.26	3290.78	3003.23	2782.25	2607.84	2352.01	2175.69	2048.79	100000
125000	11534.50	8050.41	6316.28	5282.08	4597.82	4113.48	3754.03	3477.81	3259.79	2940.02	2719.61	2560.99	125000
150000	13841.40	9660.49	7579.53	6338.50	5517.39	4936.17	4504.84	4173.37	3911.75	3528.02	3263.53	3073.19	150000
175000	16148.29	11270.57	8842.78	7394.92	6436.95	5758.86	5255.64	4868.93	4563.71	4116.02	3807.45	3585.39	175000
200000	18455.19	12880.65	10106.04	8451.33	7356.51	6581.56	6006.45	5564.49	5215.67	4704.02	4351.37	4097.58	200000
250000	23068.99	16100.81	12632.55	10564.16	9195.64	8226.95	7508.06	6955.61	6519.58	5880.03	5439.21	5121.98	250000

Amount	9.0 Years	10.0 Years	11.0 Years	12.0 Years	13.0 Years	14.0 Years	15.0 Years	16.0 Years	20.0 Years	30.0 Years	40.0 Years	50.0 Years	Amount
100	1.96	1.89	1.83	1.79	1.76	1.73	1.71	1.69	1.65	1.61	1.61	1.61	100
200	3.91	3.77	3.66	3.57	3.51	3.45	3.41	3.37	3.29	3.22	3.21	3.21	200
300	5.87	5.65	5.49	5.36	5.26	5.17	5.11	5.06	4.93	4.83	4.82	4.82	300
400	7.82	7.54	7.32	7.14	7.01	6.90	6.81	6.74	6.57	6.44	6.42	6.42	400
500	9.78	9.42	9.14	8.93	8.76	8.62	8.51	8.42	8.21	8.05	8.03	8.03	500
600	11.73	11.30	10.97	10.71	10.51	10.34	10.21	10.11	9.85	9.66	9.63	9.63	600
700	13.69	13.19	12.80	12.50	12.26	12.07	11.91	11.79	11.49	11.27	11.24	11.23	700
800	15.64	15.07	14.63	14.28	14.01	13.79	13.61	13.47	13.13	12.88	12.84	12.84	800
900	17.60	16.95	16.46	16.07	15.76	15.51	15.32	15.16	14.77	14.49	14.45	14.44	900
1000	19.55	18.84	18.28	17.85	17.51	17.24	17.02	16.84	16.41	16.10	16.05	16.05	1000
2000	39.10	37.67	36.56	35.70	35.01	34.47	34.03	33.67	32.81	32.19	32.10	32.09	2000
3000	58.64	56.50	54.84	53.54	52.52	51.70	51.04	50.51	49.21	48.29	48.15	48.13	3000
4000	78.19	75.33	73.12	71.39	70.02	68.93	68.05	67.34	65.61	64.38	64.20	64.18	4000
5000	97.74	94.16	91.40	89.23	87.52	86.16	85.06	84.18	82.01	80.47	80.25	80.22	5000
6000	117.28	112.99	109.68	107.08	105.03	103.39	102.07	101.01	98.41	96.57	96.30	96.26	6000
7000	136.83	131.82	127.95	124.93	122.53	120.62	119.09	117.85	114.82	112.66	112.35	112.30	7000
8000	156.37	150.65	146.23	142.77	140.03	137.85	136.10	134.68	131.22	128.76	128.40	128.35	8000
9000	175.92	169.48	164.51	160.62	157.54	155.08	153.11	151.52	147.62	144.85	144.45	144.39	9000
10000	195.47	188.31	182.79	178.46	175.04	172.31	170.12	168.35	164.02	160.94	160.50	160.43	10000
15000	293.20	282.47	274.18	267.69	262.56	258.46	255.18	252.52	246.03	241.41	240.75	240.65	15000
20000	390.93	376.62	365.57	356.92	350.08	344.62	340.23	336.70	328.04	321.88	320.99	320.86	20000
25000	488.66	470.78	456.97	446.15	437.60	430.77	425.29	420.87	410.04	402.35	401.24	401.08	25000
30000	586.39	564.93	548.36	535.38	525.11	516.92	510.35	505.04	492.05	482.82	481.49	481.29	30000
35000	684.12	659.09	639.75	624.61	612.63	603.08	595.41	589.21	574.06	563.29	561.73	561.50	35000
40000	781.85	753.24	731.14	713.84	700.15	689.23	680.46	673.39	656.07	643.76	641.98	641.72	40000
45000	879.58	847.40	822.53	803.07	787.67	775.38	765.52	757.56	738.07	724.23	722.23	721.93	45000
50000	977.31	941.55	913.93	892.30	875.19	861.54	850.58	841.73	820.08	804.70	802.47	802.15	50000
60000	1172.77	1129.86	1096.71	1070.76	1050.22	1033.84	1020.69	1010.08	984.10	965.64	962.97	962.57	60000
75000	1465.96	1412.32	1370.89	1338.44	1312.78	1292.30	1275.86	1262.59	1230.12	1207.05	1203.71	1203.22	75000
100000	1954.61	1883.10	1827.85	1784.59	1750.37	1723.07	1701.15	1683.46	1640.16	1609.40	1604.94	1604.29	100000
125000	2443.27	2353.87	2284.81	2230.74	2187.96	2153.83	2126.43	2104.32	2050.19	2011.75	2006.18	2005.36	125000
150000	2931.92	2824.64	2741.78	2676.88	2625.55	2584.60	2551.72	2525.18	2460.23	2414.10	2407.41	2406.43	150000
175000	3420.57	3295.42	3198.73	3123.03	3063.14	3015.36	2977.01	2946.04	2870.27	2816.45	2808.65	2807.50	175000
200000	3909.22	3766.19	3655.69	3569.17	3500.73	3446.13	3402.29	3366.91	3280.31	3218.80	3209.88	3208.57	200000
250000	4886.53	4707.74	4569.61	4461.47	4375.91	4307.66	4252.86	4208.63	4100.38	4023.50	4012.35	4010.71	250000

Amount	1.0 Year	1.5 Years	2.0 Years	2.5 Years	3.0 Years	3.5 Years	4.0 Years	4.5 Years	5.0 Years	6.0 Years	7.0 Years	8.0 Years	Amount
100	9.24	6.46	5.07	4.24	3.70	3.31	3.02	2.80	2.63	2.37	2.20	2.07	100
200	18.48	12.91	10.14	8.48	7.39	6.61	6.04	5.60	5.25	4.74	4.39	4.13	200
300	27.72	19.36	15.20	12.72	11.08	9.92	9.05	8.39	7.87	7.10	6.58	6.20	300
400	36.96	25.81	20.27	16.96	14.77	13.22	12.07	11.19	10.49	9.47	8.77	8.26	400
500	46.20	32.27	25.33	21.20	18.46	16.52	15.09	13.98	13.11	11.84	10.96	10.33	500
600	55.44	38.72	30.40	25.43	22.15	19.83	18.10	16.78	15.73	14.20	13.15	12.39	600
700	64.68	45.17	35.46	29.67	25.84	23.13	21.12	19.58	18.36	16.57	15.34	14.45	700
800	73.92	51.62	40.53	33.91	29.53	26.43	24.14	22.37	20.98	18.94	17.53	16.52	800
900	83.16	58.08	45.59	38.15	33.22	29.74	27.15	25.17	23.60	21.30	19.72	18.58	900
1000	92.40	64.53	50.66	42.39	36.91	33.04	30.17	27.96	26.22	23.67	21.91	20.65	1000
2000	184.80	129.05	101.31	84.77	73.82	66.08	60.33	55.92	52.44	47.33	43.82	41.29	2000
3000	277.19	193.57	151.96	127.15	110.73	99.12	90.50	83.88	78.65	71.00	65.72	61.93	3000
4000	369.59	258.10	202.61	169.53	147.64	132.15	120.66	111.84	104.87	94.66	87.63	82.57	4000
5000	461.98	322.62	253.26	211.91	184.55	165.19	150.83	139.79	131.09	118.32	109.54	103.22	5000
6000	554.38	387.14	303.92	254.29	221.46	198.23	180.99	167.75	157.30	141.99	131.44	123.86	6000
7000	646.77	451.67	354.57	296.67	258.37	231.27	211.16	195.71	183.52	165.65	153.35	144.50	7000
8000	739.17	516.19	405.22	339.05	295.28	264.30	241.32	223.67	209.74	189.32	175.25	165.14	8000
9000	831.56	580.71	455.87	381.43	332.19	297.34	271.49	251.62	235.95	212.98	197.16	185.79	9000
10000	923.96	645.24	506.52	423.81	369.10	330.38	301.65	279.58	262.17	236.64	219.07	206.43	10000
15000	1385.94	967.85	759.78	635.72	553.64	495.56	452.47	419.37	393.25	354.96	328.60	309.64	15000
20000	1847.91	1290.47	1013.04	847.62	738.19	660.75	603.30	559.16	524.33	473.28	438.13	412.85	20000
25000	2309.89	1613.08	1266.30	1059.52	922.74	825.94	754.12	698.95	655.42	591.60	547.66	516.07	25000
30000	2771.87	1935.70	1519.56	1271.43	1107.28	991.12	904.94	838.74	786.50	709.92	657.19	619.28	30000
35000	3233.84	2258.31	1772.82	1483.33	1291.83	1156.31	1055.77	978.52	917.58	828.24	766.72	722.49	35000
40000	3695.82	2580.93	2026.08	1695.24	1476.38	1321.50	1206.59	1118.31	1048.66	946.56	876.25	825.70	40000
45000	4157.80	2903.54	2279.34	1907.14	1660.92	1486.68	1357.41	1258.10	1179.75	1064.88	985.78	928.92	45000
50000	4619.77	3226.16	2532.60	2119.04	1845.47	1651.87	1508.24	1397.89	1310.83	1183.20	1095.31	1032.13	50000
60000	5543.73	3871.39	3039.12	2542.85	2214.56	1982.24	1809.88	1677.47	1572.99	1419.84	1314.37	1238.55	60000
75000	6929.66	4839.24	3798.90	3178.56	2768.20	2477.80	2262.35	2096.83	1966.24	1774.80	1642.96	1548.19	75000
100000	9239.54	6452.31	5065.19	4238.08	3690.94	3303.74	3016.47	2795.77	2621.65	2366.39	2190.62	2064.25	100000
125000	11549.43	8065.39	6331.49	5297.60	4613.67	4129.67	3770.58	3494.72	3277.06	2957.99	2738.27	2580.31	125000
150000	13859.31	9678.47	7597.79	6357.12	5536.40	4955.60	4524.70	4193.66	3932.47	3549.59	3285.92	3096.37	150000
175000	16169.20	11291.55	8864.08	7416.64	6459.13	5781.54	5278.81	4892.60	4587.88	4141.18	3833.58	3612.44	175000
200000	18479.08	12904.62	10130.38	8476.16	7381.87	6607.47	6032.93	5591.54	5243.29	4732.78	4381.23	4128.50	200000
250000	23098.85	16130.78	12662.97	10595.19	9227.33	8259.33	7541.16	6989.43	6554.11	5915.98	5476.53	5160.62	250000

Amount	9.0 Years	10.0 Years	11.0 Years	12.0 Years	13.0 Years	14.0 Years	15.0 Years	16.0 Years	20.0 Years	30.0 Years	40.0 Years	50.0 Years	Amount
100	1.98	1.90	1.85	1.81	1.77	1.75	1.72	1.71	1.66	1.63	1.63	1.63	100
200	3.95	3.80	3.69	3.61	3.54	3.49	3.44	3.41	3.32	3.26	3.26	3.26	200
300	5.92	5.70	5.54	5.41	5.31	5.23	5.16	5.11	4.98	4.89	4.88	4.88	300
400	7.89	7.60	7.38	7.21	7.08	6.97	6.88	6.81	6.64	6.52	6.51	6.51	400
500	9.86	9.50	9.23	9.01	8.85	8.71	8.60	8.52	8.30	8.15	8.13	8.13	500
600	11.83	11.40	11.07	10.82	10.61	10.45	10.32	10.22	9.96	9.78	9.76	9.76	600
700	13.80	13.30	12.92	12.62	12.38	12.19	12.04	11.92	11.62	11.41	11.38	11.38	700
800	15.77	15.20	14.76	14.42	14.15	13.93	13.76	13.62	13.28	13.04	13.01	13.01	800
900	17.74	17.10	16.61	16.22	15.92	15.67	15.48	15.32	14.94	14.67	14.64	14.63	900
1000	19.71	19.00	18.45	18.02	17.69	17.42	17.20	17.03	16.60	16.30	16.26	16.26	1000
2000	39.42	38.00	36.90	36.04	35.37	34.83	34.39	34.05	33.20	32.60	32.52	32.51	2000
3000	59.12	56.99	55.35	54.06	53.05	52.24	51.59	51.07	49.79	48.90	48.78	48.76	3000
4000	78.83	75.99	73.79	72.08	70.73	69.65	68.78	68.09	66.39	65.20	65.03	65.01	4000
5000	98.53	94.98	92.24	90.10	88.41	87.06	85.98	85.11	82.99	81.50	81.29	81.26	5000
6000	118.24	113.98	110.69	108.12	106.09	104.47	103.17	102.13	99.58	97.80	97.55	97.51	6000
7000	137.94	132.97	129.13	126.14	123.77	121.88	120.37	119.15	116.18	114.10	113.80	113.76	7000
8000	157.65	151.97	147.58	144.15	141.45	139.29	137.56	136.17	132.78	130.40	130.06	130.01	8000
9000	177.36	170.96	166.03	162.17	159.13	156.70	154.76	153.19	149.37	146.70	146.32	146.26	9000
10000	197.06	189.96	184.48	180.19	176.81	174.11	171.95	170.21	165.97	163.00	162.58	162.52	10000
15000	295.59	284.93	276.71	270.28	265.21	261.17	257.93	255.32	248.95	244.49	243.86	243.77	15000
20000	394.12	379.91	368.95	360.38	353.61	348.22	343.90	340.42	331.94	325.99	325.15	325.03	20000
25000	492.65	474.89	461.18	450.47	442.01	435.27	429.87	425.52	414.92	407.49	406.43	406.28	25000
30000	591.17	569.86	553.42	540.56	530.41	522.33	515.85	510.63	497.90	488.98	487.72	487.54	30000
35000	689.70	664.84	645.65	630.66	618.81	609.38	601.82	595.73	580.89	570.48	569.00	568.79	35000
40000	788.23	759.81	737.89	720.75	707.21	696.43	687.79	680.83	663.87	651.97	650.29	650.05	40000
45000	886.76	854.79	830.13	810.84	795.61	783.49	773.77	765.94	746.85	733.47	731.57	731.30	45000
50000	985.29	949.77	922.36	900.94	884.02	870.54	859.74	851.04	829.84	814.97	812.86	812.56	50000
60000	1182.34	1139.72	1106.83	1081.12	1060.82	1044.65	1031.69	1021.25	995.80	977.96	975.43	975.07	60000
75000	1477.93	1424.65	1383.54	1351.40	1326.02	1305.81	1289.61	1276.56	1244.75	1222.45	1219.29	1218.83	75000
100000	1970.57	1899.53	1844.72	1801.87	1768.03	1741.08	1719.48	1702.07	1659.67	1629.93	1625.71	1625.11	100000
125000	2463.21	2374.41	2305.90	2252.34	2210.03	2176.34	2149.34	2127.59	2074.59	2037.41	2032.14	2031.38	125000
150000	2955.85	2849.29	2767.07	2702.80	2652.04	2611.61	2579.21	2553.11	2489.50	2444.89	2438.57	2437.66	150000
175000	3448.49	3324.17	3228.25	3153.27	3094.04	3046.88	3009.08	2978.62	2904.42	2852.37	2845.00	2843.93	175000
200000	3941.14	3799.05	3689.43	3603.73	3536.05	3482.15	3438.95	3404.14	3319.33	3259.85	3251.42	3250.21	200000
250000	4926.42	4748.81	4611.79	4504.67	4420.06	4352.68	4298.68	4255.17	4149.17	4074.81	4064.28	4062.76	250000

Amount	1.0 Year	1.5 Years	2.0 Years	2.5 Years	3.0 Years	3.5 Years	4.0 Years	4.5 Years	5.0 Years	6.0 Years	7.0 Years	8.0 Years	Amount
100	9.26	6.47	5.08	4.26	3.71	3.32	3.03	2.81	2.64	2.39	2.21	2.08	100
200	18.51	12.93	10.16	8.51	7.41	6.64	6.06	5.62	5.28	4.77	4.42	4.16	200
300	27.76	19.40	15.24	12.76	11.12	9.96	9.09	8.43	7.91	7.15	6.62	6.24	300
400	37.01	25.86	20.31	17.01	14.82	13.27	12.12	11.24	10.55	9.53	8.83	8.32	400
500	46.26	32.33	25.39	21.26	18.52	16.59	15.15	14.05	13.18	11.91	11.03	10.40	500
600	55.51	38.79	30.47	25.51	22.23	19.91	18.18	16.86	15.82	14.29	13.24	12.48	600
700	64.77	45.26	35.55	29.76	25.93	23.22	21.21	19.67	18.45	16.67	15.44	14.56	700
800	74.02	51.72	40.62	34.01	29.63	26.54	24.24	22.48	21.09	19.05	17.65	16.64	800
900	83.27	58.18	45.70	38.26	33.34	29.86	27.27	25.29	23.72	21.43	19.86	18.72	900
1000	92.52	64.65	50.78	42.51	37.04	33.17	30.30	28.10	26.36	23.81	22.06	20.80	1000
2000	185.03	129.29	101.55	85.02	74.08	66.34	60.60	56.19	52.71	47.62	44.12	41.60	2000
3000	277.55	193.93	152.33	127.52	111.11	99.51	90.90	84.28	79.07	71.43	66.17	62.40	3000
4000	370.06	258.58	203.10	170.03	148.15	132.67	121.19	112.38	105.42	95.24	88.23	83.20	4000
5000	462.58	323.22	253.87	212.53	185.19	165.84	151.49	140.47	131.78	119.05	110.28	103.99	5000
6000	555.09	387.86	304.65	255.04	222.22	199.01	181.79	168.56	158.13	142.85	132.34	124.79	6000
7000	647.61	452.51	355.42	297.54	259.26	232.18	212.09	196.66	184.49	166.66	154.40	145.59	7000
8000	740.12	517.15	406.20	340.05	296.30	265.34	242.38	224.75	210.84	190.47	176.45	166.39	8000
9000	832.64	581.79	456.97	382.55	333.33	298.51	272.68	252.84	237.20	214.28	198.51	187.18	9000
10000	925.15	646.44	507.74	425.06	370.37	331.68	302.98	280.94	263.55	238.09	220.56	207.98	10000
15000	1387.73	969.65	761.61	637.58	555.55	497.51	454.46	421.40	395.33	357.13	330.84	311.97	15000
20000	1850.30	1292.87	1015.48	850.11	740.73	663.35	605.95	561.87	527.10	476.17	441.12	415.96	20000
25000	2312.88	1616.08	1269.35	1062.63	925.91	829.18	757.44	702.34	658.88	595.21	551.40	519.94	25000
30000	2775.45	1939.30	1523.22	1275.16	1111.09	995.02	908.92	842.80	790.65	714.25	661.68	623.93	30000
35000	3238.03	2262.51	1777.09	1487.68	1296.28	1160.86	1060.41	983.27	922.43	833.29	771.96	727.92	35000
40000	3700.60	2585.73	2030.96	1700.21	1481.46	1326.69	1211.90	1123.74	1054.20	952.33	882.24	831.91	40000
45000	4163.18	2908.94	2284.82	1912.73	1666.64	1492.53	1363.38	1264.20	1185.98	1071.37	992.52	935.90	45000
50000	4625.75	3232.16	2538.69	2125.26	1851.82	1658.36	1514.87	1404.67	1317.75	1190.41	1102.80	1039.88	50000
60000	5550.90	3878.59	3046.43	2550.31	2222.18	1990.03	1817.84	1685.60	1581.30	1428.49	1323.36	1247.86	60000
75000	6938.62	4848.24	3808.04	3187.89	2777.73	2487.54	2272.30	2107.00	1976.63	1785.62	1654.20	1559.82	75000
100000	9251.49	6464.31	5077.38	4250.51	3703.64	3316.72	3029.74	2809.34	2635.50	2380.82	2205.60	2079.76	100000
125000	11564.37	8080.39	6346.72	5313.14	4629.55	4145.90	3787.17	3511.67	3294.38	2976.02	2756.99	2599.70	125000
150000	13877.24	9696.47	7616.07	6375.77	5555.45	4975.08	4544.60	4214.00	3953.25	3571.23	3308.39	3119.64	150000
175000	16190.11	11312.54	8885.41	7438.39	6481.36	5804.26	5302.04	4916.33	4612.13	4166.43	3859.79	3639.58	175000
200000	18502.98	12928.62	10154.76	8501.02	7407.27	6633.44	6059.47	5618.67	5271.00	4761.63	4411.19	4159.52	200000
250000	23128.73	16160.78	12693.44	10626.27	9259.09	8291.79	7574.34	7023.33	6588.75	5952.04	5513.98	5199.40	250000

Amount	9.0 Years	10.0 Years	11.0 Years	12.0 Years	13.0 Years	14.0 Years	15.0 Years	16.0 Years	20.0 Years	30.0 Years	40.0 Years	50.0 Years	Amount
100	1.99	1.92	1.87	1.82	1.79	1.76	1.74	1.73	1.68	1.66	1.65	1.65	100
200	3.98	3.84	3.73	3.64	3.58	3.52	3.48	3.45	3.36	3.31	3.30	3.30	200
300	5.96	5.75	5.59	5.46	5.36	5.28	5.22	5.17	5.04	4.96	4.94	4.94	300
400	7.95	7.67	7.45	7.28	7.15	7.04	6.96	6.89	6.72	6.61	6.59	6.59	400
500	9.94	9.59	9.31	9.10	8.93	8.80	8.69	8.61	8.40	8.26	8.24	8.23	500
600	11.92	11.50	11.17	10.92	10.72	10.56	10.43	10.33	10.08	9.91	9.88	9.88	600
700	13.91	13.42	13.04	12.74	12.51	12.32	12.17	12.05	11.76	11.56	11.53	11.53	700
800	15.90	15.33	14.90	14.56	14.29	14.08	13.91	13.77	13.44	13.21	13.18	13.17	800
900	17.88	17.25	16.76	16.38	16.08	15.84	15.65	15.49	15.12	14.86	14.82	14.82	900
1000	19.87	19.17	18.62	18.20	17.86	17.60	17.38	17.21	16.80	16.51	16.47	16.46	1000
2000	39.74	38.33	37.24	36.39	35.72	35.19	34.76	34.42	33.59	33.01	32.93	32.92	2000
3000	59.60	57.49	55.85	54.58	53.58	52.78	52.14	51.63	50.38	49.52	49.40	49.38	3000
4000	79.47	76.65	74.47	72.77	71.43	70.37	69.52	68.83	67.17	66.02	65.86	65.84	4000
5000	99.33	95.81	93.09	90.97	89.29	87.96	86.90	86.04	83.97	82.53	82.33	82.30	5000
6000	119.20	114.97	111.70	109.16	107.15	105.55	104.28	103.25	100.76	99.03	98.79	98.76	6000
7000	139.07	134.13	130.32	127.35	125.01	123.14	121.65	120.46	117.55	115.54	115.26	115.22	7000
8000	158.93	153.29	148.94	145.54	142.86	140.74	139.03	137.66	134.34	132.04	131.72	131.68	8000
9000	178.80	172.45	167.55	163.73	160.72	158.33	156.41	154.87	151.14	148.55	148.19	148.14	9000
10000	198.66	191.61	186.17	181.93	178.58	175.92	173.79	172.08	167.93	165.05	164.65	164.60	10000
15000	297.99	287.41	279.25	272.89	267.87	263.88	260.68	258.12	251.89	247.57	246.98	246.89	15000
20000	397.32	383.21	372.33	363.85	357.15	351.83	347.58	344.15	335.85	330.10	329.30	329.19	20000
25000	496.65	479.01	465.42	454.81	446.44	439.79	434.47	430.19	419.81	412.62	411.63	411.49	25000
30000	595.98	574.81	558.50	545.77	535.73	527.75	521.36	516.23	503.77	495.14	493.95	493.78	30000
35000	695.31	670.61	651.58	636.73	625.01	615.70	608.25	602.26	587.73	577.67	576.27	576.08	35000
40000	794.64	766.41	744.66	727.69	714.30	703.66	695.15	688.30	671.69	660.19	658.60	658.38	40000
45000	893.97	862.21	837.74	818.65	803.59	791.62	782.04	774.34	755.66	742.71	740.92	740.67	45000
50000	993.29	958.01	930.83	909.61	892.88	879.57	868.93	860.37	839.62	825.24	823.25	822.97	50000
60000	1191.95	1149.61	1116.99	1091.53	1071.45	1055.49	1042.72	1032.45	1007.54	990.28	987.90	987.56	60000
75000	1489.94	1437.01	1396.24	1364.41	1339.31	1319.36	1303.40	1290.56	1259.42	1237.85	1234.87	1234.45	75000
100000	1986.58	1916.02	1861.65	1819.21	1785.75	1759.14	1737.86	1720.74	1679.23	1650.47	1646.49	1645.93	100000
125000	2483.23	2395.02	2327.06	2274.01	2232.18	2198.93	2172.32	2150.93	2099.03	2063.08	2058.11	2057.41	125000
150000	2979.87	2874.02	2792.47	2728.82	2678.62	2638.71	2606.79	2581.11	2518.84	2475.70	2469.73	2468.89	150000
175000	3476.52	3353.02	3257.88	3183.62	3125.05	3078.50	3041.25	3011.30	2938.64	2888.31	2881.35	2880.37	175000
200000	3973.16	3832.03	3723.29	3638.42	3571.49	3518.28	3475.71	3441.48	3358.45	3300.93	3292.97	3291.86	200000
250000	4966.45	4790.03	4654.11	4548.02	4464.36	4397.85	4344.64	4301.85	4198.06	4126.16	4116.22	4114.82	250000

Monthly Payment Required To Amortize A Loan

Amount	1.0 Year	1.5 Years	2.0 Years	2.5 Years	3.0 Years	3.5 Years	4.0 Years	4.5 Years	5.0 Years	6.0 Years	7.0 Years	8.0 Years	Amount
100	9.27	6.48	5.09	4.27	3.72	3.33	3.05	2.83	2.65	2.40	2.23	2.10	100
200	18.53	12.96	10.18	8.53	7.44	6.66	6.09	5.65	5.30	4.80	4.45	4.20	200
300	27.80	19.43	15.27	12.79	11.15	9.99	9.13	8.47	7.95	7.19	6.67	6.29	300
400	37.06	25.91	20.36	17.06	14.87	13.32	12.18	11.30	10.60	9.59	8.89	8.39	400
500	46.32	32.39	25.45	21.32	18.59	16.65	15.22	14.12	13.25	11.98	11.11	10.48	500
600	55.59	38.86	30.54	25.58	22.30	19.98	18.26	16.94	15.90	14.38	13.33	12.58	600
700	64.85	45.34	35.63	29.85	26.02	23.31	21.31	19.77	18.55	16.77	15.55	14.67	700
800	74.11	51.82	40.72	34.11	29.74	26.64	24.35	22.59	21.20	19.17	17.77	16.77	800
900	83.38	58.29	45.81	38.37	33.45	29.97	27.39	25.41	23.85	21.56	19.99	18.86	900
1000	92.64	64.77	50.90	42.63	37.17	33.30	30.44	28.23	26.50	23.96	22.21	20.96	1000
2000	185.27	129.53	101.80	85.26	74.33	66.60	60.87	56.46	52.99	47.91	44.42	41.91	2000
3000	277.90	194.29	152.69	127.89	111.50	99.90	91.30	84.69	79.49	71.86	66.62	62.86	3000
4000	370.54	259.06	203.59	170.52	148.66	133.19	121.73	112.92	105.98	95.82	88.83	83.82	4000
5000	463.18	323.82	254.48	213.15	185.82	166.49	152.16	141.15	132.47	119.77	111.04	104.77	5000
6000	555.81	388.58	305.38	255.78	222.99	199.79	182.59	169.38	158.97	143.72	133.24	125.72	6000
7000	648.45	453.35	356.28	298.41	260.15	233.09	213.02	197.61	185.46	167.67	155.45	146.68	7000
8000	741.08	518.11	407.17	341.04	297.31	266.38	243.45	225.84	211.96	191.63	177.65	167.63	8000
9000	833.72	582.87	458.07	383.67	334.48	299.68	273.88	254.07	238.45	215.58	199.86	188.58	9000
10000	926.35	647.64	508.96	426.30	371.64	332.98	304.31	282.30	264.94	239.53	222.07	209.54	10000
15000	1389.52	971.45	763.44	639.45	557.46	499.46	456.46	423.44	397.41	359.30	333.10	314.30	15000
20000	1852.70	1295.27	1017.92	852.60	743.28	665.95	608.61	564.59	529.88	479.06	444.13	419.07	20000
25000	2315.87	1619.09	1272.40	1065.74	929.09	832.44	760.76	705.74	662.35	598.83	555.16	523.84	25000
30000	2779.04	1942.90	1526.88	1278.89	1114.91	998.92	912.92	846.88	794.82	718.59	666.19	628.60	30000
35000	3242.21	2266.72	1781.36	1492.04	1300.73	1165.41	1065.07	988.03	927.29	838.35	777.22	733.37	35000
40000	3705.39	2590.53	2035.84	1705.19	1486.55	1331.90	1217.22	1129.18	1059.76	958.12	888.25	838.13	40000
45000	4168.56	2914.35	2290.32	1918.34	1672.37	1498.38	1369.37	1270.32	1192.23	1077.88	999.28	942.90	45000
50000	4631.73	3238.17	2544.80	2131.48	1858.18	1664.87	1521.52	1411.47	1324.70	1197.65	1110.31	1047.67	50000
60000	5558.08	3885.80	3053.75	2557.78	2229.82	1997.84	1825.83	1693.76	1589.64	1437.17	1332.38	1257.20	60000
75000	6947.59	4857.25	3817.19	3197.22	2787.27	2497.30	2282.28	2117.20	1987.05	1796.47	1665.47	1571.50	75000
100000	9263.46	6476.33	5089.59	4262.96	3716.36	3329.73	3043.04	2822.93	2649.39	2395.29	2220.62	2095.33	100000
125000	11579.32	8095.41	6361.98	5328.70	4645.45	4162.16	3803.80	3528.67	3311.74	2994.11	2775.78	2619.16	125000
150000	13895.18	9714.49	7634.38	6394.44	5574.54	4994.60	4564.56	4234.40	3974.09	3592.93	3330.93	3142.99	150000
175000	16211.04	11333.57	8906.77	7460.18	6503.63	5827.03	5325.32	4940.13	4636.43	4191.75	3886.09	3666.82	175000
200000	18526.91	12952.66	10179.17	8525.92	7432.72	6659.46	6086.08	5645.86	5298.78	4790.57	4441.24	4190.65	200000
250000	23158.63	16190.81	12723.96	10657.40	9290.90	8324.32	7607.60	7057.33	6623.48	5988.21	5551.55	5238.31	250000

Amount	9.0 Years	10.0 Years	11.0 Years	12.0 Years	13.0 Years	14.0 Years	15.0 Years	16.0 Years	20.0 Years	30.0 Years	40.0 Years	50.0 Years	Amount
100	2.01	1.94	1.88	1.84	1.81	1.78	1.76	1.74	1.70	1.68	1.67	1.67	100
200	4.01	3.87	3.76	3.68	3.61	3.56	3.52	3.48	3.40	3.35	3.34	3.34	200
300	6.01	5.80	5.64	5.51	5.42	5.34	5.28	5.22	5.10	5.02	5.01	5.01	300
400	8.02	7.74	7.52	7.35	7.22	7.11	7.03	6.96	6.80	6.69	6.67	6.67	400
500	10.02	9.67	9.40	9.19	9.02	8.89	8.79	8.70	8.50	8.36	8.34	8.34	500
600	12.02	11.60	11.28	11.02	10.83	10.67	10.54	10.44	10.20	10.03	10.01	10.01	600
700	14.02	13.53	13.16	12.86	12.63	12.45	12.30	12.18	11.90	11.70	11.68	11.67	700
800	16.03	15.47	15.03	14.70	14.43	14.22	14.06	13.92	13.60	13.37	13.34	13.34	800
900	18.03	17.40	16.91	16.53	16.24	16.00	15.81	15.66	15.29	15.04	15.01	15.01	900
1000	20.03	19.33	18.79	18.37	18.04	17.78	17.57	17.40	16.99	16.72	16.68	16.67	1000
2000	40.06	38.66	37.58	36.74	36.08	35.55	35.13	34.79	33.98	33.43	33.35	33.34	2000
3000	60.08	57.98	56.36	55.10	54.11	53.32	52.69	52.19	50.97	50.14	50.02	50.01	3000
4000	80.11	77.31	75.15	73.47	72.15	71.10	70.26	69.58	67.96	66.85	66.70	66.67	4000
5000	100.14	96.63	93.94	91.84	90.18	88.87	87.82	86.98	84.95	83.56	83.37	83.34	5000
6000	120.16	115.96	112.72	110.20	108.22	106.64	105.38	104.37	101.93	100.27	100.04	100.01	6000
7000	140.19	135.28	131.51	128.57	126.25	124.41	122.95	121.77	118.92	116.98	116.71	116.68	7000
8000	160.22	154.61	150.30	146.93	144.29	142.19	140.51	139.16	135.91	133.69	133.39	133.34	8000
9000	180.24	173.94	169.08	165.30	162.32	159.96	158.07	156.56	152.90	150.40	150.06	150.01	9000
10000	200.27	193.26	187.87	183.67	180.36	177.73	175.63	173.95	169.89	167.11	166.73	166.68	10000
15000	300.40	289.89	281.80	275.50	270.53	266.59	263.45	260.92	254.83	250.66	250.09	250.02	15000
20000	400.54	386.52	375.73	367.33	360.71	355.46	351.26	347.90	339.77	334.21	333.46	333.35	20000
25000	500.67	483.14	469.66	459.16	450.89	444.32	439.08	434.87	424.71	417.76	416.82	416.69	25000
30000	600.80	579.77	563.60	550.99	541.06	533.18	526.89	521.84	509.65	501.31	500.18	500.03	30000
35000	700.93	676.40	657.53	642.82	631.24	622.05	614.71	608.82	594.59	584.86	583.55	583.37	35000
40000	801.07	773.03	751.46	734.65	721.41	710.91	702.52	695.79	679.53	668.41	666.91	666.70	40000
45000	901.20	869.66	845.39	826.48	811.59	799.77	790.34	782.76	764.48	751.96	750.27	750.04	45000
50000	1001.33	966.28	939.32	918.31	901.77	888.64	878.15	869.74	849.42	835.51	833.64	833.38	50000
60000	1201.60	1159.54	1127.19	1101.97	1082.12	1066.36	1053.78	1043.68	1019.30	1002.62	1000.06	1000.05	60000
75000	1501.99	1449.42	1408.98	1377.46	1352.65	1332.95	1317.23	1304.60	1274.12	1253.27	1250.45	1250.07	75000
100000	2002.66	1932.56	1878.64	1836.61	1803.53	1777.27	1756.30	1739.47	1698.83	1671.02	1667.27	1666.76	100000
125000	2503.32	2415.70	2348.30	2295.77	2254.41	2221.59	2195.38	2174.34	2123.54	2088.78	2084.09	2083.44	125000
150000	3003.98	2898.84	2817.96	2754.92	2705.29	2665.90	2634.45	2609.20	2548.24	2506.53	2500.90	2500.13	150000
175000	3504.64	3381.98	3287.61	3214.07	3156.17	3110.22	3073.52	3044.07	2972.95	2924.29	2917.72	2916.82	175000
200000	4005.31	3865.12	3757.27	3673.22	3607.05	3554.54	3512.60	3478.94	3397.65	3342.04	3334.53	3333.50	200000
250000	5006.63	4831.40	4696.59	4591.53	4508.81	4443.17	4390.75	4348.67	4247.07	4177.55	4168.17	4166.88	250000

Amount	1.0 Year	1.5 Years	2.0 Years	2.5 Years	3.0 Years	3.5 Years	4.0 Years	4.5 Years	5.0 Years	6.0 Years	7.0 Years	8.0 Years	Amount
100	9.28	6.49	5.11	4.28	3.73	3.35	3.06	2.84	2.67	2.41	2.24	2.12	100
200	18.56	12.98	10.21	8.56	7.46	6.69	6.12	5.68	5.33	4.82	4.48	4.23	200
300	27.83	19.47	15.31	12.83	11.19	10.03	9.17	8.51	7.99	7.23	6.71	6.34	300
400	37.11	25.96	20.41	17.11	14.92	13.38	12.23	11.35	10.66	9.64	8.95	8.45	400
500	46.38	32.45	25.51	21.38	18.65	16.72	15.29	14.19	13.32	12.05	11.18	10.56	500
600	55.66	38.94	30.62	25.66	22.38	20.06	18.34	17.02	15.98	14.46	13.42	12.67	600
700	64.93	45.42	35.72	29.93	26.11	23.40	21.40	19.86	18.65	16.87	15.65	14.78	700
800	74.21	51.91	40.82	34.21	29.84	26.75	24.46	22.70	21.31	19.28	17.89	16.89	800
900	83.48	58.40	45.92	38.48	33.57	30.09	27.51	25.53	23.97	21.69	20.13	19.00	900
1000	92.76	64.89	51.02	42.76	37.30	33.43	30.57	28.37	26.64	24.10	22.36	21.11	1000
2000	185.51	129.77	102.04	85.51	74.59	66.86	61.13	56.74	53.27	48.20	44.72	42.22	2000
3000	278.27	194.66	153.06	128.27	111.88	100.29	91.70	85.10	79.90	72.30	67.08	63.33	3000
4000	371.02	259.54	204.08	171.02	149.17	133.72	122.26	113.47	106.54	96.40	89.43	84.44	4000
5000	463.78	324.42	255.10	213.78	186.46	167.14	152.82	141.83	133.17	120.49	111.79	105.55	5000
6000	556.53	389.31	306.11	256.53	223.75	200.57	183.39	170.20	159.80	144.59	134.15	126.66	6000
7000	649.28	454.19	357.13	299.29	261.04	234.00	213.95	198.56	186.44	168.69	156.50	147.77	7000
8000	742.04	519.07	408.15	342.04	298.33	267.43	244.51	226.93	213.07	192.79	178.86	168.88	8000
9000	834.79	583.96	459.17	384.79	335.62	300.85	275.08	255.30	239.70	216.89	201.22	189.99	9000
10000	927.55	648.84	510.19	427.55	372.92	334.28	305.64	283.66	266.34	240.98	223.57	211.10	10000
15000	1391.32	973.26	765.28	641.32	559.37	501.42	458.46	425.49	399.50	361.47	335.36	316.65	15000
20000	1855.09	1297.67	1020.37	855.09	745.83	668.56	611.28	567.32	532.67	481.96	447.14	422.19	20000
25000	2318.86	1622.09	1275.46	1068.86	932.28	835.70	764.10	709.15	665.83	602.45	558.93	527.74	25000
30000	2782.63	1946.51	1530.55	1282.63	1118.74	1002.84	916.92	850.97	799.00	722.94	670.71	633.29	30000
35000	3246.40	2270.93	1785.64	1496.41	1305.19	1169.97	1069.74	992.80	932.17	843.43	782.50	738.83	35000
40000	3710.17	2595.34	2040.73	1710.18	1491.65	1337.11	1222.55	1134.63	1065.33	963.92	894.28	844.38	40000
45000	4173.94	2919.76	2295.82	1923.95	1678.10	1504.25	1375.37	1276.46	1198.50	1084.41	1006.07	949.93	45000
50000	4637.71	3244.18	2550.91	2137.72	1864.56	1671.39	1528.19	1418.29	1331.66	1204.90	1117.85	1055.47	50000
60000	5565.26	3893.01	3061.09	2565.26	2237.47	2005.67	1833.83	1701.94	1598.00	1445.88	1341.42	1266.57	60000
75000	6956.57	4866.26	3826.36	3206.58	2796.84	2507.08	2292.28	2127.43	1997.49	1807.35	1676.78	1583.21	75000
100000	9275.42	6488.35	5101.81	4275.44	3729.11	3342.77	3056.38	2836.57	2663.32	2409.80	2235.70	2110.94	100000
125000	11594.28	8110.44	6377.26	5344.30	4661.39	4178.46	3820.47	3545.71	3329.15	3012.25	2794.63	2638.68	125000
150000	13913.13	9732.52	7652.71	6413.15	5593.67	5014.16	4584.56	4254.85	3994.98	3614.70	3353.55	3166.41	150000
175000	16231.99	11354.61	8928.16	7482.01	6525.95	5849.85	5348.66	4963.99	4660.81	4217.15	3912.48	3694.14	175000
200000	18550.84	12976.69	10203.61	8550.87	7458.22	6685.44	6112.75	5673.13	5326.64	4819.60	4471.40	4221.88	200000
250000	23188.55	16220.87	12754.51	10688.59	9322.78	8356.92	7640.93	7091.41	6658.30	6024.50	5589.25	5277.35	250000

Amount	9.0 Years	10.0 Years	11.0 Years	12.0 Years	13.0 Years	14.0 Years	15.0 Years	16.0 Years	20.0 Years	30.0 Years	40.0 Years	50.0 Years	Amount
100	2.02	1.95	1.90	1.86	1.83	1.80	1.78	1.76	1.72	1.70	1.69	1.69	100
200	4.04	3.90	3.80	3.71	3.65	3.60	3.55	3.52	3.44	3.39	3.38	3.38	200
300	6.06	5.85	5.69	5.57	5.47	5.39	5.33	5.28	5.16	5.08	5.07	5.07	300
400	8.08	7.80	7.59	7.42	7.29	7.19	7.10	7.04	6.88	6.77	6.76	6.76	400
500	10.10	9.75	9.48	9.28	9.11	8.98	8.88	8.80	8.60	8.46	8.45	8.44	500
600	12.12	11.70	11.38	11.13	10.93	10.78	10.65	10.55	10.32	10.15	10.13	10.13	600
700	14.14	13.65	13.27	12.98	12.75	12.57	12.43	12.31	12.03	11.85	11.82	11.82	700
800	16.16	15.60	15.17	14.84	14.58	14.37	14.20	14.07	13.75	13.54	13.51	13.51	800
900	18.17	17.55	17.07	16.69	16.40	16.16	15.98	15.83	15.47	15.23	15.20	15.19	900
1000	20.19	19.50	18.96	18.55	18.22	17.96	17.75	17.59	17.19	16.92	16.89	16.88	1000
2000	40.38	38.99	37.92	37.09	36.43	35.91	35.50	35.17	34.37	33.84	33.77	33.76	2000
3000	60.57	58.48	56.88	55.63	54.65	53.87	53.25	52.75	51.56	50.75	50.65	50.63	3000
4000	80.76	77.97	75.83	74.17	72.86	71.82	71.00	70.33	68.74	67.67	67.53	67.51	4000
5000	100.94	97.46	94.79	92.71	91.07	89.78	88.74	87.92	85.93	84.58	84.41	84.38	5000
6000	121.13	116.95	113.75	111.25	109.29	107.73	106.49	105.50	103.11	101.50	101.29	101.26	6000
7000	141.32	136.45	132.70	129.79	127.50	125.69	124.24	123.08	120.30	118.42	118.17	118.14	7000
8000	161.51	155.94	151.66	148.33	145.71	143.64	141.99	140.66	137.48	135.33	135.05	135.01	8000
9000	181.69	175.43	170.62	166.87	163.93	161.60	159.74	158.25	154.67	152.25	151.93	151.89	9000
10000	201.88	194.92	189.57	185.41	182.14	179.55	177.48	175.83	171.85	169.16	168.81	168.76	10000
15000	302.82	292.38	284.36	278.12	273.21	269.32	266.22	263.74	257.78	253.74	253.21	253.14	15000
20000	403.76	389.84	379.14	370.82	364.28	359.09	354.96	351.65	343.70	338.32	337.61	337.52	20000
25000	504.70	487.30	473.93	463.52	455.35	448.87	443.70	439.57	429.62	422.90	422.00	421.90	25000
30000	605.64	584.75	568.71	556.23	546.41	538.64	532.44	527.48	515.55	507.48	506.42	506.28	30000
35000	706.58	682.21	663.49	648.93	637.48	628.41	621.18	615.39	601.47	592.06	590.82	590.66	35000
40000	807.52	779.67	758.28	741.63	728.55	718.18	709.92	703.30	687.39	676.64	675.22	675.03	40000
45000	908.45	877.13	853.06	834.34	819.62	807.96	798.66	791.22	773.32	761.22	759.63	759.41	45000
50000	1009.39	974.59	947.85	927.04	910.69	897.73	887.40	879.13	859.24	845.80	844.03	843.79	50000
60000	1211.27	1169.50	1137.42	1112.45	1092.82	1077.27	1064.88	1054.95	1031.09	1014.96	1012.83	1012.55	60000
75000	1514.09	1461.88	1421.77	1390.56	1366.03	1346.59	1331.10	1318.69	1288.86	1268.70	1266.04	1265.69	75000
100000	2018.78	1949.17	1895.69	1854.07	1821.37	1795.45	1774.80	1758.25	1718.47	1691.60	1688.05	1687.58	100000
125000	2523.48	2436.46	2369.61	2317.59	2276.71	2244.32	2218.50	2197.81	2148.09	2114.50	2110.07	2109.47	125000
150000	3028.17	2923.75	2843.53	2781.11	2732.05	2693.18	2662.20	2637.38	2577.71	2537.39	2532.08	2531.37	150000
175000	3532.86	3411.04	3317.45	3244.63	3187.39	3142.04	3105.89	3076.94	3007.33	2960.29	2954.09	2953.26	175000
200000	4037.56	3898.33	3791.37	3708.14	3642.73	3590.90	3549.59	3516.50	3436.94	3383.19	3376.10	3375.15	200000
250000	5046.95	4872.91	4739.21	4635.18	4553.41	4488.63	4436.99	4395.62	4296.18	4228.99	4220.13	4218.94	250000

Amount	1.0 Year	1.5 Years	2.0 Years	2.5 Years	3.0 Years	3.5 Years	4.0 Years	4.5 Years	5.0 Years	6.0 Years	7.0 Years	8.0 Years	Amount
100	9.29	6.51	5.12	4.29	3.75	3.36	3.07	2.86	2.68	2.43	2.26	2.13	100
200	18.58	13.01	10.23	8.58	7.49	6.72	6.14	5.71	5.36	4.85	4.51	4.26	200
300	27.87	19.51	15.35	12.87	11.23	10.07	9.21	8.56	8.04	7.28	6.76	6.38	300
400	37.15	26.01	20.46	17.16	14.97	13.43	12.28	11.41	10.71	9.70	9.01	8.51	400
500	46.44	32.51	25.58	21.44	18.71	16.78	15.35	14.26	13.39	12.13	11.26	10.64	500
600	55.73	39.01	30.69	25.73	22.46	20.14	18.42	17.11	16.07	14.55	13.51	12.76	600
700	65.02	45.51	35.80	30.02	26.20	23.50	21.49	19.96	18.75	16.98	15.76	14.89	700
800	74.30	52.01	40.92	34.31	29.94	26.85	24.56	22.81	21.42	19.40	18.01	17.02	800
900	83.59	58.51	46.03	38.60	33.68	30.21	27.63	25.66	24.10	21.82	20.26	19.14	900
1000	92.88	65.01	51.15	42.88	37.42	33.56	30.70	28.51	26.78	24.25	22.51	21.27	1000
2000	185.75	130.01	102.29	85.76	74.84	67.12	61.40	57.01	53.55	48.49	45.02	42.54	2000
3000	278.63	195.02	153.43	128.64	112.26	100.68	92.10	85.51	80.32	72.74	67.53	63.80	3000
4000	371.50	260.02	204.57	171.52	149.68	134.24	122.79	114.01	107.10	96.98	90.04	85.07	4000
5000	464.37	325.02	255.71	214.40	187.10	167.80	153.49	142.52	133.87	121.22	112.55	106.34	5000
6000	557.25	390.03	306.85	257.28	224.52	201.36	184.19	171.02	160.64	145.47	135.05	127.60	6000
7000	650.12	455.03	357.99	300.16	261.94	234.91	214.89	199.52	187.42	169.71	157.56	148.87	7000
8000	743.00	520.04	409.13	343.04	299.36	268.47	245.58	228.02	214.19	193.95	180.07	170.13	8000
9000	835.87	585.04	460.27	385.92	336.77	302.03	276.28	256.53	240.96	218.20	202.58	191.40	9000
10000	928.74	650.04	511.41	428.80	374.19	335.59	306.98	285.03	267.73	242.44	225.09	212.67	10000
15000	1393.11	975.06	767.11	643.19	561.29	503.38	460.47	427.54	401.60	363.66	337.63	319.00	15000
20000	1857.48	1300.08	1022.81	857.59	748.38	671.17	613.95	570.05	535.46	484.88	450.17	425.33	20000
25000	2321.85	1625.10	1278.51	1071.99	935.48	838.96	767.44	712.56	669.33	606.09	562.71	531.66	25000
30000	2786.22	1950.12	1534.22	1286.38	1122.57	1006.76	920.93	855.07	803.19	727.31	675.25	637.99	30000
35000	3250.59	2275.14	1789.92	1500.78	1309.66	1174.55	1074.41	997.59	937.06	848.53	787.79	744.32	35000
40000	3714.96	2600.16	2045.62	1715.18	1496.76	1342.34	1227.90	1140.10	1070.92	969.75	900.33	850.65	40000
45000	4179.33	2925.18	2301.32	1929.57	1683.85	1510.13	1381.39	1282.61	1204.78	1090.96	1012.88	956.98	45000
50000	4643.70	3250.20	2557.02	2143.97	1870.95	1677.92	1534.87	1425.12	1338.65	1212.18	1125.42	1063.31	50000
60000	5572.44	3900.23	3068.43	2572.76	2245.14	2013.51	1841.85	1710.14	1606.38	1454.62	1350.50	1275.97	60000
75000	6965.55	4875.29	3835.53	3215.95	2806.42	2516.88	2302.31	2137.68	2007.97	1818.27	1688.12	1594.96	75000
100000	9287.40	6500.39	5114.04	4287.93	3741.89	3355.84	3069.74	2850.24	2677.29	2424.36	2250.83	2126.61	100000
125000	11609.25	8125.48	6392.55	5359.91	4677.36	4194.80	3837.18	3562.79	3346.61	3030.45	2813.54	2658.26	125000
150000	13931.10	9750.58	7671.06	6431.89	5612.83	5033.76	4604.61	4275.35	4015.93	3636.54	3376.24	3189.91	150000
175000	16252.95	11375.67	8949.57	7503.88	6548.30	5872.72	5372.05	4987.91	4685.26	4242.62	3938.95	3721.57	175000
200000	18574.80	13000.77	10228.08	8575.86	7483.77	6711.68	6139.48	5700.47	5354.58	4848.71	4501.65	4253.22	200000
250000	23218.50	16250.96	12785.10	10719.82	9354.71	8389.60	7674.35	7125.58	6693.22	6060.89	5627.07	5316.52	250000

Amount	9.0 Years	10.0 Years	11.0 Years	12.0 Years	13.0 Years	14.0 Years	15.0 Years	16.0 Years	20.0 Years	30.0 Years	40.0 Years	50.0 Years	Amount
100	2.04	1.97	1.92	1.88	1.84	1.82	1.80	1.78	1.74	1.72	1.71	1.71	100
200	4.07	3.94	3.83	3.75	3.68	3.63	3.59	3.56	3.48	3.43	3.42	3.42	200
300	6.11	5.90	5.74	5.62	5.52	5.45	5.39	5.34	5.22	5.14	5.13	5.13	300
400	8.14	7.87	7.66	7.49	7.36	7.26	7.18	7.11	6.96	6.85	6.84	6.84	400
500	10.18	9.83	9.57	9.36	9.20	9.07	8.97	8.89	8.70	8.57	8.55	8.55	500
600	12.21	11.80	11.48	11.23	11.04	10.89	10.77	10.67	10.43	10.28	10.26	10.26	600
700	14.25	13.77	13.39	13.11	12.88	12.70	12.56	12.44	12.17	11.99	11.97	11.96	700
800	16.28	15.73	15.31	14.98	14.72	14.51	14.35	14.22	13.91	13.70	13.68	13.67	800
900	18.32	17.70	17.22	16.85	16.56	16.33	16.15	16.00	15.65	15.41	15.38	15.38	900
1000	20.35	19.66	19.13	18.72	18.40	18.14	17.94	17.78	17.39	17.13	17.09	17.09	1000
2000	40.70	39.32	38.26	37.44	36.79	36.28	35.87	35.55	34.77	34.25	34.18	34.17	2000
3000	61.05	58.98	57.39	56.15	55.18	54.42	53.81	53.32	52.15	51.37	51.27	51.26	3000
4000	81.40	78.64	76.52	74.87	73.58	72.55	71.74	71.09	69.53	68.49	68.36	68.34	4000
5000	101.75	98.30	95.64	93.58	91.97	90.69	89.67	88.86	86.91	85.61	85.45	85.42	5000
6000	122.10	117.95	114.77	112.30	110.36	108.83	107.61	106.63	104.29	102.74	102.54	102.51	6000
7000	142.45	137.61	133.90	131.02	128.75	126.96	125.54	124.40	121.68	119.86	119.62	119.59	7000
8000	162.80	157.27	153.03	149.73	147.15	145.10	143.47	142.17	139.06	136.98	136.71	136.68	8000
9000	183.15	176.93	172.16	168.45	165.54	163.24	161.41	159.94	156.44	154.10	153.80	153.76	9000
10000	203.50	196.59	191.28	187.16	183.93	181.37	179.34	177.71	173.82	171.22	170.89	170.84	10000
15000	305.25	294.88	286.92	280.74	275.89	272.06	269.01	266.57	260.73	256.83	256.33	256.26	15000
20000	407.00	393.17	382.56	374.32	367.86	362.74	358.67	355.42	347.64	342.44	341.77	341.68	20000
25000	508.74	491.46	478.20	467.90	459.82	453.43	448.34	444.28	434.54	428.05	427.21	427.10	25000
30000	610.49	589.75	573.84	561.48	551.78	544.11	538.01	533.13	521.45	513.66	512.66	512.52	30000
35000	712.24	688.04	669.48	655.06	643.75	634.80	627.68	621.98	608.36	599.27	598.10	597.94	35000
40000	813.99	786.33	765.12	748.64	735.71	725.48	717.34	710.84	695.27	684.88	683.54	683.36	40000
45000	915.74	884.63	860.76	842.22	827.67	816.17	807.01	799.69	782.17	770.49	768.98	768.78	45000
50000	1017.48	982.92	956.40	935.80	919.63	906.85	896.68	888.55	869.08	856.10	854.42	854.20	50000
60000	1220.98	1179.50	1147.68	1122.96	1103.56	1088.22	1076.01	1066.25	1042.90	1027.31	1025.31	1025.04	60000
75000	1526.22	1474.37	1434.60	1403.70	1379.45	1360.27	1345.02	1332.82	1303.62	1284.14	1281.63	1281.30	75000
100000	2034.96	1965.83	1912.80	1871.59	1839.26	1813.70	1793.35	1777.09	1738.16	1712.19	1708.84	1708.40	100000
125000	2543.70	2457.28	2390.99	2339.49	2299.08	2267.12	2241.69	2221.36	2172.70	2140.23	2136.05	2135.50	125000
150000	3052.44	2948.74	2869.19	2807.39	2758.89	2720.54	2690.03	2665.63	2607.24	2568.28	2563.26	2562.60	150000
175000	3561.18	3440.20	3347.39	3275.29	3218.71	3173.96	3138.36	3109.90	3041.77	2996.32	2990.47	2989.70	175000
200000	4069.92	3931.65	3825.59	3743.18	3678.52	3627.39	3586.70	3554.17	3476.31	3424.37	3417.68	3416.80	200000
250000	5087.40	4914.56	4781.98	4678.98	4598.15	4534.23	4483.37	4442.71	4345.39	4280.46	4272.10	4271.00	250000

Amount	1.0 Year	1.5 Years	2.0 Years	2.5 Years	3.0 Years	3.5 Years	4.0 Years	4.5 Years	5.0 Years	6.0 Years	7.0 Years	8.0 Years	Amount
100	9.30	6.52	5.13	4.31	3.76	3.37	3.09	2.87	2.70	2.44	2.27	2.15	100
200	18.60	13.03	10.26	8.61	7.51	6.74	6.17	5.73	5.39	4.88	4.54	4.29	200
300	27.90	19.54	15.38	12.91	11.27	10.11	9.25	8.60	8.08	7.32	6.80	6.43	300
400	37.20	26.05	20.51	17.21	15.02	13.48	12.34	11.46	10.77	9.76	9.07	8.57	400
500	46.50	32.57	25.64	21.51	18.78	16.85	15.42	14.32	13.46	12.20	11.33	10.72	500
600	55.80	39.08	30.76	25.81	22.53	20.22	18.50	17.19	16.15	14.64	13.60	12.86	600
700	65.10	45.59	35.89	30.11	26.29	23.59	21.59	20.05	18.84	17.08	15.87	15.00	700
800	74.40	52.10	41.02	34.41	30.04	26.96	24.67	22.92	21.54	19.52	18.13	17.14	800
900	83.70	58.62	46.14	38.71	33.80	30.33	27.75	25.78	24.23	21.96	20.40	19.29	900
1000	93.00	65.13	51.27	43.01	37.55	33.69	30.84	28.64	26.92	24.39	22.66	21.43	1000
2000	185.99	130.25	102.53	86.01	75.10	67.38	61.67	57.28	53.83	48.78	45.32	42.85	2000
3000	278.99	195.38	153.79	129.02	112.65	101.07	92.50	85.92	80.74	73.17	67.98	64.27	3000
4000	371.98	260.50	205.06	172.02	150.19	134.76	123.33	114.56	107.66	97.56	90.64	85.70	4000
5000	464.97	325.63	256.32	215.03	187.74	168.45	154.16	143.20	134.57	121.95	113.30	107.12	5000
6000	557.97	390.75	307.58	258.03	225.29	202.14	184.99	171.84	161.48	146.34	135.96	128.54	6000
7000	650.96	455.88	358.85	301.04	262.83	235.83	215.82	200.48	188.40	170.73	158.62	149.97	7000
8000	743.96	521.00	410.11	344.04	300.38	269.52	246.66	229.12	215.31	195.12	181.28	171.39	8000
9000	836.95	586.12	461.37	387.04	337.93	303.21	277.49	257.76	242.22	219.51	203.94	192.81	9000
10000	929.94	651.25	512.63	430.05	375.47	336.90	308.32	286.40	269.13	243.90	226.60	214.24	10000
15000	1394.91	976.87	768.95	645.07	563.21	505.34	462.48	429.60	403.70	365.85	339.90	321.35	15000
20000	1859.88	1302.49	1025.26	860.09	750.94	673.79	616.63	572.79	538.26	487.80	453.20	428.47	20000
25000	2324.85	1628.11	1281.58	1075.12	938.68	842.24	770.79	715.99	672.83	609.74	566.50	535.59	25000
30000	2789.82	1953.73	1537.89	1290.14	1126.41	1010.68	924.95	859.19	807.39	731.69	679.80	642.70	30000
35000	3254.79	2279.36	1794.21	1505.16	1314.14	1179.13	1079.10	1002.38	941.96	853.64	793.10	749.82	35000
40000	3719.76	2604.98	2050.52	1720.18	1501.88	1347.58	1233.26	1145.58	1076.52	975.59	906.40	856.94	40000
45000	4184.73	2930.60	2306.84	1935.20	1689.61	1516.02	1387.42	1288.78	1211.09	1097.53	1019.70	964.05	45000
50000	4649.70	3256.22	2563.15	2150.23	1877.35	1684.47	1541.57	1431.97	1345.65	1219.48	1133.00	1071.17	50000
60000	5579.63	3907.46	3075.78	2580.27	2252.81	2021.36	1849.89	1718.37	1614.78	1463.38	1359.60	1285.40	60000
75000	6974.54	4884.33	3844.73	3225.34	2816.02	2526.70	2312.36	2147.96	2018.47	1829.22	1699.50	1606.75	75000
100000	9299.39	6512.44	5126.30	4300.45	3754.69	3368.94	3083.14	2863.94	2691.30	2438.96	2266.00	2142.33	100000
125000	11624.23	8140.54	6407.87	5375.56	4693.36	4211.17	3853.93	3579.92	3364.12	3048.70	2832.50	2677.91	125000
150000	13949.08	9768.65	7689.45	6450.67	5632.03	5053.40	4624.71	4295.91	4036.94	3658.44	3399.00	3213.50	150000
175000	16273.93	11396.76	8971.02	7525.78	6570.70	5895.64	5395.50	5011.89	4709.77	4268.18	3965.50	3749.08	175000
200000	18598.77	13024.87	10252.59	8600.89	7509.37	6737.87	6166.28	5727.87	5382.59	4877.91	4532.00	4284.66	200000
250000	23248.46	16281.08	12815.74	10751.11	9386.71	8422.34	7707.85	7159.84	6728.23	6097.39	5665.00	5355.82	250000

Amount	9.0 Years	10.0 Years	11.0 Years	12.0 Years	13.0 Years	14.0 Years	15.0 Years	16.0 Years	20.0 Years	30.0 Years	40.0 Years	50.0 Years	Amount
100	2.06	1.99	1.93	1.89	1.86	1.84	1.82	1.80	1.76	1.74	1.73	1.73	100
200	4.11	3.97	3.86	3.78	3.72	3.67	3.63	3.60	3.52	3.47	3.46	3.46	200
300	6.16	5.95	5.79	5.67	5.58	5.50	5.44	5.39	5.28	5.20	5.19	5.19	300
400	8.21	7.94	7.72	7.56	7.43	7.33	7.25	7.19	7.04	6.94	6.92	6.92	400
500	10.26	9.92	9.65	9.45	9.29	9.16	9.06	8.98	8.79	8.67	8.65	8.55	500
600	12.31	11.90	11.58	11.34	11.15	11.00	10.88	10.78	10.55	10.40	10.38	10.38	600
700	14.36	13.88	13.51	13.23	13.01	12.83	12.69	12.58	12.31	12.13	12.11	12.11	700
800	16.41	15.87	15.44	15.12	14.86	14.66	14.50	14.37	14.07	13.87	13.84	13.84	800
900	18.47	17.85	17.37	17.01	16.72	16.49	16.31	16.17	15.83	15.60	15.57	15.57	900
1000	20.52	19.83	19.30	18.90	18.58	18.32	18.12	17.96	17.58	17.33	17.30	17.30	1000
2000	41.03	39.66	38.60	37.79	37.15	36.64	36.24	35.92	35.16	34.66	34.60	34.59	2000
3000	61.54	59.48	57.90	56.68	55.72	54.96	54.36	53.88	52.74	51.99	51.89	51.88	3000
4000	82.05	79.31	77.20	75.57	74.29	73.28	72.48	71.84	70.32	69.32	69.19	69.17	4000
5000	102.56	99.13	96.50	94.46	92.87	91.60	90.60	89.80	87.90	86.64	86.49	86.47	5000
6000	123.08	118.96	115.80	113.36	111.44	109.92	108.72	107.76	105.48	103.97	103.78	103.76	6000
7000	143.59	138.78	135.10	132.25	130.01	128.24	126.84	125.72	123.06	121.30	121.08	121.05	7000
8000	164.10	158.61	154.40	151.14	148.58	146.56	144.96	143.68	140.64	138.63	138.38	138.34	8000
9000	184.61	178.43	173.70	170.03	167.15	164.88	163.08	161.64	158.21	155.96	155.67	155.64	9000
10000	205.12	198.26	193.00	188.92	185.73	183.20	181.20	179.60	175.79	173.28	172.97	172.93	10000
15000	307.68	297.39	289.50	283.38	278.59	274.80	271.80	269.40	263.69	259.92	259.45	259.39	15000
20000	410.24	396.51	386.00	377.84	371.45	366.40	362.40	359.20	351.58	346.56	345.93	345.85	20000
25000	512.80	495.64	482.49	472.30	464.31	458.00	452.99	449.00	439.47	433.20	432.41	432.31	25000
30000	615.36	594.77	578.99	566.76	557.17	549.60	543.59	538.79	527.37	519.84	518.89	518.77	30000
35000	717.92	693.89	675.49	661.21	650.03	641.20	634.19	628.59	615.26	606.48	605.37	605.23	35000
40000	820.48	793.02	771.99	755.67	742.89	732.80	724.79	718.39	703.16	693.12	691.86	691.70	40000
45000	923.04	892.15	868.49	850.13	835.75	824.40	815.38	808.19	791.05	779.76	778.34	778.16	45000
50000	1025.60	991.28	964.98	944.59	928.61	916.00	905.98	897.99	878.94	866.40	864.82	864.62	50000
60000	1230.72	1189.53	1157.98	1133.51	1114.33	1099.20	1087.18	1077.58	1054.73	1039.68	1037.78	1037.54	60000
75000	1538.40	1486.91	1447.47	1416.88	1392.91	1374.00	1358.97	1346.98	1318.41	1299.59	1297.23	1296.92	75000
100000	2051.20	1982.55	1929.96	1889.17	1857.22	1831.99	1811.96	1795.97	1757.88	1732.79	1729.63	1729.23	100000
125000	2564.00	2478.18	2412.45	2361.46	2321.52	2289.99	2264.95	2244.96	2197.35	2165.98	2162.04	2161.54	125000
150000	3076.80	2973.82	2894.94	2833.76	2785.82	2747.99	2717.93	2693.95	2636.82	2599.18	2594.45	2593.84	150000
175000	3589.60	3469.45	3377.43	3306.05	3250.13	3205.98	3170.92	3142.94	3076.29	3032.38	3026.85	3026.15	175000
200000	4102.40	3965.09	3859.92	3778.34	3714.43	3663.98	3623.91	3591.93	3515.76	3465.57	3459.26	3458.46	200000
250000	5127.99	4956.36	4824.90	4722.92	4643.04	4579.97	4529.89	4489.92	4394.70	4331.96	4324.08	4323.07	250000

Amount	1.0 Year	1.5 Years	2.0 Years	2.5 Years	3.0 Years	3.5 Years	4.0 Years	4.5 Years	5.0 Years	6.0 Years	7.0 Years	8.0 Years	Amount
100	9.32	6.53	5.14	4.32	3.77	3.39	3.10	2.88	2.71	2.46	2.29	2.16	100
200	18.63	13.05	10.28	8.63	7.54	6.77	6.20	5.76	5.42	4.91	4.57	4.32	200
300	27.94	19.58	15.42	12.94	11.31	10.15	9.29	8.64	8.12	7.37	6.85	6.48	300
400	37.25	26.10	20.56	17.26	15.08	13.53	12.39	11.52	10.83	9.82	9.13	8.64	400
500	46.56	32.63	25.70	21.57	18.84	16.92	15.49	14.39	13.53	12.27	11.41	10.80	500
600	55.87	39.15	30.84	25.88	22.61	20.30	18.58	17.27	16.24	14.73	13.69	12.95	600
700	65.18	45.68	35.97	30.20	26.38	23.68	21.68	20.15	18.94	17.18	15.97	15.11	700
800	74.50	52.20	41.11	34.51	30.15	27.06	24.78	23.03	21.65	19.63	18.25	17.27	800
900	83.81	58.73	46.25	38.82	33.91	30.44	27.87	25.90	24.35	22.09	20.54	19.43	900
1000	93.12	65.25	51.39	43.13	37.68	33.83	30.97	28.78	27.06	24.54	22.82	21.59	1000
2000	186.23	130.49	102.78	86.26	75.36	67.65	61.94	57.56	54.11	49.08	45.63	43.17	2000
3000	279.35	195.74	154.16	129.39	113.03	101.47	92.90	86.34	81.17	73.61	68.44	64.75	3000
4000	372.46	260.98	205.55	172.52	150.71	135.29	123.87	115.11	108.22	98.15	91.25	86.33	4000
5000	465.57	326.23	256.93	215.65	188.38	169.11	154.83	143.89	135.27	122.68	114.07	107.91	5000
6000	558.69	391.47	308.32	258.78	226.06	202.93	185.80	172.67	162.33	147.22	136.88	129.49	6000
7000	651.80	456.72	359.70	301.91	263.73	236.75	216.76	201.44	189.38	171.76	159.69	151.07	7000
8000	744.92	521.96	411.09	345.04	301.41	270.57	247.73	230.22	216.43	196.29	182.50	172.65	8000
9000	838.03	587.21	462.48	388.17	339.08	304.39	278.70	259.00	243.49	220.83	205.32	194.23	9000
10000	931.14	652.45	513.86	431.30	376.76	338.21	309.66	287.77	270.54	245.36	228.13	215.82	10000
15000	1396.71	978.68	770.79	646.95	565.13	507.31	464.49	431.66	405.81	368.04	342.19	323.72	15000
20000	1862.28	1304.90	1027.72	862.60	753.51	676.42	619.32	575.54	541.07	490.72	456.25	431.63	20000
25000	2327.85	1631.13	1284.65	1078.25	941.88	845.52	774.15	719.42	676.34	613.40	570.31	539.53	25000
30000	2793.42	1957.35	1541.57	1293.90	1130.26	1014.62	928.98	863.31	811.61	736.08	684.37	647.44	30000
35000	3258.99	2283.58	1798.50	1509.55	1318.63	1183.73	1083.80	1007.19	946.87	858.76	798.43	755.34	35000
40000	3724.56	2609.80	2055.43	1725.20	1507.01	1352.83	1238.63	1151.07	1082.14	981.44	912.49	863.25	40000
45000	4190.12	2936.03	2312.36	1940.84	1695.38	1521.93	1393.46	1294.96	1217.41	1104.12	1026.56	971.15	45000
50000	4655.69	3262.25	2569.29	2156.49	1883.76	1691.03	1548.29	1438.84	1352.67	1226.80	1140.62	1079.06	50000
60000	5586.83	3914.70	3083.14	2587.79	2260.51	2029.24	1857.95	1726.61	1623.21	1472.16	1368.74	1294.87	60000
75000	6983.54	4893.37	3853.93	3234.74	2825.64	2536.55	2322.43	2158.26	2029.01	1840.20	1710.92	1618.58	75000
100000	9311.38	6524.50	5138.57	4312.98	3767.51	3382.06	3096.57	2877.68	2705.34	2453.60	2281.23	2158.11	100000
125000	11639.23	8155.62	6423.21	5391.22	4709.39	4227.58	3870.72	3597.09	3381.67	3067.00	2851.53	2697.63	125000
150000	13967.07	9786.74	7707.85	6469.47	5651.27	5073.09	4644.86	4316.51	4058.01	3680.40	3421.84	3237.16	150000
175000	16294.92	11417.87	8992.49	7547.71	6593.14	5918.61	5419.00	5035.93	4734.34	4293.80	3992.14	3776.68	175000
200000	18622.76	13048.99	10277.14	8625.96	7535.02	6764.12	6193.14	5755.35	5410.68	4907.20	4562.45	4316.21	200000
250000	23278.45	16311.24	12846.42	10782.44	9418.77	8455.15	7741.43	7194.18	6763.34	6134.00	5703.06	5395.26	250000

Amount	9.0 Years	10.0 Years	11.0 Years	12.0 Years	13.0 Years	14.0 Years	15.0 Years	16.0 Years	20.0 Years	30.0 Years	40.0 Years	50.0 Years	Amount
100	2.07	2.00	1.95	1.91	1.88	1.86	1.84	1.82	1.78	1.76	1.76	1.76	100
200	4.14	4.00	3.90	3.82	3.76	3.71	3.67	3.63	3.56	3.51	3.51	3.51	200
300	6.21	6.00	5.85	5.73	5.63	5.56	5.50	5.45	5.34	5.27	5.26	5.26	300
400	8.27	8.00	7.79	7.63	7.51	7.41	7.33	7.26	7.12	7.02	7.01	7.01	400
500	10.34	10.00	9.74	9.54	9.38	9.26	9.16	9.08	8.89	8.77	8.76	8.76	500
600	12.41	12.00	11.69	11.45	11.26	11.11	10.99	10.89	10.67	10.53	10.51	10.51	600
700	14.48	14.00	13.64	13.35	13.13	12.96	12.82	12.71	12.45	12.28	12.26	12.26	700
800	16.54	16.00	15.58	15.26	15.01	14.81	14.65	14.52	14.23	14.03	14.01	14.01	800
900	18.61	18.00	17.53	17.17	16.88	16.66	16.48	16.34	16.00	15.79	15.76	15.76	900
1000	20.68	20.00	19.48	19.07	18.76	18.51	18.31	18.15	17.78	17.54	17.51	17.51	1000
2000	41.35	39.99	38.95	38.14	37.51	37.01	36.62	36.30	35.56	35.07	35.01	35.01	2000
3000	62.03	59.98	58.42	57.21	56.26	55.52	54.92	54.45	53.33	52.61	52.52	52.51	3000
4000	82.70	79.98	77.89	76.28	75.01	74.02	73.23	72.60	71.11	70.14	70.02	70.01	4000
5000	103.38	99.97	97.36	95.35	93.77	92.52	91.54	90.75	88.89	87.68	87.53	87.51	5000
6000	124.05	119.96	116.84	114.41	112.52	111.03	109.84	108.90	106.66	105.21	105.03	105.01	6000
7000	144.73	139.96	136.31	133.48	131.27	129.53	128.15	127.05	124.44	122.74	122.53	122.51	7000
8000	165.40	159.95	155.78	152.55	150.02	148.03	146.45	145.20	142.22	140.28	140.04	140.01	8000
9000	186.08	179.94	175.25	171.62	168.78	166.54	164.76	163.35	159.99	157.81	157.54	157.51	9000
10000	206.75	199.94	194.72	190.69	187.53	185.04	183.07	181.49	177.77	175.35	175.05	175.01	10000
15000	310.13	299.90	292.08	286.03	281.29	277.56	274.60	272.24	266.65	263.02	262.57	262.51	15000
20000	413.50	399.87	389.44	381.37	375.05	370.07	366.13	362.98	355.53	350.69	350.09	350.02	20000
25000	516.88	499.83	486.80	476.71	468.81	462.59	457.66	453.73	444.42	438.36	437.61	437.52	25000
30000	620.25	599.80	584.16	572.05	562.57	555.11	549.19	544.47	533.30	526.03	525.13	525.02	30000
35000	723.63	699.77	681.52	667.39	656.33	647.62	640.72	635.22	622.18	613.70	612.65	612.52	35000
40000	827.00	799.73	778.88	762.73	750.09	740.14	732.25	725.96	711.06	701.37	700.17	700.03	40000
45000	930.37	899.70	876.24	858.07	843.86	832.66	823.78	816.71	799.94	789.04	787.70	787.53	45000
50000	1033.75	999.66	973.60	953.41	937.62	925.17	915.31	907.45	888.83	876.71	875.22	875.03	50000
60000	1240.50	1199.60	1168.31	1144.09	1125.14	1110.21	1098.37	1088.94	1066.59	1052.05	1050.26	1050.04	60000
75000	1550.62	1499.49	1460.39	1430.11	1406.42	1387.76	1372.96	1361.18	1333.24	1315.06	1312.82	1312.54	75000
100000	2067.49	1999.32	1947.19	1906.81	1875.23	1850.34	1830.62	1814.90	1777.65	1753.41	1750.43	1750.06	100000
125000	2584.36	2499.15	2433.98	2383.51	2344.03	2312.93	2288.27	2268.63	2222.06	2191.76	2188.03	2187.57	125000
150000	3101.24	2998.98	2920.78	2860.21	2812.84	2775.51	2745.92	2722.35	2666.47	2630.11	2625.64	2625.08	150000
175000	3618.11	3498.81	3407.57	3336.91	3281.65	3238.10	3203.58	3176.08	3110.88	3068.46	3063.25	3062.60	175000
200000	4134.98	3998.64	3894.37	3813.61	3750.45	3700.68	3661.23	3629.80	3555.29	3506.81	3500.85	3500.11	200000
250000	5168.72	4998.30	4867.96	4767.01	4688.06	4625.85	4576.54	4537.25	4444.11	4383.51	4376.06	4375.14	250000

Monthly Payment Required To Amortize A Loan

Amount	1.0 Year	1.5 Years	2.0 Years	2.5 Years	3.0 Years	3.5 Years	4.0 Years	4.5 Years	5.0 Years	6.0 Years	7.0 Years	8.0 Years	Amount
100	9.33	6.54	5.16	4.33	3.79	3.40	3.12	2.90	2.72	2.47	2.30	2.18	100
200	18.65	13.08	10.31	8.66	7.57	6.80	6.23	5.79	5.44	4.94	4.60	4.35	200
300	27.98	19.61	15.46	12.98	11.35	10.19	9.34	8.68	8.16	7.41	6.89	6.53	300
400	37.30	26.15	20.61	17.31	15.13	13.59	12.45	11.57	10.88	9.88	9.19	8.70	400
500	46.62	32.69	25.76	21.63	18.91	16.98	15.56	14.46	13.60	12.35	11.49	10.87	500
600	55.95	39.22	30.91	25.96	22.69	20.38	18.67	17.35	16.32	14.81	13.78	13.05	600
700	65.27	45.76	36.06	30.28	26.47	23.77	21.78	20.25	19.04	17.28	16.08	15.22	700
800	74.59	52.30	41.21	34.61	30.25	27.17	24.89	23.14	21.76	19.75	18.38	17.40	800
900	83.92	58.83	46.36	38.93	34.03	30.56	28.00	26.03	24.48	22.22	20.67	19.57	900
1000	93.24	65.37	51.51	43.26	37.81	33.96	31.11	28.92	27.20	24.69	22.97	21.74	1000
2000	186.47	130.74	103.02	86.52	75.61	67.91	62.21	57.83	54.39	49.37	45.93	43.48	2000
3000	279.71	196.10	154.53	129.77	113.42	101.86	93.31	86.75	81.59	74.05	68.90	65.22	3000
4000	372.94	261.47	206.04	173.03	151.22	135.81	124.41	115.66	108.78	98.74	91.86	86.96	4000
5000	466.17	326.83	257.55	216.28	189.02	169.77	155.51	144.58	135.98	123.42	114.83	108.70	5000
6000	559.41	392.20	309.06	259.54	226.83	203.72	186.61	173.49	163.17	148.10	137.79	130.44	6000
7000	652.64	457.56	360.56	302.79	264.63	237.67	217.71	202.41	190.36	172.79	160.76	152.18	7000
8000	745.88	522.93	412.07	346.05	302.43	271.62	248.81	231.32	217.56	197.47	183.72	173.92	8000
9000	839.11	588.30	463.58	389.30	340.24	305.57	279.91	260.24	244.75	222.15	206.69	195.66	9000
10000	932.34	653.66	515.09	432.56	378.04	339.53	311.01	289.15	271.95	246.83	229.65	217.40	10000
15000	1398.51	980.49	772.63	648.83	567.06	509.29	466.51	433.72	407.92	370.25	344.48	326.09	15000
20000	1864.68	1307.32	1030.18	865.11	756.08	679.05	622.01	578.29	543.89	493.66	459.30	434.79	20000
25000	2330.85	1634.15	1287.72	1081.39	945.09	848.81	777.51	722.87	679.86	617.08	574.13	543.49	25000
30000	2797.02	1960.98	1545.26	1297.66	1134.11	1018.57	933.01	867.44	815.83	740.49	688.95	652.18	30000
35000	3263.19	2287.80	1802.80	1513.94	1323.13	1188.33	1088.52	1012.01	951.80	863.91	803.78	760.88	35000
40000	3729.36	2614.63	2060.35	1730.22	1512.15	1358.09	1244.02	1156.58	1087.77	987.32	918.60	869.58	40000
45000	4195.53	2941.46	2317.89	1946.49	1701.16	1527.85	1399.52	1301.16	1223.74	1110.73	1033.43	978.27	45000
50000	4661.69	3268.29	2575.43	2162.77	1890.18	1697.61	1555.02	1445.73	1359.71	1234.15	1148.25	1086.97	50000
60000	5594.03	3921.95	3090.52	2595.32	2268.22	2037.13	1866.02	1734.87	1631.66	1480.98	1377.90	1304.36	60000
75000	6992.54	4902.43	3863.14	3244.15	2835.27	2546.41	2332.53	2168.59	2039.57	1851.22	1722.38	1630.45	75000
100000	9323.38	6536.57	5150.86	4325.54	3780.36	3395.22	3110.04	2891.45	2719.42	2468.29	2296.50	2173.93	100000
125000	11654.23	8170.71	6438.57	5406.92	4725.45	4244.02	3887.54	3614.31	3399.28	3085.37	2870.62	2717.41	125000
150000	13985.07	9804.86	7726.28	6488.30	5670.54	5092.82	4665.05	4337.17	4079.13	3702.44	3444.75	3260.89	150000
175000	16315.92	11439.00	9014.00	7569.68	6615.63	5941.62	5442.56	5060.03	4758.99	4319.51	4018.87	3804.38	175000
200000	18646.76	13073.14	10301.71	8651.07	7560.71	6790.43	6220.07	5782.89	5438.84	4936.58	4592.99	4347.86	200000
250000	23308.45	16341.42	12877.14	10813.83	9450.89	8488.03	7775.08	7228.62	6798.55	6170.73	5741.24	5434.82	250000

Amount	9.0 Years	10.0 Years	11.0 Years	12.0 Years	13.0 Years	14.0 Years	15.0 Years	16.0 Years	20.0 Years	30.0 Years	40.0 Years	50.0 Years	Amount
100	2.09	2.02	1.97	1.93	1.90	1.87	1.85	1.84	1.80	1.78	1.78	1.78	100
200	4.17	4.04	3.93	3.85	3.79	3.74	3.70	3.67	3.60	3.55	3.55	3.55	200
300	6.26	6.05	5.90	5.78	5.68	5.61	5.55	5.51	5.40	5.33	5.32	5.32	300
400	8.34	8.07	7.86	7.70	7.58	7.48	7.40	7.34	7.19	7.10	7.09	7.09	400
500	10.42	10.09	9.83	9.63	9.47	9.35	9.25	9.17	8.99	8.88	8.86	8.86	500
600	12.51	12.10	11.79	11.55	11.36	11.22	11.10	11.01	10.79	10.65	10.63	10.63	600
700	14.59	14.12	13.76	13.48	13.26	13.09	12.95	12.84	12.59	12.42	12.40	12.40	700
800	16.68	16.13	15.72	15.40	15.15	14.95	14.80	14.68	14.38	14.20	14.17	14.17	800
900	18.76	18.15	17.69	17.33	17.04	16.82	16.65	16.51	16.18	15.97	15.95	15.94	900
1000	20.84	20.17	19.65	19.25	18.94	18.69	18.50	18.34	17.98	17.75	17.72	17.71	1000
2000	41.68	40.33	39.29	38.49	37.87	37.38	36.99	36.68	35.95	35.49	35.43	35.42	2000
3000	62.52	60.49	58.94	57.74	56.80	56.07	55.48	55.02	53.93	53.23	53.14	53.13	3000
4000	83.36	80.65	78.58	76.98	75.74	74.75	73.98	73.36	71.90	70.97	70.85	70.84	4000
5000	104.20	100.81	98.23	96.23	94.67	93.44	92.47	91.70	89.88	88.71	88.57	88.55	5000
6000	125.03	120.97	117.87	115.47	113.60	112.13	110.96	110.04	107.85	106.45	106.28	106.26	6000
7000	145.87	141.14	137.52	134.72	132.54	130.82	129.46	128.38	125.83	124.19	123.99	123.97	7000
8000	166.71	161.30	157.16	153.96	151.47	149.50	147.95	146.72	143.80	141.93	141.70	141.68	8000
9000	187.55	181.46	176.81	173.21	170.40	168.19	166.44	165.05	161.77	159.67	159.41	159.38	9000
10000	208.39	201.62	196.45	192.45	189.33	186.88	184.94	183.39	179.75	177.41	177.13	177.09	10000
15000	312.58	302.43	294.67	288.68	284.00	280.32	277.40	275.09	269.62	266.11	265.69	265.64	15000
20000	416.77	403.23	392.90	384.90	378.66	373.75	369.87	366.78	359.49	354.81	354.25	354.18	20000
25000	520.96	504.04	491.12	481.13	473.33	467.19	462.34	458.48	449.37	443.51	442.81	442.73	25000
30000	625.15	604.85	589.34	577.35	567.99	560.63	554.80	550.17	539.24	532.21	531.37	531.27	30000
35000	729.35	705.66	687.57	673.58	662.66	654.07	647.27	641.86	629.11	620.92	619.93	619.81	35000
40000	833.54	806.46	785.79	769.80	757.32	747.50	739.73	733.56	718.98	709.62	708.49	708.36	40000
45000	937.73	907.27	884.01	866.03	851.98	840.94	832.20	825.25	808.85	798.32	797.05	796.90	45000
50000	1041.92	1008.08	982.23	962.25	946.65	934.38	924.67	916.95	898.73	887.02	885.62	885.45	50000
60000	1250.30	1209.69	1178.68	1154.70	1135.98	1121.25	1109.60	1100.34	1078.47	1064.42	1062.74	1062.53	60000
75000	1562.88	1512.12	1473.35	1443.37	1419.97	1401.56	1387.00	1375.42	1348.09	1330.53	1328.17	1328.17	75000
100000	2083.84	2016.15	1964.46	1924.50	1893.29	1868.75	1849.33	1833.89	1797.45	1774.03	1771.23	1770.89	100000
125000	2604.80	2520.19	2455.58	2405.62	2366.62	2335.94	2311.66	2292.36	2246.81	2217.54	2214.03	2213.61	125000
150000	3125.75	3024.23	2946.69	2886.74	2839.94	2803.12	2773.99	2750.83	2696.17	2661.05	2656.84	2656.33	150000
175000	3646.71	3528.26	3437.81	3367.87	3313.26	3270.31	3236.32	3209.30	3145.53	3104.56	3099.64	3099.05	175000
200000	4167.67	4032.30	3928.92	3848.99	3786.58	3737.49	3698.65	3667.77	3594.89	3548.06	3542.45	3541.77	200000
250000	5209.59	5040.37	4911.15	4811.23	4733.23	4671.87	4623.31	4584.72	4493.62	4435.08	4428.06	4427.21	250000

Amount	1.0 Year	1.5 Years	2.0 Years	2.5 Years	3.0 Years	3.5 Years	4.0 Years	4.5 Years	5.0 Years	6.0 Years	7.0 Years	8.0 Years	Amount
100	9.34	6.55	5.17	4.34	3.80	3.41	3.13	2.91	2.74	2.49	2.32	2.19	100
200	18.68	13.10	10.33	8.68	7.59	6.82	6.25	5.82	5.47	4.97	4.63	4.38	200
300	28.01	19.65	15.49	13.02	11.38	10.23	9.38	8.72	8.21	7.45	6.94	6.57	300
400	37.35	26.20	20.66	17.36	15.18	13.64	12.50	11.63	10.94	9.94	9.25	8.76	400
500	46.68	32.75	25.82	21.70	18.97	17.05	15.62	14.53	13.67	12.42	11.56	10.95	500
600	56.02	39.30	30.98	26.03	22.76	20.46	18.75	17.44	16.41	14.90	13.88	13.14	600
700	65.35	45.85	36.15	30.37	26.56	23.86	21.87	20.34	19.14	17.39	16.19	15.33	700
800	74.69	52.39	41.31	34.71	30.35	27.27	24.99	23.25	21.87	19.87	18.50	17.52	800
900	84.02	58.94	46.47	39.05	34.14	30.68	28.12	26.15	24.61	22.35	20.81	19.71	900
1000	93.36	65.49	51.64	43.39	37.94	34.09	31.24	29.06	27.34	24.84	23.12	21.90	1000
2000	186.71	130.98	103.27	86.77	75.87	68.17	62.48	58.11	54.68	49.67	46.24	43.80	2000
3000	280.07	196.46	154.90	130.15	113.80	102.26	93.71	87.16	82.01	74.50	69.36	65.70	3000
4000	373.42	261.95	206.53	173.53	151.73	136.34	124.95	116.22	109.35	99.33	92.48	87.60	4000
5000	466.77	327.44	258.16	216.91	189.67	170.42	156.18	145.27	136.68	124.16	115.60	109.50	5000
6000	560.13	392.92	309.79	260.29	227.60	204.51	187.42	174.32	164.02	148.99	138.71	131.39	6000
7000	653.48	458.41	361.43	303.67	265.53	238.59	218.65	203.37	191.35	173.82	161.83	153.29	7000
8000	746.84	523.90	413.06	347.05	303.46	272.68	249.89	232.43	218.69	198.65	184.95	175.19	8000
9000	840.19	589.38	464.69	390.43	341.40	306.76	281.12	261.48	246.02	223.48	208.07	197.09	9000
10000	933.54	654.87	516.32	433.82	379.33	340.84	312.36	290.53	273.36	248.31	231.19	218.99	10000
15000	1400.31	982.30	774.48	650.72	568.99	511.26	468.53	435.79	410.04	372.46	346.78	328.48	15000
20000	1867.08	1309.74	1032.64	867.63	758.65	681.68	624.71	581.06	546.71	496.61	462.37	437.97	20000
25000	2333.85	1637.17	1290.79	1084.53	948.31	852.10	780.89	726.32	683.39	620.76	577.96	547.46	25000
30000	2800.62	1964.60	1548.95	1301.44	1137.97	1022.52	937.06	871.58	820.07	744.91	693.55	656.95	30000
35000	3267.39	2292.03	1807.11	1518.34	1327.63	1192.94	1093.24	1016.84	956.74	869.06	809.14	766.44	35000
40000	3734.16	2619.47	2065.27	1735.25	1517.30	1363.36	1249.42	1162.11	1093.42	993.21	924.73	875.93	40000
45000	4200.93	2946.90	2323.43	1952.15	1706.96	1533.78	1405.59	1307.37	1230.10	1117.36	1040.32	985.42	45000
50000	4667.70	3274.33	2581.58	2169.06	1896.62	1704.20	1561.77	1452.63	1366.77	1241.51	1155.91	1094.91	50000
60000	5601.24	3929.20	3097.90	2602.87	2275.94	2045.04	1874.12	1743.16	1640.13	1489.82	1387.09	1313.89	60000
75000	7001.55	4911.50	3872.37	3253.59	2844.93	2556.30	2342.65	2178.94	2050.16	1862.27	1733.87	1642.36	75000
100000	9335.40	6548.66	5163.16	4338.11	3793.23	3408.40	3123.53	2905.26	2733.54	2483.02	2311.82	2189.81	100000
125000	11669.24	8185.82	6453.95	5422.64	4741.54	4260.49	3904.41	3631.57	3416.93	3103.78	2889.77	2737.26	125000
150000	14003.09	9822.99	7744.74	6507.17	5689.85	5112.59	4685.29	4357.88	4100.31	3724.53	3467.73	3284.71	150000
175000	16336.94	11460.15	9035.53	7591.69	6638.15	5964.69	5466.18	5084.20	4783.70	4345.29	4045.68	3832.16	175000
200000	18670.79	13097.31	10326.32	8676.22	7586.46	6816.79	6247.06	5810.51	5467.08	4966.04	4623.63	4379.61	200000
250000	23338.48	16371.64	12907.90	10845.27	9483.07	8520.98	7808.82	7263.14	6833.85	6207.55	5779.54	5474.51	250000

Amount	9.0 Years	10.0 Years	11.0 Years	12.0 Years	13.0 Years	14.0 Years	15.0 Years	16.0 Years	20.0 Years	30.0 Years	40.0 Years	50.0 Years	Amount
100	2.11	2.04	1.99	1.95	1.92	1.89	1.87	1.86	1.82	1.80	1.80	1.80	100
200	4.21	4.07	3.97	3.89	3.83	3.78	3.74	3.71	3.64	3.59	3.59	3.59	200
300	6.31	6.10	5.95	5.83	5.74	5.67	5.61	5.56	5.46	5.39	5.38	5.38	300
400	8.41	8.14	7.93	7.77	7.65	7.55	7.48	7.42	7.27	7.18	7.17	7.17	400
500	10.51	10.17	9.91	9.72	9.56	9.44	9.35	9.27	9.09	8.98	8.97	8.96	500
600	12.61	12.20	11.90	11.66	11.47	11.33	11.21	11.12	10.91	10.77	10.76	10.76	600
700	14.71	14.24	13.88	13.60	13.38	13.22	13.08	12.98	12.73	12.57	12.55	12.55	700
800	16.81	16.27	15.86	15.54	15.30	15.10	14.95	14.83	14.54	14.36	14.34	14.34	800
900	18.91	18.30	17.84	17.49	17.21	16.99	16.82	16.68	16.36	16.16	16.13	16.13	900
1000	21.01	20.34	19.82	19.43	19.12	18.88	18.69	18.53	18.18	17.95	17.93	17.92	1000
2000	42.01	40.67	39.64	38.85	38.23	37.75	37.37	37.06	36.35	35.90	35.85	35.84	2000
3000	63.01	61.00	59.46	58.27	57.35	56.62	56.05	55.59	54.52	53.85	53.77	53.76	3000
4000	84.01	81.33	79.28	77.69	76.46	75.49	74.73	74.12	72.70	71.79	71.69	71.67	4000
5000	105.02	101.66	99.09	97.12	95.58	94.37	93.41	92.65	90.87	89.74	89.61	89.59	5000
6000	126.02	121.99	118.91	116.54	114.69	113.24	112.09	111.18	109.04	107.69	107.53	107.51	6000
7000	147.02	142.32	138.73	135.96	133.80	132.11	130.77	129.71	127.21	125.63	125.45	125.42	7000
8000	168.02	162.65	158.55	155.38	152.92	150.98	149.45	148.24	145.39	143.58	143.37	143.34	8000
9000	189.03	182.98	178.37	174.81	172.03	169.85	168.13	166.77	163.56	161.53	161.29	161.26	9000
10000	210.03	203.31	198.18	194.23	191.15	188.73	186.81	185.30	181.73	179.47	179.21	179.18	10000
15000	315.04	304.96	297.27	291.34	286.72	283.09	280.22	277.94	272.60	269.21	268.81	268.76	15000
20000	420.05	406.61	396.36	388.45	382.29	377.45	373.62	370.59	363.46	358.94	358.41	358.35	20000
25000	525.06	508.26	495.45	485.56	477.86	471.81	467.03	463.23	454.33	448.67	448.01	447.93	25000
30000	630.07	609.92	594.54	582.68	573.43	566.17	560.43	555.88	545.19	538.41	537.62	537.52	30000
35000	735.09	711.57	693.63	679.79	669.00	660.53	653.84	648.53	636.05	628.14	627.21	627.10	35000
40000	840.10	813.22	792.72	776.90	764.57	754.89	747.24	741.17	726.92	717.87	716.81	716.69	40000
45000	945.11	914.87	891.81	874.01	860.14	849.25	840.64	833.82	817.78	807.61	806.42	806.27	45000
50000	1050.12	1016.52	990.90	971.12	955.71	943.61	934.05	926.46	908.65	897.34	896.02	895.86	50000
60000	1260.14	1219.83	1189.08	1165.35	1146.85	1132.33	1120.86	1111.76	1090.37	1076.81	1075.22	1075.03	60000
75000	1575.18	1524.78	1486.35	1456.68	1433.56	1415.41	1401.07	1389.69	1362.97	1346.01	1344.02	1343.79	75000
100000	2100.24	2033.04	1981.80	1942.24	1911.41	1887.21	1868.09	1852.92	1817.29	1794.67	1792.03	1791.71	100000
125000	2625.29	2541.30	2477.25	2427.80	2389.27	2359.01	2335.11	2316.15	2271.61	2243.34	2240.03	2239.64	125000
150000	3150.35	3049.56	2972.70	2913.36	2867.12	2830.81	2802.13	2779.38	2725.93	2692.01	2688.04	2687.57	150000
175000	3675.41	3557.81	3468.14	3398.92	3344.97	3302.61	3269.15	3242.61	3180.25	3140.68	3136.04	3135.50	175000
200000	4200.47	4066.07	3963.59	3884.48	3822.82	3774.41	3736.17	3705.84	3634.57	3589.34	3584.05	3583.42	200000
250000	5250.58	5082.59	4954.49	4855.60	4778.53	4718.01	4670.22	4632.30	4543.21	4486.68	4480.06	4479.28	250000

Amount	1.0 Year	1.5 Years	2.0 Years	2.5 Years	3.0 Years	3.5 Years	4.0 Years	4.5 Years	5.0 Years	6.0 Years	7.0 Years	8.0 Years	Amount
100	9.35	6.57	5.18	4.36	3.81	3.43	3.14	2.92	2.75	2.50	2.33	2.21	100
200	18.70	13.13	10.36	8.71	7.62	6.85	6.28	5.84	5.50	5.00	4.66	4.42	200
300	28.05	19.69	15.53	13.06	11.42	10.27	9.42	8.76	8.25	7.50	6.99	6.62	300
400	37.39	26.25	20.71	17.41	15.23	13.69	12.55	11.68	11.00	10.00	9.31	8.83	400
500	46.74	32.81	25.88	21.76	19.04	17.11	15.69	14.60	13.74	12.49	11.64	11.03	500
600	56.09	39.37	31.06	26.11	22.84	20.53	18.83	17.52	16.49	14.99	13.97	13.24	600
700	65.44	45.93	36.23	30.46	26.65	23.96	21.96	20.44	19.24	17.49	16.30	15.45	700
800	74.78	52.49	41.41	34.81	30.45	27.38	25.10	23.36	21.99	19.99	18.62	17.65	800
900	84.13	59.05	46.58	39.16	34.26	30.80	28.24	26.28	24.73	22.49	20.95	19.86	900
1000	93.48	65.61	51.76	43.51	38.07	34.22	31.38	29.20	27.48	24.98	23.28	22.06	1000
2000	186.95	131.22	103.51	87.02	76.13	68.44	62.75	58.39	54.96	49.96	46.55	44.12	2000
3000	280.43	196.83	155.27	130.53	114.19	102.65	94.12	87.58	82.44	74.94	69.82	66.18	3000
4000	373.90	262.44	207.02	174.03	152.25	136.87	125.49	116.77	109.91	99.92	93.09	88.23	4000
5000	467.38	328.04	258.78	217.54	190.31	171.08	156.86	145.96	137.39	124.89	116.36	110.29	5000
6000	560.85	393.65	310.53	261.05	228.37	205.30	188.23	175.15	164.87	149.87	139.64	132.35	6000
7000	654.32	459.26	362.29	304.55	266.43	239.52	219.60	204.34	192.34	174.85	162.91	154.41	7000
8000	747.80	524.87	414.04	348.06	304.49	273.73	250.97	233.53	219.82	199.83	186.18	176.46	8000
9000	841.27	590.47	465.80	391.57	342.56	307.95	282.34	262.72	247.30	224.81	209.45	198.52	9000
10000	934.75	656.08	517.55	435.08	380.62	342.16	313.71	291.91	274.77	249.78	232.72	220.58	10000
15000	1402.12	984.12	776.33	652.61	570.92	513.24	470.56	437.87	412.16	374.67	349.08	330.86	15000
20000	1869.49	1312.16	1035.10	870.15	761.23	684.32	627.42	583.82	549.54	499.56	465.44	441.15	20000
25000	2336.86	1640.19	1293.87	1087.68	951.54	855.40	784.27	729.78	686.93	624.45	581.80	551.44	25000
30000	2804.23	1968.23	1552.65	1305.22	1141.84	1026.48	941.12	875.73	824.31	749.34	698.16	661.72	30000
35000	3271.60	2296.27	1811.42	1522.75	1332.15	1197.56	1097.97	1021.69	961.70	874.23	814.52	772.01	35000
40000	3738.97	2624.31	2070.20	1740.29	1522.45	1368.64	1254.83	1167.64	1099.08	999.12	930.88	882.30	40000
45000	4206.34	2952.34	2328.97	1957.82	1712.76	1539.72	1411.68	1313.60	1236.47	1124.01	1047.24	992.58	45000
50000	4673.71	3280.38	2587.74	2175.36	1903.07	1710.80	1568.53	1459.55	1373.85	1248.90	1163.60	1102.87	50000
60000	5608.45	3936.46	3105.29	2610.43	2283.68	2052.96	1882.24	1751.46	1648.62	1498.68	1396.31	1323.44	60000
75000	7010.56	4920.57	3881.61	3263.03	2854.60	2566.20	2352.79	2189.33	2060.78	1873.35	1745.39	1654.30	75000
100000	9347.42	6560.76	5175.48	4350.71	3806.13	3421.60	3137.06	2919.10	2747.70	2497.80	2327.19	2205.73	100000
125000	11684.27	8200.95	6469.35	5438.38	4757.66	4277.00	3921.32	3648.87	3434.62	3122.25	2908.98	2757.17	125000
150000	14021.12	9841.13	7763.22	6526.06	5709.19	5132.40	4705.58	4378.65	4121.55	3746.70	3490.78	3308.60	150000
175000	16357.97	11481.32	9057.09	7613.74	6660.72	5987.80	5489.84	5108.42	4808.47	4371.15	4072.57	3860.03	175000
200000	18694.83	13121.51	10350.96	8701.41	7612.25	6843.20	6274.11	5838.20	5495.40	4995.59	4654.37	4411.46	200000
250000	23368.53	16401.89	12938.70	10876.76	9515.32	8554.00	7842.63	7297.74	6869.24	6244.49	5817.96	5514.33	250000

Amount	9.0 Years	10.0 Years	11.0 Years	12.0 Years	13.0 Years	14.0 Years	15.0 Years	16.0 Years	20.0 Years	30.0 Years	40.0 Years	50.0 Years	Amount
100	2.12	2.05	2.00	1.97	1.93	1.91	1.89	1.88	1.84	1.82	1.82	1.82	100
200	4.24	4.10	4.00	3.93	3.86	3.82	3.78	3.75	3.68	3.64	3.63	3.63	200
300	6.36	6.15	6.00	5.89	5.79	5.72	5.67	5.62	5.52	5.45	5.44	5.44	300
400	8.47	8.20	8.00	7.85	7.72	7.63	7.55	7.49	7.35	7.27	7.26	7.26	400
500	10.59	10.25	10.00	9.81	9.65	9.53	9.44	9.36	9.19	9.08	9.07	9.07	500
600	12.71	12.30	12.00	11.77	11.58	11.44	11.33	11.24	11.03	10.90	10.88	10.88	600
700	14.82	14.35	14.00	13.73	13.51	13.34	13.21	13.11	12.87	12.71	12.69	12.69	700
800	16.94	16.40	16.00	15.69	15.44	15.25	15.10	14.98	14.70	14.53	14.51	14.51	800
900	19.06	18.45	18.00	17.65	17.37	17.16	16.99	16.85	16.54	16.34	16.32	16.32	900
1000	21.17	20.50	20.00	19.61	19.30	19.06	18.87	18.72	18.38	18.16	18.13	18.13	1000
2000	42.34	41.00	39.99	39.21	38.60	38.12	37.74	37.44	36.75	36.31	36.26	36.26	2000
3000	63.51	61.50	59.98	58.81	57.89	57.18	56.61	56.16	55.12	54.46	54.39	54.38	3000
4000	84.67	82.00	79.97	78.41	77.19	76.23	75.48	74.88	73.49	72.62	72.52	72.51	4000
5000	105.84	102.50	99.96	98.01	96.48	95.29	94.35	93.60	91.86	90.77	90.65	90.63	5000
6000	127.01	123.00	119.96	117.61	115.78	114.35	113.22	112.32	110.23	108.92	108.77	108.76	6000
7000	148.17	143.50	139.95	137.21	135.08	133.40	132.09	131.04	128.61	127.08	126.90	126.88	7000
8000	169.34	164.00	159.94	156.81	154.37	152.46	150.96	149.76	146.98	145.23	145.03	145.01	8000
9000	190.51	184.50	179.93	176.41	173.67	171.52	169.83	168.48	165.35	163.38	163.16	163.13	9000
10000	211.67	205.00	199.92	196.01	192.96	190.58	188.69	187.20	183.72	181.54	181.29	181.26	10000
15000	317.51	307.50	299.88	294.01	289.44	285.86	283.04	280.80	275.58	272.30	271.93	271.89	15000
20000	423.34	410.00	399.84	392.01	385.92	381.15	377.38	374.40	367.44	363.07	362.57	362.51	20000
25000	529.18	512.50	499.80	490.01	482.40	476.43	471.73	468.00	459.29	453.84	453.21	453.14	25000
30000	635.01	615.00	599.76	588.02	578.88	571.72	566.07	561.60	551.15	544.60	543.85	543.77	30000
35000	740.84	717.50	699.72	686.02	675.36	667.00	660.42	655.20	643.01	635.37	634.49	634.39	35000
40000	846.68	819.99	799.68	784.02	771.84	762.29	754.76	748.80	734.87	726.13	725.14	725.02	40000
45000	952.51	922.49	899.64	882.02	868.32	857.58	849.11	842.40	826.72	816.90	815.78	815.65	45000
50000	1058.35	1024.99	999.60	980.02	964.80	952.86	943.45	936.00	918.58	907.67	906.42	906.27	50000
60000	1270.02	1229.99	1199.52	1176.03	1157.75	1143.43	1132.14	1123.20	1102.30	1089.20	1087.70	1087.53	60000
75000	1587.52	1537.49	1499.39	1470.03	1447.19	1429.29	1415.18	1404.00	1377.87	1361.50	1359.62	1359.41	75000
100000	2116.69	2049.98	1999.19	1960.04	1929.59	1905.72	1886.90	1872.00	1837.16	1815.33	1812.83	1812.54	100000
125000	2645.86	2562.47	2498.99	2450.05	2411.98	2382.15	2358.63	2340.00	2296.45	2269.16	2266.04	2265.68	125000
150000	3175.03	3074.97	2998.78	2940.06	2894.38	2858.57	2830.35	2808.00	2755.74	2722.99	2719.24	2718.81	150000
175000	3704.20	3587.46	3498.58	3430.07	3376.77	3335.00	3302.07	3276.00	3215.02	3176.82	3172.45	3171.95	175000
200000	4233.37	4099.95	3998.37	3920.08	3859.17	3811.43	3773.80	3744.00	3674.31	3630.65	3625.66	3625.08	200000
250000	5291.72	5124.94	4997.97	4900.10	4823.96	4764.29	4717.25	4680.00	4592.89	4538.31	4532.07	4531.35	250000

Amount	1.0 Year	1.5 Years	2.0 Years	2.5 Years	3.0 Years	3.5 Years	4.0 Years	4.5 Years	5.0 Years	6.0 Years	7.0 Years	8.0 Years	Amount
100	9.36	6.58	5.19	4.37	3.82	3.44	3.16	2.94	2.77	2.52	2.35	2.23	100
200	18.72	13.15	10.38	8.73	7.64	6.87	6.31	5.87	5.53	5.03	4.69	4.45	200
300	28.08	19.72	15.57	13.09	11.46	10.31	9.46	8.80	8.29	7.54	7.03	6.67	300
400	37.44	26.30	20.76	17.46	15.28	13.74	12.61	11.74	11.05	10.06	9.38	8.89	400
500	46.80	32.87	25.94	21.82	19.10	17.18	15.76	14.67	13.81	12.57	11.72	11.11	500
600	56.16	39.44	31.13	26.18	22.92	20.61	18.91	17.60	16.58	15.08	14.06	13.34	600
700	65.52	46.02	36.32	30.55	26.74	24.05	22.06	20.54	19.34	17.59	16.40	15.56	700
800	74.88	52.59	41.51	34.91	30.56	27.48	25.21	23.47	22.10	20.11	18.75	17.78	800
900	84.24	59.16	46.70	39.27	34.38	30.92	28.36	26.40	24.86	22.62	21.09	20.00	900
1000	93.60	65.73	51.88	43.64	38.20	34.35	31.51	29.33	27.62	25.13	23.43	22.22	1000
2000	187.19	131.46	103.76	87.27	76.39	68.70	63.02	58.66	55.24	50.26	46.86	44.44	2000
3000	280.79	197.19	155.64	130.90	114.58	103.05	94.52	87.99	82.86	75.38	70.28	66.66	3000
4000	374.38	262.92	207.52	174.54	152.77	137.40	126.03	117.32	110.48	100.51	93.71	88.87	4000
5000	467.98	328.65	259.40	218.17	190.96	171.75	157.54	146.65	138.10	125.64	117.13	111.09	5000
6000	561.57	394.38	311.27	261.80	229.15	206.10	189.04	175.98	165.72	150.76	140.56	133.31	6000
7000	655.17	460.11	363.15	305.44	267.34	240.44	220.55	205.31	193.34	175.89	163.99	155.52	7000
8000	748.76	525.83	415.03	349.07	305.53	274.79	252.05	234.64	220.96	201.01	187.41	177.74	8000
9000	842.35	591.56	466.91	392.70	343.72	309.14	283.56	263.97	248.58	226.14	210.84	199.96	9000
10000	935.95	657.29	518.79	436.34	381.91	343.49	315.07	293.30	276.19	251.27	234.26	222.18	10000
15000	1403.92	985.93	778.18	654.50	572.86	515.23	472.60	439.95	414.29	376.90	351.39	333.26	15000
20000	1871.89	1314.58	1037.57	872.67	763.81	686.97	630.13	586.60	552.38	502.53	468.52	444.35	20000
25000	2339.86	1643.22	1296.96	1090.84	954.77	858.71	787.66	733.25	690.48	628.16	585.65	555.43	25000
30000	2807.84	1971.86	1556.35	1309.00	1145.72	1030.46	945.19	879.90	828.57	753.79	702.78	666.52	30000
35000	3275.81	2300.51	1815.74	1527.17	1336.67	1202.20	1102.72	1026.55	966.67	879.42	819.91	777.60	35000
40000	3743.78	2629.15	2075.13	1745.33	1527.62	1373.94	1260.25	1173.19	1104.76	1005.05	937.04	888.69	40000
45000	4211.75	2957.79	2334.52	1963.50	1718.58	1545.68	1417.78	1319.84	1242.86	1130.68	1054.17	999.77	45000
50000	4679.72	3286.44	2593.91	2181.67	1909.53	1717.42	1575.31	1466.49	1380.95	1256.31	1171.30	1110.86	50000
60000	5615.67	3943.72	3112.69	2618.00	2291.43	2060.91	1890.37	1759.79	1657.14	1507.57	1405.56	1333.03	60000
75000	7019.58	4929.65	3890.87	3272.50	2864.29	2576.13	2362.96	2199.73	2071.42	1884.46	1756.95	1666.29	75000
100000	9359.44	6572.87	5187.82	4363.33	3819.05	3434.84	3150.61	2932.98	2761.90	2512.62	2342.60	2221.71	100000
125000	11699.30	8216.09	6484.77	5454.16	4773.81	4293.55	3938.26	3666.22	3452.37	3140.77	2928.25	2777.14	125000
150000	14039.16	9859.30	7781.73	6544.99	5728.57	5152.26	4725.92	4399.46	4142.84	3768.92	3513.90	3332.57	150000
175000	16379.02	11502.52	9078.68	7635.82	6683.33	6010.97	5513.57	5132.71	4833.31	4397.08	4099.55	3887.99	175000
200000	18718.88	13145.74	10375.64	8726.65	7638.10	6869.68	6301.22	5865.95	5523.79	5025.23	4685.19	4443.42	200000
250000	23398.60	16432.17	12969.54	10908.31	9547.62	8587.10	7876.52	7332.44	6904.73	6281.54	5856.49	5554.27	250000

Amount	9.0 Years	10.0 Years	11.0 Years	12.0 Years	13.0 Years	14.0 Years	15.0 Years	16.0 Years	20.0 Years	30.0 Years	40.0 Years	50.0 Years	Amount
100	2.14	2.07	2.02	1.98	1.95	1.93	1.91	1.90	1.86	1.84	1.84	1.84	100
200	4.27	4.14	4.04	3.96	3.90	3.85	3.82	3.79	3.72	3.68	3.67	3.67	200
300	6.40	6.21	6.05	5.94	5.85	5.78	5.72	5.68	5.58	5.51	5.51	5.51	300
400	8.54	8.27	8.07	7.92	7.80	7.70	7.63	7.57	7.43	7.35	7.34	7.34	400
500	10.67	10.34	10.09	9.89	9.74	9.63	9.53	9.46	9.29	9.18	9.17	9.17	500
600	12.80	12.41	12.10	11.87	11.69	11.55	11.44	11.35	11.15	11.02	11.01	11.01	600
700	14.94	14.47	14.12	13.85	13.64	13.47	13.35	13.24	13.00	12.86	12.84	12.84	700
800	17.07	16.54	16.14	15.83	15.59	15.40	15.25	15.13	14.86	14.69	14.67	14.67	800
900	19.20	18.61	18.15	17.81	17.54	17.32	17.16	17.03	16.72	16.53	16.51	16.51	900
1000	21.34	20.67	20.17	19.78	19.48	19.25	19.06	18.92	18.58	18.36	18.34	18.34	1000
2000	42.67	41.34	40.34	39.56	38.96	38.49	38.12	37.83	37.15	36.72	36.68	36.67	2000
3000	64.00	62.01	60.50	59.34	58.44	57.73	57.18	56.74	55.72	55.08	55.01	55.01	3000
4000	85.33	82.68	80.67	79.12	77.92	76.98	76.24	75.65	74.29	73.44	73.35	73.34	4000
5000	106.66	103.35	100.84	98.90	97.40	96.22	95.29	94.56	92.86	91.80	91.69	91.67	5000
6000	128.00	124.02	121.00	118.68	116.87	115.46	114.35	113.47	111.43	110.16	110.02	110.01	6000
7000	149.33	144.69	141.17	138.46	136.35	134.70	133.41	132.38	130.00	128.52	128.36	128.34	7000
8000	170.66	165.36	161.34	158.24	155.83	153.95	152.47	151.29	148.57	146.88	146.70	146.67	8000
9000	191.99	186.03	181.50	178.02	175.31	173.19	171.52	170.21	167.14	165.24	165.03	165.01	9000
10000	213.32	206.70	201.67	197.79	194.79	192.43	190.58	189.12	185.71	183.60	183.37	183.34	10000
15000	319.98	310.05	302.50	296.69	292.18	288.65	285.87	283.67	278.56	275.40	275.05	275.01	15000
20000	426.64	413.40	403.33	395.58	389.57	384.86	381.16	378.23	371.42	367.20	366.73	366.68	20000
25000	533.30	516.75	504.16	494.48	486.96	481.07	476.44	472.79	464.27	459.00	458.41	458.35	25000
30000	639.96	620.10	604.99	593.37	584.35	577.29	571.73	567.34	557.12	550.80	550.09	550.02	30000
35000	746.62	723.44	705.83	692.27	681.74	673.50	667.02	661.90	649.98	642.60	641.78	641.68	35000
40000	853.28	826.79	806.66	791.16	779.13	769.71	762.31	756.45	742.83	734.40	733.46	733.35	40000
45000	959.94	930.14	907.49	890.06	876.52	865.93	857.60	851.01	835.68	826.20	825.14	825.02	45000
50000	1066.60	1033.49	1008.32	988.95	973.91	962.14	952.88	945.57	928.53	918.00	916.82	916.69	50000
60000	1279.92	1240.19	1209.98	1186.74	1168.69	1154.57	1143.46	1134.68	1114.24	1101.60	1100.18	1100.03	60000
75000	1599.90	1550.23	1512.48	1483.43	1460.86	1443.21	1429.32	1418.35	1392.80	1376.99	1375.23	1375.03	75000
100000	2133.20	2066.97	2016.63	1977.90	1947.81	1924.28	1905.76	1891.13	1857.06	1835.99	1833.64	1833.37	100000
125000	2666.49	2583.72	2520.79	2472.37	2434.77	2405.35	2382.20	2363.91	2321.33	2294.99	2292.05	2291.71	125000
150000	3199.79	3100.46	3024.95	2966.85	2921.72	2886.41	2858.64	2836.69	2785.59	2753.98	2750.45	2750.06	150000
175000	3733.09	3617.20	3529.11	3461.32	3408.67	3367.48	3335.08	3309.47	3249.86	3212.98	3208.86	3208.40	175000
200000	4266.39	4133.94	4033.26	3955.79	3895.62	3848.55	3811.52	3782.25	3714.12	3671.97	3667.27	3666.74	200000
250000	5332.98	5167.43	5041.58	4944.74	4869.53	4810.69	4764.40	4727.81	4642.65	4589.97	4584.09	4583.42	250000

Amount	1.0 Year	1.5 Years	2.0 Years	2.5 Years	3.0 Years	3.5 Years	4.0 Years	4.5 Years	5.0 Years	6.0 Years	7.0 Years	8.0 Years	Amount
100	9.38	6.59	5.21	4.38	3.84	3.45	3.17	2.95	2.78	2.53	2.36	2.24	100
200	18.75	13.17	10.41	8.76	7.67	6.90	6.33	5.90	5.56	5.06	4.72	4.48	200
300	28.12	19.76	15.61	13.13	11.50	10.35	9.50	8.85	8.33	7.59	7.08	6.72	300
400	37.49	26.34	20.81	17.51	15.33	13.80	12.66	11.79	11.11	10.11	9.44	8.96	400
500	46.86	32.93	26.01	21.88	19.16	17.25	15.83	14.74	13.89	12.64	11.80	11.19	500
600	56.23	39.51	31.21	26.26	23.00	20.69	18.99	17.69	16.66	15.17	14.15	13.43	600
700	65.61	46.10	36.41	30.64	26.83	24.14	22.15	20.63	19.44	17.70	16.51	15.67	700
800	74.98	52.68	41.61	35.01	30.66	27.59	25.32	23.58	22.21	20.22	18.87	17.91	800
900	84.35	59.27	46.81	39.39	34.49	31.04	28.48	26.53	24.99	22.75	21.23	20.14	900
1000	93.72	65.85	52.01	43.76	38.32	34.49	31.65	29.47	27.77	25.28	23.59	22.38	1000
2000	187.43	131.70	104.01	87.52	76.64	68.97	63.29	58.94	55.53	50.55	47.17	44.76	2000
3000	281.15	197.55	156.01	131.28	114.96	103.45	94.93	88.41	83.29	75.83	70.75	67.14	3000
4000	374.86	263.40	208.01	175.04	153.28	137.93	126.57	117.88	111.05	101.10	94.33	89.51	4000
5000	468.58	329.25	260.01	218.80	191.60	172.41	158.21	147.35	138.81	126.38	117.91	111.89	5000
6000	562.29	395.10	312.02	262.56	229.92	206.89	189.86	176.82	166.57	151.65	141.49	134.27	6000
7000	656.01	460.95	364.02	306.32	268.24	241.37	221.50	206.29	194.33	176.93	165.07	156.65	7000
8000	749.72	526.80	416.02	350.08	306.56	275.85	253.14	235.76	222.09	202.20	188.65	179.02	8000
9000	843.44	592.65	468.02	393.84	344.88	310.33	284.78	265.22	249.86	227.48	212.23	201.40	9000
10000	937.15	658.50	520.02	437.60	383.20	344.82	316.42	294.69	277.62	252.75	235.81	223.78	10000
15000	1405.73	987.75	780.03	656.40	574.80	517.22	474.63	442.04	416.42	379.13	353.71	335.67	15000
20000	1874.30	1317.00	1040.04	875.20	766.40	689.63	632.84	589.38	555.23	505.50	471.62	447.55	20000
25000	2342.87	1646.25	1300.05	1093.99	958.00	862.03	791.05	736.73	694.04	631.87	589.52	559.44	25000
30000	2811.45	1975.50	1560.06	1312.79	1149.60	1034.44	949.26	884.07	832.84	758.25	707.42	671.33	30000
35000	3280.02	2304.75	1820.06	1531.59	1341.20	1206.84	1107.47	1031.41	971.65	884.62	825.32	783.21	35000
40000	3748.59	2634.00	2080.07	1750.39	1532.80	1379.25	1265.68	1178.76	1110.45	1010.99	943.23	895.10	40000
45000	4217.17	2963.25	2340.08	1969.19	1724.40	1551.65	1423.89	1326.10	1249.26	1137.37	1061.13	1006.99	45000
50000	4685.74	3292.50	2600.09	2187.98	1916.00	1724.06	1582.10	1473.45	1388.07	1263.74	1179.03	1118.87	50000
60000	5622.89	3951.00	3120.11	2625.58	2299.20	2068.87	1898.52	1768.14	1665.68	1516.49	1414.84	1342.65	60000
75000	7028.61	4938.75	3900.13	3281.97	2874.00	2586.08	2373.15	2210.17	2082.10	1895.61	1768.55	1678.31	75000
100000	9371.48	6584.99	5200.17	4375.96	3832.00	3448.11	3164.20	2946.89	2776.13	2527.48	2358.06	2237.74	100000
125000	11714.35	8231.24	6500.22	5469.95	4789.99	4310.13	3955.25	3683.61	3470.16	3159.35	2947.57	2797.18	125000
150000	14057.22	9877.49	7800.26	6563.94	5747.99	5172.16	4746.30	4420.33	4164.19	3791.22	3537.09	3356.61	150000
175000	16400.08	11523.74	9100.30	7657.93	6705.99	6034.18	5537.35	5157.05	4858.22	4423.08	4126.60	3916.04	175000
200000	18742.95	13169.98	10400.34	8751.92	7663.99	6896.21	6328.40	5893.77	5552.25	5054.95	4716.12	4475.48	200000
250000	23428.69	16462.48	13000.43	10939.90	9579.98	8620.26	7910.49	7367.22	6940.32	6318.69	5895.14	5594.35	250000

Amount	9.0 Years	10.0 Years	11.0 Years	12.0 Years	13.0 Years	14.0 Years	15.0 Years	16.0 Years	20.0 Years	30.0 Years	40.0 Years	50.0 Years	Amount
100	2.15	2.09	2.04	2.00	1.97	1.95	1.93	1.92	1.88	1.86	1.86	1.86	100
200	4.30	4.17	4.07	4.00	3.94	3.89	3.85	3.83	3.76	3.72	3.71	3.71	200
300	6.45	6.26	6.11	5.99	5.90	5.83	5.74	5.74	5.64	5.57	5.57	5.57	300
400	8.60	8.34	8.14	7.99	7.87	7.78	7.70	7.65	7.51	7.43	7.42	7.42	400
500	10.75	10.43	10.18	9.98	9.84	9.72	9.63	9.56	9.39	9.29	9.28	9.28	500
600	12.90	12.51	12.21	11.98	11.80	11.66	11.55	11.47	11.27	11.14	11.13	11.13	600
700	15.05	14.59	14.24	13.98	13.77	13.61	13.48	13.38	13.14	13.00	12.99	12.98	700
800	17.20	16.68	16.28	15.97	15.73	15.55	15.40	15.29	15.02	14.86	14.84	14.84	800
900	19.35	18.76	18.31	17.97	17.70	17.49	17.33	17.20	16.90	16.71	16.69	16.69	900
1000	21.50	20.85	20.35	19.96	19.67	19.43	19.25	19.11	18.77	18.57	18.55	18.55	1000
2000	43.00	41.69	40.69	39.92	39.33	38.86	38.50	38.21	37.54	37.14	37.09	37.09	2000
3000	64.50	62.53	61.03	59.88	58.99	58.29	57.74	57.31	56.31	55.70	55.64	55.63	3000
4000	85.99	83.37	81.37	79.84	78.65	77.72	76.99	76.42	75.08	74.27	74.18	74.17	4000
5000	107.49	104.21	101.71	99.80	98.31	97.15	96.24	95.52	93.85	92.84	92.73	92.71	5000
6000	128.99	125.05	122.05	119.75	117.97	116.58	115.48	114.62	112.62	111.40	111.27	111.26	6000
7000	150.49	145.89	142.39	139.71	137.63	136.01	134.73	133.73	131.39	129.97	129.82	129.80	7000
8000	171.98	166.73	162.74	159.67	157.29	155.44	153.98	152.83	150.16	148.53	148.36	148.34	8000
9000	193.48	187.57	183.08	179.63	176.95	174.86	173.22	171.93	168.93	167.10	166.90	166.88	9000
10000	214.98	208.41	203.42	199.59	196.61	194.29	192.47	191.03	187.70	185.67	185.45	185.42	10000
15000	322.47	312.61	305.12	299.38	294.92	291.44	288.70	286.55	281.55	278.50	278.17	278.13	15000
20000	429.95	416.81	406.83	399.17	393.22	388.58	384.94	382.06	375.40	371.34	370.89	370.84	20000
25000	537.44	521.01	508.54	498.96	491.53	485.73	481.17	477.58	469.25	464.17	463.62	463.55	25000
30000	644.93	625.21	610.24	598.75	589.83	582.87	577.40	573.09	563.10	557.00	556.34	556.26	30000
35000	752.42	729.41	711.95	698.54	688.14	680.01	673.64	668.61	656.95	649.84	649.06	648.97	35000
40000	859.90	833.61	813.66	798.33	786.44	777.16	769.87	764.12	750.80	742.67	741.78	741.68	40000
45000	967.39	937.81	915.36	898.12	884.74	874.30	866.10	859.64	844.65	835.50	834.50	834.39	45000
50000	1074.88	1042.01	1017.07	997.91	983.05	971.45	962.34	955.15	938.50	928.33	927.23	927.10	50000
60000	1289.85	1250.42	1220.48	1197.49	1179.66	1165.74	1154.80	1146.18	1126.20	1114.00	1112.67	1112.52	60000
75000	1612.32	1563.02	1525.60	1496.86	1474.57	1457.17	1443.50	1432.73	1407.75	1392.50	1390.84	1390.65	75000
100000	2149.75	2084.02	2034.13	1995.81	1966.09	1942.89	1924.67	1910.30	1877.00	1856.66	1854.45	1854.20	100000
125000	2687.19	2605.03	2542.66	2494.76	2457.61	2428.61	2405.83	2387.87	2346.25	2320.83	2318.06	2317.75	125000
150000	3224.63	3126.03	3051.20	2993.71	2949.14	2914.33	2887.00	2865.45	2815.50	2784.99	2781.67	2781.30	150000
175000	3762.06	3647.03	3559.73	3492.66	3440.66	3400.05	3368.17	3343.02	3284.75	3249.16	3245.28	3244.85	175000
200000	4299.50	4168.04	4068.26	3991.61	3932.18	3885.77	3849.33	3820.59	3754.00	3713.32	3708.89	3708.40	200000
250000	5374.38	5210.05	5085.32	4989.51	4915.22	4857.22	4811.66	4775.74	4692.50	4641.65	4636.11	4635.50	250000

Amount	1.0 Year	1.5 Years	2.0 Years	2.5 Years	3.0 Years	3.5 Years	4.0 Years	4.5 Years	5.0 Years	6.0 Years	7.0 Years	8.0 Years	Amount
100	9.39	6.60	5.22	4.39	3.85	3.47	3.18	2.97	2.80	2.55	2.38	2.26	100
200	18.77	13.20	10.43	8.78	7.69	6.93	6.36	5.93	5.59	5.09	4.75	4.51	200
300	28.16	19.80	15.64	13.17	11.54	10.39	9.54	8.89	8.38	7.63	7.13	6.77	300
400	37.54	26.39	20.86	17.56	15.38	13.85	12.72	11.85	11.17	10.17	9.50	9.02	400
500	46.92	32.99	26.07	21.95	19.23	17.31	15.89	14.81	13.96	12.72	11.87	11.27	500
600	56.31	39.59	31.28	26.34	23.07	20.77	19.07	17.77	16.75	15.26	14.25	13.53	600
700	65.69	46.18	36.49	30.73	26.92	24.23	22.25	20.73	19.54	17.80	16.62	15.78	700
800	75.07	52.78	41.71	35.11	30.76	27.70	25.43	23.69	22.33	20.34	18.99	18.04	800
900	84.46	59.38	46.92	39.50	34.61	31.16	28.61	26.65	25.12	22.89	21.37	20.29	900
1000	93.84	65.98	52.13	43.89	38.45	34.62	31.78	29.61	27.91	25.43	23.74	22.54	1000
2000	187.68	131.95	104.26	87.78	76.90	69.23	63.56	59.22	55.81	50.85	47.48	45.08	2000
3000	281.51	197.92	156.38	131.66	115.35	103.85	95.34	88.83	83.72	76.28	71.21	67.62	3000
4000	375.35	263.89	208.51	175.55	153.80	138.46	127.12	118.44	111.62	101.70	94.95	90.16	4000
5000	469.18	329.86	260.63	219.44	192.25	173.07	158.90	148.05	139.52	127.12	118.68	112.70	5000
6000	563.02	395.83	312.76	263.32	230.70	207.69	190.67	177.65	167.43	152.55	142.42	135.23	6000
7000	656.85	461.80	364.88	307.21	269.15	242.30	222.45	207.26	195.33	177.97	166.15	157.77	7000
8000	750.69	527.78	417.01	351.09	307.60	276.92	254.23	236.87	223.24	203.40	189.89	180.31	8000
9000	844.52	593.75	469.13	394.98	346.05	311.53	286.01	266.48	251.14	228.82	213.63	202.85	9000
10000	938.36	659.72	521.26	438.87	384.50	346.14	317.79	296.09	279.04	254.24	237.36	225.39	10000
15000	1407.53	989.57	781.89	658.30	576.75	519.21	476.68	444.13	418.56	381.36	356.04	338.08	15000
20000	1876.71	1319.43	1042.51	877.73	769.00	692.28	635.57	592.17	558.08	508.48	474.72	450.77	20000
25000	2345.88	1649.29	1303.14	1097.16	961.25	865.35	794.46	740.21	697.60	635.60	593.40	563.46	25000
30000	2815.06	1979.14	1563.77	1316.59	1153.49	1038.42	953.35	888.25	837.12	762.72	712.07	676.15	30000
35000	3284.24	2309.00	1824.39	1536.02	1345.74	1211.49	1112.24	1036.30	976.64	889.84	830.75	788.84	35000
40000	3753.41	2638.86	2085.02	1755.45	1537.99	1384.56	1271.13	1184.34	1116.16	1016.96	949.43	901.53	40000
45000	4222.59	2968.71	2345.65	1974.88	1730.24	1557.63	1430.02	1332.38	1255.68	1144.07	1068.11	1014.22	45000
50000	4691.76	3298.57	2606.27	2194.31	1922.49	1730.70	1588.91	1480.42	1395.20	1271.19	1186.79	1126.91	50000
60000	5630.12	3958.28	3127.53	2633.17	2306.98	2076.84	1906.69	1776.50	1674.24	1525.43	1424.14	1352.29	60000
75000	7037.64	4947.85	3909.41	3291.47	2883.73	2596.05	2383.37	2220.63	2092.80	1906.79	1780.18	1690.37	75000
100000	9383.52	6597.13	5212.54	4388.62	3844.97	3461.40	3177.82	2960.84	2790.40	2542.38	2373.57	2253.82	100000
125000	11729.40	8246.41	6515.68	5485.77	4806.21	4326.75	3972.27	3701.04	3488.00	3177.98	2966.96	2817.27	125000
150000	14075.28	9895.69	7818.81	6582.93	5767.45	5192.09	4766.73	4441.25	4185.60	3813.57	3560.35	3380.73	150000
175000	16421.16	11544.98	9121.95	7680.08	6728.69	6057.44	5561.18	5181.46	4883.20	4449.16	4153.74	3944.18	175000
200000	18767.04	13194.26	10425.08	8777.24	7689.93	6922.79	6355.64	5921.67	5580.79	5084.76	4747.13	4507.63	200000
250000	23458.80	16492.82	13031.35	10971.54	9612.41	8653.49	7944.54	7402.08	6975.99	6355.95	5933.91	5634.54	250000

Amount	9.0 Years	10.0 Years	11.0 Years	12.0 Years	13.0 Years	14.0 Years	15.0 Years	16.0 Years	20.0 Years	30.0 Years	40.0 Years	50.0 Years	Amount
100	2.17	2.11	2.06	2.02	1.99	1.97	1.95	1.93	1.90	1.88	1.88	1.88	100
200	4.34	4.21	4.11	4.03	3.97	3.93	3.89	3.86	3.80	3.76	3.76	3.76	200
300	6.50	6.31	6.16	6.05	5.96	5.89	5.84	5.79	5.70	5.64	5.63	5.63	300
400	8.67	8.41	8.21	8.06	7.94	7.85	7.78	7.72	7.59	7.51	7.51	7.51	400
500	10.84	10.51	10.26	10.07	9.93	9.81	9.72	9.65	9.49	9.39	9.38	9.38	500
600	13.00	12.61	12.32	12.09	11.91	11.77	11.67	11.58	11.39	11.27	11.26	11.26	600
700	15.17	14.71	14.37	14.10	13.90	13.74	13.61	13.51	13.28	13.15	13.13	13.13	700
800	17.34	16.81	16.42	16.12	15.88	15.70	15.55	15.44	15.18	15.02	15.01	15.01	800
900	19.50	18.92	18.47	18.13	17.86	17.66	17.50	17.37	17.08	16.90	16.88	16.88	900
1000	21.67	21.02	20.52	20.14	19.85	19.62	19.44	19.30	18.97	18.78	18.76	18.76	1000
2000	43.33	42.03	41.04	40.28	39.69	39.24	38.88	38.60	37.94	37.55	37.51	37.51	2000
3000	65.00	63.04	61.56	60.42	59.54	58.85	58.31	57.89	56.91	56.33	56.26	56.26	3000
4000	86.66	84.05	82.07	80.56	79.38	78.47	77.75	77.19	75.88	75.10	75.02	75.01	4000
5000	108.32	105.06	102.59	100.69	99.23	98.08	97.19	96.48	94.85	93.87	93.77	93.76	5000
6000	129.99	126.07	123.11	120.83	119.07	117.70	116.62	115.78	113.82	112.65	112.52	112.51	6000
7000	151.65	147.08	143.62	140.97	138.91	137.31	136.06	135.07	132.79	131.42	131.27	131.26	7000
8000	173.31	168.09	164.14	161.11	158.76	156.93	155.49	154.37	151.76	150.19	150.03	150.01	8000
9000	194.98	189.11	184.66	181.24	178.60	176.54	174.93	173.66	170.73	168.97	168.78	168.76	9000
10000	216.64	210.12	205.17	201.38	198.45	196.16	194.37	192.96	189.70	187.74	187.53	187.51	10000
15000	324.96	315.17	307.76	302.07	297.67	294.24	291.55	289.43	284.55	281.61	281.29	281.26	15000
20000	433.28	420.23	410.34	402.76	396.89	392.31	388.73	385.91	379.40	375.47	375.06	375.01	20000
25000	541.59	525.28	512.92	503.45	496.11	490.39	485.91	482.38	474.25	469.34	468.82	468.76	25000
30000	649.91	630.34	615.51	604.13	595.33	588.47	583.09	578.86	569.10	563.21	562.58	562.51	30000
35000	758.23	735.40	718.09	704.82	694.55	686.55	680.27	675.33	663.94	657.07	656.34	656.26	35000
40000	866.55	840.45	820.68	805.51	793.77	784.62	777.45	771.81	758.79	750.94	750.11	750.02	40000
45000	974.87	945.51	923.26	906.20	892.99	882.70	874.63	868.28	853.64	844.81	843.87	843.77	45000
50000	1083.18	1050.56	1025.84	1006.89	992.21	980.78	971.81	964.76	948.49	938.67	937.63	937.52	50000
60000	1299.82	1260.68	1231.01	1208.26	1190.66	1176.93	1166.18	1157.71	1138.19	1126.41	1125.16	1125.02	60000
75000	1624.77	1575.84	1538.76	1510.33	1488.32	1471.16	1457.72	1447.14	1422.73	1408.01	1406.44	1406.28	75000
100000	2166.36	2101.12	2051.68	2013.77	1984.42	1961.55	1943.62	1929.51	1896.98	1877.34	1875.26	1875.03	100000
125000	2707.95	2626.40	2564.60	2517.21	2480.53	2451.94	2429.53	2411.89	2371.22	2346.68	2344.07	2343.79	125000
150000	3249.54	3151.68	3077.52	3020.65	2976.63	2942.32	2915.43	2894.27	2845.46	2816.01	2812.88	2812.55	150000
175000	3791.13	3676.96	3590.44	3524.09	3472.73	3432.71	3401.34	3376.64	3319.70	3285.35	3281.70	3281.30	175000
200000	4332.72	4202.24	4103.36	4027.53	3968.84	3923.09	3887.24	3859.02	3793.95	3754.68	3750.51	3750.06	200000
250000	5415.90	5252.80	5129.20	5034.41	4961.05	4903.87	4859.05	4823.78	4742.43	4693.35	4688.13	4687.57	250000

Amount	1.0 Year	1.5 Years	2.0 Years	2.5 Years	3.0 Years	3.5 Years	4.0 Years	4.5 Years	5.0 Years	6.0 Years	7.0 Years	8.0 Years	Amount
100	9.40	6.61	5.23	4.41	3.86	3.48	3.20	2.98	2.81	2.56	2.39	2.27	100
200	18.80	13.22	10.45	8.81	7.72	6.95	6.39	5.95	5.61	5.12	4.78	4.54	200
300	28.19	19.83	15.68	13.21	11.58	10.43	9.58	8.93	8.42	7.68	7.17	6.81	300
400	37.59	26.44	20.90	17.61	15.44	13.90	12.77	11.90	11.22	10.23	9.56	9.08	400
500	46.98	33.05	26.13	22.01	19.29	17.38	15.96	14.88	14.03	12.79	11.95	11.35	500
600	56.38	39.66	31.35	26.41	23.15	20.85	19.15	17.85	16.83	15.35	14.34	13.62	600
700	65.77	46.27	36.58	30.81	27.01	24.33	22.35	20.83	19.64	17.91	16.73	15.89	700
800	75.17	52.88	41.80	35.22	30.87	27.80	25.54	23.80	22.44	20.46	19.12	18.16	800
900	84.57	59.49	47.03	39.62	34.73	31.28	28.73	26.78	25.25	23.02	21.51	20.43	900
1000	93.96	66.10	52.25	44.02	38.58	34.75	31.92	29.75	28.05	25.58	23.90	22.70	1000
2000	187.92	132.19	104.50	88.03	77.16	69.50	63.83	59.50	56.10	51.15	47.79	45.40	2000
3000	281.87	198.28	156.75	132.04	115.74	104.25	95.75	89.25	84.15	76.72	71.68	68.10	3000
4000	375.83	264.38	209.00	176.06	154.32	138.99	127.66	119.00	112.19	102.30	95.57	90.80	4000
5000	469.78	330.47	261.25	220.07	192.90	173.74	159.58	148.75	140.24	127.87	119.46	113.50	5000
6000	563.74	396.56	313.50	264.08	231.48	208.49	191.49	178.49	168.29	153.44	143.35	136.20	6000
7000	657.69	462.65	365.75	308.10	270.06	243.23	223.41	208.24	196.33	179.02	167.24	158.90	7000
8000	751.65	528.75	418.00	352.11	308.64	277.98	255.32	237.99	224.38	204.59	191.13	181.60	8000
9000	845.61	594.84	470.25	396.12	347.22	312.73	287.24	267.74	252.43	230.16	215.03	204.30	9000
10000	939.56	660.93	522.50	440.13	385.80	347.48	319.15	297.49	280.48	255.74	238.92	227.00	10000
15000	1409.34	991.40	783.74	660.20	578.70	521.21	478.72	446.23	420.71	383.60	358.37	340.50	15000
20000	1879.12	1321.86	1044.99	880.26	771.60	694.95	638.30	594.97	560.95	511.47	477.83	453.99	20000
25000	2348.90	1652.32	1306.24	1100.33	964.49	868.68	797.87	743.71	701.18	639.34	597.28	567.49	25000
30000	2818.68	1982.79	1567.48	1320.39	1157.39	1042.42	957.44	892.45	841.42	767.20	716.74	680.99	30000
35000	3288.45	2313.25	1828.73	1540.46	1350.29	1216.15	1117.02	1041.19	981.65	895.07	836.20	794.48	35000
40000	3758.23	2643.72	2089.98	1760.52	1543.19	1389.89	1276.59	1189.93	1121.89	1022.93	955.65	907.98	40000
45000	4228.01	2974.18	2351.22	1980.59	1736.08	1563.63	1436.16	1338.67	1262.12	1150.80	1075.11	1021.48	45000
50000	4697.79	3304.64	2612.47	2200.65	1928.98	1737.36	1595.74	1487.41	1402.36	1278.67	1194.56	1134.98	50000
60000	5637.35	3965.57	3134.96	2640.78	2314.78	2084.83	1914.88	1784.89	1682.83	1534.40	1433.48	1361.97	60000
75000	7046.68	4956.96	3918.70	3300.98	2893.47	2606.04	2393.60	2231.11	2103.53	1918.00	1791.84	1702.46	75000
100000	9395.58	6609.28	5224.93	4401.30	3857.96	3474.72	3191.47	2974.82	2804.71	2557.33	2389.12	2269.95	100000
125000	11744.47	8261.60	6531.16	5501.62	4822.45	4343.40	3989.34	3718.52	3505.88	3196.66	2986.40	2837.43	125000
150000	14093.36	9913.92	7837.40	6601.95	5786.94	5212.07	4787.20	4462.22	4207.06	3835.99	3583.68	3404.92	150000
175000	16442.25	11566.24	9143.63	7702.27	6751.42	6080.75	5585.07	5205.92	4908.23	4475.32	4180.96	3972.40	175000
200000	18791.15	13218.56	10449.86	8802.59	7715.91	6949.43	6382.94	5949.63	5609.41	5114.65	4778.24	4539.89	200000
250000	23488.93	16523.20	13062.32	11003.24	9644.89	8686.79	7978.67	7437.03	7011.76	6393.31	5972.80	5674.86	250000

Amount	9.0 Years	10.0 Years	11.0 Years	12.0 Years	13.0 Years	14.0 Years	15.0 Years	16.0 Years	20.0 Years	30.0 Years	40.0 Years	50.0 Years	Amount
100	2.19	2.12	2.07	2.04	2.01	1.99	1.97	1.95	1.92	1.90	1.90	1.90	100
200	4.37	4.24	4.14	4.07	4.01	3.97	3.93	3.90	3.84	3.80	3.80	3.80	200
300	6.55	6.36	6.21	6.10	6.01	5.95	5.89	5.85	5.76	5.70	5.69	5.69	300
400	8.74	8.48	8.28	8.13	8.02	7.93	7.86	7.80	7.67	7.60	7.59	7.59	400
500	10.92	10.60	10.35	10.16	10.02	9.91	9.82	9.75	9.59	9.50	9.49	9.48	500
600	13.10	12.71	12.42	12.20	12.02	11.89	11.78	11.70	11.51	11.39	11.38	11.38	600
700	15.29	14.83	14.49	14.23	14.02	13.87	13.74	13.65	13.42	13.29	13.28	13.28	700
800	17.47	16.95	16.56	16.26	16.03	15.85	15.71	15.60	15.34	15.19	15.17	15.17	800
900	19.65	19.07	18.63	18.29	18.03	17.83	17.67	17.54	17.26	17.09	17.07	17.07	900
1000	21.84	21.19	20.70	20.32	20.03	19.81	19.63	19.49	19.17	18.99	18.97	18.96	1000
2000	43.67	42.37	41.39	40.64	40.06	39.61	39.26	38.98	38.34	37.97	37.93	37.92	2000
3000	65.50	63.55	62.08	60.96	60.09	59.41	58.88	58.47	57.51	56.95	56.89	56.88	3000
4000	87.33	84.74	82.78	81.28	80.12	79.22	78.51	77.96	76.68	75.93	75.85	75.84	4000
5000	109.16	105.92	103.47	101.59	100.14	99.02	98.14	97.44	95.85	94.91	94.81	94.80	5000
6000	130.99	127.10	124.16	121.91	120.17	118.82	117.76	116.93	115.02	113.89	113.77	113.76	6000
7000	152.82	148.28	144.85	142.23	140.20	138.62	137.39	136.42	134.19	132.87	132.73	132.72	7000
8000	174.65	169.47	165.55	162.55	160.23	158.43	157.01	155.91	153.36	151.85	151.69	151.67	8000
9000	196.48	190.65	186.24	182.86	180.26	178.23	176.64	175.39	172.53	170.83	170.65	170.63	9000
10000	218.31	211.83	206.93	203.18	200.28	198.03	196.27	194.88	191.70	189.81	189.61	189.59	10000
15000	327.46	317.75	310.40	304.77	300.42	297.04	294.40	292.32	287.55	284.71	284.41	284.38	15000
20000	436.61	423.66	413.86	406.36	400.56	396.06	392.53	389.76	383.40	379.61	379.22	379.18	20000
25000	545.76	529.57	517.33	507.95	500.70	495.07	490.66	487.20	479.25	474.51	474.02	473.97	25000
30000	654.91	635.49	620.79	609.54	600.84	594.08	588.79	584.63	575.10	569.41	568.82	568.76	30000
35000	764.06	741.40	724.25	711.13	700.98	693.09	686.92	682.07	670.95	664.32	663.63	663.56	35000
40000	873.21	847.31	827.72	812.71	801.12	792.11	785.05	779.51	766.79	759.22	758.43	758.35	40000
45000	982.36	953.23	931.18	914.30	901.26	891.12	883.18	876.95	862.64	854.12	853.23	853.14	45000
50000	1091.51	1059.14	1034.65	1015.89	1001.40	990.13	981.31	974.39	958.49	949.02	948.04	947.93	50000
60000	1309.82	1270.97	1241.57	1219.07	1201.68	1188.16	1177.58	1169.26	1150.19	1138.82	1137.64	1137.52	60000
75000	1637.27	1588.71	1551.97	1523.84	1502.10	1485.19	1471.97	1461.58	1437.73	1423.53	1422.05	1421.90	75000
100000	2183.02	2118.28	2069.29	2031.78	2002.80	1980.26	1962.62	1948.77	1916.98	1898.04	1896.07	1895.86	100000
125000	2728.78	2647.85	2586.61	2539.72	2503.50	2475.32	2453.28	2435.96	2396.22	2372.54	2370.08	2369.83	125000
150000	3274.53	3177.41	3103.93	3047.67	3004.20	2970.38	2943.93	2923.15	2875.46	2847.05	2844.10	2843.79	150000
175000	3820.29	3706.98	3621.25	3555.61	3504.90	3465.45	3434.59	3410.35	3354.71	3321.56	3318.12	3317.76	175000
200000	4366.04	4236.55	4138.57	4063.55	4005.60	3960.51	3925.24	3897.54	3833.95	3796.07	3792.13	3791.72	200000
250000	5457.55	5295.69	5173.21	5079.44	5007.00	4950.64	4906.55	4871.92	4792.43	4745.08	4740.16	4739.65	250000

Amount	1.0 Year	1.5 Years	2.0 Years	2.5 Years	3.0 Years	3.5 Years	4.0 Years	4.5 Years	5.0 Years	6.0 Years	7.0 Years	8.0 Years	Amount
100	9.41	6.63	5.24	4.42	3.88	3.49	3.21	2.99	2.82	2.58	2.41	2.29	100
200	18.82	13.25	10.48	8.83	7.75	6.98	6.42	5.98	5.64	5.15	4.81	4.58	200
300	28.23	19.87	15.72	13.25	11.62	10.47	9.62	8.97	8.46	7.72	7.22	6.86	300
400	37.64	26.49	20.95	17.66	15.49	13.96	12.83	11.96	11.28	10.29	9.62	9.15	400
500	47.04	33.11	26.19	22.07	19.36	17.45	16.03	14.95	14.10	12.87	12.03	11.44	500
600	56.45	39.73	31.43	26.49	23.23	20.93	19.24	17.94	16.92	15.44	14.43	13.72	600
700	65.86	46.36	36.67	30.90	27.10	24.42	22.44	20.93	19.74	18.01	16.84	16.01	700
800	75.27	52.98	41.90	35.32	30.97	27.91	25.65	23.92	22.56	20.58	19.24	18.29	800
900	84.67	59.60	47.14	39.73	34.84	31.40	28.85	26.90	25.38	23.16	21.65	20.58	900
1000	94.08	66.22	52.38	44.14	38.71	34.89	32.06	29.89	28.20	25.73	24.05	22.87	1000
2000	188.16	132.43	104.75	88.28	77.42	69.77	64.11	59.78	56.39	51.45	48.10	45.73	2000
3000	282.23	198.65	157.12	132.42	116.13	104.65	96.16	89.67	84.58	77.17	72.15	68.59	3000
4000	376.31	264.86	209.50	176.56	154.84	139.53	128.21	119.56	112.77	102.90	96.19	91.45	4000
5000	470.39	331.08	261.87	220.70	193.55	174.41	160.26	149.45	140.96	128.62	120.24	114.31	5000
6000	564.46	397.29	314.24	264.84	232.26	209.29	192.31	179.33	169.15	154.34	144.29	137.17	6000
7000	658.54	463.51	366.62	308.98	270.97	244.17	224.37	209.22	197.34	180.07	168.34	160.03	7000
8000	752.62	529.72	418.99	353.12	309.68	279.05	256.42	239.11	225.53	205.79	192.38	182.89	8000
9000	846.69	595.93	471.36	397.26	348.39	313.93	288.47	269.00	253.72	231.51	216.43	205.76	9000
10000	940.77	662.15	523.74	441.40	387.10	348.81	320.52	298.89	281.91	257.24	240.48	228.62	10000
15000	1411.15	993.22	785.60	662.10	580.65	523.21	480.78	448.33	422.86	385.85	360.71	342.92	15000
20000	1881.53	1324.29	1047.47	882.80	774.20	697.62	641.03	597.77	563.81	514.47	480.95	457.23	20000
25000	2351.91	1655.36	1309.34	1103.50	967.75	872.02	801.29	747.21	704.77	643.08	601.18	571.53	25000
30000	2822.29	1986.44	1571.20	1324.20	1161.30	1046.42	961.55	896.65	845.72	771.70	721.42	685.84	30000
35000	3292.68	2317.51	1833.07	1544.90	1354.85	1220.83	1121.81	1046.09	986.67	900.31	841.66	800.15	35000
40000	3763.06	2648.58	2094.94	1765.60	1548.39	1395.23	1282.06	1195.54	1127.62	1028.93	961.89	914.45	40000
45000	4233.44	2979.65	2356.80	1986.30	1741.94	1569.63	1442.32	1344.98	1268.58	1157.54	1082.13	1028.76	45000
50000	4703.82	3310.72	2618.67	2207.00	1935.49	1744.04	1602.58	1494.42	1409.53	1286.16	1202.36	1143.06	50000
60000	5644.58	3972.87	3142.40	2648.40	2322.59	2092.84	1923.09	1793.30	1691.43	1543.39	1442.84	1371.68	60000
75000	7055.73	4966.08	3928.00	3310.50	2903.23	2616.05	2403.87	2241.62	2114.29	1929.24	1803.54	1714.59	75000
100000	9407.65	6621.44	5237.34	4414.00	3870.98	3488.07	3205.15	2988.83	2819.05	2572.32	2404.72	2286.12	100000
125000	11759.55	8276.80	6546.67	5517.50	4838.72	4360.08	4006.44	3736.04	3523.81	3215.39	3005.90	2857.65	125000
150000	14111.45	9932.16	7856.00	6620.99	5806.46	5232.10	4807.73	4483.24	4228.58	3858.47	3607.08	3429.18	150000
175000	16463.36	11587.52	9165.33	7724.49	6774.21	6104.11	5609.01	5230.45	4933.34	4501.55	4208.26	4000.71	175000
200000	18815.27	13242.88	10474.67	8827.99	7741.95	6976.13	6410.30	5977.66	5638.10	5144.63	4809.44	4572.24	200000
250000	23519.09	16553.60	13093.33	11034.99	9677.44	8720.16	8012.87	7472.07	7047.62	6430.78	6011.80	5715.30	250000

Amount	9.0 Years	10.0 Years	11.0 Years	12.0 Years	13.0 Years	14.0 Years	15.0 Years	16.0 Years	20.0 Years	30.0 Years	40.0 Years	50.0 Years	Amount
100	2.20	2.14	2.09	2.05	2.03	2.00	1.99	1.97	1.94	1.92	1.92	1.92	100
200	4.40	4.28	4.18	4.10	4.05	4.00	3.97	3.94	3.88	3.84	3.84	3.84	200
300	6.60	6.41	6.27	6.15	6.07	6.00	5.95	5.91	5.82	5.76	5.76	5.76	300
400	8.80	8.55	8.35	8.20	8.09	8.00	7.93	7.88	7.75	7.68	7.67	7.67	400
500	11.00	10.68	10.44	10.25	10.11	10.00	9.91	9.85	9.69	9.60	9.59	9.59	500
600	13.20	12.82	12.53	12.30	12.13	12.00	11.89	11.81	11.63	11.52	11.51	11.51	600
700	15.40	14.95	14.61	14.35	14.15	14.00	13.88	13.78	13.56	13.44	13.42	13.42	700
800	17.60	17.09	16.70	16.40	16.17	16.00	15.86	15.75	15.50	15.35	15.34	15.34	800
900	19.80	19.22	18.79	18.45	18.20	18.00	17.84	17.72	17.44	17.27	17.26	17.26	900
1000	22.00	21.36	20.87	20.50	20.22	20.00	19.82	19.69	19.38	19.19	19.17	19.17	1000
2000	44.00	42.71	41.74	41.00	40.43	39.99	39.64	39.37	38.75	38.38	38.34	38.34	2000
3000	66.00	64.07	62.61	61.50	60.64	59.98	59.45	59.05	58.12	57.57	57.51	57.51	3000
4000	87.99	85.42	83.48	82.00	80.85	79.97	79.27	78.73	77.49	76.75	76.68	76.67	4000
5000	109.99	106.78	104.35	102.50	101.07	99.96	99.09	98.41	96.86	95.94	95.85	95.84	5000
6000	131.99	128.13	125.22	123.00	121.28	119.95	118.90	118.09	116.23	115.13	115.02	115.01	6000
7000	153.99	149.49	146.09	143.49	141.49	139.94	138.72	137.77	135.60	134.32	134.19	134.17	7000
8000	175.98	170.84	166.96	163.99	161.70	159.93	158.54	157.45	154.97	153.50	153.36	153.34	8000
9000	197.98	192.20	187.83	184.49	181.92	179.92	178.35	177.13	174.34	172.69	172.52	172.51	9000
10000	219.98	213.55	208.70	204.99	202.13	199.91	198.17	196.81	193.71	191.88	191.69	191.67	10000
15000	329.96	320.33	313.05	307.48	303.19	299.86	297.25	295.21	290.56	287.81	287.54	287.51	15000
20000	439.95	427.10	417.39	409.97	404.25	399.81	396.34	393.62	387.41	383.75	383.38	383.34	20000
25000	549.94	533.87	521.74	512.46	505.31	499.76	495.42	492.02	484.26	479.69	479.22	479.18	25000
30000	659.92	640.65	626.09	614.96	606.37	599.71	594.50	590.42	581.11	575.62	575.07	575.01	30000
35000	769.91	747.42	730.43	717.45	707.43	699.66	693.59	688.83	677.96	671.56	670.91	670.85	35000
40000	879.90	854.20	834.78	819.94	808.50	799.61	792.67	787.23	774.81	767.50	766.76	766.68	40000
45000	989.88	960.97	939.13	922.43	909.56	899.56	891.75	885.63	871.66	863.43	862.60	862.51	45000
50000	1099.87	1067.74	1043.47	1024.92	1010.62	999.51	990.84	984.04	968.51	959.37	958.44	958.35	50000
60000	1319.84	1281.29	1252.17	1229.91	1212.74	1199.41	1189.00	1180.84	1162.21	1151.24	1150.13	1150.02	60000
75000	1649.80	1601.61	1565.21	1537.38	1515.92	1499.26	1486.25	1476.05	1452.76	1439.05	1437.66	1437.52	75000
100000	2199.74	2135.48	2086.94	2049.84	2021.23	1999.01	1981.67	1968.07	1937.01	1918.74	1916.88	1916.69	100000
125000	2749.67	2669.35	2608.68	2562.30	2526.54	2498.77	2477.08	2460.09	2421.26	2398.42	2396.10	2395.87	125000
150000	3299.60	3203.22	3130.41	3074.76	3031.84	2998.52	2972.50	2952.10	2905.51	2878.10	2875.32	2875.04	150000
175000	3849.54	3737.09	3652.15	3587.22	3537.15	3498.27	3467.92	3444.12	3389.76	3357.78	3354.54	3354.21	175000
200000	4399.47	4270.96	4173.88	4099.68	4042.46	3998.02	3963.33	3936.14	3874.01	3837.47	3833.76	3833.38	200000
250000	5499.34	5338.70	5217.35	5124.60	5053.07	4997.53	4954.16	4920.17	4842.51	4796.83	4792.20	4791.73	250000

Amount	1.0 Year	1.5 Years	2.0 Years	2.5 Years	3.0 Years	3.5 Years	4.0 Years	4.5 Years	5.0 Years	6.0 Years	7.0 Years	8.0 Years	Amount
100	9.42	6.64	5.25	4.43	3.89	3.51	3.22	3.01	2.84	2.59	2.43	2.31	100
200	18.84	13.27	10.50	8.86	7.77	7.01	6.44	6.01	5.67	5.18	4.85	4.61	200
300	28.26	19.91	15.75	13.29	11.66	10.51	9.66	9.01	8.51	7.77	7.27	6.91	300
400	37.68	26.54	21.00	17.71	15.54	14.01	12.88	12.02	11.34	10.35	9.69	9.21	400
500	47.10	33.17	26.25	22.14	19.43	17.51	16.10	15.02	14.17	12.94	12.11	11.52	500
600	56.52	39.81	31.50	26.57	23.31	21.01	19.32	18.02	17.01	15.53	14.53	13.82	600
700	65.94	46.44	36.75	30.99	27.19	24.52	22.54	21.03	19.84	18.12	16.95	16.12	700
800	75.36	53.07	42.00	35.42	31.08	28.02	25.76	24.03	22.67	20.70	19.37	18.42	800
900	84.78	59.71	47.25	39.85	34.96	31.52	28.97	27.03	25.51	23.29	21.79	20.73	900
1000	94.20	66.34	52.50	44.27	38.85	35.02	32.19	30.03	28.34	25.88	24.21	23.03	1000
2000	188.40	132.68	105.00	88.54	77.69	70.03	64.38	60.06	56.67	51.75	48.41	46.05	2000
3000	282.60	199.01	157.50	132.81	116.53	105.05	96.57	90.09	85.01	77.63	72.62	69.08	3000
4000	376.79	265.35	210.00	177.07	155.37	140.06	128.76	120.12	113.34	103.50	96.82	92.10	4000
5000	470.99	331.69	262.49	221.34	194.21	175.08	160.95	150.15	141.68	129.37	121.02	115.12	5000
6000	565.19	398.02	314.99	265.61	233.05	210.09	193.14	180.18	170.01	155.25	145.23	138.15	6000
7000	659.38	464.36	367.49	309.87	271.89	245.11	225.33	210.21	198.35	181.12	169.43	161.17	7000
8000	753.58	530.69	419.99	354.14	310.73	280.12	257.51	240.23	226.68	206.99	193.63	184.19	8000
9000	847.78	597.03	472.48	398.41	349.57	315.13	289.70	270.26	255.01	232.87	217.84	207.22	9000
10000	941.98	663.37	524.98	442.68	388.41	350.15	321.89	300.29	283.35	258.74	242.04	230.24	10000
15000	1412.96	995.05	787.47	664.01	582.61	525.22	482.83	450.44	425.02	388.11	363.06	345.36	15000
20000	1883.95	1326.73	1049.96	885.35	776.81	700.29	643.78	600.58	566.69	517.47	484.08	460.47	20000
25000	2354.93	1658.41	1312.44	1106.68	971.01	875.36	804.72	750.72	708.36	646.84	605.10	575.59	25000
30000	2825.92	1990.09	1574.93	1328.02	1165.21	1050.44	965.66	900.87	850.03	776.21	726.11	690.71	30000
35000	3296.90	2321.77	1837.42	1549.35	1359.41	1225.51	1126.61	1051.01	991.71	905.57	847.13	805.83	35000
40000	3767.89	2653.45	2099.91	1770.69	1553.61	1400.58	1287.55	1201.15	1133.38	1034.94	968.15	920.94	40000
45000	4238.87	2985.13	2362.39	1992.03	1747.81	1575.65	1448.49	1351.30	1275.05	1164.31	1089.17	1036.06	45000
50000	4709.86	3316.81	2624.88	2213.36	1942.01	1750.72	1609.43	1501.44	1416.72	1293.68	1210.19	1151.18	50000
60000	5651.83	3980.17	3149.86	2656.03	2330.41	2100.87	1931.32	1801.73	1700.06	1552.41	1452.22	1381.41	60000
75000	7064.78	4975.21	3937.32	3320.04	2913.02	2626.08	2414.15	2252.16	2125.08	1940.51	1815.28	1726.76	75000
100000	9419.71	6633.62	5249.76	4426.72	3884.02	3501.44	3218.86	3002.88	2833.43	2587.35	2420.37	2302.35	100000
125000	11774.63	8292.02	6562.19	5533.40	4855.02	4376.80	4023.58	3753.60	3541.79	3234.18	3025.46	2877.94	125000
150000	14129.56	9950.42	7874.63	6640.07	5826.03	5252.16	4828.29	4504.32	4250.15	3881.02	3630.55	3453.52	150000
175000	16484.48	11608.83	9187.07	7746.75	6797.03	6127.52	5633.01	5255.04	4958.51	4527.85	4235.65	4029.11	175000
200000	18839.41	13267.23	10499.51	8853.43	7768.03	7002.88	6437.72	6005.75	5666.86	5174.69	4840.74	4604.70	200000
250000	23549.26	16584.04	13124.38	11066.79	9710.04	8753.60	8047.15	7507.19	7083.58	6468.36	6050.92	5755.87	250000

Amount	9.0 Years	10.0 Years	11.0 Years	12.0 Years	13.0 Years	14.0 Years	15.0 Years	16.0 Years	20.0 Years	30.0 Years	40.0 Years	50.0 Years	Amount
100	2.22	2.16	2.11	2.07	2.04	2.02	2.01	1.99	1.96	1.94	1.94	1.94	100
200	4.44	4.31	4.21	4.14	4.08	4.04	4.01	3.98	3.92	3.88	3.88	3.88	200
300	6.65	6.46	6.32	6.21	6.12	6.06	6.01	5.97	5.88	5.82	5.82	5.82	300
400	8.87	8.62	8.42	8.28	8.16	8.08	8.01	7.95	7.83	7.76	7.76	7.76	400
500	11.09	10.77	10.53	10.34	10.20	10.09	10.01	9.94	9.79	9.70	9.69	9.69	500
600	13.30	12.92	12.63	12.41	12.24	12.11	12.01	11.93	11.75	11.64	11.63	11.63	600
700	15.52	15.07	14.74	14.48	14.28	14.13	14.01	13.92	13.70	13.58	13.57	13.57	700
800	17.74	17.23	16.84	16.55	16.32	16.15	16.01	15.90	15.66	15.52	15.51	15.51	800
900	19.95	19.38	18.95	18.62	18.36	18.17	18.01	17.89	17.62	17.46	17.44	17.44	900
1000	22.17	21.53	21.05	20.68	20.40	20.18	20.01	19.88	19.58	19.40	19.38	19.38	1000
2000	44.33	43.06	42.10	41.36	40.80	40.36	40.02	39.75	39.15	38.79	38.76	38.76	2000
3000	66.50	64.59	63.14	62.04	61.20	60.54	60.03	59.63	58.72	58.19	58.14	58.13	3000
4000	88.66	86.11	84.19	82.72	81.59	80.72	80.04	79.50	78.29	77.58	77.51	77.51	4000
5000	110.83	107.64	105.24	103.40	101.99	100.90	100.04	99.38	97.86	96.98	96.89	96.88	5000
6000	132.99	129.17	126.28	124.08	122.39	121.07	120.05	119.25	117.43	116.37	116.27	116.26	6000
7000	155.16	150.70	147.33	144.76	142.78	141.25	140.06	139.12	137.00	135.77	135.64	135.63	7000
8000	177.32	172.22	168.38	165.44	163.18	161.43	160.07	159.00	156.57	155.16	155.02	155.01	8000
9000	199.49	193.75	189.42	186.12	183.58	181.61	180.07	178.87	176.14	174.55	174.40	174.38	9000
10000	221.65	215.28	210.47	206.80	203.98	201.79	200.08	198.75	195.71	193.95	193.77	193.76	10000
15000	332.48	322.92	315.70	310.20	305.96	302.68	300.12	298.12	293.56	290.92	290.66	290.63	15000
20000	443.30	430.55	420.93	413.60	407.95	403.57	400.16	397.49	391.42	387.89	387.54	387.51	20000
25000	554.13	538.19	526.17	516.99	509.93	504.46	500.19	496.86	489.27	484.86	484.43	484.38	25000
30000	664.95	645.83	631.40	620.39	611.92	605.35	600.23	596.23	587.12	581.84	581.31	581.26	30000
35000	775.78	753.46	736.63	723.79	713.90	706.24	700.27	695.60	684.98	678.81	678.20	678.14	35000
40000	886.60	861.10	841.86	827.19	815.89	807.13	800.31	794.97	782.83	775.78	775.08	775.01	40000
45000	997.43	968.74	947.10	930.58	917.87	908.02	900.34	894.34	880.68	872.75	871.97	871.89	45000
50000	1108.25	1076.37	1052.33	1033.98	1019.86	1008.91	1000.38	993.71	978.54	969.72	968.85	968.76	50000
60000	1329.90	1291.65	1262.79	1240.78	1223.83	1210.69	1200.46	1192.45	1174.24	1163.67	1162.62	1162.52	60000
75000	1662.38	1614.56	1578.49	1550.97	1529.78	1513.36	1500.57	1490.56	1467.80	1454.58	1453.28	1453.14	75000
100000	2216.50	2152.74	2104.65	2067.96	2039.71	2017.82	2000.76	1987.41	1957.07	1939.44	1937.70	1937.52	100000
125000	2770.62	2690.92	2630.81	2584.94	2549.63	2522.27	2500.95	2484.26	2446.33	2424.30	2422.12	2421.90	125000
150000	3324.75	3229.11	3156.97	3101.93	3059.56	3026.72	3001.13	2981.12	2935.60	2909.16	2906.55	2906.28	150000
175000	3878.87	3767.29	3683.13	3618.92	3569.49	3531.17	3501.32	3477.97	3424.87	3394.02	3390.97	3390.66	175000
200000	4433.00	4305.48	4209.30	4135.91	4079.41	4035.63	4001.51	3974.82	3914.13	3878.88	3875.39	3875.04	200000
250000	5541.24	5381.84	5261.62	5169.88	5099.26	5044.53	5001.89	4968.52	4892.66	4848.60	4844.24	4843.80	250000

Amount	1.0 Year	1.5 Years	2.0 Years	2.5 Years	3.0 Years	3.5 Years	4.0 Years	4.5 Years	5.0 Years	6.0 Years	7.0 Years	8.0 Years	Amount
100	9.44	6.65	5.27	4.44	3.90	3.52	3.24	3.02	2.85	2.61	2.44	2.32	100
200	18.87	13.30	10.53	8.88	7.80	7.03	6.47	6.04	5.70	5.21	4.88	4.64	200
300	28.30	19.94	15.79	13.32	11.70	10.55	9.70	9.06	8.55	7.81	7.31	6.96	300
400	37.73	26.59	21.05	17.76	15.59	14.06	12.94	12.07	11.40	10.41	9.75	9.28	400
500	47.16	33.23	26.32	22.20	19.49	17.58	16.17	15.09	14.24	13.02	12.19	11.60	500
600	56.60	39.88	31.58	26.64	23.39	21.09	19.40	18.11	17.09	15.62	14.62	13.92	600
700	66.03	46.53	36.84	31.08	27.28	24.61	22.63	21.12	19.94	18.22	17.06	16.24	700
800	75.46	53.17	42.10	35.52	31.18	28.12	25.87	24.14	22.79	20.82	19.49	18.55	800
900	84.89	59.82	47.36	39.96	35.08	31.64	29.10	27.16	25.64	23.43	21.93	20.87	900
1000	94.32	66.46	52.63	44.40	38.98	35.15	32.33	30.17	28.48	26.03	24.37	23.19	1000
2000	188.64	132.92	105.25	88.79	77.95	70.30	64.66	60.34	56.96	52.05	48.73	46.38	2000
3000	282.96	199.38	157.87	133.19	116.92	105.45	96.98	90.51	85.44	78.08	73.09	69.56	3000
4000	377.28	265.84	210.49	177.58	155.89	140.60	129.31	120.68	113.92	104.10	97.45	92.75	4000
5000	471.59	332.29	263.11	221.98	194.86	175.75	161.64	150.85	142.40	130.13	121.81	115.94	5000
6000	565.91	398.75	315.74	266.37	233.83	210.90	193.96	181.02	170.88	156.15	146.17	139.12	6000
7000	660.23	465.21	368.36	310.77	272.80	246.04	226.29	211.19	199.35	182.17	170.53	162.31	7000
8000	754.55	531.67	420.98	355.16	311.77	281.19	258.61	241.36	227.83	208.20	194.89	185.49	8000
9000	848.87	598.13	473.60	399.56	350.74	316.34	290.94	271.53	256.31	234.22	219.25	208.68	9000
10000	943.18	664.58	526.22	443.95	389.71	351.49	323.27	301.70	284.79	260.25	243.61	231.87	10000
15000	1414.77	996.87	789.33	665.92	584.57	527.23	484.90	452.55	427.18	390.37	365.41	347.80	15000
20000	1886.36	1329.16	1052.44	887.90	779.42	702.97	646.53	603.40	569.57	520.49	487.22	463.73	20000
25000	2357.95	1661.45	1315.55	1109.87	974.28	878.72	808.16	754.24	711.97	650.61	609.02	579.66	25000
30000	2829.54	1993.74	1578.66	1331.84	1169.13	1054.46	969.79	905.09	854.36	780.73	730.82	695.59	30000
35000	3301.13	2326.03	1841.77	1553.81	1363.98	1230.20	1131.42	1055.94	996.75	910.85	852.63	811.52	35000
40000	3772.72	2658.32	2104.88	1775.79	1558.84	1405.94	1293.05	1206.79	1139.14	1040.97	974.43	927.45	40000
45000	4244.31	2990.61	2367.99	1997.76	1753.69	1581.68	1454.68	1357.64	1281.54	1171.09	1096.23	1043.38	45000
50000	4715.89	3322.90	2631.10	2219.73	1948.55	1757.43	1616.31	1508.48	1423.93	1301.21	1218.03	1159.31	50000
60000	5659.07	3987.48	3157.32	2663.68	2338.25	2108.91	1939.57	1810.18	1708.71	1561.45	1461.64	1391.18	60000
75000	7073.84	4984.35	3946.65	3329.59	2922.82	2636.14	2424.46	2262.72	2135.89	1951.82	1827.05	1738.97	75000
100000	9431.78	6645.80	5262.19	4439.46	3897.09	3514.85	3232.61	3016.96	2847.85	2602.42	2436.06	2318.62	100000
125000	11789.73	8307.25	6577.74	5549.32	4871.36	4393.56	4040.76	3771.20	3559.82	3253.02	3045.08	2898.28	125000
150000	14147.67	9968.70	7893.29	6659.18	5845.63	5272.27	4848.91	4525.44	4271.78	3903.63	3654.09	3477.93	150000
175000	16505.62	11630.15	9208.83	7769.05	6819.90	6150.98	5657.06	5279.68	4983.74	4554.23	4263.11	4057.59	175000
200000	18863.56	13291.60	10524.38	8878.91	7794.17	7029.69	6465.21	6033.92	5695.70	5204.83	4872.12	4637.24	200000
250000	23579.45	16614.50	13155.47	11098.63	9742.71	8787.11	8081.51	7542.40	7119.63	6506.04	6090.15	5796.55	250000

Amount	9.0 Years	10.0 Years	11.0 Years	12.0 Years	13.0 Years	14.0 Years	15.0 Years	16.0 Years	20.0 Years	30.0 Years	40.0 Years	50.0 Years	Amount
100	2.24	2.18	2.13	2.09	2.06	2.04	2.02	2.01	1.98	1.97	1.96	1.96	100
200	4.47	4.35	4.25	4.18	4.12	4.08	4.04	4.02	3.96	3.93	3.92	3.92	200
300	6.70	6.52	6.37	6.26	6.18	6.11	6.06	6.03	5.94	5.89	5.88	5.88	300
400	8.94	8.69	8.49	8.35	8.24	8.15	8.08	8.03	7.91	7.85	7.84	7.84	400
500	11.17	10.86	10.62	10.44	10.30	10.19	10.10	10.04	9.89	9.81	9.80	9.80	500
600	13.40	13.03	12.74	12.52	12.35	12.22	12.12	12.05	11.87	11.77	11.76	11.76	600
700	15.64	15.20	14.86	14.61	14.41	14.26	14.14	14.05	13.85	13.73	13.71	13.71	700
800	17.87	17.37	16.98	16.69	16.47	16.30	16.16	16.06	15.82	15.69	15.67	15.67	800
900	20.10	19.54	19.11	18.78	18.53	18.33	18.18	18.07	17.80	17.65	17.63	17.63	900
1000	22.34	21.71	21.23	20.87	20.59	20.37	20.20	20.07	19.78	19.61	19.59	19.59	1000
2000	44.67	43.41	42.45	41.73	41.17	40.74	40.40	40.14	39.55	39.21	39.18	39.17	2000
3000	67.00	65.11	63.68	62.59	61.75	61.10	60.60	60.21	59.32	58.81	58.76	58.76	3000
4000	89.34	86.81	84.90	83.45	82.33	81.47	80.80	80.28	79.09	78.41	78.35	78.34	4000
5000	111.67	108.51	106.13	104.31	102.92	101.84	101.00	100.34	98.86	98.01	97.93	97.92	5000
6000	134.00	130.21	127.35	125.17	123.50	122.20	121.20	120.41	118.63	117.62	117.52	117.51	6000
7000	156.34	151.91	148.57	146.03	144.08	142.57	141.40	140.48	138.41	137.22	137.10	137.09	7000
8000	178.67	173.61	169.80	166.89	164.66	162.94	161.60	160.55	158.18	156.82	156.69	156.67	8000
9000	201.00	195.31	191.02	187.76	185.25	183.30	181.79	180.62	177.95	176.42	176.27	176.26	9000
10000	223.34	217.01	212.25	208.62	205.83	203.67	201.99	200.68	197.72	196.02	195.86	195.84	10000
15000	335.00	325.51	318.37	312.92	308.74	305.50	302.99	301.02	296.58	294.03	293.78	293.76	15000
20000	446.67	434.01	424.49	417.23	411.65	407.34	403.98	401.36	395.44	392.04	391.71	391.68	20000
25000	558.33	542.52	530.61	521.53	514.56	509.17	504.98	501.70	494.29	490.04	489.63	489.59	25000
30000	670.00	651.02	636.73	625.84	617.47	611.00	605.97	602.04	593.15	588.05	587.56	587.51	30000
35000	781.66	759.52	742.85	730.14	720.39	712.84	706.96	702.38	692.01	686.06	685.48	685.43	35000
40000	893.33	868.02	848.97	834.45	823.30	814.67	807.96	802.72	790.87	784.07	783.41	783.35	40000
45000	1004.99	976.52	955.09	938.76	926.21	916.50	908.95	903.06	889.72	882.07	881.33	881.26	45000
50000	1116.66	1085.03	1061.21	1043.06	1029.12	1018.33	1009.95	1003.40	988.58	980.08	979.26	979.18	50000
60000	1339.99	1302.03	1273.45	1251.67	1234.94	1222.00	1211.94	1204.08	1186.30	1176.10	1175.11	1175.02	60000
75000	1674.99	1627.54	1591.81	1564.59	1543.68	1527.50	1514.92	1505.10	1482.87	1470.12	1468.89	1468.77	75000
100000	2233.31	2170.05	2122.41	2086.12	2058.23	2036.66	2019.89	2006.79	1977.16	1960.16	1958.52	1958.36	100000
125000	2791.64	2712.56	2653.01	2607.65	2572.79	2545.83	2524.86	2508.49	2471.44	2450.20	2448.14	2447.94	125000
150000	3349.97	3255.07	3183.61	3129.18	3087.35	3054.99	3029.83	3010.19	2965.73	2940.24	2937.77	2937.53	150000
175000	3908.30	3797.58	3714.21	3650.70	3601.91	3564.16	3534.80	3511.88	3460.02	3430.27	3427.40	3427.12	175000
200000	4466.62	4340.09	4244.81	4172.23	4116.46	4073.32	4039.77	4013.58	3954.31	3920.31	3917.03	3916.71	200000
250000	5583.28	5425.11	5306.01	5215.29	5145.58	5091.65	5049.72	5016.98	4942.88	4900.39	4896.28	4895.88	250000

Amount	1.0 Year	1.5 Years	2.0 Years	2.5 Years	3.0 Years	3.5 Years	4.0 Years	4.5 Years	5.0 Years	6.0 Years	7.0 Years	8.0 Years	Amount
100	9.45	6.66	5.28	4.46	3.92	3.53	3.25	3.04	2.87	2.62	2.46	2.34	100
200	18.89	13.32	10.55	8.91	7.83	7.06	6.50	6.07	5.73	5.24	4.91	4.67	200
300	28.34	19.98	15.83	13.36	11.74	10.59	9.74	9.10	8.59	7.86	7.36	7.01	300
400	37.78	26.64	21.10	17.81	15.65	14.12	12.99	12.13	11.45	10.48	9.81	9.34	400
500	47.22	33.29	26.38	22.27	19.56	17.65	16.24	15.16	14.32	13.09	12.26	11.68	500
600	56.67	39.95	31.65	26.72	23.47	21.17	19.48	18.19	17.18	15.71	14.72	14.01	600
700	66.11	46.61	36.93	31.17	27.38	24.70	22.73	21.22	20.04	18.33	17.17	16.35	700
800	75.56	53.27	42.20	35.62	31.29	28.23	25.98	24.25	22.90	20.95	19.62	18.68	800
900	85.00	59.93	47.48	40.07	35.20	31.76	29.22	27.28	25.77	23.56	22.07	21.02	900
1000	94.44	66.58	52.75	44.53	39.11	35.29	32.47	30.32	28.63	26.18	24.52	23.35	1000
2000	188.88	133.16	105.50	89.05	78.21	70.57	64.93	60.63	57.25	52.36	49.04	46.70	2000
3000	283.32	199.74	158.24	133.57	117.31	105.85	97.40	90.94	85.87	78.53	73.56	70.05	3000
4000	377.76	266.32	210.99	178.09	156.41	141.14	129.86	121.25	114.50	104.71	98.08	93.40	4000
5000	472.20	332.90	263.74	222.62	195.51	176.42	162.32	151.56	143.12	130.88	122.59	116.75	5000
6000	566.64	399.48	316.48	267.14	234.62	211.70	194.79	181.87	171.74	157.06	147.11	140.10	6000
7000	661.08	466.06	369.23	311.66	273.72	246.98	227.25	212.18	200.37	183.23	171.63	163.45	7000
8000	755.51	532.64	421.98	356.18	312.82	282.27	259.72	242.49	228.99	209.41	196.15	186.80	8000
9000	849.95	599.22	474.72	400.70	351.92	317.55	292.18	272.80	257.61	235.58	220.67	210.15	9000
10000	944.39	665.80	527.47	445.23	391.02	352.83	324.64	303.11	286.24	261.76	245.18	233.50	10000
15000	1416.58	998.70	791.20	667.84	586.53	529.25	486.96	454.67	429.35	392.63	367.77	350.25	15000
20000	1888.78	1331.60	1054.93	890.45	782.04	705.66	649.28	606.22	572.47	523.51	490.36	466.99	20000
25000	2360.97	1664.50	1318.67	1113.06	977.55	882.07	811.60	757.77	715.58	654.39	612.95	583.74	25000
30000	2833.16	1997.40	1582.40	1335.67	1173.06	1058.49	973.92	909.33	858.70	785.26	735.54	700.49	30000
35000	3305.36	2330.30	1846.13	1558.28	1368.56	1234.90	1136.24	1060.88	1001.81	916.14	858.13	817.23	35000
40000	3777.55	2663.20	2109.86	1780.89	1564.07	1411.31	1298.56	1213.44	1144.93	1047.02	980.72	933.98	40000
45000	4249.74	2996.09	2373.59	2003.50	1759.58	1587.73	1460.88	1363.99	1288.04	1177.89	1103.31	1050.73	45000
50000	4721.94	3329.00	2637.33	2226.11	1955.09	1764.14	1623.19	1515.54	1431.16	1308.77	1225.90	1167.48	50000
60000	5666.32	3994.80	3164.79	2671.33	2346.11	2116.97	1947.83	1818.65	1717.39	1570.52	1471.08	1400.97	60000
75000	7082.90	4993.50	3955.99	3339.16	2932.63	2646.21	2434.79	2273.31	2146.73	1963.15	1838.85	1751.21	75000
100000	9443.87	6658.00	5274.65	4452.22	3910.18	3528.28	3246.38	3031.08	2862.31	2617.53	2451.80	2334.95	100000
125000	11804.84	8322.50	6593.31	5565.27	4887.72	4410.34	4057.98	3788.85	3577.88	3271.91	3064.75	2918.68	125000
150000	14165.80	9987.00	7911.97	6678.32	5865.26	5292.41	4869.57	4546.62	4293.46	3926.30	3677.70	3502.42	150000
175000	16526.77	11651.50	9230.63	7791.38	6842.80	6174.48	5681.17	5304.39	5009.04	4580.68	4290.65	4086.15	175000
200000	18887.74	13316.00	10549.29	8904.43	7820.35	7056.55	6492.76	6062.16	5724.61	5235.06	4903.60	4669.89	200000
250000	23609.67	16645.00	13186.61	11130.53	9775.43	8820.68	8115.95	7577.69	7155.76	6543.82	6129.50	5837.36	250000

Amount	9.0 Years	10.0 Years	11.0 Years	12.0 Years	13.0 Years	14.0 Years	15.0 Years	16.0 Years	20.0 Years	30.0 Years	40.0 Years	50.0 Years	Amount
100	2.26	2.19	2.15	2.11	2.08	2.06	2.04	2.03	2.00	1.99	1.98	1.98	100
200	4.51	4.38	4.29	4.21	4.16	4.12	4.08	4.06	4.00	3.97	3.96	3.96	200
300	6.76	6.57	6.43	6.32	6.24	6.17	6.12	6.08	6.00	5.95	5.94	5.94	300
400	9.01	8.75	8.57	8.42	8.31	8.23	8.16	8.11	7.99	7.93	7.92	7.92	400
500	11.26	10.94	10.71	10.53	10.39	10.28	10.20	10.14	9.99	9.91	9.90	9.90	500
600	13.51	13.13	12.85	12.63	12.47	12.34	12.24	12.16	11.99	11.89	11.88	11.88	600
700	15.76	15.32	14.99	14.74	14.54	14.39	14.28	14.19	13.99	13.87	13.86	13.86	700
800	18.01	17.50	17.13	16.84	16.62	16.45	16.32	16.21	15.98	15.85	15.84	15.84	800
900	20.26	19.69	19.27	18.94	18.70	18.50	18.36	18.24	17.98	17.83	17.82	17.82	900
1000	22.51	21.88	21.41	21.05	20.77	20.56	20.40	20.27	19.98	19.81	19.80	19.80	1000
2000	45.01	43.75	42.81	42.09	41.54	41.12	40.79	40.53	39.95	39.62	39.59	39.59	2000
3000	67.51	65.63	64.21	63.13	62.31	61.67	61.18	60.79	59.92	59.43	59.38	59.38	3000
4000	90.01	87.50	85.61	84.18	83.08	82.23	81.57	81.05	79.90	79.24	79.18	79.17	4000
5000	112.51	109.38	107.02	105.22	103.85	102.78	101.96	101.32	99.87	99.05	98.97	98.96	5000
6000	135.02	131.25	128.42	126.26	124.61	123.34	122.35	121.58	119.84	118.86	118.76	118.76	6000
7000	157.52	153.12	149.82	147.31	145.38	143.89	142.74	141.84	139.81	138.67	138.56	138.55	7000
8000	180.02	175.00	171.22	168.35	166.15	164.45	163.13	162.10	159.79	158.48	158.35	158.34	8000
9000	202.52	196.87	192.62	189.39	186.92	185.00	183.52	182.36	179.76	178.28	178.14	178.13	9000
10000	225.02	218.75	214.03	210.44	207.69	205.56	203.91	202.63	199.73	198.09	197.94	197.92	10000
15000	337.53	328.12	321.04	315.65	311.53	308.34	305.86	303.94	299.60	297.14	296.90	296.88	15000
20000	450.04	437.49	428.05	420.87	415.37	411.12	407.82	405.25	399.46	396.18	395.87	395.84	20000
25000	562.55	546.86	535.06	526.09	519.21	513.89	509.77	506.56	499.32	495.22	494.84	494.80	25000
30000	675.06	656.23	642.07	631.30	623.05	616.67	611.72	607.87	599.19	594.27	593.80	593.76	30000
35000	787.57	765.60	749.08	736.52	726.89	719.45	713.68	709.18	699.05	693.31	692.77	692.72	35000
40000	900.07	874.97	856.09	841.74	830.73	822.23	815.63	810.49	798.91	792.36	791.74	791.68	40000
45000	1012.58	984.34	963.10	946.95	934.57	925.00	917.58	911.80	898.78	891.40	890.70	890.64	45000
50000	1125.09	1093.71	1070.11	1052.17	1038.41	1027.78	1019.53	1013.11	998.64	990.44	989.67	989.60	50000
60000	1350.11	1312.45	1284.13	1262.60	1246.09	1233.34	1223.44	1215.73	1198.37	1188.53	1187.60	1187.51	60000
75000	1687.63	1640.56	1605.16	1578.25	1557.61	1541.67	1529.30	1519.66	1497.96	1485.66	1484.50	1484.39	75000
100000	2250.18	2187.41	2140.22	2104.33	2076.81	2055.56	2039.06	2026.21	1997.27	1980.88	1979.33	1979.19	100000
125000	2812.72	2734.26	2675.27	2630.41	2596.01	2569.44	2548.83	2532.77	2496.59	2476.10	2474.17	2473.98	125000
150000	3375.26	3281.11	3210.32	3156.49	3115.21	3083.33	3058.59	3039.32	2995.91	2971.32	2969.00	2968.78	150000
175000	3937.81	3827.96	3745.37	3682.58	3634.41	3597.22	3568.36	3545.87	3495.22	3466.54	3463.83	3463.57	175000
200000	4500.35	4374.81	4280.43	4208.66	4153.61	4111.11	4078.12	4052.42	3994.54	3961.76	3958.66	3958.37	200000
250000	5625.44	5468.51	5350.53	5260.82	5192.01	5138.88	5097.65	5065.53	4993.17	4952.19	4948.33	4947.96	250000

Monthly Payment Required To Amortize A Loan

Amount	1.0 Year	1.5 Years	2.0 Years	2.5 Years	3.0 Years	3.5 Years	4.0 Years	4.5 Years	5.0 Years	6.0 Years	7.0 Years	8.0 Years	Amount
100	9.46	6.68	5.29	4.47	3.93	3.55	3.27	3.05	2.88	2.64	2.47	2.36	100
200	18.92	13.35	10.58	8.93	7.85	7.09	6.53	6.10	5.76	5.27	4.94	4.71	200
300	28.37	20.02	15.87	13.40	11.77	10.63	9.79	9.14	8.64	7.90	7.41	7.06	300
400	37.83	26.69	21.15	17.86	15.70	14.17	13.05	12.19	11.51	10.54	9.88	9.41	400
500	47.28	33.36	26.44	22.33	19.62	17.71	16.31	15.23	14.39	13.17	12.34	11.76	500
600	56.74	40.03	31.73	26.79	23.54	21.26	19.57	18.28	17.27	15.80	14.81	14.11	600
700	66.20	46.70	37.01	31.26	27.47	24.80	22.83	21.32	20.14	18.43	17.28	16.46	700
800	75.65	53.37	42.30	35.72	31.39	28.34	26.09	24.37	23.02	21.07	19.75	18.82	800
900	85.11	60.04	47.59	40.19	35.31	31.88	29.35	27.41	25.90	23.70	22.21	21.17	900
1000	94.56	66.71	52.88	44.65	39.24	35.42	32.61	30.46	28.77	26.33	24.68	23.52	1000
2000	189.12	133.41	105.75	89.30	78.47	70.84	65.21	60.91	57.54	52.66	49.36	47.03	2000
3000	283.68	200.11	158.62	133.95	117.70	106.26	97.81	91.36	86.31	78.99	74.03	70.54	3000
4000	378.24	266.81	211.49	178.60	156.94	141.67	130.41	121.81	115.08	105.31	98.71	94.06	4000
5000	472.80	333.52	264.36	223.25	196.17	177.09	163.01	152.27	143.84	131.64	123.38	117.57	5000
6000	567.36	400.22	317.23	267.90	235.40	212.51	195.62	182.72	172.61	157.97	148.06	141.08	6000
7000	661.92	466.92	370.10	312.55	274.63	247.93	228.22	213.17	201.38	184.29	172.74	164.60	7000
8000	756.48	533.62	422.97	357.20	313.87	283.34	260.82	243.62	230.15	210.62	197.41	188.11	8000
9000	851.04	600.32	475.84	401.85	353.10	318.76	293.42	274.08	258.92	236.95	222.09	211.62	9000
10000	945.60	667.03	528.72	446.50	392.33	354.18	326.02	304.53	287.68	263.27	246.76	235.14	10000
15000	1418.40	1000.54	793.07	669.75	588.50	531.26	489.03	456.79	431.52	394.91	370.14	352.70	15000
20000	1891.20	1334.05	1057.43	893.00	784.66	708.35	652.04	609.05	575.36	526.54	493.52	470.27	20000
25000	2363.99	1667.56	1321.78	1116.25	980.83	885.44	815.05	761.31	719.20	658.18	616.90	587.83	25000
30000	2836.79	2001.07	1586.14	1339.50	1176.99	1062.52	978.06	913.57	863.04	789.81	740.28	705.40	30000
35000	3309.59	2334.58	1850.49	1562.75	1373.15	1239.61	1141.07	1065.83	1006.88	921.44	863.66	822.96	35000
40000	3782.39	2668.09	2114.85	1786.00	1569.32	1416.70	1304.08	1218.10	1150.72	1053.08	987.04	940.53	40000
45000	4255.19	3001.60	2379.20	2009.25	1765.48	1593.78	1467.09	1370.36	1294.55	1184.71	1110.42	1058.10	45000
50000	4727.98	3335.11	2643.56	2232.50	1961.65	1770.87	1630.10	1522.62	1438.40	1316.35	1233.80	1175.66	50000
60000	5673.58	4002.13	3172.27	2679.00	2353.98	2125.04	1956.12	1827.14	1726.08	1579.61	1480.55	1410.79	60000
75000	7091.97	5002.66	3965.34	3348.75	2942.47	2656.30	2445.14	2283.92	2157.60	1974.52	1850.69	1763.49	75000
100000	9455.96	6670.22	5287.11	4465.00	3923.29	3541.73	3260.19	3045.23	2876.80	2632.69	2467.59	2351.32	100000
125000	11819.95	8337.77	6608.89	5581.25	4904.11	4427.17	4075.23	3806.54	3596.00	3290.86	3084.48	2939.15	125000
150000	14183.94	10005.32	7930.67	6697.49	5884.93	5312.60	4890.28	4567.84	4315.20	3949.03	3701.38	3526.97	150000
175000	16547.93	11672.87	9252.45	7813.74	6865.75	6198.03	5705.33	5329.15	5034.40	4607.20	4318.27	4114.80	175000
200000	18911.92	13340.43	10574.22	8929.99	7846.58	7083.46	6520.37	6090.46	5753.60	5265.37	4935.17	4702.63	200000
250000	23639.90	16675.53	13217.78	11162.49	9808.22	8854.33	8150.46	7613.07	7192.00	6581.71	6168.96	5878.29	250000

Amount	9.0 Years	10.0 Years	11.0 Years	12.0 Years	13.0 Years	14.0 Years	15.0 Years	16.0 Years	20.0 Years	30.0 Years	40.0 Years	50.0 Years	Amount
100	2.27	2.21	2.16	2.13	2.10	2.08	2.06	2.05	2.02	2.01	2.01	2.01	100
200	4.54	4.41	4.32	4.25	4.20	4.15	4.12	4.10	4.04	4.01	4.01	4.01	200
300	6.81	6.62	6.48	6.37	6.29	6.23	6.18	6.14	6.06	6.01	6.01	6.01	300
400	9.07	8.82	8.64	8.50	8.39	8.30	8.24	8.19	8.07	8.01	8.01	8.01	400
500	11.34	11.03	10.80	10.62	10.48	10.38	10.30	10.23	10.09	10.01	10.01	10.01	500
600	13.61	13.23	12.95	12.74	12.58	12.45	12.35	12.28	12.11	12.01	12.01	12.01	600
700	15.87	15.44	15.11	14.86	14.67	14.53	14.41	14.32	14.13	14.02	14.01	14.01	700
800	18.14	17.64	17.27	16.99	16.77	16.60	16.47	16.37	16.14	16.02	16.01	16.01	800
900	20.41	19.85	19.43	19.11	18.86	18.68	18.53	18.42	18.16	18.02	18.01	18.01	900
1000	22.68	22.05	21.59	21.23	20.96	20.75	20.59	20.46	20.18	20.02	20.01	20.01	1000
2000	45.35	44.10	43.17	42.46	41.91	41.49	41.17	40.92	40.35	40.04	40.01	40.01	2000
3000	68.02	66.15	64.75	63.68	62.87	62.24	61.75	61.38	60.53	60.05	60.01	60.01	3000
4000	90.69	88.20	86.33	84.91	83.82	82.98	82.34	81.83	80.70	80.07	80.01	80.01	4000
5000	113.36	110.25	107.91	106.13	104.78	103.73	102.92	102.29	100.88	100.09	100.01	100.01	5000
6000	136.03	132.29	129.49	127.36	125.73	124.47	123.50	122.75	121.05	120.10	120.01	120.01	6000
7000	158.70	154.34	151.07	148.59	146.68	145.22	144.08	143.20	141.22	140.12	140.02	140.01	7000
8000	181.37	176.39	172.65	169.81	167.64	165.96	164.67	163.66	161.40	160.13	160.02	160.01	8000
9000	204.04	198.44	194.23	191.04	188.59	186.71	185.25	184.12	181.57	180.15	180.02	180.01	9000
10000	226.71	220.49	215.81	212.26	209.55	207.45	205.83	204.57	201.75	200.17	200.02	200.01	10000
15000	340.07	330.73	323.72	318.39	314.32	311.18	308.75	306.86	302.62	300.25	300.03	300.01	15000
20000	453.42	440.97	431.62	424.52	419.09	414.90	411.66	409.14	403.49	400.33	400.03	400.01	20000
25000	566.78	551.21	539.52	530.65	523.86	518.63	514.57	511.42	504.36	500.41	500.04	500.01	25000
30000	680.13	661.45	647.43	636.78	628.63	622.35	617.49	613.71	605.23	600.49	600.05	600.01	30000
35000	793.48	771.69	755.33	742.91	733.40	726.08	720.40	715.99	706.10	700.57	700.06	700.01	35000
40000	906.84	881.93	863.23	849.04	838.17	829.80	823.31	818.27	806.97	800.65	800.06	800.01	40000
45000	1020.19	992.17	971.14	955.17	942.94	933.52	926.23	920.56	907.84	900.73	900.07	900.01	45000
50000	1133.55	1102.41	1079.04	1061.30	1047.52	1037.25	1029.14	1022.84	1008.71	1000.81	1000.08	1000.01	50000
60000	1360.26	1322.89	1294.85	1273.56	1257.26	1244.70	1234.97	1227.41	1210.45	1200.97	1200.09	1200.01	60000
75000	1700.32	1653.61	1618.56	1591.94	1571.57	1555.87	1543.71	1534.26	1513.06	1501.21	1500.12	1500.02	75000
100000	2267.09	2204.81	2158.07	2122.59	2095.43	2074.49	2058.28	2045.67	2017.41	2001.61	2000.15	2000.02	100000
125000	2833.86	2756.02	2697.59	2653.24	2619.28	2593.11	2572.85	2557.09	2521.77	2502.01	2500.19	2500.02	125000
150000	3400.63	3307.22	3237.11	3183.88	3143.14	3111.74	3087.42	3068.51	3026.12	3002.41	3000.23	3000.03	150000
175000	3967.40	3858.42	3776.62	3714.53	3666.99	3630.36	3601.98	3579.92	3530.47	3502.81	3500.27	3500.03	175000
200000	4534.17	4409.62	4316.14	4245.18	4190.85	4148.98	4116.55	4091.34	4034.82	4003.21	4000.30	4000.03	200000
250000	5667.72	5512.03	5395.17	5306.47	5238.56	5186.22	5145.69	5114.17	5043.53	5004.02	5000.38	5000.04	250000

Amount	1.0 Year	1.5 Years	2.0 Years	2.5 Years	3.0 Years	3.5 Years	4.0 Years	4.5 Years	5.0 Years	6.0 Years	7.0 Years	8.0 Years	Amount
100	9.47	6.69	5.30	4.48	3.94	3.56	3.28	3.06	2.90	2.65	2.49	2.37	100
200	18.94	13.37	10.60	8.96	7.88	7.12	6.55	6.12	5.79	5.30	4.97	4.74	200
300	28.41	20.05	15.90	13.44	11.81	10.67	9.83	9.18	8.68	7.95	7.46	7.11	300
400	37.88	26.73	21.20	17.92	15.75	14.23	13.10	12.24	11.57	10.60	9.94	9.48	400
500	47.35	33.42	26.50	22.39	19.69	17.78	16.38	15.30	14.46	13.24	12.42	11.84	500
600	56.81	40.10	31.80	26.87	23.62	21.34	19.65	18.36	17.35	15.89	14.91	14.21	600
700	66.28	46.78	37.10	31.35	27.56	24.89	22.92	21.42	20.24	18.54	17.39	16.58	700
800	75.75	53.46	42.40	35.83	31.50	28.45	26.20	24.48	23.14	21.19	19.87	18.95	800
900	85.22	60.15	47.70	40.31	35.43	32.00	29.47	27.54	26.03	23.84	22.36	21.31	900
1000	94.69	66.83	53.00	44.78	39.37	35.56	32.75	30.60	28.92	26.48	24.84	23.68	1000
2000	189.37	133.65	106.00	89.56	78.73	71.11	65.49	61.19	57.83	52.96	49.67	47.36	2000
3000	284.05	200.48	158.99	134.34	118.10	106.66	98.23	91.79	86.74	79.44	74.51	71.04	3000
4000	378.73	267.30	211.99	179.12	157.46	142.21	130.97	122.38	115.66	105.92	99.34	94.71	4000
5000	473.41	334.13	264.98	223.89	196.83	177.77	163.71	152.98	144.57	132.40	124.18	118.39	5000
6000	568.09	400.95	317.98	268.67	236.19	213.32	196.45	183.57	173.48	158.88	149.01	142.07	6000
7000	662.77	467.78	370.98	313.45	275.55	248.87	229.19	214.16	202.40	185.36	173.84	165.75	7000
8000	757.45	534.60	423.97	358.23	314.92	284.42	261.93	244.76	231.31	211.84	198.68	189.42	8000
9000	852.13	601.42	476.97	403.01	354.28	319.97	294.67	275.35	260.22	238.31	223.51	213.10	9000
10000	946.81	668.25	529.96	447.78	393.65	355.53	327.41	305.95	289.14	264.79	248.35	236.78	10000
15000	1420.21	1002.37	794.94	671.67	590.47	533.29	491.11	458.92	433.70	397.19	372.52	355.16	15000
20000	1893.62	1336.49	1059.92	895.56	787.29	711.05	654.81	611.89	578.27	529.58	496.69	473.55	20000
25000	2367.02	1670.61	1324.90	1119.45	984.11	888.81	818.51	764.86	722.84	661.98	620.86	591.94	25000
30000	2840.42	2004.74	1589.88	1343.34	1180.93	1066.57	982.21	917.83	867.40	794.37	745.03	710.32	30000
35000	3313.83	2338.86	1854.86	1567.23	1377.75	1244.33	1145.91	1070.80	1011.97	926.76	869.20	828.71	35000
40000	3787.23	2672.98	2119.84	1791.12	1574.57	1422.09	1309.61	1223.77	1156.54	1059.16	993.37	947.10	40000
45000	4260.63	3007.10	2384.82	2015.01	1771.40	1599.85	1473.31	1376.74	1301.10	1191.55	1117.54	1065.48	45000
50000	4734.04	3341.22	2649.80	2238.90	1968.22	1777.61	1637.01	1529.71	1445.67	1323.95	1241.71	1183.87	50000
60000	5680.84	4009.47	3179.76	2686.68	2361.86	2133.13	1964.42	1835.65	1734.80	1588.73	1490.05	1420.64	60000
75000	7101.05	5011.83	3974.70	3358.35	2952.32	2666.42	2455.52	2294.56	2168.50	1985.92	1862.56	1775.80	75000
100000	9468.07	6682.44	5299.60	4477.80	3936.43	3555.22	3274.02	3059.42	2891.33	2647.89	2483.41	2367.74	100000
125000	11835.08	8353.05	6624.50	5597.25	4920.53	4444.02	4092.53	3824.27	3614.16	3309.86	3104.27	2959.67	125000
150000	14202.10	10023.66	7949.40	6716.69	5904.64	5332.83	4911.03	4589.12	4336.99	3971.83	3725.12	3551.60	150000
175000	16569.11	11694.27	9274.30	7836.14	6888.75	6221.63	5729.54	5353.97	5059.83	4633.80	4345.97	4143.53	175000
200000	18936.13	13364.87	10599.20	8955.59	7872.85	7110.44	6548.04	6118.83	5782.66	5295.77	4966.82	4735.47	200000
250000	23670.16	16706.09	13248.99	11194.49	9841.06	8888.04	8185.05	7648.53	7228.32	6619.71	6208.53	5919.33	250000

Amount	9.0 Years	10.0 Years	11.0 Years	12.0 Years	13.0 Years	14.0 Years	15.0 Years	16.0 Years	20.0 Years	30.0 Years	40.0 Years	50.0 Years	Amount
100	2.29	2.23	2.18	2.15	2.12	2.10	2.08	2.07	2.04	2.03	2.03	2.03	100
200	4.57	4.45	4.36	4.29	4.23	4.19	4.16	4.14	4.08	4.05	4.05	4.05	200
300	6.86	6.67	6.53	6.43	6.35	6.29	6.24	6.20	6.12	6.07	6.07	6.07	300
400	9.14	8.89	8.71	8.57	8.46	8.38	8.32	8.27	8.16	8.09	8.09	8.09	400
500	11.43	11.12	10.88	10.71	10.58	10.47	10.39	10.33	10.19	10.12	10.11	10.11	500
600	13.71	13.34	13.06	12.85	12.69	12.57	12.47	12.40	12.23	12.14	12.13	12.13	600
700	15.99	15.56	15.24	14.99	14.80	14.66	14.55	14.46	14.27	14.16	14.15	14.15	700
800	18.28	17.78	17.41	17.13	16.92	16.75	16.63	16.53	16.31	16.18	16.17	16.17	800
900	20.56	20.01	19.59	19.27	19.03	18.85	18.70	18.59	18.35	18.21	18.19	18.19	900
1000	22.85	22.23	21.76	21.41	21.15	20.94	20.78	20.66	20.38	20.23	20.21	20.21	1000
2000	45.69	44.45	43.52	42.82	42.29	41.87	41.56	41.31	40.76	40.45	40.42	40.42	2000
3000	68.53	66.67	65.28	64.23	63.43	62.81	62.33	61.96	61.13	60.68	60.63	60.63	3000
4000	91.37	88.90	87.04	85.64	84.57	83.74	83.11	82.61	81.51	80.90	80.84	80.84	4000
5000	114.21	111.12	108.80	107.05	105.71	104.68	103.88	103.26	101.88	101.12	101.05	101.05	5000
6000	137.05	133.34	130.56	128.46	126.85	125.61	124.66	123.91	122.26	121.35	121.26	121.26	6000
7000	159.89	155.56	152.32	149.87	147.99	146.55	145.43	144.57	142.64	141.57	141.47	141.46	7000
8000	182.73	177.79	174.08	171.28	169.13	167.48	166.21	165.22	163.01	161.79	161.68	161.67	8000
9000	205.57	200.01	195.84	192.69	190.27	188.42	186.98	185.87	183.39	182.02	181.89	181.88	9000
10000	228.41	222.23	217.60	214.09	211.41	209.35	207.76	206.52	203.76	202.24	202.10	202.09	10000
15000	342.61	333.35	326.40	321.14	317.12	314.03	311.63	309.78	305.64	303.36	303.15	303.13	15000
20000	456.81	444.46	435.20	428.18	422.82	418.70	415.51	413.04	407.52	404.47	404.20	404.17	20000
25000	571.02	555.57	544.00	535.23	528.53	523.37	519.39	516.30	509.40	505.59	505.25	505.22	25000
30000	685.22	666.69	652.80	642.27	634.23	628.05	623.26	619.55	611.28	606.71	606.30	606.26	30000
35000	799.42	777.80	761.60	749.32	739.93	732.72	727.14	722.81	713.16	707.82	707.34	707.30	35000
40000	913.62	888.91	870.39	856.36	845.64	837.39	831.02	826.07	815.03	808.94	808.39	808.34	40000
45000	1027.83	1000.03	979.19	963.41	951.34	942.07	934.89	929.33	916.91	910.06	909.44	909.39	45000
50000	1142.03	1111.14	1087.99	1070.45	1057.05	1046.74	1038.77	1032.59	1018.79	1011.17	1010.49	1010.43	50000
60000	1370.43	1333.37	1305.59	1284.54	1268.46	1256.09	1246.52	1239.10	1222.55	1213.41	1212.59	1212.51	60000
75000	1713.04	1666.71	1631.98	1605.67	1585.57	1570.11	1558.15	1548.88	1528.19	1516.76	1515.73	1515.64	75000
100000	2284.05	2222.27	2175.98	2140.90	2114.09	2093.47	2077.53	2065.17	2037.58	2022.34	2020.97	2020.85	100000
125000	2855.06	2777.84	2719.97	2676.12	2642.61	2616.84	2596.92	2581.46	2546.97	2527.93	2526.22	2526.06	125000
150000	3426.07	3333.41	3263.96	3211.34	3171.13	3140.21	3116.30	3097.75	3056.37	3033.51	3031.46	3031.27	150000
175000	3997.09	3888.97	3807.96	3746.57	3699.65	3663.57	3635.68	3614.04	3565.76	3539.10	3536.70	3536.48	175000
200000	4568.10	4444.54	4351.95	4281.79	4228.18	4186.94	4155.06	4130.33	4075.15	4044.68	4041.94	4041.70	200000
250000	5710.12	5555.67	5439.94	5352.24	5285.22	5233.67	5193.83	5162.91	5093.94	5055.85	5052.43	5052.12	250000

Monthly Payment Required To Amortize A Loan

Amount	1.0 Year	1.5 Years	2.0 Years	2.5 Years	3.0 Years	3.5 Years	4.0 Years	4.5 Years	5.0 Years	6.0 Years	7.0 Years	8.0 Years	Amount
100	9.49	6.70	5.32	4.50	3.95	3.57	3.29	3.08	2.91	2.67	2.50	2.39	100
200	18.97	13.39	10.63	8.99	7.90	7.14	6.58	6.15	5.82	5.33	5.00	4.77	200
300	28.45	20.09	15.94	13.48	11.85	10.71	9.87	9.23	8.72	7.99	7.50	7.16	300
400	37.93	26.78	21.25	17.97	15.80	14.28	13.16	12.30	11.63	10.66	10.00	9.54	400
500	47.41	33.48	26.57	22.46	19.75	17.85	16.44	15.37	14.53	13.32	12.50	11.93	500
600	56.89	40.17	31.88	26.95	23.70	21.42	19.73	18.45	17.44	15.98	15.00	14.31	600
700	66.37	46.87	37.19	31.44	27.65	24.99	23.02	21.52	20.35	18.65	17.50	16.69	700
800	75.85	53.56	42.50	35.93	31.60	28.55	26.31	24.59	23.25	21.31	20.00	19.08	800
900	85.33	60.26	47.81	40.42	35.55	32.12	29.60	27.67	26.16	23.97	22.50	21.46	900
1000	94.81	66.95	53.13	44.91	39.50	35.69	32.88	30.74	29.06	26.64	25.00	23.85	1000
2000	189.61	133.90	106.25	89.82	79.00	71.38	65.76	61.48	58.12	53.27	49.99	47.69	2000
3000	284.41	200.85	159.37	134.72	118.49	107.07	98.64	92.21	87.18	79.90	74.98	71.53	3000
4000	379.21	267.79	212.49	179.63	157.99	142.75	131.52	122.95	116.24	106.53	99.98	95.37	4000
5000	474.01	334.74	265.61	224.54	197.48	178.44	164.40	153.69	145.30	133.16	124.97	119.21	5000
6000	568.82	401.69	318.73	269.44	236.98	214.13	197.28	184.42	174.36	159.79	149.96	143.06	6000
7000	663.62	468.63	371.85	314.35	276.48	249.82	230.16	215.16	203.42	186.42	174.95	166.90	7000
8000	758.42	535.58	424.97	359.25	315.97	285.50	263.04	245.90	232.48	213.05	199.95	190.74	8000
9000	853.22	602.53	478.09	404.16	355.47	321.19	295.91	276.63	261.54	239.69	224.94	214.58	9000
10000	948.02	669.47	531.21	449.07	394.96	356.88	328.79	307.37	290.59	266.32	249.93	238.42	10000
15000	1422.03	1004.21	796.82	673.60	592.44	535.31	493.19	461.05	435.89	399.47	374.90	357.63	15000
20000	1896.04	1338.94	1062.42	898.13	789.92	713.75	657.58	614.73	581.18	532.63	499.86	476.84	20000
25000	2370.05	1673.67	1328.03	1122.66	987.40	892.19	821.98	768.41	726.48	665.78	624.83	596.05	25000
30000	2844.06	2008.41	1593.63	1347.19	1184.88	1070.62	986.37	922.09	871.77	798.94	749.79	715.26	30000
35000	3318.07	2343.14	1859.24	1571.72	1382.36	1249.06	1150.77	1075.78	1017.07	932.10	874.75	834.47	35000
40000	3792.07	2677.87	2124.84	1796.25	1579.84	1427.50	1315.16	1229.46	1162.36	1065.25	999.72	953.68	40000
45000	4266.08	3012.61	2390.45	2020.78	1777.32	1605.93	1479.55	1383.14	1307.66	1198.41	1124.68	1072.89	45000
50000	4740.09	3347.34	2656.05	2245.31	1974.80	1784.37	1643.95	1536.82	1452.95	1331.56	1249.65	1192.10	50000
60000	5688.11	4016.81	3187.26	2694.37	2369.76	2141.24	1972.74	1844.18	1743.54	1597.88	1499.58	1430.52	60000
75000	7110.14	5021.01	3984.08	3367.97	2962.19	2676.55	2465.92	2305.23	2179.42	1997.34	1874.47	1788.15	75000
100000	9480.18	6694.68	5312.10	4490.62	3949.59	3568.73	3287.89	3073.63	2905.90	2663.12	2499.29	2384.20	100000
125000	11850.22	8368.34	6640.13	5613.27	4936.99	4460.92	4109.86	3842.04	3632.37	3328.90	3124.11	2980.25	125000
150000	14220.27	10042.01	7968.15	6735.93	5924.38	5353.10	4931.84	4610.45	4358.84	3994.68	3748.93	3576.30	150000
175000	16590.31	11715.68	9296.18	7858.58	6911.78	6245.28	5753.81	5378.86	5085.32	4660.46	4373.75	4172.35	175000
200000	18960.35	13389.35	10624.20	8981.23	7899.18	7137.46	6575.78	6147.26	5811.79	5326.24	4998.57	4768.40	200000
250000	23700.44	16736.68	13280.25	11226.54	9873.97	8921.83	8219.72	7684.08	7264.73	6657.80	6248.21	5960.50	250000

Amount	9.0 Years	10.0 Years	11.0 Years	12.0 Years	13.0 Years	14.0 Years	15.0 Years	16.0 Years	20.0 Years	30.0 Years	40.0 Years	50.0 Years	Amount
100	2.31	2.24	2.20	2.16	2.14	2.12	2.10	2.09	2.06	2.05	2.05	2.05	100
200	4.61	4.48	4.39	4.32	4.27	4.23	4.20	4.17	4.12	4.09	4.09	4.09	200
300	6.91	6.72	6.59	6.48	6.40	6.34	6.30	6.26	6.18	6.13	6.13	6.13	300
400	9.21	8.96	8.78	8.64	8.54	8.45	8.39	8.34	8.24	8.18	8.17	8.17	400
500	11.51	11.20	10.97	10.80	10.67	10.57	10.49	10.43	10.29	10.22	10.21	10.21	500
600	13.81	13.44	13.17	12.96	12.80	12.68	12.59	12.51	12.35	12.26	12.26	12.26	600
700	16.11	15.68	15.36	15.12	14.93	14.79	14.68	14.60	14.41	14.31	14.30	14.30	700
800	18.41	17.92	17.56	17.28	17.07	16.90	16.78	16.68	16.47	16.35	16.34	16.34	800
900	20.71	20.16	19.75	19.44	19.20	19.02	18.88	18.77	18.52	18.39	18.38	18.38	900
1000	23.02	22.40	21.94	21.60	21.33	21.13	20.97	20.85	20.58	20.44	20.42	20.42	1000
2000	46.03	44.80	43.88	43.19	42.66	42.25	41.94	41.70	41.16	40.87	40.84	40.84	2000
3000	69.04	67.20	65.82	64.78	63.99	63.38	62.91	62.55	61.74	61.30	61.26	61.26	3000
4000	92.05	89.60	87.76	86.37	85.32	84.50	83.88	83.39	82.32	81.73	81.68	81.67	4000
5000	115.06	111.99	109.70	107.97	106.64	105.63	104.85	104.24	102.89	102.16	102.09	102.09	5000
6000	138.07	134.39	131.64	129.56	127.97	126.75	125.81	125.09	123.47	122.59	122.51	122.51	6000
7000	161.08	156.79	153.58	151.15	149.30	147.88	146.78	145.93	144.05	143.02	142.93	142.92	7000
8000	184.09	179.19	175.52	172.74	170.63	169.00	167.75	166.78	164.63	163.45	163.35	163.34	8000
9000	207.10	201.58	197.46	194.34	191.96	190.13	188.72	187.63	185.20	183.88	183.77	183.76	9000
10000	230.11	223.98	219.40	215.93	213.28	211.25	209.69	208.47	205.78	204.31	204.18	204.17	10000
15000	345.16	335.97	329.09	323.89	319.92	316.88	314.53	312.71	308.67	306.47	306.27	306.26	15000
20000	460.22	447.96	438.79	431.85	426.56	422.50	419.37	416.94	411.56	408.62	408.36	408.34	20000
25000	575.27	559.95	548.49	539.82	533.20	528.13	524.21	521.18	514.45	510.78	510.45	510.42	25000
30000	690.32	671.94	658.18	647.78	639.84	633.75	629.05	625.41	617.33	612.93	612.54	612.51	30000
35000	805.37	783.93	767.88	755.74	746.48	739.38	733.89	729.65	720.22	715.08	714.63	714.59	35000
40000	920.43	895.91	877.58	863.70	853.12	845.00	838.73	833.88	823.11	817.24	816.72	816.68	40000
45000	1035.48	1007.90	987.27	971.67	959.76	950.62	943.58	938.12	926.00	919.39	918.81	918.76	45000
50000	1150.53	1119.89	1096.97	1079.63	1066.40	1056.25	1048.42	1042.35	1028.89	1021.55	1020.90	1020.84	50000
60000	1380.64	1343.87	1316.36	1295.55	1279.68	1267.50	1258.10	1250.82	1234.66	1225.85	1225.08	1225.01	60000
75000	1725.80	1679.83	1645.45	1619.44	1599.60	1584.37	1572.62	1563.53	1543.33	1532.32	1531.35	1531.26	75000
100000	2301.06	2239.78	2193.93	2159.25	2132.80	2112.49	2096.83	2084.70	2057.77	2043.09	2041.80	2041.68	100000
125000	2876.33	2799.72	2742.41	2699.06	2666.00	2640.62	2621.04	2605.87	2572.21	2553.86	2552.24	2552.10	125000
150000	3451.59	3359.66	3290.90	3238.88	3199.20	3168.74	3145.24	3127.05	3086.65	3064.63	3062.69	3062.52	150000
175000	4026.85	3919.61	3839.38	3778.69	3732.40	3696.86	3669.45	3648.22	3601.09	3575.40	3573.14	3572.94	175000
200000	4602.12	4479.55	4387.86	4318.50	4265.59	4224.98	4193.65	4169.39	4115.54	4086.17	4083.59	4083.36	200000
250000	5752.65	5599.44	5484.82	5398.12	5331.99	5281.23	5242.07	5211.74	5144.42	5107.71	5104.48	5104.20	250000

24.50%   Page 158   Monthly Payment Required To Amortize A Loan   Page 158   **24.50%**

Amount	1.0 Year	1.5 Years	2.0 Years	2.5 Years	3.0 Years	3.5 Years	4.0 Years	4.5 Years	5.0 Years	6.0 Years	7.0 Years	8.0 Years	Amount
100	9.50	6.71	5.33	4.51	3.97	3.59	3.31	3.09	2.93	2.68	2.52	2.41	100
200	18.99	13.42	10.65	9.01	7.93	7.17	6.61	6.18	5.85	5.36	5.04	4.81	200
300	28.48	20.13	15.98	13.52	11.89	10.75	9.91	9.27	8.77	8.04	7.55	7.21	300
400	37.97	26.83	21.30	18.02	15.86	14.33	13.21	12.36	11.69	10.72	10.07	9.61	400
500	47.47	33.54	26.63	22.52	19.82	17.92	16.51	15.44	14.61	13.40	12.58	12.01	500
600	56.96	40.25	31.95	27.03	23.78	21.50	19.82	18.53	17.53	16.08	15.10	14.41	600
700	66.45	46.95	37.28	31.53	27.74	25.08	23.12	21.62	20.45	18.75	17.61	16.81	700
800	75.94	53.66	42.60	36.03	31.71	28.66	26.42	24.71	23.37	21.43	20.13	19.21	800
900	85.44	60.37	47.93	40.54	35.67	32.25	29.72	27.80	26.29	24.11	22.64	21.61	900
1000	94.93	67.07	53.25	45.04	39.63	35.83	33.02	30.88	29.21	26.79	25.16	24.01	1000
2000	189.85	134.14	106.50	90.07	79.26	71.65	66.04	61.76	58.41	53.57	50.31	48.02	2000
3000	284.77	201.21	159.74	135.11	118.89	107.47	99.06	92.64	87.62	80.36	75.46	72.03	3000
4000	379.70	268.28	212.99	180.14	158.52	143.30	132.08	123.52	116.82	107.14	100.61	96.03	4000
5000	474.62	335.35	266.24	225.18	198.14	179.12	165.09	154.40	146.03	133.92	125.77	120.04	5000
6000	569.54	402.42	319.48	270.21	237.77	214.94	198.11	185.28	175.23	160.71	150.92	144.05	6000
7000	664.47	469.49	372.73	315.25	277.40	250.76	231.13	216.16	204.44	187.49	176.07	168.05	7000
8000	759.39	536.56	425.97	360.28	317.03	286.59	264.15	247.04	233.64	214.28	201.22	192.06	8000
9000	854.31	603.63	479.22	405.32	356.65	322.41	297.17	277.91	262.85	241.06	226.37	216.07	9000
10000	949.23	670.70	532.47	450.35	396.28	358.23	330.18	308.79	292.05	267.84	251.53	240.08	10000
15000	1423.85	1006.04	798.70	675.52	594.42	537.35	495.27	463.19	438.08	401.76	377.29	360.11	15000
20000	1898.46	1341.39	1064.93	900.70	792.56	716.46	660.36	617.58	584.10	535.68	503.05	480.15	20000
25000	2373.08	1676.74	1331.16	1125.87	990.70	895.57	825.45	771.98	730.13	669.60	628.81	600.18	25000
30000	2847.69	2012.08	1597.39	1351.04	1188.84	1074.69	990.54	926.37	876.15	803.52	754.57	720.22	30000
35000	3322.31	2347.43	1863.62	1576.21	1386.98	1253.80	1155.63	1080.76	1022.18	937.44	880.33	840.25	35000
40000	3796.92	2682.77	2129.85	1801.39	1585.11	1432.91	1320.72	1235.16	1168.20	1071.36	1006.09	960.29	40000
45000	4271.54	3018.12	2396.08	2026.56	1783.25	1612.03	1485.81	1389.55	1314.23	1205.28	1131.85	1080.32	45000
50000	4746.15	3353.47	2662.31	2251.73	1981.39	1791.14	1650.90	1543.95	1460.25	1339.20	1257.61	1200.36	50000
60000	5695.38	4024.16	3194.78	2702.08	2377.67	2149.37	1981.08	1852.73	1752.30	1607.04	1509.13	1440.43	60000
75000	7119.22	5030.20	3993.47	3377.60	2972.08	2686.71	2476.34	2315.92	2190.38	2008.80	1886.41	1800.54	75000
100000	9492.30	6706.93	5324.62	4503.46	3962.78	3582.27	3301.79	3087.89	2920.50	2678.40	2515.21	2400.71	100000
125000	11865.37	8383.66	6655.78	5629.32	4953.47	4477.84	4127.24	3859.86	3650.62	3348.00	3144.01	3000.89	125000
150000	14238.44	10060.39	7986.93	6755.19	5944.16	5373.41	4952.68	4631.83	4380.75	4017.60	3772.81	3601.07	150000
175000	16611.52	11737.12	9318.08	7881.05	6934.86	6268.98	5778.13	5403.80	5110.87	4687.20	4401.61	4201.24	175000
200000	18984.59	13413.85	10649.24	9006.91	7925.55	7164.54	6603.57	6175.77	5840.99	5356.80	5030.41	4801.42	200000
250000	23730.74	16767.31	13311.55	11258.64	9906.94	8955.68	8254.47	7719.71	7301.24	6696.00	6288.01	6001.78	250000

Amount	9.0 Years	10.0 Years	11.0 Years	12.0 Years	13.0 Years	14.0 Years	15.0 Years	16.0 Years	20.0 Years	30.0 Years	40.0 Years	50.0 Years	Amount
100	2.32	2.26	2.22	2.18	2.16	2.14	2.12	2.11	2.08	2.07	2.07	2.07	100
200	4.64	4.52	4.43	4.36	4.31	4.27	4.24	4.21	4.16	4.13	4.13	4.13	200
300	6.96	6.78	6.64	6.54	6.46	6.40	6.35	6.32	6.24	6.20	6.19	6.19	300
400	9.28	9.03	8.85	8.72	8.61	8.53	8.47	8.42	8.32	8.26	8.26	8.26	400
500	11.60	11.29	11.06	10.89	10.76	10.66	10.59	10.53	10.39	10.32	10.32	10.32	500
600	13.91	13.55	13.28	13.07	12.91	12.79	12.70	12.63	12.47	12.39	12.38	12.38	600
700	16.23	15.81	15.49	15.25	15.07	14.93	14.82	14.73	14.55	14.45	14.44	14.44	700
800	18.55	18.06	17.70	17.43	17.22	17.06	16.93	16.84	16.63	16.52	16.51	16.51	800
900	20.87	20.32	19.91	19.60	19.37	19.19	19.05	18.94	18.71	18.58	18.57	18.57	900
1000	23.19	22.58	22.12	21.78	21.52	21.32	21.17	21.05	20.78	20.64	20.63	20.63	1000
2000	46.37	45.15	44.24	43.56	43.04	42.64	42.33	42.09	41.56	41.28	41.26	41.26	2000
3000	69.55	67.72	66.36	65.33	64.55	63.95	63.49	63.13	62.34	61.92	61.88	61.88	3000
4000	92.73	90.30	88.48	87.11	86.07	85.27	84.65	84.18	83.12	82.56	82.51	82.51	4000
5000	115.91	112.87	110.60	108.89	107.58	106.58	105.81	105.22	103.90	103.20	103.14	103.13	5000
6000	139.09	135.44	132.72	130.66	129.10	127.90	126.97	126.26	124.68	123.83	123.76	123.76	6000
7000	162.27	158.02	154.84	152.44	150.61	149.21	148.14	147.30	145.46	144.47	144.39	144.38	7000
8000	185.45	180.59	176.96	174.22	172.13	170.53	169.30	168.35	166.24	165.11	165.01	165.01	8000
9000	208.64	203.16	199.08	195.99	193.64	191.84	190.46	189.39	187.02	185.75	185.64	185.63	9000
10000	231.82	225.74	221.20	217.77	215.16	213.16	211.62	210.43	207.80	206.39	206.27	206.26	10000
15000	347.72	338.60	331.79	326.65	322.74	319.74	317.43	315.64	311.70	309.58	309.40	309.38	15000
20000	463.63	451.47	442.39	435.53	430.31	426.32	423.24	420.86	415.60	412.77	412.53	412.51	20000
25000	579.55	564.34	552.99	544.42	537.89	532.89	529.04	526.07	519.50	515.96	515.66	515.63	25000
30000	695.44	677.20	663.58	653.30	645.47	639.47	634.85	631.28	623.40	619.15	618.79	618.76	30000
35000	811.34	790.07	774.18	762.18	753.05	746.05	740.66	736.50	727.30	722.34	721.92	721.88	35000
40000	927.25	902.94	884.78	871.06	860.62	852.63	846.47	841.71	831.20	825.54	825.05	825.01	40000
45000	1043.16	1015.80	995.37	979.95	968.20	959.20	952.28	946.92	935.10	928.73	928.18	928.13	45000
50000	1159.06	1128.67	1105.97	1088.83	1075.78	1065.78	1058.08	1052.14	1038.99	1031.92	1031.31	1031.26	50000
60000	1390.87	1354.40	1327.16	1306.59	1290.93	1278.94	1269.70	1262.56	1246.79	1238.30	1237.57	1237.51	60000
75000	1738.59	1693.00	1658.95	1633.24	1613.67	1598.67	1587.12	1578.20	1558.49	1547.88	1546.97	1546.89	75000
100000	2318.12	2257.33	2211.93	2177.65	2151.55	2131.56	2116.16	2104.27	2077.98	2063.83	2062.62	2062.51	100000
125000	2897.65	2821.66	2764.92	2722.06	2689.44	2664.44	2645.20	2630.33	2597.48	2579.79	2578.27	2578.14	125000
150000	3477.18	3386.00	3317.90	3266.48	3227.33	3197.33	3174.24	3156.40	3116.97	3095.75	3093.93	3093.77	150000
175000	4056.70	3950.33	3870.88	3810.89	3765.21	3730.22	3703.28	3682.46	3636.47	3611.70	3609.58	3609.40	175000
200000	4636.23	4514.66	4423.86	4355.30	4303.10	4263.11	4232.32	4208.53	4155.96	4127.66	4125.23	4125.02	200000
250000	5795.29	5643.32	5529.83	5444.12	5378.87	5328.88	5290.40	5260.66	5194.95	5159.57	5156.54	5156.28	250000

Amount	1.0 Year	1.5 Years	2.0 Years	2.5 Years	3.0 Years	3.5 Years	4.0 Years	4.5 Years	5.0 Years	6.0 Years	7.0 Years	8.0 Years	Amount
100	9.51	6.72	5.34	4.52	3.98	3.60	3.32	3.11	2.94	2.70	2.54	2.42	100
200	19.01	13.44	10.68	9.04	7.96	7.20	6.64	6.21	5.88	5.39	5.07	4.84	200
300	28.52	20.16	16.02	13.55	11.93	10.79	9.95	9.31	8.81	8.09	7.60	7.26	300
400	38.02	26.88	21.35	18.07	15.91	14.39	13.27	12.41	11.75	10.78	10.13	9.67	400
500	47.53	33.60	26.69	22.59	19.88	17.98	16.58	15.52	14.68	13.47	12.66	12.09	500
600	57.03	40.32	32.03	27.10	23.86	21.58	19.90	18.62	17.62	16.17	15.19	14.51	600
700	66.54	47.04	37.37	31.62	27.84	25.18	23.21	21.72	20.55	18.86	17.72	16.93	700
800	76.04	53.76	42.70	36.14	31.81	28.77	26.53	24.82	23.49	21.55	20.25	19.34	800
900	85.54	60.48	48.04	40.65	35.79	32.37	29.85	27.92	26.42	24.25	22.79	21.76	900
1000	95.05	67.20	53.38	45.17	39.76	35.96	33.16	31.03	29.36	26.94	25.32	24.18	1000
2000	190.09	134.39	106.75	90.33	79.52	71.92	66.32	62.05	58.71	53.88	50.63	48.35	2000
3000	285.14	201.58	160.12	135.49	119.28	107.88	99.48	93.07	88.06	80.82	75.94	72.52	3000
4000	380.18	268.77	213.49	180.66	159.04	143.84	132.63	124.09	117.41	107.75	101.25	96.70	4000
5000	475.23	335.96	266.86	225.82	198.80	179.80	165.79	155.11	146.76	134.69	126.56	120.87	5000
6000	570.27	403.16	320.23	270.98	238.56	215.76	198.95	186.14	176.11	161.63	151.87	145.04	6000
7000	665.31	470.35	373.61	316.15	278.32	251.71	232.10	217.16	205.46	188.57	177.19	169.21	7000
8000	760.36	537.54	426.98	361.31	318.08	287.67	265.26	248.18	234.82	215.50	202.50	193.39	8000
9000	855.40	604.73	480.35	406.47	357.84	323.63	298.42	279.20	264.17	242.44	227.81	217.56	9000
10000	950.45	671.92	533.72	451.64	397.60	359.59	331.58	310.22	293.52	269.38	253.12	241.73	10000
15000	1425.67	1007.88	800.58	677.45	596.40	539.38	497.36	465.33	440.27	404.06	379.68	362.59	15000
20000	1900.89	1343.84	1067.44	903.27	795.20	719.17	663.15	620.44	587.03	538.75	506.24	483.46	20000
25000	2376.11	1679.80	1334.29	1129.08	994.00	898.96	828.93	775.55	733.79	673.43	632.80	604.32	25000
30000	2851.33	2015.76	1601.15	1354.90	1192.80	1078.76	994.72	930.66	880.54	808.12	759.35	725.18	30000
35000	3326.55	2351.72	1868.01	1580.72	1391.60	1258.55	1160.50	1085.76	1027.30	942.81	885.91	846.05	35000
40000	3801.77	2687.68	2134.87	1806.53	1590.40	1438.34	1326.29	1240.87	1174.06	1077.49	1012.47	966.91	40000
45000	4276.99	3023.64	2401.72	2032.35	1789.20	1618.13	1492.08	1395.98	1320.81	1212.18	1139.03	1087.77	45000
50000	4752.22	3359.60	2668.58	2258.16	1988.00	1797.92	1657.86	1551.09	1467.57	1346.86	1265.59	1208.64	50000
60000	5702.66	4031.51	3202.30	2709.79	2385.59	2157.51	1989.43	1861.31	1761.08	1616.24	1518.70	1450.36	60000
75000	7128.32	5039.39	4002.87	3387.24	2981.99	2696.88	2486.79	2326.63	2201.35	2020.29	1898.38	1812.95	75000
100000	9504.43	6719.19	5337.16	4516.32	3975.99	3595.84	3315.72	3102.17	2935.14	2693.72	2531.17	2417.27	100000
125000	11880.53	8398.98	6671.45	5645.40	4969.98	4494.80	4144.65	3877.72	3668.92	3367.15	3163.96	3021.59	125000
150000	14256.64	10078.78	8005.73	6774.48	5963.98	5393.76	4973.57	4653.26	4402.70	4040.58	3796.75	3625.90	150000
175000	16632.74	11758.57	9340.02	7903.56	6957.97	6292.72	5802.50	5428.80	5136.49	4714.01	4429.54	4230.22	175000
200000	19008.85	13438.37	10674.31	9032.64	7951.97	7191.68	6631.43	6204.34	5870.27	5387.44	5062.33	4834.54	200000
250000	23761.06	16797.96	13342.89	11290.80	9939.96	8989.60	8289.29	7755.43	7337.84	6734.30	6327.91	6043.17	250000

Amount	9.0 Years	10.0 Years	11.0 Years	12.0 Years	13.0 Years	14.0 Years	15.0 Years	16.0 Years	20.0 Years	30.0 Years	40.0 Years	50.0 Years	Amount
100	2.34	2.28	2.23	2.20	2.18	2.16	2.14	2.13	2.10	2.09	2.09	2.09	100
200	4.68	4.55	4.46	4.40	4.35	4.31	4.28	4.25	4.20	4.17	4.17	4.17	200
300	7.01	6.83	6.69	6.59	6.52	6.46	6.41	6.38	6.30	6.26	6.26	6.26	300
400	9.35	9.10	8.92	8.79	8.69	8.61	8.55	8.50	8.40	8.34	8.34	8.34	400
500	11.68	11.38	11.15	10.99	10.86	10.76	10.68	10.62	10.50	10.43	10.42	10.42	500
600	14.02	13.65	13.38	13.18	13.03	12.91	12.82	12.75	12.59	12.51	12.51	12.51	600
700	16.35	15.93	15.61	15.38	15.20	15.06	14.95	14.87	14.69	14.60	14.59	14.59	700
800	18.69	18.20	17.84	17.57	17.37	17.21	17.09	17.00	16.79	16.68	16.67	16.67	800
900	21.02	20.48	20.07	19.77	19.54	19.36	19.22	19.12	18.89	18.77	18.76	18.76	900
1000	23.36	22.75	22.30	21.97	21.71	21.51	21.36	21.24	20.99	20.85	20.84	20.84	1000
2000	46.71	45.50	44.60	43.93	43.41	43.02	42.72	42.48	41.97	41.70	41.67	41.67	2000
3000	70.06	68.25	66.90	65.89	65.12	64.52	64.07	63.72	62.95	62.54	62.51	62.51	3000
4000	93.41	91.00	89.20	87.85	86.82	86.03	85.43	84.96	83.93	83.39	83.34	83.34	4000
5000	116.77	113.75	111.50	109.81	108.52	107.54	106.78	106.20	104.92	104.23	104.18	104.17	5000
6000	140.12	136.50	133.80	131.77	130.23	129.04	128.14	127.44	125.90	125.08	125.01	125.01	6000
7000	163.47	159.25	156.10	153.73	151.93	150.55	149.49	148.68	146.88	145.93	145.85	145.84	7000
8000	186.82	182.00	178.40	175.69	173.63	172.06	170.85	169.91	167.86	166.77	166.68	166.67	8000
9000	210.17	204.75	200.70	197.65	195.34	193.56	192.20	191.15	188.84	187.62	187.51	187.51	9000
10000	233.53	227.50	223.00	219.61	217.04	215.07	213.56	212.39	209.83	208.46	208.35	208.34	10000
15000	350.29	341.24	334.50	329.42	325.56	322.60	320.33	318.58	314.74	312.69	312.52	312.51	15000
20000	467.05	454.99	446.00	439.22	434.07	430.14	427.11	424.78	419.65	416.92	416.69	416.67	20000
25000	583.81	568.74	557.50	549.03	542.59	537.67	533.89	530.97	524.56	521.15	520.86	520.84	25000
30000	700.57	682.48	669.00	658.83	651.11	645.20	640.66	637.16	629.47	625.38	625.04	625.01	30000
35000	817.33	796.23	780.50	768.64	759.63	752.73	747.44	743.36	734.38	729.61	729.21	729.17	35000
40000	934.09	909.98	892.00	878.44	868.14	860.27	854.22	849.55	839.29	833.84	833.38	833.34	40000
45000	1050.85	1023.72	1003.49	988.25	976.66	967.80	960.99	955.74	944.20	938.07	937.55	937.51	45000
50000	1167.61	1137.47	1114.99	1098.05	1085.18	1075.33	1067.77	1061.94	1049.11	1042.29	1041.72	1041.68	50000
60000	1401.14	1364.96	1337.99	1317.66	1302.21	1290.40	1281.32	1274.32	1258.93	1250.75	1250.07	1250.01	60000
75000	1751.42	1706.20	1672.49	1647.07	1627.76	1613.00	1601.65	1592.90	1573.67	1563.44	1562.58	1562.51	75000
100000	2335.22	2274.93	2229.98	2196.10	2170.35	2150.66	2135.53	2123.87	2098.22	2084.58	2083.44	2083.35	100000
125000	2919.03	2843.67	2787.48	2745.12	2712.94	2688.32	2669.42	2654.84	2622.78	2605.73	2604.30	2604.18	125000
150000	3502.83	3412.40	3344.97	3294.14	3255.52	3225.99	3203.30	3185.80	3147.33	3126.87	3125.16	3125.02	150000
175000	4086.64	3981.13	3902.46	3843.17	3798.11	3763.65	3737.18	3716.77	3671.88	3648.02	3646.02	3645.85	175000
200000	4670.44	4549.86	4459.96	4392.19	4340.69	4301.32	4271.06	4247.74	4196.44	4169.16	4166.88	4166.69	200000
250000	5838.05	5687.33	5574.95	5490.24	5425.87	5376.64	5338.83	5309.67	5245.55	5211.45	5208.60	5208.36	250000

GLOSSARY

Acceleration Clause: A clause in a mortgage stipulating, if certain defined conditions occur, any amount of money still outstanding is due and payable at once.

Adjustable Rate Mortgage (ARM): The interest rate of a mortgage which varies during the term of the mortgage.

Amortization: Repaying a loan through a series of installment payments.

Annual Interest Rate: An amount of money that the principal will earn over the period of a year, when multiplied by the principal.

Balloon Note: A note that usually calls for a final payment greater than the regular payments.

Blanket Mortgage: One mortgage covering more than one parcel of real estate.

Conventional Mortgage: A mortgage not insured by a governmental agency.

Discount Points: A charge, made by the lending institution to the borrower, based on the mortgage amount. A point is one percent of the principal mortgage amount.

Federal Housing Administration (FHA) Mortgage: Mortgage loan insured by the Federal Housing Administration.

First Mortgage: The first mortgage on a property.

Flexible Payment Mortgage (FPM): Mortgage with payments that vary over the term of the mortgage.

Graduated Payment Mortgage (GPM): Mortgage with payments that increase in a specified manner over the term of the mortgage.

Interest: An amount of money earned by the principal over a specified period of time.

Interest Rate: A percentage that, when multiplied by the principal, determines the amount of money that the principal earns over a period of time, usually one year.

Mortgage: A legal document that establishes real estate as the security for the loan which finances that real estate.

Mortgagee: The institution or person who is the lender or creditor on a mortgage loan.

Mortgagor: The institution or person who is the borrower or debtor on a mortgage loan.

Open-End Mortgage: Provides for additional amounts to be loaned to the borrower without the need to create a new mortgage.

Prepayment Clause: A clause in a mortgage enabling the borrower to pay off the mortgage before the end of the term.

Reverse Annuity Mortgage (RAM): Mortgage that allows a borrower to draw on the current equity of the property.

Rollover Mortgage (ROM): Provides for the renegotiation of the interest rate and payment terms.

Shared Appreciation Mortgage (SAM): Provides for the lender to receive a share in the appreciation of residential real estate. In return, the borrower is given a lower interest rate.

Veterans Administration (VA) Mortgage: A mortgage made to veterans by a lender for residential real estate, insured by the Veterans Administration.